Anti-Scientific Americans

Anti-Scientific Americans

The Prevalence, Origins, and Political Consequences of Anti-Intellectualism in the US

MATTHEW MOTTA

OXFORD
UNIVERSITY PRESS

Oxford University Press is a department of the University of Oxford.
It furthers the University's objective of excellence in research, scholarship,
and education by publishing worldwide. Oxford is a registered trade mark of
Oxford University Press in the UK and in certain other countries.

Published in the United States of America by Oxford University Press
198 Madison Avenue, New York, NY 10016, United States of America.

© Oxford University Press 2024

All rights reserved. No part of this publication may be reproduced, stored in a retrieval system,
or transmitted, in any form or by any means, without the prior permission in writing of Oxford
University Press, or as expressly permitted by law, by license or under terms agreed with the
appropriate reprographics rights organization. Inquiries concerning reproduction outside the scope
of the above should be sent to the Rights Department, Oxford University Press, at the address above.

You must not circulate this work in any other form and you must impose this same condition on any acquirer

Library of Congress Cataloging-in-Publication Data

Names: Motta, Matt, author.
Title: Anti-Scientific Americans : the prevalence, origins, and political
consequences of anti-intellectualism in the US / Matt Motta, PhD.,
Assistant Professor, Dept. of Health Law, Policy, & Management,
Boston University.
Other titles: Prevalence, origins, and political consequences of
anti-intellectualism in the United States
Description: New York, NY : Oxford University Press, [2024] | Includes
bibliographical references.
Identifiers: LCCN 2024009066 (print) | LCCN 2024009067 (ebook) |
ISBN 9780197788813 (paperback) | ISBN 9780197788806 (hardback) |
ISBN 9780197788837 (epub)
Subjects: LCSH: Science—Political aspects—United States. |
Science and state—United States. | Anti-intellectualism—United States. |
National characteristics, American.
Classification: LCC Q175.52.U6 M68 2024 (print) | LCC Q175.52.U6 (ebook) |
DDC 303.48/30973—dc23/eng/20240523
LC record available at https://lccn.loc.gov/2024009066
LC ebook record available at https://lccn.loc.gov/2024009067

To Daria, DJ, Elizabeth, Kory, & Morgan – for navigating a global pandemic together, and for supporting me while I wrote this book.

And to my parents, Joyce & Robert, and my sister, Gabriella – for teaching me how to trust fully, question constructively, and to know when to do both at the same time.

ACKNOWLEDGMENTS

I first set pen to paper to write this book early in the morning on March 12*th*, 2021. It's a date that I think I'll hold with me for the rest of my life.

You might be wondering why I have any recollection *at all* of the date that I began writing this book. That's a fair question. After all, I began the process of both collecting and analyzing the data that form this book's empirical backbone several years earlier. There's nothing inherently special about that date.

For me, though, March 12*th* is a very special date. I began writing that morning with a nervous and excited energy unlike anything I'd ever experienced before in my life. After spending several months in isolation due to the onset of a global pandemic, March 12*th* was the day I received my first dose of the COVID-19 vaccine.

The promise of one day returning to life as usual, the *status quo ante COVID* as I like to call it, inspired me to begin writing that morning. But it's the lessons that I hope we can take from the COVID-19 pandemic, or the *status quo post COVID* that continue to motivate my work every day.

To that end, I am forever indebted to the work of our first responders and essential workers who risked their personal safety and well-being in order to keep us safe throughout the darkest days of the COVID-19 pandemic. In a time of unprecedented uncertainty, their selflessness and perseverance allowed people like me to write books like this one from the comfort and safety of my own home. I will always be grateful for their sacrifice.

I am also profoundly thankful for the people in my life who supported me throughout the process of writing this book. I could not have done this without the friends I made at every stage of my academic career: from Minneapolis, New Haven, Tulsa, Boston, and all of the exciting places we now call home. I am especially indebted to my friends and colleagues Robert Ralston and Dom Stecula for their years of social, emotional, and intellectual support while writing this book. Thanks for being attentive sounding boards, prudent problem-solvers, and even better friends.

This book is also the culmination of skills and passions I developed over the course my academic and professional training. I am so lucky to have spent many happy and productive years at Wesleyan University (where I did my undergraduate work), the University of Minnesota (where I earned my PhD), as well as the Annenberg Public Policy Center at the University of Pennsylvania and Yale Law School (where I did my postdoctoral work). I could not have written this book without the academic and professional mentorship of Joanne Miller, Paul Goren, Howie Lavine, Kathleen Hall Jamieson, and Dan Kahan. I am especially indebted to Erika Franklin Fowler, for introducing me to the process of conducting social science research, as a college student. To all my mentors: thanks for encouraging me to take risks, try new things, and – above all – to believe in myself.

Moreover, I now work in a different academic field (public health) than I did when starting this project. I am truly thankful for my colleagues, mentors, and friends at Boston University's School of Public Health – especially my longtime collaborator and friend Tim Callaghan – for giving me the space, resources, and time necessary to finish writing this book. I could not have done this without your support, guidance, and friendship.

I am also forever grateful to those who supported my research by providing me with the resources necessary to collect, clean, and analyze the data featured throughout this book. I began writing this book when I was an assistant professor at Oklahoma State University. I am profoundly thankful for OSU's willingness to fund several of the public opinion surveys featured in this book, and for providing me with access to databases necessary to carry out this research. I am also indebted to the anonymous peer reviewers at Oxford University Press who provided feedback on this book, and to those at the ANES, NORC, and iPoll databases who do the hard work to make many of the secondary data sources for this data available for public use.

Finally, I could not have written this book without a lifetime of support from my parents – Joyce & Robert Motta. Your hard work and sacrifice gave me the opportunity to pursue a career in academia. Thanks for making this project and all others possible.

CONTENTS

1. Anti-Scientific Americans? 1

CONCEPTUALIZING ANTI-INTELLECTUALISM 3

It's Personal: Anti-Intellectualism as an Affective and
Group-Based Phenomenon 4

Expert Dislike and Distrust 6

WHO IS AN EXPERT? MEASURING ANTI-EXPERT ATTITUDES 10

Experts and Intellectuals: The Eye of the Beholder Approach 11

The Scientific Community: A More-Narrow Approach 12

How Anti-Intellectualism Relates to Populism 15

WHAT'S AT STAKE? 18

THE PLAN OF THIS BOOK 19

A WORD OF CAUTION: EXPERTS ARE PEOPLE TOO 24

2. The Nature and Origins of Anti-Intellectualism 28

UNDERSTANDING ANTI-INTELLECTUALISM: AN AFFECTIVE
AND GROUP-CENTRIC THEORY 29

Psychologically Unpacking the Group-Based Origins of Expert
Dislike and Distrust 30

Applying SIT, SCT, and ITT to Anti-Intellectual Attitude
Endorsement 32

The Political Psychological Inputs and Policy-Relevant
Outputs of Anti-Intellectual Attitude Endorsement 33

STATIC INPUTS: WHO HOLDS ANTI-INTELLECTUAL ATTITUDES? 35

Republican Partisan Identity and Symbolic Ideology 37

Preferences for Limited Government 43

Religiosity 44

The Tea Party and the Temporal Dynamics of Asymmetric
Polarization 46

DYNAMIC INPUTS: WHAT MOTIVATES CHANGE IN
ANTI-INTELLECTUALISM? 52

Knowledge of Basic Scientific Facts 54

Interest in Scientific Research 56

EXPERTS' POLICY INFLUENCE: THE BIDIRECTIONALITY THESIS 57

TESTING THE GROUP-CENTRIC MODEL: A PREVIEW 63

3. Validating Two Approaches to Measuring Anti-Intellectual Attitude Endorsement in Public-Opinion Surveys 65

A REFRESHER: TWO APPROACHES TO MEASURING ANTI-INTELLECTUAL
ATTITUDE ENDORSEMENT 67

THE PUBLIC-OPINION DATA: AN OVERVIEW 68

GSS Time Series Studies (1974–2018) 70

GSS Panel Studies (2006–2010, 2008–2012, 2010–2014) 70

CSPP Panel Study (2016) 72

ANES Pilot Study (2019) and 2020 Time Series Study 75

Science and Policy Rolling Cross-Sectional Study
(2020–2021) 76

VALIDATING THE TWO MICRO-LEVEL INDICATORS OF
ANTI-INTELLECTUALISM 77

Content Validation, Part 1: Americans' Definitions of Expertise
and How Scientists Contribute to It 80

Content Validation, Part 2: How Anti-Intellectual Thought Underpins
Evaluations of Scientists 82

CONCLUSION 90

4. The Prevalence of Anti-Intellectual Attitudes 91

MACRO ANTI-INTELLECTUALISM DATABASE (1944–2021) 93

THE PROBLEM WITH PREVALENCE 97

A PERVASIVE PROBLEM OR AN OVERHYPED MYTH? 102

A PLURALISTIC PREVALENCE ASSESSMENT 106

CONCLUSION 110

5. Origin Story Part I: Explaining Between-Person Differences in Anti-Intellectual Attitude Endorsement 112

ANALYTICAL STRATEGY: DETECTING BETWEEN-PERSON
DIFFERENCES IN ANTI-INTELLECTUAL ATTITUDE ENDORSEMENT 114

Measures and Data 117

Contents

MODEL INPUT STABILITY ASSESSMENT   121

RESULTS   123

Partisan Identity   124

Ideology   127

Limited-Government Attitudes   129

Religiosity   131

Reverse Causality Assessment   133

"Taxed Enough by Academics?" Attitude Polarization and
the Rise of the Tea Party   136

CONCLUSION   139

6. Origin Story Part II: Change in Anti-Intellectual Attitude Endorsement   141

ANALYTICAL STRATEGY   143

DATA AND MEASURES   144

RESULTS   145

Reverse Causality Assessment   147

Exploring the Effects of Expert Contact in
Higher-Educational Settings   148

CONCLUSION   150

7. The Bidirectionality Thesis: Hofstadter's Forgotten Prediction   152

TESTING THE BIDIRECTIONALITY THESIS   155

DATA AND MEASURES   156

Data   156

Measuring General Expert Policy Role Orientations   156

RESULTS   160

CONCLUSION   164

8. Anti-Intellectualism and Its Pernicious Policy Consequences   166

ANTI-INTELLECTUALISM AND THE REJECTION OF EVIDENCE-BASED
POLICY   167

Climate Science   176

Public Health   179

Economics   184

ELITE RESPONSIVENESS TO PUBLIC ANTI-INTELLECTUALISM   186

Measuring Expert Influence in the Policymaking Process   188

Climate Science   192

Economics   195
Public Health   196
Robustness Checks   197
CONCLUSION   197

9. What's Next, Doc?   199

JUST ASKING QUESTIONS: EMERGING STRAINS OF
ANTI-INTELLECTUALISM   202

TOWARD A UNIFIED APPROACH FOR IMPROVING TRUST IN EXPERTS   206

Restoring Faith in Experts: A Unified Approach   206

A Brief Note on System-Level Reforms   210

IS AMERICAN ANTI-INTELLECTUALISM EXCEPTIONAL?   211

LIMITATIONS AND DIRECTIONS FOR FUTURE RESEARCH   214

IT'S PERSONAL: CONCLUDING REFLECTIONS ON THE
STATE OF ANTI-INTELLECTUAL ATTITUDE ENDORSEMENT
IN THE UNITED STATES   216

Appendix Materials For "Anti-Scientific Americans: The Prevalence,
Origins, and Political Consequences of Anti-Intellectualism in the US"   219
References   299
Index   319

1

Anti-Scientific Americans?

Americans' distaste for scientific and medical experts was on full display during one of the deadliest pandemics in recent human history.

For example, Dr. John Anderson of Washington State reported regularly being spat at by passersby on the streets of Spokane, Washington, during his tenure as a state public health official. His offense? Dr. Anderson recommended that the city ban indoor gatherings and adopt mask-wearing mandates to curtail the spread of a deadly virus.

And after local health officials testified before the Portland, Oregon, city council in favor of instituting a city-wide mask mandate, he and his proposal were labeled as "autocratic" by a local city councilor who refused to be "muzzled with a mask like a hydrophobic dog" (Navarro, 2020). Even the federal government in Washington, DC, potentially at the urging of a president who had himself became infected with the virus (Coll, 2020), downplayed the severity of the virus (Little, 2020). Some suggested that the spread of the virus was in decline during a period of peak transmission and referred to the disease as "just the flu" (Shapiro, 2020).

Incidents such as these occurred throughout the COVID-19 pandemic—a period during which Americans occupied state capitols to protest Centers for Disease Control (CDC) recommendations regarding mask mandates and restrictions on indoor shopping/dining. Leading public health figures routinely received threats of bodily harm, and even a sitting president frequently and publicly declared himself at odds with its own administration's health experts.

However, the incidents described here were *not* episodes from the recent COVID-19 pandemic. Instead, they are scenes from the 1918 influenza (Spanish flu) pandemic (Deshais, 2019) that killed, by some estimates, nearly 5 percent of the global population.

Amid an unprecedented global public health crisis, some Americans chose not to listen to experts but to instead defy them. One hundred years later, we did it again.

Anti-intellectualism, a term originally coined by Richard Hofstadter in a Pulitzer Prize–winning 1963 book on the subject, concerns the extent to which Americans dislike and distrust people who can credibly claim superior knowledge of a specialized subject (*experts*). Anti-intellectualism has received a substantial amount of both scholarly and popular attention in recent years (e.g., Nichols, 2017; Motta, 2018a; Merkley, 2020). And for good reason. Americans' negative attitudes toward scientists, academics, and other experts may help us better understand why some people support politicians who denigrate experts (e.g., former President Donald Trump, who routinely derided even his own expert advisors while in office), accept misinformation about vaccine safety and effectiveness of pseudoscientific remedies, and oppose the advice that experts lend when attempting to inform policymaking about the environment, public health, the economy, and much more.

What is missing from past efforts to study anti-intellectualism, however, is a cohesive effort to conceptualize what anti-intellectualism is, offer a unified theory as to why some people are more likely to hold anti-intellectual attitudes than others, and understand how it both shapes and is shaped by contemporary politics. Also missing from past research is an effort to track just how many Americans have endorsed anti-intellectual attitudes over the past century, robustly assess its potential causes, and synthesize its pernicious impact on American politics across a wide range of policy issues.

In this book, I aim to do all of these things.

Throughout the book, I offer a novel, unifying theoretical framework that conceptualizes what anti-intellectualism is (and what it is not), considers why some people are more likely to hold these views than others, and evaluates how anti-intellectualism both shapes and is shaped by opposition to the role that experts play in American public life. I empirically test the model's core predictions by bringing together hundreds of public-opinion surveys, spanning several decades, capable of measuring the prevalence, correlates, and policy consequences of anti-intellectual attitude endorsement.

In testing the model, I show that while anti-intellectualism has pervaded American public life for decades, partisan polarization in anti-intellectual attitude endorsement is a fairly recent phenomenon and is likely attributable to recent political movements that cast doubt on the importance of scientific expertise. I also show that anti-intellectualism is associated with opposition to evidence-based policies in a wide range of policy domains (including health, environmental, and economic policy) and that policymakers are less likely to consult scientific experts in periods when public anti-intellectual sentiment is comparatively high. Perhaps most importantly, I conclude by considering how insights from this book can be used to reduce anti-intellectual attitude endorsement and restore Americans' faith in experts.

My hope is that this book can advance what we understand about anti-intellectualism by offering a conceptually unified and empirically pluralistic assessment of its causes and policy consequences.

Before I can do this, however, I first need to define what anti-intellectualism is. And to do that, I first want to revisit how it is that historian Richard Hofstadter conceptualized anti-intellectualism when he introduced the term in his seminal work on the subject.

Conceptualizing Anti-Intellectualism

Throughout this book, I conceptualize anti-intellectualism as the *dislike and distrust of experts*. Specifically, I consider someone to hold anti-intellectual attitudes if they express negative feelings toward people who can credibly lay claim to superior knowledge in academic or scientific fields (i.e., *experts*).

This conceptualization of anti-intellectualism is both affective and group focused. In other words, it pertains to negative views of experts *as people*. In the pages that follow, I draw on scholarly research from across the social sciences to unpack why I believe that the highly personalized negativity toward experts offers a suitable working definition for what it means to hold anti-intellectual attitudes.

This definition, of course, raises some important questions. Why focus on experts (as a group) as opposed to expertise (i.e., the appreciation of subject-area knowledge)? Who counts as an expert? Is anti-intellectualism any different from the dislike and distrust of elites more generally?

These are important questions. In what follows, I take them up one by one.

First, I argue that although scholars have employed several different and useful standards to study anti-intellectualism in the past, the dislike and distrust of experts (1) has historical roots in Hofstadter's conceptualization of the term and (2) is uniquely appropriate for the study of politics. Next, I discuss two standards I use to determine who counts as an expert (recognizing that these accounts, while incomplete, provide sufficient leverage for exploring the questions I hope to answer in this book). Third, and finally, I discuss how anti-intellectualism relates to populism and anti-elite attitudes more broadly. Therein, I discuss why I expect anti-intellectualism to have unique, policy-relevant effects in ways that populism might not.

With a definition of anti-intellectualism elaborated, I then briefly discuss what's at stake—why it *matters* if Americans hold anti-intellectual attitudes and the potential policy impacts of anti-intellectualism. I conclude the chapter by discussing how this book studies the prevalence, origins, and policy consequences of anti-intellectualism.

It's Personal: Anti-Intellectualism as an Affective and Group-Based Phenomenon

Americans' dislike and distrust of experts extends far beyond disdain for the findings of scientific research, the machinations of higher-education institutions, or aversions to critical thought. *It's personal.*

In Chapter 2, I present a new theoretical model for understanding what anti-intellectualism is and why some people are more likely than others to hold anti-intellectual attitudes. Central to this model is the idea that many Americans dislike experts *as people.* In that chapter, I discuss why some Americans might be motivated to view experts as an unlikable social group with interests at odds with their own and how this can, in turn, engender negative feelings toward that group. The highly personal nature of expert dislike and distrust implies that anti-intellectualism is both affective and group focused in nature. It is *affective* because it pertains to the negative feelings and emotions that Americans harbor toward different types of experts. Additionally, anti-intellectualism is *group focused* because experts—the targets of dislike and distrust—are social beings that some Americans might view as having interests or exhibiting behaviors that are at odds with their own.

While I unpack the political psychological underpinnings of this idea more fully in Chapter 2, a recent high-profile demonstration of Americans' dislike and distrust of scientific experts can help demonstrate the affective and group-based nature of anti-intellectual attitude endorsement in the United States.

In spring 2016, scientists, academics, and those who support them (Fisher, 2018) gathered in cities across the United States to participate in March for Science protests. Sociological reflections on the march argue that its primary motivation was unique in the sense that it did not result from opposition to one specific policy but to a collection of anticipated policy maneuvers and hostile rhetoric from (at the time) newly elected President Donald Trump. These words and potential policy actions seemingly threatened the sovereignty and integrity of scientific inquiry in the United States (Brulle, 2018).

Concerning issues related to the environment, for example, the former president cast doubt on the scholarly consensus about the reality of human-caused climate change and attacked climate scientists (whom he regularly referred to as "hoaxsters") by claiming that they were "having a lot of fun" perpetuating an (alleged) climate hoax (Schulman, 2016). Trump transformed his anti-scientist rhetoric into policy-relevant action early on in his presidency by withdrawing from the US Paris climate accord (the Paris Agreement, a global partnership aimed at curbing greenhouse gas emissions), barring government scientists from attending and presenting research at environmental conferences, and appointing fossil-fuel industry insiders to key posts (e.g., Scott Pruitt – who worked with political supporters from the fossil fuel industry to sue environmental regulatory agencies throughout his time as Attorney General of Oklahoma (Biesecker & Kealoha Causey 2017) – as head of the Environmental Protection Agency) traditionally focused on environmental protection (Carter et al., 2020).

Just as scientists bore the brunt of many of the former president's attacks on science, they were also the public face of the March for Science. Popular press coverage of the march, for example, often drew attention to *who* was doing the marching. For example, media outlets curated slideshows that celebrated the often-quirky signage present at the march and penned reports documenting the attendance of famous scientists and science popularizers at events across the country (e.g., Bill Nye, Neil deGrasse Tyson; Gibson, 2017).

At the same time, however, several social scientists (e.g., Nyhan, 2017; Mullin, 2017) asked whether the march would risk politicizing public views toward science and scientists.

Political scientist Megan Mullin (2017), for example, asked whether the events might "depict scientists as a liberal constituency," thereby engendering political conflict.

Arguably, that's precisely what happened. In a panel survey that interviewed Americans just before and just after the march, I found that Americans' attitudes toward scientists did indeed become more politically polarized following the events (Motta, 2018c). Self-identified liberals came to hold more positive views toward scientists, while conservatives came to hold more negative views.

Importantly, though, *Americans' attitudes toward scientific research did not change.* Consistent with the idea that Americans were reacting to the march's public face (i.e., scientists and those who support them), I documented evidence of affective polarization toward scientists and other experts *as social groups* but not toward the type of work that these individuals do. Politicization, of course, was not the march's stated intention (Yong, 2017), nor was it necessarily the goal of those who attended the events. For example, some attendees even brought signs claiming that science is "not political."

On some level, that's true. Scientific *inquiry* is not necessarily political in nature. But as this example illustrates, *scientists* clearly are—both with respect to not only how they are seen in the general public but also with respect to the actions they took protesting the Trump presidency (and through the political activities of the unprecedented number of scientists who sought elected office in the years that followed) (Motta, 2020).

At this point, however, it is important to note that my affective and group-based approach stands in contrast to several existing conceptualizations of anti-intellectualism in the United States. In fact, while my understanding of anti-intellectualism borrows much from Richard Hofstadter's pioneering work on the topic, it is nevertheless at odds with some of the ways that he conceptualized the phenomenon. In the discussion that follows, I summarize how it is that Hofstadter initially conceptualized anti-intellectualism and note areas in which my approach differs from his.

Expert Dislike and Distrust

A necessary first step toward understanding how anti-intellectual sentiments might lead Americans to reject policy efforts to mitigate the effects of a changing climate, refuse to vaccinate against communicable disease, or support shutting credentialed experts out of the policymaking process is to conceptually unpack why I define anti-intellectualism as the dislike and distrust of experts. Perhaps the most sensible place to start is with Richard Hofstadter's conceptualization of the term. His work, after all, played an essential role in popularizing the term.

Hofstadter's (1963) initial work on anti-intellectualism did many things well. It profiled the history and social consequences of anti-intellectualism (particularly those pertaining to education). It also offered novel insights into why ordinary Americans might come to hold anti-intellectual views.

What Hofstadter's work did not do, however, is offer a singular standard by which scholars can conceptualize anti-intellectualism. Instead, scholars of Hofstadter have argued that his work produces three different characterizations of anti-intellectualism (Rigney, 1991).

One form of anti-intellectualism is what Rigney terms "anti-rationalism," or the devaluation of critical thought and reasoned discourse. One reason why Americans might come to hold anti-rational views is that they see critical thinking and the scientific method as posing a challenge to matters of religious faith. Hofstadter argued that opponents of teaching evolution in public schools often invoked attempts to appeal to Americans' anti-rational sentiments. For example, Hofstadter profiled a Georgia state representative who once claimed that "there isn't another book [other than the Bible] that it is necessary for anyone to read, and therefore I am opposed to all libraries" (Hofstadter, 1966, p 124).

While anti-rationalism is certainly an important component of the development of anti-intellectual thought, there are at least two reasons why it may not be the most appropriate definition for the contemporary study of politics and policy.

The first is conceptual. Hofstadter recognizes that anti-rationalism may be motivated by feelings that rational thought is "dispassionate" or "cold." These affective appraisals of rational thought are difficult, I argue, to distinguish from the people (experts) who are *participating in reasoned thought.*

In a rebuke of modernity and rational thought, for example, Hofstadter cites a 1920's statement from the Ku Klux Klan that contrasts, as Hofstadter puts it, the "cold intellectualism" of experts from the emotional and instinctive appeal of ordinary people (pp 124–125). The statement argues—fusing concerns about both rational thought *and* those who employ it into a single critique—that basic human instincts can be better trusted than the "fine-haired reasoning of the denatured intellectuals." (p 125).

Evidence of this fusion exists today as well. Recent social psychological research has found that Americans tend to view scientists, academics, and other researchers as colder and more dispassionate than the American public more generally (Rutjens & Heine, 2016; see also Rutjens, Sutton, & van der Lee, 2018). This pattern of effects is likely due to suspicions that rational thought and scientific inquiry are incongruous with the social and moral values of ordinary people (Sutton, Petterson, & Rutjens, 2019). Correspondingly, both Hofstadter's own analysis and contemporary research seem to recognize that it is difficult to disentangle negative views of rational thought from those who engage in it.

A second issue with defining anti-intellectualism as anti-rationalism concerns its practical application to politics and current policy debates. If anti-intellectualism were to be defined as anti-rationalism, we would expect that people who more strongly value or express rational thought should be more likely to hold positive views toward scientists, academics, and other experts. They might also be more likely to support the policy-relevant recommendations of experts' research and advice. As I go on to unpack at length in Chapter 2, however, this may not be the case.

People who are themselves more inclined (or better able) to solve problems via critical thinking, as opposed to intuition (Oliver & Wood, 2018), may have the cognitive skillset necessary to appreciate the process by which experts reach consensus on even politically divisive topics. This is the core prediction of what psychologists and science communication researchers call the *knowledge deficit model* (Sturgis & Allum, 2004).

However, people who strongly value critical thought could also use their reasoning skills to *reject* scientific and expert consensus. In other words, they can use their deep knowledge or reasoning skills develop sophisticated counterarguments (Petty & Caccioppo, 1986; Chaiken, 1987) that refute experts' policy recommendations in service of their deeply held political, religious, or cultural beliefs that are at odds with consensus (Kahan, 2015, 2017c; Osmundsen et al., 2021). Correspondingly, studies on *directionally motivated reasoning* (i.e., the tendency to arrive at conclusions consistent with one's previously held beliefs; see Kunda, 1990; Kraft, Lodge, & Taber, 2015) suggest that critical thinking is something of a double-edged sword, meaning that both of these potential outcomes are possible. The application of anti-rationalism to contemporary policy-relevant debates is therefore unclear and may be unable to generate parsimonious predictions about the role that anti-intellectualism plays in American political life.

A second form of anti-intellectualism that Rigney identifies in Hofstadter's work is what he terms "unreflective instrumentalism." *Unreflective instrumentalism* concerns the extent to which Americans value ideas that promote short-term and practical payoffs as opposed to utopian, philosophical ideals.

Unreflective instrumentalism is not necessarily a rejection of rational thought. After all, scholarly and expert research can certainly be applied toward practical and policy-focused ends. Instead, Hofstadter is concerned about Americans' discomfort with philosophical ideals that promote visions of desirable political and social states that may be at odds with industrial, production-based capitalism.

While unreflective instrumentalism is again important to understanding how Hofstadter conceptualized anti-intellectualism, it is not especially germane to the questions I hope to answer in this book. As I discuss in more detail shortly, anti-intellectualism is most problematic when it shapes how Americans think about politics and public policy. Policies that I study in this book—such as efforts to reduce industrial carbon emissions to help combat human-caused climate change—may be *motivated* by abstract ideals (e.g., protecting vulnerable populations from insufficiently regulated corporate polluters). However, these policies are not themselves necessarily matters of philosophy in practical application. Consequently, Hofstadter's anti-rational conceptualization of anti-intellectualism is less well-suited for the investigation I undertake in this book.

Related to anti-rationalism is the possibility that technological advancements, such as the accessibility of information about highly specialized subjects on the internet, have empowered people to *feel* as if they can credibly lay claim to superior knowledge about a subject, despite lacking requisite educational and other skill-refining experiences (Nichols, 2017). Sometimes referred to as *meta-ignorance* or the *Dunning-Kruger effect* (Dunning, 2011; Pennycook et al., 2017), Americans may believe that they know as much or more than medical doctors about the proximal cause of a skin rash after spending an hour or two on WebMD, even if objective assessments of their expertise (e.g., factual knowledge tests) suggest the contrary.

The Dunning Kruger effect has certainly been shown motivate the rejection of evidence-based vaccine policy (e.g., Motta, Callaghan, & Sylvester, 2018), policy-relevant considerations concerning genetically modified food (Fernbach et al., 2019), and a wide range of other politically relevant topics (Anson, 2018) such as susceptibility to political misinformation (Lyons et al., 2021). However, it too is perhaps not the best way to define anti-intellectualism. Specifically, meta-ignorance has a somewhat conflictual relationship with how Americans think about expertise.

On the one hand, meta-ignorance rejects established, institutionalized knowledge in favor of more-democratic methods of accumulating knowledge about complex topics. In other words, people who exhibit meta-ignorance may also be more likely to harbor some amount of skepticism toward scientists and other experts (Motta, Callaghan, & Sylvester, 2018). This makes the Dunning-Kruger effect a potentially attractive way to conceptualize anti-intellectual thought in contemporary public life.

On the other hand, though, people who exhibit meta-ignorance may nevertheless value the scientific method, academic research, and the pursuit of expert information. Somewhat paradoxically, people who exhibit meta-ignorance may be using the very same tools used to distinguish institutionalized expertise from lay knowledge in their pursuit of specialized knowledge. Many of us, for example, know people who think that they comprehend more than the scientific community about the potential link between childhood vaccines and autism after glancing through a handful of abstracts from scientific studies on Google Scholar and forming an opinion about the state of scientific consensus on the issue.

What this implies is that people who claim to know more than experts may be producing incorrect assessments of how much they know relative to subject-matter experts. But the process (i.e., the consultation of academic studies) by which they arrive at those conclusions may represent an embrace—not a rejection—of the scientific method and other forms of expert inquiry. Meta-ignorance therefore is not *necessarily* wholesale rejection of expertise or the knowledge-generating process.

Consequently, I turn to the third and final definition of anti-intellectualism present in Hofstadter's work. This is what Rigney terms "anti-elitism." *Anti-elitism* refers to the dislike and distrust of academics, scientists, and other experts. As I and others have noted in previous work (Motta 2018a; Merkley, 2020), the *dislike and distrust of experts, as people* offers arguably the most useful way to study the political and policy consequences of anti-intellectualism.

Writing at the height of the McCarthy era in US politics, Hofstadter was astutely aware of (and concerned about) what seemed to be a burgeoning association between right-wing politics and the denigration of experts. Hofstadter was especially concerned about public response to the 1952 and 1956 presidential election contests between Dwight Eisenhower and Adlai Stevenson. Stevenson, an Ivy League–educated attorney and former governor, frequently found himself the subject of attacks linking his intellectual *bona fides* to anxiety about communism.

For example, when members of the faculty at Columbia University published an opinion piece endorsing Stevenson for president, journalists at the *New York Daily News* published an McCarthy-style exposé suggesting that some co-signers of the piece may have had communist loyalties (p 226). Hofstadter argues that incidents like this one helped solidify a linkage between Stevenson's intellectualism and "anti-American" communist values, ultimately costing him support in his bids for the presidency.

Interestingly, Stevenson directly acknowledged a link between his intellectualism and his supposed communist loyalties when joking about deeply personal McCarthy-style attacks on the campaign trail. As Hofstadter reviews in *The Rise of the Expert*, pundits regularly attacked not just Stevenson's supposed communist sympathies but *who he was as a person*. Popular press pundits labeled Stevenson's voice and diction as "feminine" in an effort (according to Hofstadter) to cast doubt on his political competencies (p 227). Notably, for example, after one conservative pundit labeled Stevenson as an "egghead"—a comment on both his intellectual mannerisms and his baldness—Stevenson invoked perhaps the most famous passage from the *Communist Manifesto* by quipping, "Eggheads of the world, you have nothing to lose but your yolks!"

For Hofstadter, then, anti-intellectualism was about more than just the rejection of (or failure to engage in) rational thought. Anti-intellectualism represented the denigration of experts in a deeply personal manner and in a way that maps at least in part onto prevailing sources of political disagreement.

Therein lies, in my view, the clearest application of anti-intellectualism to US politics. As I review in Chapter 2, the stereotypes and affective (i.e., feeling-based) appraisals Americans place on many politically relevant groups in society are thought to play a pivotal role in shaping how they think about both abstract political ideas and their positions on many concrete social and political issues (Ellis & Stimson, 2012; Achen & Bartels, 2017). Correspondingly, the expression of negative affect toward experts have been shown to be associated with the rejection of scientific consensus on politically polarizing issues and the tendency to vote for candidates who themselves denigrate experts (e.g., Donald Trump in 2016, George Wallace in 1968; see Motta, 2018a).

Thus, I argue that conceptualizing anti-intellectualism as the dislike and distrust of experts is the most suitable way to study anti-intellectualism in relation to politics and public policy. To this point, however, I have not yet defined who exactly *counts* as an expert when attempting to survey public anti-intellectual attitude endorsement. I take up that question next.

Who Is an Expert? Measuring Anti-Expert Attitudes

Throughout this book, I consider people to be *experts* if they can credibly make claim to hold superior knowledge on a particular subject or in a particular field (Nichols, 2017). On some level, this is an intuitive definition. Most medical doctors can credibly claim to have the academic training and technical skillset necessary to differentiate between the common cold and chronic respiratory illness. Economists are better suited to formulate predictions about how the size and scope of social safety net reforms might impact the country's unemployment rate.

At the same time, of course, my definition is an exceptionally broad way to think about expertise. Many, perhaps most, people have high levels of competency in *some* area.

A farmer, for example, can make credible claims of superior knowledge about the dynamics of crop rotation. An accountant is more familiar with the ins and outs of federal and state tax regulations than most of us ever hope or care to know. And professional basketball referees better understand the minutiae of what can be considered goaltending better than any of us watching the game at home (however tempted we might be to assert the contrary when our team is on the receiving end of what we assume is a bad call).

Conceptually, then, expertise is—almost by definition—a very inclusive concept. However, its inclusiveness can make expertise a tricky concept to measure empirically. Consequently, I think it is necessary to draw some boundaries with respect to defining expertise in application to anti-intellectualism.

Before I do so, however, I want to make clear that operationalizing expertise is, necessarily, an imperfect exercise. Perfection is not my goal. Instead, I hope to adopt a measurement strategy—suitable for administration in surveys of the American public—that is both practical and conceptually justifiable.

With that being said, I take two approaches to measuring expertise in this book. The first is the most general. It simply asks people to report their opinions about experts and intellectuals (i.e., allowing readers to provide their own conceptualization of expertise when answering questions about their trustworthiness). The second is somewhat narrower. It instead relies on survey questions that include targets (i.e., the subjects being evaluated) labeled as scientists (e.g., asking people to report the extent to which they trust the scientific community in particular).

Both of these standards share the important advantage of having been employed broadly in past research on anti-intellectualism (Motta, 2018a; Merkley, 2020; Motta & Callaghan, 2020; Merkley & Loewen, 2021). More importantly, as I detail here, I think that both sets of measures are conceptually justifiable as well.

Experts and Intellectuals: The Eye of the Beholder Approach

The first way I operationalize expertise is fairly broad in substantive scope. This approach makes no effort to define what expertise is for the person being asked to render a judgment. Instead, this approach relies on widely used survey questions that ask Americans to assess how they feel about experts and intellectuals in general (bringing their own conceptualizations of expertise to bear when doing so).

This eye of the beholder approach has the obvious advantage of being much broader in application than focusing on specific groups of experts alone. However, there is an important drawback. Because everyone has the opportunity to define expertise in their own way, it's impossible to ensure that every survey respondent is thinking about expertise in the same way when answering questions designed to measure anti-intellectualism.

Fortunately, as I document in Chapter 3, many Americans appear to be in agreement when it comes to identifying several core components of what it means to be an expert. In both open-ended writing tasks and multiple-answer survey questions, I find that many Americans define expertise as being indicative of holding legitimate claims to superior knowledge in a particular subject area.

In Chapter 3 I also document substantial evidence of overlap regarding Americans' conceptualizations of and attitudes toward experts and intellectuals (in general) and attitudes toward the scientific community (specifically). As I expand on in the following section, the analyses presented in Chapter 3 help further establish the idea that although the two approaches I take to measuring anti-intellectualism in this book are substantively distinct from one another, they nevertheless share a great deal in common with respect to how Americans *think* about each one.

The Scientific Community: A More-Narrow Approach

The second approach I take to measuring anti-intellectual attitude endorsement focuses on Americans' attitudes toward the scientific community.

The decision to include scientists in this measurement procedure may strike some as counterintuitive. If anti-intellectualism pertains to the dislike and distrust of many different types of people who can credibly claim to hold superior knowledge in a particular area (i.e., experts as a general class of people), why include measures that ask Americans to report their attitudes toward the scientific community specifically (i.e., one particular type of expert)?

This question has two answers. The first is practical and much less satisfying. Indicators of Americans' dislike and distrust toward scientists are widely available in a wealth of high-quality public-opinion polls dating back to the early 1970s. This enables me to study many of the time-varying and historical objectives I hope to study in this book (outlined in Chapter 2).

However, there's a much broader—and, I hope, more satisfying—answer to this question as well: *anti-intellectual thought underlies how Americans think about both experts and intellectuals (as general categories) and scientists (specifically)*. Like attitudes toward expertise more generally, attitudes toward the scientific community are both conceptually and empirically likely to display highly personal manifestations of expert negativity.

Conceptually, scientists offer an important way that Americans interact with expertise in both their personal and political lives. As I review in Chapter 2, this idea is present in Hofstadter's work, who recognized that while major developments in science and technology were making Americans' lives simpler, they simultaneously took away a sense of agency over their day-to-day lives and made Americans dependent on experts. For example, while advances in preventive medicine have improved our collective well-being and life expectancy, anyone who has anxiously awaited the results of a diagnostic blood test or medical procedure knows how helpless and anxiety inducing it can feel to depend on medical and scientific experts (lab technicians, physicians, etc.) to render a judgment about one's health. For Hofstadter, this loss of agency—resulting from advances in science and technology—has contributed to Americans' negative attitudes toward experts.

Furthermore, a clear comprehension of contemporary governance in the United States necessitates an understanding of scientific progress and those involved in its advancement. As I discuss in more detail in Chapter 2, some science historians consider scientists to be so instrumental to the functioning of government that they constitute a "fifth branch" of government (Jassanoff, 1998). Indeed, the United States has several federal offices devoted to promoting evidence-based policy and applying insights from scientific research to solving major policy issues, such as the Office of Science and Technology Policy.

Policy-relevant science and evidence-based medicine also touched all of our lives throughout the COVID-19 pandemic. The pandemic represented an exceptional period in which, according to some polls, over 90 percent of Americans could both identify and formulate an opinion about the former director of the National Institute of Allergy and Infectious Diseases (NIAID's Dr. Anthony Fauci; Hamel et al., 2020). Deference to scientific experts was also a major issue in the 2020 presidential election campaign (Maxmen et al., 2020), and one of President-Elect Biden's first actions upon securing the presidency was to assemble a team of science advisors to help inform pandemic-related policies (Subbaraman et al., 2021). The COVID-19 pandemic, then, represented a period in which the policy relevance of medical expertise became a seemingly omnipresent part of our everyday lives.

There is an empirical argument to be made on this front as well. As I show in Chapter 3, measures of anti-intellectual attitude endorsement that pertain to experts and intellectuals and to scientists are tightly linked to one another. Specifically, I argue that:

1. **Both measures used throughout this book are strongly associated with one another**. This means that Americans who display highly negative attitudes toward scientists are also very likely to display negative attitudes toward experts/intellectuals more generally (and vice versa). In other words, despite the fact that these are—at least on their face—two substantively different

ways to conceptualize expertise, many Americans tend to think about them *in the same way*.

2. **Attitudes toward scientists, experts, and intellectuals are collectively psychologically motivated by anti-intellectual thought.** In Chapter 3, I present both qualitative and quantitative evidence suggesting that the reason why measures of negative attitudes toward scientists and experts/intellectuals more generally are highly correlated is because anti-intellectual thought underlies Americans' conceptualization of both groups. There I show that when Americans are asked to define *expertise* as a general construct, many spontaneously choose to provide examples of scientists as part of that definition. I also provide evidence suggesting that many Americans harbor negative feelings toward both groups—for example, by viewing both scientists and intellectuals' interests as at odds with those of ordinary people, and by characterizing both groups as "elitist"—and that Americans who express negative attitudes toward one group more often than not tend to do so toward the other group too.

3. **Anti-expert and anti-scientist attitudes are similarly predictive of evaluations toward specific scientists and other experts.** Perhaps unsurprisingly, given their conceptual similarities, I conclude Chapter 3 by presenting evidence that the measures of attitudes toward both scientists and experts/intellectuals are similarly predictive of attitudes toward *specific* scientists and other experts. For example, people earning high scores on both measures are more likely to hold negative views not only toward famous public health experts like Dr. Fauci but also toward economists like Federal Reserve Chair Janet Yellen. This means that Americans' attitudes toward the two groups are not only similarly motivated by anti-intellectual thought but also similar in their politically relevant *effects*.

Simply put, the decision to take both a general and a specific approach to measuring Americans' anti-intellectual attitudes allows me to provide new answers to a more ambitious series of questions and is both conceptually and empirically reflective of the idea that the basic elements of anti-intellectual thought described throughout this chapter likely underlie both measures. Correspondingly, the two measures are highly correlated with one another and similarly predictive of politically relevant outcomes. While these two measures are certainly not identical in either construction or motivation, they are nevertheless similarly capable of capturing anti-intellectual attitude endorsement in American public life.

Consequently, studying how Americans feel about scientists seems like a reasonable standard for measuring anti-intellectualism. As I review in Chapter 3, measures based on this conceptualization of who counts as an expert have the added benefit of being available in dozens of public-opinion surveys conducted since the 1970s. Whereas it may be possible to develop alternative measures of anti-intellectualism *today*, it is difficult to do the same for historical periods. A narrower approach therefore makes it more possible to trace the opinion dynamics of anti-intellectual attitudes over time.

How Anti-Intellectualism Relates to Populism

Some might ask whether the definition of anti-intellectualism that I make use of throughout this book is conceptually distinct from the broader, populist mistrust of government, business, scientists, and other elites. *Populism*, as Oliver & Rahn (2016) conceptualize it in their important work on the subject, concerns the extent to which people feel that the interests of a "nefarious elite" are at odds with those of a comparatively more-virtuous general public. Populism, both in the United States and cross-nationally (Mudde & Kaltwasser, 2017), can thereby be thought about as the extent to which people prefer an expanded role for ordinary people—or, conversely, express suspicion about the role of elite actors—in many different forms of public life.

Readers may be particularly interested in how anti-intellectualism differs from science-related populism. Science-related populism is a specific form of populist sentiment (similar to that described by Oliver and Rahn and observed cross-nationally by Mudde and Kaltwasser) resulting from the perceived misalignment of interests between a "nefarious academic elite" and ordinary people (Mede & Schäfer, 2020). This perceived misalignment causes people to question whether academic experts can be considered legitimate sources of scientific knowledge and motivates demands for elevating folk and popular wisdom (Motta & Callaghan, 2020) as a legitimate source of scientific authority. Differentiating anti-intellectualism from science-related populism is especially important, given that scientists and academics are—at least in part—the types of experts that I study in this book.

Anti-intellectualism, as I conceptualize it in this book, can be contrasted from both general and science-related populist sentiment in the following ways.

First, experts, as noted earlier, play an important role in American public life. Consequently, for Oliver and Rahn, anti-intellectualism (which they term *expert mistrust*) is one of three dimensions that constitute contemporary populism in the United States. The other dimensions include *national affiliation* (i.e., feelings of patriotism and nationalism) and *anti-elite* sentiments (i.e., distrust of government and a lack of confidence in one's ability to influence it) as important components of populist opinion in the United States.

While expert mistrust may help us better understand the recent appeal of populist sentiments in the United States, I argue that there is good reason to suspect that the relationship between anti-intellectualism and populism may be more complex. In his studies of Hofstadter's work, for example, Rigney (1991) argues that Hofstadter was both aware of and concerned about the presence of anti-intellectualism in populist movements.

At the same time, however, Rigney discusses how intellectuals on both the ideological left and right have often *embraced* populist ideals, such as the importance of popular governance. As Rigney notes, Hofstadter recognized the populist tendencies of experts and intellectuals when he wrote about the "unresolvable conflict between the elite character of [their] own class and [their] democratic aspirations." (pp 407–408). For Hofstadter, populism was something that intellectuals *themselves* value, despite the potential for tension with the elite role that they play in American public life.

Moreover, some who see anti-intellectualism as a subcomponent of populist attitude endorsement might argue that both populism (generally) and anti-intellectualism (specifically) share in common the dislike and distrust of elites. After all, academics, scientists, and other experts are typically members of a social stratum that has elite doctoral-level training in their area of specialization, an educational background shared by just under 2 percent of the population more broadly (Wilson, 2017). They also theoretically occupy a meritocratic social space that rewards advancement—albeit imperfectly (i.e., in a way that reflects existing class, gender, and racial inequalities in American public life; Turner, Gonzalez, & Wong, 2011; Cundiff et al., 2018)—on the basis of the production and dissemination of knowledge.

In this way, anti-intellectual sentiment may be at least partially motivated by the dislike and distrust of elites thought to inspire populist attitude endorsement (in general) and science-related populism (in particular). Yet here too there is an important theoretical tension between the two groups of concepts. As Oliver & Rahn (2016) report in their work on populist attitude endorsement in the American public, the social, psychological, and political origins of expert mistrust are categorically different from negative attitudes toward elites more generally.

For example, those who dislike and distrust experts—in contrast to those who dislike elites more generally—may actually *hold some elites in high esteem*. As Oliver and Rahn note, fundamentalist religious beliefs play a much stronger role in motivating expert mistrust than they do that of anti-elite attitudes. This may reflect the idea that fundamentalists are more likely to strongly value the word of sacred religious texts—and those elites who communicate them (i.e., faith leaders within one's own congregation or high-profile public religious figures)— over that of scientific, academic, and other forms of expertise.

In fact, it may well be the case that elites are *instrumental* in driving anti-intellectual sentiment in the public, especially in the present day. For example, as

I expand on in much more detail in Chapter 2, attitudes toward scientific consensus, higher education, and expertise more generally have become politically and socially contentious among partisan elites (e.g., elected officials, political pundits). Members of the public who hold these figures that espouse anti-intellectual views in high esteem—likely, as I argue later on in this book, the result of their allegiances to one political party over another—may then be more likely to hold negative views toward experts.

Consequently, while anti-intellectualism is nevertheless (at least on some level) motivated by the negative feelings toward elites thought to underlie populist sentiment (in general)—and science-related populist sentiment (in particular)—it may also be *facilitated* by a selective trust in certain types of elites. This implies that anti-intellectualism may be more the result of contemporary social and political disagreement, and the dislike of experts on a highly personal level, than it is the blanket dislike and distrust of meritocracy, wealth, or academic credentials themselves.

The experience of Dr. Joshua Cuevas—a faculty member at the University of North Georgia who was subjected to threats of both psychological and bodily harm after commenting on a social media post about the 2016 election—helps to further exemplify this basic point.

In a piece that he penned recounting the incident, Dr. Cuevas wrote:

> This disdain toward academia can be attributed, in part, to the dissonance between certain ideologies and information derived from academic research in areas such as climate change, evolution, and gun violence. The elitism that some in the profession may project when trying to convince others that we are "right" exacerbates the friction, and those of us in higher education increasingly find ourselves the target of hostilities. (Joshua 2018)

For Dr. Cuevas, then, anti-elite sentiment plays something of a secondary and exacerbating role in motivating the distaste for, in this case, academic elites. Instead, he felt as if the vitriol he experienced was more the result of contemporary social and political dynamics, perhaps *exacerbated* by some academics' insistence on "being right." This account, while anecdotal, nevertheless supplements an argument I will make throughout this book (i.e., that anti-intellectualism is the result of several interrelated areas of social and political disagreement in American public life and not necessarily a subcomponent of populism).

Ultimately, resolving the theoretical tensions between populism and anti-intellectualism is an enormous question and likely lies outside the purview of what I can accomplish in this book. Instead, I opt to study the origins and policy relevance of anti-intellectualism *independently* of populism. As I note in Chapter 3, however, I make an effort to contrast the nature and effects of anti-intellectualism from other broader measures of populism whenever available data make it possible for me to do so.

What's at Stake?

Negative attitudes toward experts are problematic in and of themselves, but anti-intellectualism becomes *politically consequential* when people choose to act on it. High levels of anti-intellectual attitude endorsement might not be so problematic, for example, if it does not play a role in shaping how Americans think about politics and policy.

Unfortunately, however, anti-intellectualism has several important and politically relevant effects. Past research finds, for example, that people who endorse anti-intellectual attitudes are more likely to vote for political candidates who are themselves hostile to experts and the role that they play in the policymaking process (Motta, 2018a). Anti-intellectualism is also associated with the rejection of scientific consensus on salient policy issues like climate change (Motta, 2018a; Merkley, 2020) and noncompliance with expert-recommended health behavior (Merkley & Loewen, 2021).

These findings may seem fairly obvious. It is perhaps unsurprising that people who hold negative views toward experts are less willing to defer to experts in their everyday lives or to value the role that they might play in shaping public policy.

However, there is still much we still don't know about anti-intellectualism and its policy influence. As I describe at length in Chapter 2, for example, most research on anti-intellectualism is correlational. This makes it difficult to tease out whether anti-intellectualism causes people to develop more negative attitudes about experts' policy influence, whether policy attitudes shape anti-intellectualism, or whether both might be simultaneously true.

More generally, the field lacks a unified conceptual theory that attempts to not only understand why some people are more likely to hold anti-intellectual attitudes than others but also to study factors that contribute to shifts in anti-intellectualism over time. Whether political elites are responsive to fluctuations in anti-intellectual opinion, the prevalence of anti-intellectual attitude endorsement, and the scope of policies that anti-intellectualism might influence have not been thoroughly investigated in prior research.

This book attempts to answer those questions by bringing together a diverse collection of data to test a novel and unified theoretical model that explains where anti-intellectualism comes from and why we should care about it.

The Plan of This Book

Having just defined what anti-intellectualism is and explaining the general approach I take to measuring anti-intellectual attitude endorsement in public-opinion research, this book proceeds as follows. Chapter 2 proposes a novel, unified, and group-centric theory for understanding the potential causes and consequences of anti-intellectualism. The theoretical model makes predictions about (1) the socio-political factors that explain differences between people in their willingness to endorse anti-intellectual attitudes, (2) how epistemic abilities and motivations might lead people to change anti-intellectual attitudes over time, and (3) the dynamic relationship between opposition to the role that experts play in the policymaking process and anti-intellectualism.

Drawing on previous political psychological research, the model suggests that partisan affiliation with the Republican party, ideological conservatism, and limited-government attitudes can help explain individual differences in anti-intellectual attitude endorsement. Similarly, the model predicts that socio-cultural factors like religiosity can help explain who holds anti-intellectual attitudes and who does not.

In contrast to previous work on anti-intellectualism, the model also argues that political polarization with respect to anti-intellectual attitude acceptance is a fairly (and, in fact, almost exclusively) recent phenomenon. I argue that partisan and ideological polarization tracks closely with changes in how Republican political elites have framed discussions about experts in recent years. This argument pushes back on the findings of past work, which posits that the political polarization of anti-intellectual attitudes began in the 1980s and has either (1) grown steadily over time or (2) arose in response to the presidencies of Ronald Reagan and George W. Bush. I offer a conceptual alternative, making the case that the (more recent) Tea Party movement's embrace of rhetorical strategies that denigrate scientific experts accelerated political polarization and is uniquely responsible for this development.

Moreover, as people rarely change their political and religious orientations over time, the model proposes that these factors are more likely to explain differences in anti-intellectual attitude endorsement between people rather than within-person change over time. More mutable factors, such as how much people know about the basics of scientific research and (especially) interest in scientific topics, should better explain why some come to hold more anti-intellectual attitudes over time.

Finally, the model attempts to apply an often-overlooked prediction from Hofstadter's 1963 book to contemporary American life, arguing that anti-intellectual attitudes both shape and are shaped by aversions to the role that experts play in the policymaking process. While much social science research looks at the effect of anti-intellectual attitudes on a variety of political and policy-relevant outcomes, few consider the possibility that the relationship may function in reverse. Hofstadter, however, argued that Americans' negative feelings toward experts is due, at least in part, to discomfort with the increasingly powerful role that scientists and other experts play in governing not only our own personal lives (e.g., requiring medical specialists to diagnose bodily ailments) but also our democracy (e.g., policies informed by increasingly complex technical knowledge and expert input). Consequently, I propose that the relationship between anti-intellectualism and aversion to the role that experts play in the policymaking process is *bidirectional*. I refer to this prediction as the Bidirectionality Thesis throughout the book.

Chapter 3 details (in a nontechnical way) the two ways I measure anti-intellectual attitude endorsement in public-opinion surveys. In addition to offering a brief summary of the different public-opinion datasets I rely on throughout this book to test several key elements of my theoretical model, the chapter's primary goal is to put forward a data-driven exploration of the various factors Americans consider when evaluating the different types of experts referenced in each measurement approach (a *content validation* exercise), whether people tend to earn similar scores across measures (*convergent validation*), and the extent to which each measure is associated with contemporary manifestations of anti-intellectualism in American public life (*predictive validation*). I find that each of these two measures (while substantively distinct) nevertheless share much in common and are both valid indicators of anti-intellectual attitude endorsement.

For those readers interested in the nearly fifty years' worth of micro-level public-opinion data I rely on throughout the book, as well as technical information about the estimation strategies I use to test my theoretical expectations, I have written a technical compendium for this chapter that you can find in the appendix. As a general matter, I believe that each dataset, estimation approach, and measure of anti-intellectual attitude endorsement brings a unique set of advantages and disadvantages to studying each element of the theoretical model. Consequently, I conclude Chapter 3 by making the case that while no single study is perfectly suited to study the questions I hope to answer, they *collectively* provide a pluralistic and empirically robust approach for doing so.

Chapter 4 then provides a data-driven overview of the prevalence of anti-intellectual attitude endorsement in American public life. I begin by discussing how I am able to use public-opinion data to devise aggregated measures of public anti-intellectual sentiments spanning the majority of the past century. Across hundreds of aggregated cross-sectional surveys ranging from 1944 to 2021, employing a wide range of measurement and sampling strategies, I show that—although anti-intellectualism fluctuates to some degree over time—approximately one third of

Americans tend to hold anti-intellectual attitudes at any given time. I also offer new evidence of an uptick in public anti-intellectual attitude endorsement on the eve of the candidacies of George Wallace and Donald Trump (two prominent presidential candidates who frequently invoked anti-intellectual rhetoric on the campaign trail and, as I discuss in the chapter, often did so in surprisingly similar ways).

After assessing the contemporary prevalence of anti-intellectual attitude endorsement, I offer tests of each portion of the theory outlined in Chapter 2.

Chapter 5 begins by assessing the determinants of differences in anti-intellectualism between people. Across dozens of cross-sectional studies, I find that—consistent with theoretical expectations—highly temporally stable socio-political factors such as political orientations (partisanship, ideology) and religiosity can help explain why some people hold anti-intellectual attitudes while others do not. Specifically, I find that Republicans, political conservatives, people who prefer a smaller role for government in everyday life, and highly religious people are more likely to hold anti-intellectual attitudes.

Although some of these correlates of anti-intellectualism have been studied in previous correlational work, Chapter 5 advances previous research by supplementing cross-sectional analyses (using panel data) to show that these effects are not reverse causal. People, for example, do not choose to become Republicans because they hold negative views toward experts; they hold negative views toward experts because they are Republicans.

Importantly, Chapter 5 also advances previous work by demonstrating that the strong influence of political partisanship, ideology, and limited-government attitudes on anti-intellectual attitude endorsement is a recent phenomenon. Contrary to previous work on the subject, which suggests that political polarization in anti-intellectual attitude endorsement has either increased steadily since the 1980s or in response to discrete political events (i.e., the anti-science policies pursued by presidents Ronald Reagan and George W. Bush), I find that the popularity of the Tea Party movement, following the election of Barack Obama in 2008, played a critical role in linking right-wing politics and anti-intellectual attitudes. I also devise new tests of this proposition not possible in previous research on the subject.

Across dozens of multivariate statistical tests, I find that the political polarization of anti-intellectual attitude endorsement accelerated following the election of Barack Obama. Polarization was relatively rare prior to the 2010 Tea Party wave midterm election, with Republicans and Democrats expressing similar attitudes toward experts until the mid-2000s, and I find that polarization became significantly more common in its aftermath. I further substantiate this point by showing that Tea Party–identifying Republicans were more likely than all other Republicans to endorse anti-intellectual sentiments during the Obama presidency. In addition to advancing insights from previous work on the sources of partisan polarization with respect to anti-intellectual attitude endorsement, this underscores the politically pernicious impact of the Tea Party movement on US opinion in an understudied area.

Chapter 6 goes on to offer a novel exploration into how *epistemic abilities* (i.e., knowledge of basic scientific facts) and *motivations* (i.e., interest in scientific topics) shape within-person change in anti-intellectual attitude endorsement over time. I find that while both science knowledge and interest are correlated with anti-intellectualism in cross-sectional surveys, only gains in science interest are associated with decreased anti-intellectualism in panel surveys. This latter finding is consistent with recent work from a growing literature on the political psychology of science interest and curiosity.

I also show that these effects are particularly strong for survey panelists who are currently in the process of receiving a college degree. This pattern of results is consistent with insights from political socialization research proposing that exposure to new people and ideas in college—including experts and intellectuals—may stimulate both interest in academic research and those who produce it. At the same time, I find little evidence that change in the (theoretically quite stable) socio-political factors that can help us better understand between-person differences in anti-intellectual attitude endorsement (Chapter 5) explains individual-level change in anti-intellectual attitude endorsement.

Correspondingly, Chapter 6 helps differentiate the correlates of anti-intellectualism that are useful for explaining differences between people from those who can help us understand why people embrace more (or less) anti-intellectual attitudes over time. It also serves as the basis for a series of recommendations that I make in the book's conclusion regarding how to design effective strategic communication interventions that facilitate trust in scientists and other experts.

Chapter 7 offers a general test of the dynamic relationship between anti-intellectual attitude endorsement and opposition to the role that experts play in the policymaking process. I begin the chapter with a contemporary example of Hofstadter's often-overlooked expectations: drawing on how Governor Ron DeSantis's (R-FL) opposition to Dr. Anthony Fauci's policy influence in the Biden White House during the COVID-19 pandemic informed his anti-expert rhetoric and health-policy maneuvers.

I then show, consistent with theoretical expectations (and again making use of panel data), that preferences regarding experts' roles in the policymaking process and anti-intellectual attitude endorsement are co-constitutive. People who become more anti-intellectual are less likely to want experts to exert a strong influence on shaping public policies. At the same time, people prefer a smaller policy role for experts tend to embrace more general negativity toward expertise. These findings are the first to highlight the bidirectional nature of anti-intellectualism and its policy consequences, in line with Hofstadter's overlooked predictions, and serve as an important conceptual context for understanding the analyses presented in Chapters 8.

Chapter 8 takes a multifaceted look at the impact anti-intellectualism has on contemporary American social and political life. This a discussion includes how anti-intellectualism shapes support for expert-backed policies and the role that experts play in the policymaking process in three distinct areas: the macroeconomic performance, public health policy during and after the COVID-19 pandemic, and the politics of climate-change denial. My hope, in doing this, is not to provide an exhaustive list of the potential policy domains in which anti-intellectualism might have an impact. Instead, my goal is to demonstrate that anti-intellectualism has a powerful influence on policymaking in the United States in a diverse range of policy areas.

I begin Chapter 8 by studying anti-intellectualism in relation to macroeconomic policy orientations. At the micro and cross-sectional level, I find that anti-intellectualism is associated with the devaluation of economists' policy-relevant expertise on issues related to unemployment and taxation. I also present new evidence that shows the correlation between widespread shifts in anti-intellectualism and legislative consultation with experts on matters pertaining to economic policy. Specifically, I find that in periods of heightened public anti-intellectual attitude endorsement Congress tends to invite fewer testimonies from experts on macroeconomic issues.

I then investigate the link between anti-intellectual attitude endorsement and public evaluations of scientific consensus on climate change, as well as support for evidence-based policies aimed at mitigating and adapting to its pernicious effects. I again find that anti-intellectualism (at the individual level) is associated with the rejection of scientific consensus on climate change and opposition to efforts to mitigate or adapt to climate change. Likewise, in the aggregate, I find that increased anti-intellectual attitude endorsement is associated with less congressional solicitation of expert input on climate-focused legislation (measured as congressional hearing counts on environmental issues, which I both conceptually and empirically validate as a strong proxy for expert involvement in the legislative process).

Finally, I study the association between anti-intellectual attitudes and public health attitudes/behavior throughout and beyond the COVID-19 pandemic, including the acceptance of pandemic-related misinformation, compliance with expert-recommended health behaviors (e.g., social distancing, mask wearing, and vaccine uptake), and more-general support for expert-backed health policies (e.g., childhood vaccine mandates in public schools). I again find that anti-intellectualism is strongly associated with opposition to expert consensus and health recommendations.

Collectively, the findings presented in Chapter 8 suggest that anti-intellectualism poses two important challenges to American governance. It not only fosters opposition toward the involvement of experts in policymaking but also influences the actions of political leaders in Congress .

Chapter 9 concludes by summarizing the lessons learned from the analyses presented in this book and suggests directions for future research. In Chapter 9, I conclude that anti-intellectualism is the product of both socio-political and epistemic forces. It both shapes and is shaped by views about the role that experts play in the policymaking process. Most notably, anti-intellectualism generates opposition among both political elites and the broader American public to the influence of experts on policy matters in several critical areas.

Consequently, I suggest that one question scholars should explore in the future is how to reduce anti-intellectual attitude acceptance. In contrast to "piecemeal" efforts to boost trust in scientists and other experts suggested in previous research, I point to analyses presented in Chapter 6 as offering a potentially unified approach to combating anti-intellectualism. I suggest that efforts to stimulate Americans' interest in and curiosity about science, technology, and related matters could help mitigate the extent to which Americans express negativity toward experts. I also discuss how social scientists might put this approach to the test in future research. More generally, I suggest several different directions for future research on the study of anti-intellectualism, including the possibility of contextualizing anti-intellectual attitude endorsement in the United States, cross-nationally. I provide some preliminary insights in this regard, drawn on recent data that illustrates Americans' skepticism toward experts as being comparatively typical among residents of other wealthy liberal democracies.

A Word of Caution: Experts Are People Too

Before moving on, I want to be careful to say that my objective in this book is not to claim that deference to experts is *always* desirable. People with superior knowledge about a variety of subjects have been shown to be subject to the same evaluative biases (Kahneman & Klein, 2009; Kahneman, 2011) as most other people. Experts also experience the temptation to arrive at decisions that reinforce their previously held beliefs, both within (Beattie & Snider, 2019) and outside (Kahan, 2015) their areas of expertise.

Consequently, expert predictions may, in some situations, perform no better than the general public at making predictions about future events (Ungar et al., 2012). More generally, academics, from time to time, engage in fraudulent research practices (Jamieson, 2018; Jamieson et al., 2019). And while most scientists may be primarily motivated by producing rigorous and substantively impactful research (Funk, Rainie, & Page, 2015), they are not necessarily immune from taking academic prestige and career-related considerations into account.

Experts, in other words, are people too. It is important that we recognize their potential fallibility.

Additionally, I am not claiming that experts are a monolithic group who uniformly agree on the policy-relevant recommendations they might provide. For example, some medical doctors hold skeptical views toward vaccine safety (Callaghan et al., 2022). Some climate scientists think that humans are not primarily responsible for changes in average global temperatures (Carlton et al., 2015). While these individuals hold views outside of the mainstream of what other experts in their respective fields consider to be true, it is nevertheless important to recognize that well-educated and highly skilled people can reasonably disagree, from time to time, about matters of consensus.

This, of course, is not to say that unanimity is required for experts to make meaningful policy recommendations. Instead, what is most important is attempting to formulate policies that align with widely held views in expert communities that are supported by rigorously and transparently substantiated empirical data.

Instead, I encourage what we might call a *healthy skepticism* of expert advice and scientific research. Skepticism, after all, lies at the heart of the scientific method. Social scientists (like myself) test every hypothesis that we expect to be true against the possibility that we might be wrong. Peer reviewers draw on substantively similar knowledge bases to critique work in their fields. And we achieve scholarly consensus not on the basis of a single study but by weighing the balance of evidence, accumulated over time, that either supports or fails to support a particular point of view.

My hope is that Americans and policymakers alike employ similar principles when deciding just how much they ought to defer to subject-matter experts. This does *not* mean—as I discuss in this book—that it is acceptable to shut experts out of the policymaking process or that negative attitudes toward who they are as people are justified.

Healthy skepticism instead begs both experts and the public to engage in productive discourse about the role that expertise ought to play in American public life. For experts, this means trying to communicate the results of their research and their policy-relevant views and advice in ways that anyone can understand. By doing so, they provide insight, in accessible language, into the process by which they "know what they know." We need to then use that information to evaluate the soundness of the evidence and the policy prescriptions that experts might make. Is a particular viewpoint shared by most people who are experts in this field? Did experts consider the possibility that they might be wrong or try to detect fraud? Asking and answering these questions can help promote a useful form of evidence-based skepticism.

As an example of what it might mean to employ healthy skepticism in practice, consider the case of the Food and Drug Administration's (FDA) approval of BioGen's Aducanumab (also known as Aduhelm). Aduhelm is an intravenous preventive treatment for Alzheimer's that, initially, was found to have so little impact on staving off cognitive decline that the drug's clinical trials were suspended (Mullard, 2021). After drug manufacturers provided new analyses suggesting some—albeit very minimal—effectiveness of the drug in high doses (Abbott 2019) FDA regulators granted the drug a pathway to accelerated approval (FDA, 2021).

The FDA's decision was met with both optimism and ire.

For those suffering from Alzheimer's, either personally or through the experiences of a loved one, the drug offered new hope in the fight against a (presently) incurable illness. However, some experts—including an FDA advisory committee comprised of medical and scientific professionals—raised concerns that the drug's minimal effectiveness did not justify its high price: over $50,000 per year (Hensley, Hamilton, & Wamsley, 2021). Some health experts, such as former Clinton administration director of the Department of Health and Human Services, Donna Shalala, raised further questions about whether a "revolving door" (Piller, 2018) relationship between FDA regulators—some of whom had worked with BioGen in the past (Feuerstein, Herper, & Garde, 2021)—and private industry might have created a perverse incentive for the government to perform the logistical maneuvers necessary to give the drug a "second chance" at approval despite evidence of minimal effectiveness (Garde & Florko, 2021).

The Aduhelm case offers a useful opportunity to put the principles of healthy skepticism into action. In this case, there appears to be a legitimate, research-oriented case for doubting the (potential) career or profit-seeking intentions of scientists at the FDA. While the drug's low levels of effectiveness (backed by scientific research) and the fact that some regulators had previously worked with BioGen *does not necessarily imply* nefarious intent, it nevertheless suggests a reasonable possibility of such. Opposition to the drug's approval from members of the scientific community further underscores the legitimacy of these considerations. Healthy skepticism of scientists' intentions in the Aduhelm case can be contrasted with, for example, those questioning the motives of government scientists and regulators who approved mRNA and other COVID-19 vaccines for emergency use during the pandemic. Backed by rigorous clinical trial data suggesting that widespread vaccination was both a highly effective and safe way to prevent infection from COVID-19—thereby having the potential to put a global pandemic that, as of this writing, has claimed over a million American lives into a state of decline—regulators were on solid scientific and normative ground to approve these vaccines for public use. In contrast to those whom we might call *blanket skeptics* (e.g., people who believe that government scientists and other regulatory experts have "something to gain" from approving demonstrably life-saving vaccines), healthy skepticism questions experts' motives and intentions on a case-by-case basis and in the absence of compelling evidence to the contrary.

Unfortunately, though, for many Americans, suspicions about experts' intentions look less like the (arguably healthier) standards we might reasonably apply to the Aduhelm case and more like the blanket skepticism applied to government regulators during the COVID-19 pandemic. For many Americans, negative attitudes toward the scientific community are both highly personal, resentful, and—as I demonstrate throughout this book—ultimately not constructive. This book aims to better understand the origins and policy consequences of anti-intellectualism so that, as a society, we might one day make responsible decisions based on the best available expert evidence.

Anti-Scientific Americans: The Prevalence, Origins, and Political Consequences of Anti-Intellectualism in the US.
Matthew Motta, Oxford University Press. © Oxford University Press 2024. DOI: 10.1093/9780197788844.003.0001

2

The Nature and Origins
of Anti-Intellectualism

How Americans feel about experts *as people* lies at the conceptual heart of what it means to hold anti-intellectual attitudes. Consequently, understanding how people come to hold negative views toward experts (as a group) is essential for understanding (1) where anti-intellectualism comes from and (2) how it might influence politics and public policy.

My goal in this chapter is to offer a unified conceptual framework for understanding the origins and policy consequences of anti-intellectualism. This is no easy task. In fact, my efforts to offer a unified theory of where anti-intellectualism comes from, and why it matters, enter into an area of academic uncertainty and active debate.

Whereas many have considered the potential correlates of anti-intellectualism, few have attempted to study how these factors might lead to change in anti-intellectualism over time. This distinction is important.

On the one hand, some highly stable individual-level attitudes—such as the political party with which people identify—might be well suited to explain why some people hold anti-intellectual attitudes while others do not (e.g., due to increasing political conflict over how partisan elites view expertise) but comparatively less well suited to explain why people change their views toward scientists and experts over time (i.e., because partisan affiliations themselves are unlikely to change much over time for most people). On the other hand, more-malleable attitudes that are comparatively more likely to change over time—such as the extent to which people take an interest in scientific research (which may stimulate open-minded thinking about even politically contentious expert policy recommendations)—may be better suited (i.e., sufficiently variable) to explain why some people come to hold less versus more anti-intellectual attitudes over time.

Moreover, whereas past research often treats anti-intellectualism as an exogenous influence on policy attitudes and related behaviors, few consider the possibility that the reverse might be true. In other words, it could be the case that uneasiness about the role that experts play in the policymaking process not only is influenced by anti-intellectualism but could *itself* motivate anti-intellectual attitude endorsement. Interestingly, Richard Hofstadter initially raised this possibility in his pioneering 1963 book on anti-intellectualism. However, it has gone relatively unexplored in the years following the book's publication.

Throughout this chapter, I offer a new, *group-centric theory* that aims to better explain causes and consequences of anti-intellectual sentiment.

The idea that anti-intellectualism is both affective and group based—i.e., that it pertains to negative affect expressed toward experts (as a social group)—has received some attention in previous research (e.g., Motta, 2018a; Merkley, 2020; Barker, DeTamble, & Marietta, 2022; Lunz-Trujillo, 2022). This work, however, varies considerably with respect to how it conceptualizes the psychological underpinnings of anti-intellectualism as an affective and group-based phenomenon.

Barker and colleagues (2022), for example, draw a conceptual distinction between identifying as an intellectual (e.g., holding advanced academic degrees, self-identifying as a "nerd") and the affective negativity toward experts. Others, like Lunz-Trujillo (2022), see anti-intellectualism as (at least in part) the result of identity-based conflict in socio-political domains that do not necessarily pertain to scientific, academic, and other forms of expertise (e.g., rural social identification).

What I aim to do throughout this book is to provide a more-general account of where anti-intellectualism comes from and how it impacts contemporary American public life.

In what follows, I first offer a very general psychological account of how expert negativity may arise from group-based conflict. Then I turn to the specifics. Using this more-general psychological discussion as a backdrop, I discuss how many different socio-political attitudes, identities, and behaviors can help explain (1) why some people are more likely to express anti-intellectual attitudes than others and (2) why some people come to hold more (or fewer) negative attitudes toward scientists and experts over time. I then consider Hofstadter's understudied predictions regarding how anti-intellectualism and opposition to the role that experts play in the policy-making process might influence one another, which I term the *Bidirectionality Thesis*. Collectively, these predictions offer a novel and conceptually unified framework for understanding the origins and policy consequences of anti-intellectualism.

Understanding Anti-Intellectualism: An Affective and Group-Centric Theory

My characterization of anti-intellectualism as an affective and group-based phenomenon begins with a simple premise. Experts, as *people*, are an important and recognizable social group in American public life (Barker, DeTamble, and Marietta, 2022; Lunz-Trujillo, 2022).

From this very basic principle stems the idea that some Americans may choose whether to incorporate this group into how it is that they understand *their own* sense of self in their social worlds. Allegiances to experts—or to those who challenge them—can thereby provide people with both psychological and material benefits.

Before delving into the psychological theories and research that support this general idea, I want to first think about the type of person who conceptualizes experts (as a social group) as being part of their own identity. Someone who views expertise as essential to their self-concept might be the type of person who adorns their office bookshelves with a Dr. Fauci bobblehead or lights a Grace Hopper prayer candle in the background during a Zoom meeting (all of which, by the way, are available for purchase at the local independent bookstore across the street from my apartment). They might also be the types of people who take it upon themselves to make plans with like-minded friends to attend public lectures or book signings from famous scientists.

These behaviors signal to others that they are on the same *team* (i.e., that they hold similar views about expertise and the role that experts play in public life). This might afford individual opportunities for people to engage with others who share their views and thereby feel as if they belong to a social group of their own.

We might observe a similar pattern among those who view skepticism of scientists, academics, and other experts as essential to understanding their sense of self. These people may be the types who wear "Arrest Fauci!" t-shirts (which I recently saw in the Salt Lake City airport while writing this passage) or who attach "INFOWARS" bumper stickers to their cars. They might also be the kind of people who organize events protesting the implementation of vaccine and other public health measures in schools at local school board meetings. Again, both sets of actions provide people with the opportunity to signal which team they are on and to reap the psychological benefits associated with belonging to a group of others who think similarly.

Group membership, of course, is not entirely positive. The integration of experts into one's understanding of their own self-concept could potentially breed *negative affect* toward those who think differently about that group and the role that they play in public life. This basic psychological process lies at the heart of my conceptualization of anti-intellectualism as an affective and group-based phenomenon.

Psychologically Unpacking the Group-Based Origins of Expert Dislike and Distrust

To understand why anti-intellectualism is both affective and group based, we first need to unpack three widely used acronyms in the study of social psychology: Social Identity Theory, Self-Categorization Theory, and Integrated Threat

Theory. Together these three social psychological theories help explain why some people choose to incorporate experts into how they understand their place in American social life and explain why some express highly personalized negativity toward experts.

Social Identity Theory (SIT) is the idea that people derive self-esteem from belonging to social groups (Tajfel, 1974; Abrams and Hogg, 1988). Psychologists argue that the "need to belong" is a fundamental human motivation (Fiske 2000, 2018; Fasce et al., 2023 that may have evolutionary roots pertaining to the benefits of group membership with respect to survival (e.g., the sharing of communal resources and organization to ward off human and animal threats; see Tooby and Cosmides, 2010; Clark et al., 2019). According to SIT, the more that being a member of a social group helps to satisfy this fundamental human motivation, the more likely we are to integrate that group into our own identity (Huddy, 2003; Huddy & Bankert, 2017).

Self-Categorization Theory (SCT) provides a mechanism by which individuals can seek out groups with which to identify. SCT predicts that people are aware of group norms, reputations, and potential members on the basis of generalizations about who belongs to those groups (Turner et al., 1987). This enables people to figure out whether an existing social group might be amenable to accepting people like them. Jointly, SIT and SCT predict that once a relevant group is identified people become more likely to adhere to the norms and behaviors that this group expresses in everyday social life, including those actions that advance the group's social and material status (Huddy & Bankert, 2017). This process not only allows people to feel a sense of belonging within the group but also helps signal to others that they are a loyal member of the group (Huddy, 2001, 2003).

The actions that group members take on, in the name of social cohesion, can be either promotional or antagonistic in nature. When group members participate in the traditions and norms associated with that group, their actions largely serve to bolster the in-group (i.e., the group to which they belong). Loyal Red Sox fans, for example, will enthusiastically sing Neil Diamond's *Sweet Caroline* during the seventh-inning stretch of a home game at Fenway Park.

Groups, however, may identify the existence of *other* social groups with motivations, attitudes, and behaviors that are perceived to be at odds with their own. SIT and SCT predict that people may take up actions aimed at *denigrating* out-groups (e.g., chanting "Yankees suck!" in the stands at Fenway Park during a rivalry game between New York and Boston).

Integrated Threat Theory (ITT) helps explain why group members take actions that both bolster the in-group and denigrate one or several out-groups (Stephan & Stephan, 2013; Fasce et al., 2021). When people feel as if an out-group poses a credible threat—either material (*realistic threat*, in ITT parlance) or psychological (*symbolic threat*)—to their in-group, they are more likely to express attitudes and behaviors that harm the other group (Grieve & Hogg 1999; Fasce et al., 2021). Anxious sports fans fearing a potential loss, for example, might resort to subjecting one another to verbal or physical abuse prior to a touted rivalry game.

Applying SIT, SCT, and ITT to Anti-Intellectual Attitude Endorsement

Taking these three ideas together, we can next see how anti-intellectualism is likely both an affective and group-based phenomenon.

According to these three social psychological theories, some people choose to signal to others that they hold negative views toward scientists, intellectuals, and other experts (SCT). This helps them feel as if they belong (SIT) to groups organized around the rejection of science and expertise (e.g., online COVID-19 medical conspiracy theory communities). As an evidence-based demonstration of this principle in a related application, my colleagues Krissy Lunz-Trujillo, Tim Callaghan, Steven Sylvester, and I (2021) have shown that many people who hold skeptical views toward scientific consensus on issues related to vaccine safety seek belonging from organized anti-vaccine communities and consider the "anti-vax" label to be a central component of their social identity (anti-vaccine social identity, or AVSID).

Fearing that experts might pose either a material or psychological threat to the group (ITT)—e.g., by producing research that debunks pseudoscientific beliefs—group members might then take up attitudes and behaviors (SCT) that aim to denigrate the out-group, such as by attending "mask-burning" events (Olmos, 2021) or vaccine-mandate protests (Forman, 2021) or by threatening physical violence against medical doctors (Elassar, Lavandera, & Killough, 2021). Turning again to our (2021) research on anti-vaccine social identity, we find that those for whom AVSID is most central to their self-concept are more likely to oppose vaccine mandates in public schools.

This, of course, is not to say that all people who hold negative attitudes toward experts are members of groups *specifically* organized around the rejection of science and other forms of expertise. Identification with many other socially and politically relevant groups may play a role in fueling expert negativity. For example, people who strongly socially identify as members of rural communities have been shown to be more likely to hold negative views toward experts (Lunz-Trujillo, 2022). According to Lunz-Trujillo (2022) people who socially identify as members of rural communities might come to view experts as a dislikable out-group, such that they fear that scientists, academics, and other experts— whom they see as being comparatively more likely to be from urban areas—as making an effort to tell people in urban areas how to live their lives (i.e., by making evidence-based arguments and policies that impose value systems that are at odds with those of individuals living in urban areas).

Here it is worthwhile to note the important (yet complicated) role that partisan social identity might play in shaping anti-intellectual attitudes. As I discuss in much more detail later in this chapter, the rejection of expertise (broadly) and several policy-relevant aspects of scientific consensus (e.g., the reality of anthropogenic climate change, the public health threats posed by COVID-19) have become entangled with partisanship in the United States, such that Republicans at both the elite and mass level are more likely to reject many forms of expertise.

Correspondingly, some may harbor negative attitudes toward experts not because they belong to groups *specifically* focused on the rejection of expertise but because they are members of a political "team" for whom holding these views can help signify group membership. In this way, partisan social identity—i.e., the tendency to view one's affiliation with one of the major political parties in the United States as central to one's sense of self (Huddy, Mason, & Aarøe, 2015; Mason, 2018)—might motivate out-group animosity (Iyengar, Sood, & Lelkes, 2012) toward social groups deemed to be affiliated with the "other side" (Mason & Wronski, 2018), which may include negative feelings toward experts (Kahan, 2017c).

However, while partisan social identity offers a useful lens for understanding the prevalence of anti-intellectual attitudes *today*, it is important to note that this may not have always been the case. As I review later in this chapter, and demonstrate in Chapter 5, there was a time when attitudes toward experts were not distinctly partisan in nature. In fact, for *most* of the past forty years, Republicans and Democrats have held similar views about scientists and the role that science plays in public life. Correspondingly, while it is worthwhile to consider how intersecting social identities might influence negative feelings toward experts, it may be the case that partisan social identity does so only in recent years.

The psychological underpinnings of how we feel toward experts, of course, raises several important questions. Why are some people more likely to hold positive (or negative) views toward experts than others? In what ways might we observe the political consequences of expert negativity? Can affect toward experts itself be shaped by considerations about the role that experts play in the policymaking process? How might anti-intellectualism impact Americans' views about contemporary policy debates?

I answer these questions by proposing a new theoretical model—grounded in the principle that anti-expert attitudes are both affective and group centric— that aims to unpack the origins and policy consequences of anti-intellectualism.

The Political Psychological Inputs and Policy-Relevant Outputs of Anti-Intellectual Attitude Endorsement

My efforts to understand the nature and origins of anti-intellectual attitude endorsement consist of two parts: (1) *inputs* (factors that shape *why* some people hold negative feelings toward experts and (2) *outputs* (the relationship between anti-expert attitudes and opposition to experts' influence in the policymaking process). Proposing a unified, group-centric theory of anti-intellectualism is important because such a theory can help resolve areas of uncertainty and debate in previous research on the subject.

Before doing so, however, it is important to reiterate that this book is not the first to study the factors that shape anti-intellectual attitude endorsement and its potential policy consequences. However, previous research is often agnostic about the temporal dynamics that underlie the causes and consequences of anti-intellectualism. Specifically, most past research on anti-intellectualism is often *correlational*. This means that scholars typically assume that anti-intellectualism is the product of socio-political inputs, such as Americans' political views and religiosity. I summarize in detail what several of those inputs might be in the pages that follow.

However, fewer researchers (if any) have tested whether this assumption is accurate. Presently it is uncertain whether these factors simply explain *static differences* between people who hold (or do not hold) anti-intellectual attitudes, *dynamic differences* within people whose levels of anti-intellectual attitude endorsement change over time, or some combination of the two. Fewer still have considered the possibility that many of the inputs that we consider to be causes of anti-intellectualism might themselves be shaped by changes in negative feelings toward experts. Social scientists refer to this latter point as the possibility of *reverse causality*.

The same can be said of much research on the policy-relevant outputs of anti-intellectual attitude endorsement. Some longitudinal studies (i.e., surveys that interview the same people several times) find that as people become more anti-intellectual over time they tend to also become more likely to spurn expert-backed health-behavior recommendations (Merkley & Loewen, 2021). However, as I review shortly, studies like this are the exception to most research on the subject and represent only a limited selection of policy-relevant areas that anti-intellectualism might impact. There may instead be good theoretical reason to consider the *bidirectionality* of a relationship between anti-intellectualism and policy-relevant attitudes, such that change in one may inspire change in the other.

Figure 2.1 takes this complicated brew of potential relationships between the phenomena I hope to study in this book and offers a distilled summary of the group-centric model I plan to advance. Moving from left to right, the model summarizes the relationship between two different classes of factors that can potentially explain anti-intellectual attitude endorsement (inputs). These include foundational and highly stable socio-political attitudes (static inputs), and less-malleable epistemic competencies and motivations (dynamic inputs). I hypothesize that the former set of static inputs (path a) are best suited to explain why

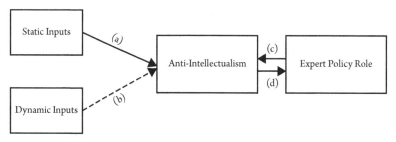

Figure 2.1 Theoretical Model Summary

some people hold anti-intellectual attitudes while others do not (i.e., *between-person* differences in anti-intellectualism). I then hypothesize that the latter set of dynamic inputs (path b) are best suited to explain *within-person* change in anti-intellectualism.

Moving further to the right, the model then summarizes the potential policy outputs of anti-intellectual attitude endorsement. Here the theory becomes a bit more conceptually complex. As path c indicates, anti-intellectualism should have policy-relevant consequences, such as the discounting of expertise in the policymaking process. However, uneasiness about experts' policy relevancy might further engender opposition toward the scientific community (path d). In other words, the relationship between anti-intellectualism and its potential policy consequences ought to be *bidirectional*.

For the remainder of this chapter, I summarize how past psychological research on intergroup processes and social science research on the correlates of anti-intellectualism motivate each step of the conceptual model outlined here. I also lay a conceptual framework that builds the case that the Tea Party movement of the late 2000s is primarily responsible for the strong levels of partisan polarization in anti-intellectual attitude endorsement that we see today.

This argument stands in some contrast to work arguing that polarization has been increasing gradually over time (or even that it just began in the late 1980s). Both discussions help lay the theoretical foundation for many of the empirical tests I conduct throughout this book.

Static Inputs: Who Holds Anti-Intellectual Attitudes?

The first class of socio-political factors that could potentially shape anti-intellectual attitude endorsement are what I refer to in Figure 2.1 as *static inputs*. Static inputs include political factors such as individuals' partisan identity, symbolic ideological attachments, and preferences for limited government. It also includes social factors like how frequently one attends religious services (i.e., religiosity), irrespective of denomination or one's particular religious persuasion. In the following sections, I explain why each of these factors might be associated with anti-intellectual attitude endorsement and review relevant literature attempting to understand those relationships.

Before I do so, though, it is important to note that although these static inputs are diverse in scope, they nevertheless share two important attributes in common. First, all factors are generally thought to be quite stable throughout the life course. Past political psychological research, for example, suggests that people rarely change their partisan affiliations (Campbell et al., 1960; Converse, 1964), and when they do they tend to change not the party with which they affiliate but the strength of those partisan attachments (Miller, 1991; Green & Palmquist, 1990, 1994). Preferences for limited government (Goren, 2005, 2013), symbolic ideological orientations (Kinder & Kalmoe, 2017), and religiosity (particularly in adulthood; Argue, Johnson, & White, 1999; Margolis, 2018) are also thought to be generally stable.

Second, all of the aforementioned static inputs are thought to give structure to politically relevant preferences (and not vice versa). In other words, these factors antecede the development of specific policy preferences. Political and sociological research finds, for example, that young children often share the political affiliations (Beck & Jennings, 1975; Jennings & Markus, 1984; Jennings, Stoker, & Bowers, 2009) and religious orientations of their parents (although note that, consistent with life cycle theories of religious socialization, some adolescents may briefly rebel against the religious traditions in which they were socialized before determining whether to return; Margolis, 2018). Although many of these effects are likely attributable to early experiences in childhood, bio-political research further suggests that partisan and ideological identities may even be, to some degree, heritable (Alford, Funk, & Hibbing, 2005; Hatemi et al., 2009).

Correspondingly, integrated bio-anthropological theories of political behavior (Smith et al., 2011) suggest that partisanship, limited-government orientations, religious preferences, and (to a lesser extent) symbolic ideological attachments are causally prior to the development of feelings toward specific political issues and specific politically relevant groups. Partisan identity, for example, is thought to be central to individuals' self-concept and senses of political identity (Green, Palmquist, & Schickler, 2004; Mason, 2018). Consequently, partisanship can be thought about as a "perceptual screen" (Campbell et al., 1960), playing a foundational role in shaping how Americans consume and perceive political information (Taber & Lodge, 2006; Kahan et al., 2012) and facilitating directionally motivated reasoning (Kunda, 1990)—i.e., the drive to arrive at conclusions consistent with one's partisanship (Lodge & Taber, 2013; Leeper & Slothuus, 2014)—about a wide range of political and policy matters (Bolsen, Druckman, & Cook, 2014; Kraft, Lodge, & Taber, 2015).

Due to their relatively static and politically foundational nature, Americans' partisan identities, symbolic ideological attachments, limited-government preferences, and religious orientations may play an important role in explaining why some people are more likely to hold anti-intellectual attitudes than others. Whether this is true, of course, hinges on the extent to which each factor is conceptually applicable to negative feelings toward scientific and academic experts. I take up this subject in detail shortly.

It is also briefly worth noting what the aforementioned factors should *not* explain with respect to anti-intellectual attitude endorsement. Because static inputs rarely change over time, it is unlikely that these factors would be associated with *change* in anti-intellectualism. That is, when individuals become more or less anti-intellectual over time, it is unlikely that they are doing so because they are changing (for example) their partisan allegiances or outlook on the role that government ought to play in people's lives. Other more-malleable factors that I discuss later in this chapter may be more likely to have this effect.

With these two points in mind, I next discuss why partisan identification with the Republican Party, ideological conservatism, preferences for smaller government, and more-frequent religious service attendance should all help explain why some Americans hold anti-intellectual attitudes while others do not.

Republican Partisan Identity and Symbolic Ideology

A Hostile Legacy

In recent years, Republican politicians have taken increasingly vocal stands in opposition to scientific and other forms of expert-consensus on policy relevant issues. While tracing the full history of Republican elites' opposition to scientific and academic experts is outside the purview of this book (see journalist Chris Mooney's excellent 2006 work for a fuller exploration of this phenomenon), prominent examples of this dynamic are both plentiful and helpful for understanding why some Americans hold anti-intellectual attitudes.

Of course, former President Trump is not the first GOP politician to strategically denigrate experts to accomplish their political goals. For example, Dwight Eisenhower—who once described intellectuals as people who "takes more words than necessary to tell what he knows" and noted that he was "deathly afraid of being considered highbrow"—may have been reluctant to publicly reject his party's McCarthyist attacks on the credibility of scientists, academics, and other experts due to his strategic efforts to be seen as a "no-nonsense" and "ordinary guy" on the campaign trail (Lim, 2008). This allowed Eisenhower—who, ironically, once served as president of Columbia University—to draw a distinction between himself and his frequent critic (and presidential campaign opponent) Adlai Stevenson, who was comparatively more popular in intellectual circles. As Hofstadter put it, McCarthyist attacks on Stevenson's character, in part, likely contributed to his electoral demise and "felt like a repudiation by plebiscite of American intellectuals and of intellect itself."

Republicans' disdain for expertise, and willingness to use it to achieve their political goals, also extends beyond the McCarthy era. Consider, for example, the case of President Richard Nixon. Following the lead of the Truman administration, who left office two decades earlier, it had become customary for presidents to appoint an advisor to provide them with advice related to science-relevant policy issues.

Presidents on both sides of the partisan aisle typically picked high-profile scientists with national reputations to fill this role. For example, Harry Truman (a Democrat) began this trend by soliciting policy advice from Manhattan Project alumnus Vannevar Bush (Miri, 2021). Dwight Eisenhower (a Republican) formalized the science advisor position by appointing another Manhattan Project vet, James Killian, to advise the president on how to regulate science-related activities pertaining to the space race and the recent establishment of NASA (Levitan, 2016.

Upon taking office for his first term in 1969, Nixon chose Lee Alvin DuBridge—a Cal-Tech physicist with both a sterling and high-profile reputation in the scientific community (Levitan, 2016)—to serve as his science advisor. It did not take long, however, for the scientific community to question whether Nixon was heeding DuBridge's policy-relevant advice. Throughout the early 1970s, science funding in the United States declined both steadily and precipitously compared to the previous presidential administrations (Boffey, Carter, & Hamilton, 1970), causing some to question whether Nixon's science advisor had any sway in the White House. DuBridge resigned the post shortly thereafter (Levitan, 2016).

Nixon, a man of many political enemies (Perlstein, 2008), apparently had no interest in taking advice from scientific experts (Greenberg, 1973). This may be due in part to his highly personal resentment of the scientific community. Nixon viewed scientists as being hostile to his administration's policy goals. This was true both in science-related domains—for example, Nixon allegedly viewed government scientists who raised environmental concerns about his proposed supersonic transport program as "vipers" (Mooney, 2006)—and for issues outside of the realm of science funding and education (e.g., the idea that scientists and academics were uniformly opposed to his handling of the Vietnam War). Consequently, journalistic accounts of his administration's views toward scientists and academics suggested that Nixon held rather personal resentment toward the scientific community.

Foreshadowing a move that would become all too common in the Trump administration decades later, Nixon took strategic action to limit experts' influence in the White House. Rather than disband the science advisor position, Nixon replaced DuBridge with Bell Labs alumnus Edward E. David—a man whom the *New York Times* once characterized as "" as Dave Levitan (2016) points out in his retrospective on the affair.

David was, unsurprisingly, ineffective in the position (Levitan, 2016) and resigned the post shortly after Nixon took action to reduce his already-limited influence in the White House. His resignation occurred amid a flurry of resignations and the forced departures of other high-profile experts tapped to advise the administration, including Nixon's ousting of former Surgeon General Jesse Steinfeld, who publicly challenged the administration's stance on the hazards of smoking (Yardley, 2014). That was by design. Nixon's administration— fueled by personal resentment of academics' opposition to (among other issues) his handling of the Vietnam War—took strategic action to limit experts' policy influence in order to preserve his own public image and policy agenda (Levitan, 2016).

Moreover, since the late 1980s, Republican politicians have strategically (and politically) aligned themselves with fossil-fuel producers' efforts to downplay the role that humans play in facilitating climate change (an industry that stands to lose revenue if alternative-energy solutions to climate change were to gain widespread adoption). Anti-climate interest groups have attempted to manufacture doubt about the reality of human-caused climate change via aggressive lobbying efforts, financially supporting politicians (which, today, primarily consists of GOP political elites) who recirculate disputed or inaccurate talking points on partisan cable news programs and even funding scientific research aimed at debunking anthropogenic climate change (Mooney, 2006; McCright & Dunlap, 2000, 2010; Merkley & Stecula, 2018, 2020).

Similarly, George W. Bush's presidential administration gained significant attention for its efforts to curtail scientists' ability to fund life-saving stem cell research (Murugan, 2009). Political pressure from the Christian Right—a voting bloc critical to his election and reelection (Claassen & Povtak, 2010), and who were concerned about the possibility of using aborted fetuses in this line of research—likely played an important role in motivating the Bush administration's decisions on this issue (Wertz, 2002). Republican state legislatures' efforts to penalize campus protest and regulate perceived bias in what professors say in the classroom (Peters, 2019), as well as late-Senator Tom Coburn's efforts to defund some social science research programs at the National Science Foundation due to fears of political bias (Mervis, 2014), further exemplify the right's distrust of scientific, academic, and other experts.

The campaigns and presidency of Donald Trump offer perhaps the clearest and most recent glimpse into how GOP elites have strategically embraced anti-expert rhetoric and policy ideals. Echoing the rhetorical strategy of former Alabama Governor George Wallace in the 1968 presidential election, Donald Trump routinely derided climate scientists and medical experts both prior to and throughout his first bid for the White House in 2016 (Motta, 2018a). While in office, the former president took more than a year and a half to appoint a director for the significantly reduced Office of Science and Technology Policy (Mervis, 2020), selected former Oklahoma Attorney General Scott Pruitt—who denies scientific consensus on human caused climate change (Chiacu & Volcovici, 2017)—to lead the Environmental Protection Agency and facilitate its rollback of environmental protection regulations (Irfan, 2018), and routinely clashed with experts from his own administration on defense (Shane, 2019), economic (Schneider, 2020), and public health issues (Stableford, 2021).

These examples illustrate the strategic usefulness of anti-intellectual rhetoric, and actions that curtail experts' policy influence, to help political elites accomplish their policy and electoral goals. Here, however, it is important to foreshadow an argument I make later on in this chapter and substantiate later in this book: Americans' hostility toward experts has become grounds for partisan contestation only in recent years. This more-recent trend has occurred in tandem with expansive efforts from GOP elites and GOP-affiliated groups to cast doubt on scientific and other forms of expertise. As I discuss in Chapter 5, the Tea Party movement, spearheaded by GOP political elites like the former Alaska governor Sarah Palin and former Fox News commentator Glenn Beck, prompted significant questioning of scientists' personal and political motivations.

Relatedly, it is important to recognize that in the recent past elite Democrats too have expressed some amount of skepticism and negative affect toward the expert community. Retrospections on the Johnson administration, for example, suggest that he—like Nixon—grew suspicious of his own high-profile science advisors' opposition to his handling of the Vietnam War. Moreover, George Wallace, as the founder of the American Independent Party, attacked academics and experts from outside of the conventional two-party system. Today, Robert F. Kennedy Jr.—a prominent vaccine skeptic who mounted a primary challenge to incumbent President Joe Biden in the 2024 Democratic presidential primaries—represents an example of a (relatively) well-known Democrat who embraces strong skepticism toward scientific and medical experts.

Animosity toward scientists and experts was never a purely partisan phenomenon, and nor is it today. What has changed in recent years, however, is that the denigration of experts has become both frequent and decisively one-sided. This

The Nature and Origins of Anti-Intellectualism

in turn may be influencing the attitudes that the American public holds toward experts and expertise.

Connecting Anti-Expert Partisan Rhetoric to Public Opinion

Today Republican elites' hostility toward experts is channeled through to the public via partisan media sources. Right-leaning online and television news outlets (e.g., Fox News) have been shown to be comparatively more likely than mainstream or left-leaning sources to feature testimony from non-expert or denialist sources on issues such as climate change (Feldman et al., 2012; Merkley & Stecula, 2018), promote misinformation about climate and health-related issues (e.g., Motta, Stecula, & Farhart, 2020; Simonov et al., 2020), and—more generally—to give a platform to GOP politicians who promote anti-expert rhetoric. Conceptually, although I lack the data necessary to test this possibility directly in this book, partisan media viewership can therefore be thought of as exhibiting a *mediating influence* in the theoretical model I outline in this chapter (because media exposure provides partisans with the opportunity to connect their previously existing political orientations to the way that they feel about experts).

As a result, people who self-identify as members of the Republican Party may come to view experts as a group that holds interests hostile to their own. And, as I reviewed previously, this may, in turn, breed animosity toward experts as a social group.

Specifically, partisans' exposure to anti-expert rhetoric can politicize public opinion toward experts via the following process. First, because people tend to place higher levels of trust in communicators from their own partisan team, they tend to be more likely to adopt the political views and policy stances held by politicians who share their partisan allegiances (Lenz, 2013; Druckman, Petersen, & Slothuus, 2018). Scholars of mass communication refer to this phenomenon as a *source credibility effect* (Hovland & Weiss, 1951; Whitehead, 1968; Pornpitakpan, 2004). Consequently, partisans exposed to messages that challenge expert opinion and expertise have been shown to be more likely to adopt those viewpoints as their own (Darmofal, 2005).

This implies that Republicans in the public who are attentive (via the media they consume) to differences in how Democrats and Republicans talk about these issues should update their views accordingly (Zaller, 1992; Stroud, 2010, 2011). In other words, because they are both exposed to elite communication that portrays expertise in a negative light and find the partisans who deliver those messages to be credible, Republicans should therefore become more likely to hold negative views toward experts and reject policy relevant expertise (Krosnick & MacInnis, 2010; Feldman et al., 2012; Hopkins & Ladd, 2014;

Merkley & Stecula, 2018, 2020; Motta, Stecula, & Farhart, 2020; Stecula et al., 2020; Simonov et al., 2020).

Moreover, Republicans may be even more motivated to update their views toward experts and expertise in response to communication from partisan elites with whom they *disagree* (Nicholson, 2012). Studies on public acceptance of anthropogenic climate change, for example, find that Republicans' *resistance* to *Democratic pro-climate messaging* may play an even stronger role in shaping their views than does partisans' acceptance of within-party messages on both sides of the partisan aisle (Merkley & Stecula, 2020).

Of course, Republicans are not alone in this regard. The politicization of science takes place on the ideological left too (albeit toward a very different end). Like Republicans, Democrats exposed to messaging defending science and other forms of expertise from fellow members of the Democratic Party should be more likely to accept those viewpoints as their own. This further widens the gulf between Democrats' and Republicans' views of expertise.

The result of this process is that, over time, self-identified Republicans in the public have become increasingly likely to share views about experts that mirror those of partisan elites. For example, in an expansive survey of Americans' views toward deference to experts on more than a dozen policy-relevant topics, Blank & Shaw (2015) find that Republicans in the public are less likely to defer to policy recommendations of experts on issues such as the safety of genetically modified food, childhood vaccine mandates, the legitimacy of teaching birth-control education and evolution in public schools, efforts to combat the AIDS pandemic, and the importance of regulating fossil-fuel emissions.

Relatedly, people who hold symbolically conservative ideological views—i.e., people who self-identify with conservative rather than liberal symbolic labels (Ellis & Stimson, 2012), which are highly reflective of partisan identification with the GOP (Bafumi & Shapiro, 2009)—have become increasingly likely to hold negative views toward the scientific community (Gauchat, 2012) and toward scientists who weigh in on politically controversial topics like climate change (Kahan, 2015; Gauchat, O'Brien, & Mirosa, 2017), even though they may nevertheless respect the process of generating scientific knowledge itself (Mann & Schleifer, 2020). Correspondingly, Republicans and ideological conservatives are thought to be more likely to embrace anti-intellectual views (i.e., to express negative attitudes toward scientists and other experts more generally) (Oliver & Rahn, 2016; Motta, 2018a; Merkley, 2020).

Collectively, then, these lines of research suggest that—at least in contemporary American political life—both self-identified Republicans and ideological conservatives in the mass public may come to hold negative views toward experts as a social group with interests perceived to be at odds with their own, thereby facilitating the endorsement of anti-intellectual attitudes.

Preferences for Limited Government

Related to (yet conceptually distinct from) the identity politics of partisan team-spersonship in the United States is the idea that people who prefer that the federal government take on a smaller regulatory role might also be more likely to hold negative views toward the scientific community.

Conceptually, people with preferences for more-limited government might see expert input on policy-relevant issues as providing the federal government with justification to expand its regulatory focus and thereby a pose threat to preferences for less-expansive federal oversight (Kahan, 2010; Lewandowsky, Oberauer, & Gignac, 2013). For example, as Kahan notes in his (2010) work outlining cultural cognitive dynamics of science-relevant attitudes, climate scientists' research suggesting that human-caused carbon emissions are responsible for climate change might lead the federal government to consider policies that expand the government's regulatory focus regarding fuel-efficiency standards, penalties on corporate polluters, and related policies. Consequently, climate science—and those who produce it—may pose a threat to people who prefer a smaller role for government intervention in our daily lives.

Likewise, research suggesting that vaccines are instrumental in stopping the spread of communicable disease could lead federal and state governments to consider widescale or mandatory vaccination programs. This could breed distrust about vaccine safety and opposition to government vaccine mandates (Kahan et al., 2010; Velan et al., 2012; Maaravi et al., 2021). Correspondingly, people with stronger preferences for limited government have been shown to be more likely to hold negative views toward medical experts who support mandatory vaccination programs (Kahan, 2010). More generally, individualistic and limited-government attitudes are also associated with the rejection of scientific evidence about the safety of nanotechnology (Kahan et al., 2008, 2009) and human-caused climate change (Kahan, 2010; Kahan et al., 2012; Lewandowsky, Oberaur, & Gignac, 2013).

Taken together, past research suggests that limited-government views may be a plausible candidate to help explain why some people come to hold anti-intellectual attitudes while others do not. Before reaching that conclusion, however, it is worth briefly contrasting limited-government views from a concept I discuss in more detail shortly: preferences regarding expert involvement in the policymaking process (expert policy role; i.e., paths c and d in Figure 2.1).

Whereas limited-government attitudes (as a static input into the theoretical model) pertain to Americans' *general* preferences for limited government, views about the role that experts ought to play in the policymaking process (as an output) are more specialized in focus (i.e., pertaining specifically to the policy influence of scientists, doctors, academics, and other experts). It would be unsurprising, then, if limited-government views are associated with opposition to experts' policy role. People who prefer smaller levels of government intervention should be opposed to regulatory action in many different applications, including the role that experts play in the policymaking process. Thus, in addition to serving as a potential input for explaining differences in anti-intellectual attitude endorsement, it is important that I account for limited-government views when assessing the relationship between anti-intellectualism and expert influence in government. I take up that possibility later in this book in Chapter 7.

At the same time, some might ask whether limited-government views themselves ought to be considered a policy output of anti-intellectual attitudes. Some might argue, for example, that negative attitudes toward scientists and other experts—given their prominence in the process of making decisions about complex and technical policy issues—facilitate distrust in government more broadly. As noted earlier in this chapter, preferences for the role that government plays in people's lives are thought to be related to bedrock psychological orientations about the optimal structure of society and therefore causally prior to the development of specific political orientations and policy attitudes (Smith et al., 2011). Correspondingly, as mentioned earlier, limited-government views have been both theorized to bias political cognition about science-relevant policy (Kahan, 2010), and—when experimentally manipulated in laboratory settings—engender negative feelings toward scientists (Kahan, 2014).

Taken together, I suspect that limited-government attitudes are a plausible candidate to explain between-person differences in anti-intellectual attitude endorsement. While suggestions that limited-government attitudes might also result from anti-intellectual attitude endorsement are plausible, it is unclear whether those expectations might play out in reality.

Still I recognize that the interrelatedness of limited-government orientations (in general) and preferences regarding experts' policy influence presents a conceptually thorny issue. Consequently, as I discuss later in this book, I will construct empirical tests that enable me to assess whether my expectations regarding limited-government attitudes (and all other elements of the theoretical model that I hope to test) have been misspecified. This means that I can test for the possibility that limited-government attitudes may best function as a policy output of anti-intellectual attitude endorsement, as opposed to an input capable of inspiring within-person change in expert negativity.

Religiosity

Finally, I suspect that Americans for whom religion occupies a central role in their daily lives, or for whom religion is a central component of their sense of self, may be more likely to harbor negative feelings toward scientists, academics, and other experts. Conceptually, highly religious people—irrespective of denomination—may come to express negativity toward experts because they view scientific, academic, and other evidence-based advice as being at odds with the teachings of trusted religious leaders. This may be true not only on matters of faith but also in application to social and political issues that might be related to religious teaching and dogma.

Of course, it is important to note that academic, scientific, and other forms of expertise do not necessarily conflict with religious preferences. It is certainly true that Americans are comparatively more likely to perceive scientific experts, for example, as being less likely to value religion in their personal lives than other professions or the American public more generally (Besley, 2015; see also Rutjens & Heine, 2016, who find that Americans are comparatively more likely to view scientists as immoral). Whether these perceptions align with reality, however, is an open question. Past research also finds that while scientists tend to be less religious than the American public more generally, approximately one in five—compared to about one in two in the general public—report attending religious services at least once a month (Masci, 2009; Scheitle, Johnson, & Ecklund, 2018).

Scientists and other experts may be therefore *less* religious than the American public. However, many nevertheless value religion in their personal lives.

Still, when experts' research or policy recommendations are at odds with religious teachings—such as human versus divine agency over the stewardship of the environment (Sachdeva, 2016; Jenkins, Berry, & Kreider, 2018), or the evolutionary origins of human life from primates (Kahan, 2017a; Weisberg et al., 2018)—scientists, academics, and other experts might pose a challenge to the social, cultural, and political authority of religious leaders (Gauchat, 2008; Scheitle, Johnson, & Ecklund, 2018). In other words, they present highly religious people with a difficult choice. Should they defer to religious dogma as relayed by those who share their faith or to those with subject-area scientific, academic, or other competencies?

Consistent with the predictions of intergroup conflict research discussed earlier in this chapter, many choose the former. This may in turn facilitate expert animosity. For example, past research finds that, irrespective of denomination, people who attend religious services more regularly—which is a commonly used indicator of religiosity (Brossard et al., 2009; Gauchat, 2012; Scheitle, Johnson, & Ecklund, 2018)—tend to hold more-negative views toward the scientific community in general (Gauchat, 2012; Motta, 2018a).

Perhaps unsurprisingly, highly religious Americans are *especially* likely to hold negative views toward experts when matters of science and faith conflict. Blank & Shaw (2015) find that highly religious people are more likely to harbor negative feelings toward scientists who advocate for birth-control education, the teaching of evolution in public schools, and scientific funding for stem cell research. These positions may conflict with certain beliefs about divine creation (e.g., shaped in the image of a deity by divine forces) and the sanctity of human life (e.g., by making use of tissue from aborted fetuses, which some consider to be a form of human life, to experiment with stem cells). Relatedly, whereas highly religious people tend to be neither more nor less knowledgeable about basic facts related to the physical sciences, they are comparatively more polarized in their willingness to accept that humans descended from primates (Kahan, 2017a).

Religiosity is also associated with negative views toward climate scientists (Blank & Shaw, 2015) and disbelief in global warming (McCright & Dunlap, 2011). This, again, may be fairly self-evident, as claims of human-caused climate change may threaten views of divine omnipotence in controlling events that take place on earth. However, when matters of science and faith are less obviously in conflict, highly religious people have been shown to be neither more nor less likely to hold negative feelings toward experts. For example, highly religious people and less-religious people alike tend to hold similar policy views on issues related to the promotion of alternative energy, responding to public health crises like the AIDS pandemic or childhood obesity, or concerns about genetically modified food safety (Blank & Shaw, 2015).

Consequently, people who value religion as being more central to their daily lives should be more likely to hold negative feelings toward experts both in general and especially in fields that challenge the teachings and expertise religious authorities. Thus, religiosity represents a plausible static input for explaining differences between people in anti-intellectual attitude acceptance.

The Tea Party and the Temporal Dynamics of Asymmetric Polarization

Having reviewed how several sets of socio-political attitudes, identities, and behaviors might contribute to anti-intellectual attitude endorsement, some might ask whether partisan asymmetries in anti-intellectual attitude endorsement that I have discussed throughout this chapter might be stronger today than they were decades ago. This is an important question and, in my view, is worthy of significant reflection.

Believe it or not, in the not too distant past—throughout the 1970s and 1980s, to be exact—Democrats and Republicans held similar attitudes toward experts and efforts to fund government scientific research (Glazer, 2021). In fact, there was even a time when scientific research was seen as advancing traditionally *conservative* policy priorities, particularly with respect to military technology. Scientific research was once seen as integral to the US military's efforts to end World War II and to keep pace with Russian technological advancements throughout the Cold War (O'Brien & Noy, 2020; Glazer, 2021).

Anecdotal evidence provides plenty of reason to speculate that the *asymmetric polarization* (Mann & Ornstein, 2012; Grossman & Hopkins, 2016) in the proliferation of negative attitudes toward experts on the political right is a relatively recent development. From Senator Chuck Grassley's suggestion that President Obama's Affordable Care Act would establish panels of government "death panel" ombudsmen who could decide whether or not to "pull the plug on grandma" (Holan, 2009), to President Trump's entertainment of the idea that consuming bleach might stave off viral infections during the COVID-19 pandemic (much to the, very public, chagrin his own administration's health experts; Riotta, 2021), GOP elites regularly showcase their dislike and distrust of scientists and other experts. I review some of these anecdotal episodes in more detail in Chapter 5.

In addition to the possibility that anti-intellectualism has become increasingly popular on the political right in contemporary US politics, there is also good conceptual reason to doubt that this link manifested itself as strongly as it does today in the not-too-distant past. Some of the most prominent anti-intellectual elites of the twentieth and twenty-first century, for example, do not fit in neatly with expectations of asymmetric polarization.

For example, George Wallace—who, as I discuss in more detail in Chapter 4, frequently took to mocking "pointy-headed intellectuals" in campaign stump speeches—was a prominent Democrat before founding the American Independent Party. Donald Trump—whose hostility to experts I discuss throughout this book—also identified as an Independent many years prior to his run for the White House in 2016. Even throughout his run for the White House, Trump held a relatively inconsistent and (arguably) ideologically incoherent mix of positions on major policy issues in the decades before he first sought elected office. He formerly embraced a larger role for the federal government (as opposed to limited-government conservative priorities) by expressing support for increasing taxes on the wealthy, universal health care, and government protection of abortion rights (Schwarz, 2015).

What the examples of Wallace, Grassley, and Trump suggest is that expecting Republicans, conservatives, and people who favor a smaller role for the federal government to be more likely to harbor negative attitudes toward experts may be a *time-bound* proposition. GOP elites like Senator Grassley and the contemporary political manifestations of Donald Trump's brand of politics may espouse political rhetoric that is colored with a distinctly anti-intellectual hue. However, this was not necessarily the case for noted anti-intellectual politicians of the past like George Wallace and may not even fit in neatly with Donald Trump's previous political experiences. This therefore raises an important question: when exactly did the Republican Party become associated with anti-intellectualism?

Previous attempts to answer this question present a conflicting pattern of results. Some researchers argue that the Reagan and (George W) Bush administrations represented pivotal moments in the Republican "war on science" and the acceleration of asymmetric polarization (Mooney, 2006). Mooney cites, for example, the Reagan administration's public and private disagreements with recommendations from the Office of Technology Assessment regarding several of the administration's nuclear defense policy proposals, which may have inspired conservative opposition to the office that ultimately led its demise in 1995. In fact, to this day, the episode is sometimes referred to as "Reagan's revenge" (Mooney, 2005, 2006). Mooney also cites the Bush administration's attempts to ban federal funding for embryonic stem cell research, which ultimately led to the discontinuation of several research programs aimed at producing therapeutic treatments for diseases like Parkinson's (Murugan, 2009) and chronic cardiovascular diseases (Lenzer, 2007). For Mooney, instances like these provide evidence that the link between right-wing politics and anti-intellectualism began to crystalize during these two presidencies.

However, other efforts to systematically study whether the *public* became more likely to express negative attitudes toward scientists and experts during the Reagan and second Bush administrations provides only mixed evidence in favor of Mooney's view. Gauchat (2012) documents that while more-conservative Americans did indeed become more likely to hold negative views toward scientists during the Reagan and (George W) Bush administrations, they *also* became more likely to do so in the intervening years between the two presidencies. Negative attitudes toward scientists also became more prominent on the right in the post-Bush period. What Gauchat's work implies, therefore, is that the link between right-wing political identification and the embrace of anti-intellectual attitudes has developed continuously over time. Bivariate analyses suggest that this trend likely began in the mid-1980s, started exhibiting signs of polarization (i.e., a stark difference in opinion between Democrats and Republicans) by the mid-1990s, and has increased steadily over time (see also Motta, 2018a).

One understandable limitation of Gauchat's work, however, is that it necessarily—as the piece was published in 2012—only studies questions about the temporal dynamics of asymmetric polarization through 2010. This leaves open the possibility that some political phenomenon may have significantly strengthened the ties between Republican identification, conservatism, and limited-government beliefs in more-recent years.

Additionally, and more technically, Gauchat's work does offer a multivariate assessment of how partisanship (in particular) has shaped anti-intellectual attitude endorsement over time (i.e., using statistical models that account for other

The Nature and Origins of Anti-Intellectualism

influences that could explain why some people hold anti-scientist attitudes while others do not). For those interested in the technical specifics, Gauchat's models are structured such that they (1) test for a linear time trend and (2) compare that to models that assume nonlinear time trends at two moments (the post-Reagan years and the post-Bush years, per Mooney's predictions). A modeling strategy that allows for the detection of nonlinear time trends in each of *many* years, in contrast, would be flexible enough to determine if certain historical moments stand out with respect to the influence they have on asymmetric polarization.

Enter, the Tea Party. The Tea Party (T-E-A standing for "taxed enough already," a reference to protests of overseas taxation in Boston Harbor following the imposition of the British Tea Act in 1773) was a grassroots political movement that arose as a reaction to Barack Obama winning the presidency in 2008. In particular, Tea Party activists were concerned that ordinary people would be tasked with footing the bill for the Obama administration's first-term agenda, especially its ambitious efforts to overhaul the US health-care system via the Affordable Care Act (ACA). GOP elites feared that these actions would offer handouts to social groups—typically seen as advantaging racial and ethnic minority populations (Gillens, 2009; Winter, 2008)—deemed undeserving of government aid (Williamson, Skocpol, & Coggin, 2011; see also, Skocpol & Williamson, 2016). Fear and resentment of government spending on groups considered unworthy in turn mapped onto Americans' negative racial attitudes and partisan loyalties (Parker & Barreto, 2014).

Although it has no formal founder, Tea Party activists consider Republican politicians like former Alaska Governor Sarah Palin and former Minnesota Representative Michele Bachmann (who organized the short-lived Congressional Tea Party Caucus) and conservative media personalities like Glenn Beck to be some of the movements most important members (Gardner, 2010). At the height of the movement's popularity in 2010, over a third of Americans—and over 60 percent of Republicans—indicated that they held favorable views of the Tea Party (Sullivan, 2013). Correspondingly, the movement was highly politically influential. The Tea Party is widely credited with helping Republicans earn a landslide victory in the 2010 midterm elections, helped launch the political careers of Senator Rand Paul (Kentucky) and Senator Marco Rubio (Florida) (Good, 2013; Zernike, 2015), and—arguably—is partially responsible for the political ascendency of former President Donald Trump (Rohlinger & Bunnage, 2017; Gervais & Morris, 2018).

Yet while the Tea Party was ostensibly formed to advance limited-government ideals, the movement became much more than that. Recent social science research suggests that people affiliated with the Tea Party were more likely to hold negative views about the scientific community (Hamilton, Hartter, & Saito, 2015). They were also more likely to accept conspiracy theories—promoted by

Tea Party elites—alleging cooperation between (Democratic) politicians and medical experts to harm ordinary people (Haltinner & Sarathchandra, 2017). As Skocpol and Williamson write in their seminal book (2016, p 80) on the topic, Tea Party elites acted to portray climate scientists as architects of an elaborate hoax designed by "scientists and bureaucrats, as a prelude to extend the reach of their power."

One episode, in particular, helps demonstrate how prominent Tea Party activists came to embrace rhetorical strategies that featured suspicion toward scientists and other experts: the so-called death panels rumor. This widely accepted rumor (Berinsky, 2017) suggested that the Affordable Care Act would create bureaus of public health experts, at the behest of the Obama administration, responsible for determining whether certain people filing insurance claims were sufficiently valuable to society to receive the medical treatments they requested. According to those circulating the rumor, the purported objective of these efforts was to reduce the ACA's substantial budgetary costs.

The death panel theory's origins are, to some degree, unclear. Some suggest that the rumor began following the New York lieutenant governor's misreading of the ACA as containing passages that make mandatory "required counseling sessions" that tell seniors how to "end their life sooner" (Holan, 2009).

How the term become popularized, however, is much easier to identify. It was Sarah Palin who first coined the term *death panels*, claiming that government-appointed health-care officials—"[Obama's] bureaucrats," as Palin put it—who could determine whether or not someone is worthy of health care based on their "level of productivity in society" (Gonyea, 2017).

Palin's comments directly tie a (fictional) group of health-policy experts to the Obama administration's alleged nefarious intentions. Despite the inaccuracy of these claims, which were labeled as nonpartisan fact-checking group PolitiFact's Lie of the Year in 2009 (Holan, 2009), many Americans nevertheless came to accept them as true (Berinsky, 2017). During the lead-up to the 2012 presidential election, nearly 40 percent of Americans claimed to see truth in the rumor according to some polls (Viebeck, 2012). The death panels rumor may have therefore provided Tea Party supporters with the opportunity to link their preferences for smaller government, partisan identities, and distrust of the Obama administration more generally to how they feel about experts.

Correspondingly, in a memoir published several years after his presidency, former President Obama accused Palin of bringing "dark spirits that had long been lurking on the edges of the modern Republican Party" and included a direct reference to her "anti-intellectual" rhetoric (Fearnow, 2020; Obama, 2020). Similarly, when reflecting on their coverage of Sarah Palin's ascendency to stardom in the GOP, CBS journalists Katie Couric and Brian Goldsmith

The Nature and Origins of Anti-Intellectualism

suggested that Palin's "contempt for experts and elites" was a defining component of her political brand (Couric & Goldsmith, 2018).

Further demonstrative of a link between the Tea Party's preferences for smaller government and negative attitudes toward experts are the comments of prominent conservative pundit Rush Limbaugh—whom former Republican Representative Joe Walsh, elected during the 2010 Tea Party wave, described as essential for amplifying the Tea Party movement's political messaging (Walsh, 2021). Limbaugh considered scientific and academic experts to be part of what he called "the four corners of deceit," suggesting that:

> Government, academia, science and media. Those institutions are now corrupt and exist by virtue of deceit. That's how they promulgate themselves; it is how they prosper.
>
> —Nature Editorial Board, 2010

For Limbaugh, then, distrust of academic and scientific experts is inextricably tied up with suspicions about the trustworthiness of the federal government. Tea Party activists saw the government as willing to deploy scientists and other experts—which, as I noted in Chapter, 1, some social scientists characterize as being so influential that they constitute a fifth branch of government (Jasanoff, 1998)—to achieve their nefarious policy goals. And as the death panels example helps demonstrate, fears that experts might become "tools" of elite Democrats to carry out a murderous health-policy agenda have in turn influenced how Tea Party supporters view scientific, medical, and other experts. Tellingly, Limbaugh once quipped that Palin was "dead right" to draw attention to rumored death panels in the ACA (Gonyea, 2017).

Synthesizing the evidence outlined here, I suspect that the Tea Party movement represents a pivotal turning point in the politicization of anti-intellectual attitudes. Like Gauchat, I recognize that the attitudes of Republicans, conservatives, and those favoring a smaller role for government intervention toward experts had been souring for at least a few decades prior to the emergence of the Tea Party. And similarly to Mooney, I believe that specific political events can significantly accelerate the asymmetric polarization of negative attitudes toward experts and scientists.

However, I suspect that the Tea Party movement's willingness to draw a direct and highly visible connection between government distrust and skepticism toward scientists (and other experts) may have considerably *accelerated* the link between right-wing politics in the United States and expert dislike and distrust. I offer a series of empirical tests designed to address this possibility in Chapter 5.

Correspondingly, the rise of the Tea Party (as a political movement) represents something of an exogenous shock to the role that the static inputs outlined in my theoretical model—Republican Party identification and symbolic conservatism, in particular—might play in giving rise to anti-intellectual attitude endorsement. The Tea Party movement did not, on its own, politicize how Americans feel about experts. However, it helped to clarify the connections between negative attitudes toward experts and longstanding political values on the ideological right, thereby exacerbating politicization. In this way, the Tea Party might be thought of as exhibiting a *moderating influence* on the model's static inputs.

Dynamic Inputs: What Motivates Change in Anti-Intellectualism?

In addition to the previously mentioned static inputs that can help us better understand why some people hold anti-intellectual attitudes (and why others do not), the affective and group-centric theoretical model that I outlined in Figure 2.1 also recognizes the possibility that comparatively more-malleable dynamic inputs might help explain why some people come to hold more (or fewer) negative views toward scientists, academics, and other experts over time.

In particular, I think two dynamic inputs are particularly good candidates to explain why some people tend to exhibit change in the extent to which they hold anti-intellectual attitudes over time. Those are (1) interest in scientific research and (2) the knowledge of basic scientific facts.

Unlike the socio-political factors discussed previously—which are central to individuals' social and political identities and consequently unlikely to change much over time—*epistemic factors* (i.e., pertaining to the pursuit and expression of knowledge) like science interest and knowledge have been shown to be considerably more malleable (Motta, 2019). Although more longitudinal research on the dynamics of science interest and knowledge is badly needed, extant research suggests that what people know and want to know about science can change in response to early-life educational experiences (Shumow & Miller, 2001; Englund et al., 2004; Pellegrino, 2013; Potvin & Hasni, 2014; Dejarnette, 2016).

Science knowledge and interest might also fluctuate in adulthood as people seek out or are otherwise exposed to science-relevant information in popular media or via educational experiences (Falk, Storksdieck, & Dierking, 2007). Past research suggests, for example, that adults who choose to watch science and nature-related programs on television tend to be more interested in and knowledgeable about science, even when accounting for the possibility that more knowledgeable and interested people are more likely to consume those programs (Nisbet et al., 2002). Knowledge and interest (of both science and other topics) may also be co-constitutive. This means that because interest may provide an incentive to acquire additional factual information about a subject—e.g., by drawing attention deficits in one's knowledge on a subject of interest (Loewenstein, 1994; Golman & Loewenstein, 2015)—and because some baseline level of knowledge may be necessary in order to explore one's interest in a particular subject, change in either one may inspire change in the other.

For my purposes in this book, the most important point emerging from this literature is that both science knowledge and interest may be fairly malleable over time. Correspondingly, as these epistemic factors are more dynamic and prone to change over time, they might help us better understand individual-level fluctuations in anti-intellectualism (i.e., change within people over time). Whether knowledge and interest might *also* play a role in explaining differences between individuals is an open empirical question (and one I test later in this book). However, to the degree that increased science knowledge or interest ought to engender more positive feelings toward scientists and experts, it is clear that both factors are candidates to explain why adults revise their anti-intellectual attitudes over time. Specifically, I suspect that as people become more knowledgeable or interested in science, they will become less likely to hold anti-intellectual attitudes. I discuss why I expect each set of dynamic inputs to have this effect in the pages that follow.

Before moving on, I want to address a question that some might have at this point. If my goal is to understand what motivates or ameliorates negative feelings toward *many* different types of experts over time, why focus on the study of scientific knowledge and interest specifically? My reasoning for doing so is twofold. First, as a practical matter, most prior research on this subject—and, as I discuss in Chapters 3 and 6, most available *public-opinion data*—pertains to the dynamics of trust in science and scientific experts. Conceptually, I note in Chapter 6 that domain-specific knowledge and interest in many different areas should have positive effects on how people feel toward experts beyond the sciences. However, putting this possibility to the empirical test is, at least at present, quite difficult.

Fortunately, though, I do at least have the opportunity to offer at least indirect evidence of the effects of science knowledge and interest (specifically) on feelings toward experts more generally. While science interest is no substitute for domain-specific interests and knowledge relevant to different types of experts that might be worth studying (e.g., an understanding of or interest in basic elements of finance and business for economic experts), I provide new evidence in Chapter 3 that American's affective feelings toward scientific experts are highly conceptually and empirically related to their feelings toward experts in other areas. This provides a conceptual and empirical basis—albeit a preliminary one—that the effects of knowledge and interest that I document in Chapter 6 may extend beyond how Americans feel toward scientists.

With these caveats in mind, I next review why gains in both science knowledge and interest may facilitate trust in experts.

Knowledge of Basic Scientific Facts

The extent to which people lack knowledge about basic scientific facts could help explain why some people are more likely to harbor negative attitudes toward scientific and other experts.

Early work on what has come to be known as the *knowledge-deficit model* suggests that support for experts, the research they produce, and the policy recommendations they make is conditional on what people know about science and the scientific method (Sturgis & Allum, 2004; Allum et al., 2008). Conceptually, people who appreciate how the scientific method works, and those who understand basic facts about science, should be more tolerant of debate and uncertainty about scientific findings and appreciative of the process by which experts achieve scholarly consensus.

Correspondingly, past work finds that the knowledge of basic scientific facts is associated with positive views toward the scientific community (Besley, 2015; Gauchat, 2011, 2012) and support of funding for scientific research (Gauchat, 2015). Conversely, people who think that they know more than scientists and medical doctors—despite evidence to the contrary (i.e., low objective knowledge; what social psychologists refer to as a *Dunning-Kruger effect*; Dunning, 2011)—are also less likely to view experts as credible sources of information about vaccine safety and oppose expert-backed universal vaccination policies (Motta et al., 2018) and more likely to reject expert consensus on the safety of genetically modified food (Fernbach et al., 2019) and accept or seek out misinformation related to politics and other topics (Anson, 2018; Lyons et al., 2021).

However, while the effects of high science knowledge are generally positive (and the effects of low knowledge are generally negative), they are often quite modest and are typically studied in correlational settings (see Allum et al., 2008 for a review). Additionally, while more research is needed to study the effects of *change* in science knowledge with respect to each of the aforementioned indicators of trust in scientists and experts, I have detected only mixed evidence (at best) that gains in science knowledge are associated with increased support for funding scientific research in past work on the subject (Motta, 2019).

Perhaps unsurprisingly, then, the idea that opposition to scientific and other forms of expertise can be offset by acquiring knowledge is not without important conceptual challenges. Political psychological theories of motivated reasoning (Kunda, 1990; Kraft, Lodge, & Taber, 2015) predict that when people hold political, cultural, or religious views that are at odds with expert recommendations and scientific research, they may use their superior understanding of basic scientific facts to *reject* the authority of scientific experts (Kahan et al., 2012, 2017; Kahan, 2015a, 2015b, 2017a, 2017b).

Work from Dan Kahan and colleagues, for example, finds that ideological conservatives who both comprehend basic scientific facts and are familiar with the reasoning processes underlying the scientific method are more likely than conservatives who are comparatively less knowledgeable to reject scientific consensus on the origins and risks posed by human-caused climate change (Kahan et al., 2012, 2017; Kahan, 2015a, 2015b). Conservatives who view climate change as comparatively lower risk to human life are in turn less likely to hold positive views toward scientists who suggest that climate change is human caused (Kahan, 2015a, 2015b). Similar patterns of results have been observed with respect to views on the risks posed by fracking, private gun possession, and other politically and culturally divisive issues (see Kahan, 2015a and Kahan et al., 2017 for a review). Collectively, this work implies that knowledge is (at best) *not* a panacea for alleviating distrust and may (at worst) exacerbate partisan and other forms of division regarding how Americans think about scientists and expertise.

Another potential critique of the knowledge-deficit model is the possibility that advances in internet accessibility have democratized information about a wide range of highly specialized subjects. People today may feel empowered to use information available online to "do their own research" to challenge expert evidence about a particular subject. For example, people who are motivated to reject an unpleasant clinical diagnosis made by their personal physician may be motivated by confirmation bias to turn to websites like WebMD to explore alternate diagnoses that they might apply to themselves (see Swire-Thompson & Lazer, 2020 for a review). These individuals do not necessarily *lack* knowledge of basic scientific facts and the scientific method—and may indeed need to draw on basic scientific principles in order to conduct searches on sites like WebMD or to comprehend its content—but are instead *motivated* to arrive at conclusions at odds with expert-provided evidence and recommendations.

Relatedly, people who subscribe to popular wisdom about the basics of science and medicine—whether encountered in online socially mediated settings or in the form of "folk theories" passed down intergenerationally (e.g., the idea that eating chicken soup can cure the common cold)—may feel as if that knowledge acts as a suitable substitute for information disseminated by scientific and other expert authorities. In both cases, neither doing one's own research nor subscribing to popular wisdom *necessarily* implies that individuals lack knowledge about the basics of science and the scientific method. Instead, it suggests that they feel empowered to elevate other forms of knowledge to the level of information purveyed by subject-area experts.

Still it is important to note that the motivated-reasoning account is *also* not without important conceptual challenges. Whereas some (like Kahan and colleagues) argue that knowledge and basic scientific-reasoning skills enable people to seek out and justify information that is inconsistent with scientific consensus on divisive topics (if they are sufficiently motivated to do so), others find that the very same type of critical-reasoning skills tend to be associated with increased ability to discern factually correct from fraudulent claims about science and politics (Pennycook & Rand, 2019; Pennycook et al., 2021).

Recent attempts to synthesize this debate point to a motivated reasoning account as being more plausible on, at least, highly politically polarizing issues (Osmudsen et al., 2021). However, resolving this matter is, quite simply, outside the purview of this book. Instead, I prefer to think of knowledge as conceptually representing something of a double-edged sword. On the one hand, knowledge enables people to *reject* expertise if they are so inclined by political, social, or cultural allegiances to do so. On the other hand, knowledge nevertheless endows people with greater competencies to separate fact from fiction. Figuring out the boundary conditions under which a motivated-reasoning account is more plausible than an information-deficit account (and vice versa) is an important task for future research.

Despite the findings from the previously discussed research, this debate highlights the possibility that as people become more knowledgeable about basic scientific facts, they may develop more-positive attitudes toward scientists and other experts, thereby making it a suitable dynamic input for understanding anti-intellectualism. However, it is important to recognize that this relationship may mask political and cultural polarization in views toward scientific expertise and consensus. Thus, if I do observe a (general) relationship between what people know about science and their views toward experts, it will be important to then assess whether these relationships might mask political and other forms of knowledge-based polarization.

Interest in Scientific Research

Another plausible dynamic input that could explain why some people come to hold more (or less) anti-intellectual attitudes over time is the extent to which Americans are *interested* in science and scientific research. People who are highly interested in science are thought to be pluralistic with respect to a wide variety of scientific claims, due to their enjoyment of engaging with many different types of scientific information. Correspondingly, they tend to be more accepting of findings from scientific research that might run contrary to their ideological, cultural, and other allegiances (Kahan et al., 2016, 2017). As a more general matter, people who are more interested in science have been found to be more cognitively open-minded than those who express less interest (Motta et al., 2019).

As a result, a growing body of literature finds that interest in consuming science-related information is associated with the acceptance of scientific consensus about the risks and origins of human-caused climate change, even among those most likely to reject those claims on the ideological right (Kahan et al., 2017). Science interest is also associated with increased positivity toward the scientific community, both between-people in correlational studies (e.g., Besley, 2015) and within-people (i.e., dynamically over time) as well. Demonstrative of this latter point, I have found in past research on the dynamics of science interest that young adults who are more interested in science in middle-school years tend to hold more-positive views toward climate scientists in adulthood (Motta, b). The extent to which change in science interest might facilitate trust in scientists and other experts in adulthood is at present, however, an open question. Consistent with the expectation that they might, however, I find that increases in science interest in adulthood is also associated with increased support for funding scientific research (Motta, 2019).

Taken together, available evidence suggests that science interest is a plausible candidate to explain dynamic change in anti-intellectual attitude endorsement. It also occupies a special role in the group-centric model. Of all the factors outlined so far, science interest is both (1) relatively malleable and (2) a theoretically strong candidate to explain why some people come to hold fewer (vs. more) anti-intellectual attitudes over time (more so than science knowledge, given the theoretical tension between knowledge deficit and the motivated rejection of science).

Science interest therefore offers a unique opportunity to potentially *decrease* anti-intellectual attitude endorsement in the United States. In other words, if it is possible to devise educational or communication interventions that can increase science interest (at either young ages or in adulthood), it may be possible to combat the pernicious policy effects of anti-intellectualism. I consider this possibility to some extent in Chapter 6 when discussing the effect of change in science interest and knowledge on anti-intellectual attitude endorsement and again in this book's conclusion when outlining an agenda for future research on anti-intellectualism. For now, I conclude this chapter by discussing Hofstadter's "forgotten" thesis: what the group-centric model predicts about how anti-intellectualism might both shape and potentially be shaped by views toward the role that experts play in the policymaking process.

Experts' Policy Influence: The Bidirectionality Thesis

The final element of the group-centric model I have outlined throughout this chapter concerns the *consequences* of anti-intellectual attitude endorsement. In particular, it is important to conceptually unpack the relationship between anti-intellectualism and the role that experts play in the policymaking process. Often, this relationship is assumed to be unidirectional, such that anti-intellectualism exerts an exogenous influence on policy orientations.

This, of course, is a plausible assumption. Intuitively, Americans who dislike and distrust experts should also be less likely to think that a group they hold in comparatively low esteem ought to have less say in how the federal government structures its responses to pressing policy concerns. They might also see less of a role for highly specialized knowledge in addressing those problems.

Surprisingly, though, few studies have investigated the relationship between anti-intellectualism and the *influence* that experts have in the policymaking process. Moreover, the precious few that do are (necessarily) limited in application. For example, Gauchat, O'Brien, & Mirosa (2017) find that people who doubt climate scientists' understanding of environmental issues and ethical integrity are less likely to think that they ought to play a role in making decisions related to global warming. More generally, people who feel that climate scientists, medical experts, and economists have Americans' best interests in mind have been shown to be more likely to express support for these groups' influence in the policymaking process in each area (O'Brien, 2013).

Comparatively more research, however, has documented a relationship between negative feelings toward experts and outcomes *related* to experts' influence in the policymaking process.

These studies typically focus on the link between anti-intellectualism and opinions concerning opposition to evidence-based policies and the rejection of policy-relevant misinformation (two subjects I take up later in this book). Most of these studies, to be clear, do not necessarily purport to study anti-intellectualism and its policy-relevant effects. Nor do they all measure negative attitudes toward experts in the same way. Nevertheless, by studying the relationship between negative views toward experts and opposition to experts' policy-relevant recommendations, they provide a useful base of knowledge for making predictions about the policy implications of anti-intellectual attitude endorsement.

For example, past work has found that people who hold negative views toward experts are more likely to support political candidates who express hostility toward scientists and other experts (Oliver & Rahn, 2016; Motta, 2018a). These individuals are also more likely to reject scientific consensus on policy-relevant issues like climate change and the safety of genetically modified food (Kellstedt et al., 2008; Hmielowski et al., 2014; Motta, 2018b; Merkley, 2020; see also, Fernbach et al., 2019); exhibit non-compliance with expert-backed health behaviors, such as wearing masks, social distancing, and choosing to vaccinate during the COVID-19 pandemic (Merkley & Lowenstein, 2021; Callaghan et al., 2021; Lindholt et al., 2021); accept misinformation about the safety of childhood vaccines and forego vaccinating both themselves and their children against vaccine-preventable diseases (Featherstone et al., 2019; Stecula, Kuru, & Jamieson, 2020; Motta 2020, 2021a); and oppose efforts to mitigate the effects of climate change (Huber, Fenseld, & Bernauer, 2020).

Unfortunately, most prior work in this area (my own included) does not account for the possibility that anti-expert attitudes might themselves be the product of opposition to the relevance of expertise in the policymaking sphere. There are, of course, some important exceptions. Merkley & Loewen (2021), for example, use longitudinal data to show that while change in anti-intellectual attitude endorsement is associated with decreased compliance with expert-recommended health behavior during the COVID-19 pandemic, the reverse pattern of effects does not appear to hold true. Additionally, in past research I have found that Americans' support for former President Trump (who routinely derided experts both on the campaign trail and throughout his time in the White House) did not tend to increase for those who came to hold more negative views toward experts over time (Motta, 2018a).

These examples are exceptions to conventional practices discussed earlier, and as just two studies, they are necessarily limited in their policy scope. More importantly, neither directly assesses the link between change in anti-intellectual attitude endorsement and more general views about experts' policy influence.

Limitations of prior research aside, there is nevertheless good theoretical reason to suspect that anti-intellectualism could *itself* be influenced by Americans' views on the role that experts ought to play in the policymaking process. Hofstadter recognized this possibility in his foundational work on anti-intellectualism in American public life.

According to Hofstadter, technological advancements have made Americans dependent on experts. Our dependence on experts could, in turn, motivate negative feelings toward people who can credibly lay claim to superior knowledge on matters relevant to not just our personal lives but to our social and political worlds as well.

Before turning to Hofstadter's expectations about the relationship between anti-intellectualism and experts' influence in the policymaking process, I want to first consider a contemporary application of this phenomenon.

Take, for example, the relationship I have with the laptop (a now-ancient 2015 MacBook Air) that I am currently using to write this book. The machine can run software programs that I did not design, using programming languages with which I'm unfamiliar. It can do this because it contains a processing device that I could never myself re-create and was assembled using highly technical systems that I might need college-level course training just to *describe* intelligibly. If my laptop were to break, I'd need to book an appointment with an aptly named (for the purposes of this book) "Genius" to diagnose the problem. I might then need to ship the device back to the company for repairs, while nearly every aspect of my computer-mediated work and social life is put on hold.

I am consequently dependent, in no small way, on the expertise of others to go about just this one task in my daily life. Imagine, then, if my computer *and* my smartphone were to malfunction on the same day. Or the mobile application on my smartphone that controls the air-conditioning unit that is, at the time of this writing on a scorching-hot Oklahoma summer day, keeping my apartment livable It's perhaps unsurprising, then, to see how my anger and frustration might spill over—a phenomenon psychologists refer to as *affect transfer* (Lodge & Taber, 2013)—to influence my feelings toward people who hold the highly specialized knowledge I so badly need.

The same dynamics are also true of contemporary democratic governance in the United States. As the nature of policy challenges Americans must face have grown more technical in recent years, so too has the process of creating policy solutions via effective self-governance. The size and scope of American bureaucracy has consequently grown to address increasingly complex domestic and global challenges, which means that experts have become an indispensable component of contemporary democratic governance, so much so that some consider scientists and other experts to function as a "fifth branch" of US government (Jasanoff, 1998).

As our policy challenges have become more complex, Americans also see an important place for technocracy (i.e., the idea that people with subject-area expertise should have a greater influence in government action in those areas) in US policymaking. Nowlin (2021) finds, for example, that individuals who hold more ideologically liberal political views tend to be more supportive of technocratic policymaking for tackling highly technical issues related to climate change and energy policy.

Consequently, Congress regularly calls on climate scientists, medical experts, economists, and other experts to provide expert testimony about pressing issues such as the risks of human-caused climate change, public health strategies for combating the coronavirus pandemic, and macroeconomic policy (Liu et al., 2015; Maher et al., 2020). Moreover, both federal and state legislatures often rely on interest groups to provide them with expert advice on complex policy issues (Hall & Deardorff, 2006), as do policymakers within executive bureaucracies (Hall & Miler, 2008). Scientists and other experts are even running for elected office in record number, motivated in part by the desire to facilitate evidence-based policymaking in Washington (Motta, 2021b).

Perhaps in no way is the policy relevance of experts clearer than with President Biden's selection of a COVID Response task force. Prior to his first day in office, then President-Elect Biden made headlines by selecting a team of doctors, epidemiologists, and other health-care experts to assist the administration to craft policies that could be implemented quickly to help stop the spread of the novel coronavirus.

These actions stand in sharp contrast to those of Biden's predecessor. Although he also assembled a response team composed of scientific experts, former President Trump routinely dismissed his team's policy authority. Trump challenged the expertise and credibility of key figures on the team, consulted outside non-expert sources to provide him with pandemic-related information (including untested treatments like hydroxychloroquine, which the president allegedly both took himself and promoted in public statements), attempted to influence the extent to which government researchers and advisors could speak with the press, and effectively disbanded the team's public presence just months into the onset of the pandemic (Swan, 2020; Rutledge, 2020). Trump even encouraged Americans to protest evidence-based social-distancing measures (Dyer, 2020a, 2020b), which may have played a role in inspiring a Michigan militia to plot to overthrow the state capitol and kidnap the Democratic governor, Gretchen Whitmer (Katov, 2021).

In sharp contrast, whereas the Trump administration was dismissive and arguably hostile to the policy advice of scientific experts, the Biden campaign and transition team made expert deference a key component of their electoral and governing strategy (Maxmen et al., 2020; Subbaraman et al., 2021). In an unprecedented but (perhaps) unsurprising move from researchers and academics across many scholarly fields, Donald Trump's candidacy drew strong opposition from leading scholarly journals like the *New England Journal of Medicine* and *Nature*. Biden's victory was celebrated by scientists around the world (Tollefson, 2020).

The COVID-19 pandemic interrupted all of our lives in ways many of us may have never thought possible. It injected uncertainty into our abilities to accomplish even the most basic tasks, such as picking up groceries, seeing friends and loved ones, and even procuring an adequate supply of toilet paper. It exacted, for many, unprecedented loss, suffering, and psychological discomfort. It changed our lives in ways that few, if any, of us will soon forget.

And yet some of us chose to lash out at those with the technical expertise necessary to guide sound policy responses to the pandemic. Some chose to spurn expert-backed public health recommendations and to refuse life-saving vaccines.

Richard Hofstadter anticipated the possibility that the increasing complexity of democratic self-governance can breed negativity toward scientists and other experts. Hofstadter observed that early in the nation's development Americans believed that nearly anyone who was eligible to vote in democratic elections (which, of course, was a highly exclusionary group for much of American history) would be capable of themselves playing a role in making important policy decisions. This "populistic dream" implied that nearly anyone could directly influence the size, shape, and direction of government. Hofstadter summarizes Americans' visions of empowerment by writing:

> In the original American populistic dream, the omnicompetence of the common [person] was fundamental and indispensable. It was believed that [they] could, without much special preparation, pursue the professions and run the government.
>
> —Hofstadter, 1963, 34

These visions, however, were just that. Hofstadter recognized that contemporary democratic governance affords Americans fewer and fewer opportunities to participate in the governing process. Responding to complicated policy challenges implies that governing is not the domain of the "common person"—either through their votes, activism, or perhaps even pursuit of elected office—but of bureaucrats and others who have acquired highly specialized technical expertise.

Correspondingly, Hofstadter goes on to claim:

> Once the intellectual was greatly ridiculed because [they] were not needed; now, [they are] fiercely resented *because they are needed too much.*
> —Hofstadter 1963, 34 *Author's emphasis in italics*

Thus, for Hofstadter, it is the uneasiness Americans experience with respect to deferring to experts that breeds negative attitudes toward experts. We dislike experts because we are dependent on them to improve our lives in times of crisis, to resume life "as normal," from something as trivial as a 2015 MacBook Air running out of hard drive space to the gravity of responding to a global pandemic.

What Hofstadter's work implies, then, is that anti-intellectualism and the role that experts play in the policymaking process is bidirectional: a two-way street, so to speak. Intuitively, and consistent with prior research, how Americans feel about experts' policy-relevance is shaped in part by anti-intellectual forces. Hofstadter reminds us, however, that the loss of Americans' "populistic dream"—resulting from negative feelings toward the role that experts play in contemporary American governance—might further exacerbate the expression of anti-intellectual attitudes.

Consequently, the group-centric model I outlined throughout this chapter accounts both for the possibility that anti-intellectualism influences policy orientations and vice versa. I refer to this proposition as the Bidirectionality Thesis throughout the remainder of this book. In what follows, I discuss how it is that I put the Bidirectionality Thesis, and all other theoretical claims that I outlined in this chapter, to the empirical test.

Testing the Group-Centric Model: A Preview

Testing the theoretical model outlined in this chapter is no small task. To put the predictions outlined in Figure 2.1 to the empirical test, I rely on three different types of data. Although I summarize each of these data sources in significantly more detail in Chapter 3, I want to offer a brief introduction to what these data are and how I make use of the data in testing my theoretical expectations.

The first type of data I use in this book are what social scientists refer to as panel or longitudinal public opinion survey data. Panel studies interview the same respondents at several time points, making it possible to track how changes in opinions and reported behaviors change over time.

Panel data are useful for several reasons. First, they allow me to test every element of the group-centric theory outlined in Figure 2.1. For example, when testing the Bidirectionality Thesis (paths c and d), I can determine whether anti-intellectualism measured early on in the panel survey is associated with policy views years later, whether the reverse is true, or whether we observe relatively equal amounts of change in both directions. Panel data are also useful for testing path b, as they allow me to assess how changes in epistemic factors like science knowledge and interest might in turn influence change in anti-intellectual attitude endorsement. Finally, panel data allow me to assess whether the static (a) and dynamic (b) paths outlined in the figure might be reverse causal (i.e., that they move in the opposite direction). Ruling out reverse causation is important in order to establish each of the aforementioned potential influence as inputs rather than potential outputs of holding anti-intellectual attitudes.

Additionally, I rely on cross-sectional survey data—i.e., studies that interview people at a single point in time—to supplement the panel studies. While panel data are necessary to test each of the claims outlined in Figure 2.1, they are not necessarily *sufficient*. As panel studies are time intensive, costly, and laborious to administer, few have the opportunity to carry them out. Consequently, panel studies that ask the questions necessary to study the questions outlined here are relatively difficult to find. This makes it difficult to offer an exhaustive assessment of how anti-intellectualism might, for example, be related to Americans' policy orientations (i.e., because any given panel necessarily asks about a subset of potentially relevant issues). Consequently, establishing support for the theory in a handful panel studies, I then rely on data from dozens of cross-sectional studies that expand the focus of the book's policy scope.

Finally, in addition to micro-level public-opinion data, I also draw on time-varying macro-level indicators of both anti-intellectualism and evidence of the influence that experts have in the policymaking process (specifically measures of congressional testimony from scientists and experts). As I discuss in the next chapter, these data are useful for several reasons, including the ability to contextualize the importance of anti-intellectualism in American political life by demonstrating whether fluctuations in how Americans *feel* about experts have a tangible impact on policymaking in the United States.

In the next chapter, I discuss how I plan to put this possibility—and all others referenced in this chapter—to the empirical test.

Anti-Scientific Americans: The Prevalence, Origins, and Political Consequences of Anti-Intellectualism in the US.
Matthew Motta, Oxford University Press. © Oxford University Press 2024. DOI: 10.1093/9780197788844.003.0002

3

Validating Two Approaches to Measuring Anti-Intellectual Attitude Endorsement in Public-Opinion Surveys

To this point, I have presented a definition of how I conceptualize anti-intellectualism, discussed its potential relevance to contemporary American political life, and outlined an affective and group-based theoretical model that explores both the origins and policy consequences of expert negativity. However, I am yet to fully discuss how I plan to put this theoretical model to the empirical test.

As alluded to earlier, I primarily (but not exclusively, as you will see in Chapter 8) test my theoretical expectations via analyses of *individual* survey respondents (i.e., at the micro level). My goal in this chapter is to provide a sense of how I plan to assess the socio-political origins and policy consequences of anti-intellectual attitude endorsement at the *micro* level.

To do this, it is essential that I attempt to both describe and validate my approach for measuring anti-intellectual attitude endorsement among individual survey respondents. As I detail below, I primarily take two approaches to measuring anti-intellectualism in the public. One takes a fairly broad view of what it means to be an *expert*, and the other operationalizes expertise more narrowly.

In this chapter, I discuss each of these two measurement strategies and what they look like in application across the dozens of micro-level public-opinion surveys that I make use of in this book. I begin by providing a general overview of each of the individual datasets that I employ and important details about how each study was conducted. These include survey sampling protocols, sample sizes, fielding dates, and an assessment of the extent to which each one is a representative reflection of the American public's views.

After discussing each dataset, I then describe in detail both the broader and narrower measurement strategies that I take to assess anti-intellectual attitude endorsement in the American public. Throughout this discussion, I note which surveys feature each set of questions and consider the potential benefits and drawbacks of each approach.

Perhaps most importantly, I conclude this chapter by providing evidence that each of these two measures is a *valid* indicator of expert dislike and distrust in the American public. In addition to discussing (conceptually) why I believe that each measure is an appropriate indicator of Americans' endorsement of anti-intellectual attitudes, I present three sets of analyses that consider (1) the extent to which survey respondents might interpret the groups referenced in each question in similar ways (*content validation*), (2) whether these two indicators of anti-intellectual attitude endorsement are empirically associated with one another (*convergent validation*), and (3) the degree to which each measure is correlated with attitudes toward experts in economic, health, climate, and other areas (*predictive validation*).

If survey respondents (a) view each of these measures in similar ways, (b) earn similar scores on each set of questions, and (c) if scores on both measures are similarly diagnostic with respect to whether people express negative attitudes toward experts in contemporary American public life, I believe that I will have strong evidence in favor of the view that each measure is a valid indicator of anti-intellectualism. As I demonstrate throughout this chapter, this is exactly what I find.

Two final points bear mentioning before moving on. First, I recognize that some readers may be interested in learning more about the analytical strategies (i.e., estimation approaches and procedures) that I use to test key elements of my theoretical expectations. As these details are sometimes quite technical in nature, I have written a compendium to this chapter that describes my methodological approach in much greater detail. This information can be found in the appendix.

Second, and more generally, I want to express both intellectual and analytical humility about the claims I make in this book and about the methodological approaches I take to substantiate them. No single dataset, measure, or analytical strategy is *perfectly* capable of testing the theories outlined in this book. As I review throughout this chapter, each dataset and analytical approach contributes a unique set of strengths and limitations.

As a general matter, I tend to err on the side of methodological pluralism, not perfection. No one dataset or measurement strategy tells the full story about where anti-intellectualism comes from, how prevalent it is, or how it shapes contemporary American politics. Instead, I hope to summarize how complementary patterns of results observed across many datasets, employing a variety of analytical approaches, advance our understanding of anti-intellectualism.

A Refresher: Two Approaches to Measuring Anti-Intellectual Attitude Endorsement

As noted in Chapter 1, I take two approaches to measuring anti-intellectualism in the micro level using public-opinion data. One approach is more general in orientation and asks respondents to report the extent to which they trust the insights of ordinary people over experts and intellectuals, derived from Oliver & Rahn's (2016) work on populism and expert mistrust. Here it is important to note that administration of this question varies slightly across three of the public-opinion databases I make use of in this study (i.e., the ANES, CSPP, and SciPol studies that I discuss in detail shortly; see Table 3.1). Later in this chapter, when describing how I make use of data from each public-opinion survey, I note all potential deviations from Oliver and Rahn's original formulation of the question.

As a general guide, however, original construction of the question is constructed as follows:

I'd rather put my trust in the wisdom of ordinary people than the opinions of experts and intellectuals.

<1> Strongly Agree

<2> Agree

<3> Neither Agree nor Disagree

<4> Disagree

<5> Strongly Disagree

*Taken from the 2016 CSPP Study

Throughout this book, I will (for brevity) refer to this as the *trust in experts* or simply *experts* question used to measure anti-intellectual attitude endorsement. Note that although Oliver and Rahn's version of this question refers to both experts and intellectuals, other iterations drop the "and intellectuals" language. As I document throughout this book, when testing my theoretical expectations, both approaches to constructing this question tend to produce highly similar results.

The second approach—featured in the GSS studies—is more specific in substantive orientation and asks respondents to report the extent to which they trust the scientific community. Specifically, that question asks:

I am going to name some institutions in this country. As far as the people running these institutions are concerned, would you say you have a great deal of confidence, only some confidence, or hardly any confidence at all in them?

Scientific Community

\<1\> Great Deal
\<2\> Only Some
\<3\> Hardly Any

*Taken from the GSS Time Series

Although I argued in Chapter 1 that both of these indicators are *conceptually* appropriate indicators of anti-intellectualism, and while both have been used extensively in past research, I recognize that neither of the two is perfectly capable of capturing anti-intellectualism as a construct on its own. Moreover, it may be unclear at this point how the two indicators relate to one another.

In what follows, I offer both a conceptual and empirical discussion of how these two measures relate to one another and the degree to which each one can be thought about as a valid indicator of anti-intellectual attitude endorsement. Before doing this, however, it is important to detail how each of these measures is constructed in the micro-level public-opinion surveys I use throughout this book and to provide background information on each one of these studies.

The Public-Opinion Data: An Overview

The public-opinion data I draw on throughout this book come from several different collections of sources. What all data sources have in common is that they make at least some effort to quantify the extent to which the US public holds anti-intellectual attitudes by asking respondents to directly report these attitudes in public-opinion surveys.

However, each source differs along several important dimensions. These include (1) when each study was fielded, (2) how they measure anti-intellectualism, and (3) the number of times they attempt to observe change in anti-intellectualism (and other factors) over time.

I provide a comprehensive summary of each dataset, and the differences between them, in Table 3.1. Note that I reference Table 3.1 throughout this book when describing the different data sources I consult in each chapter.

In addition to listing each public-opinion data source, the table also reports the valid number of non-missing observations in each study (*valid* = the total number of people who, at a bare minimum, answered questions used to measure anti-intellectualism), whether the survey interviewed respondents at multiple time points (*temporal variance*), the measure of anti-intellectualism included in each study (*AI target*), and how I employ each dataset in service of testing my theoretical expectations outlined in Chapter 2 (*usage*). I describe each of the datasets in additional detail and discuss both their benefits and limitations in the pages that follow.

Table 3.1 **Dataset Summary**

Name	Year(s)	Valid N	Temporal Variance	AI Target	Usage
GSS Time Series	1974–2018	40,784	Cross-Sectional	Scientists	Correlational Hypothesis Testing: Socio-Political Origins, Epistemic Origins, and Expert Policy Role Preferences.
ANES 2020 Pilot	2019	3,464	Cross-Sectional	Experts	Correlational Hypothesis Testing (Socio-Political Origins and Policy Consequences)
ANES 2020 Time Series	2020	7,360	Cross-Sectional	Experts	Correlational Hypothesis Testing (Socio-Political Origins and Policy Consequences)
SciPol RXC	2020–2021	6,495	Cross-Sectional	Sci./Exp.	Correlational Hypothesis Testing (Socio-Political Origins and Policy Consequences)
GSS Panel Studies	2006–2010 2008–2012 2010–2014	2,513	Pooled Longitudinal	Scientists	Dynamic Hypothesis Testing (Long); Reverse Causality Checks (Wide). Socio-Political and Epistemic Origins, and Expert Policy Role Prefer-ences *Note: Pooled across panels due to balloting structure.*
CSPP Panel Study	2016	1,571	Longitudinal	Experts	Dynamic Hypothesis Testing (Long); Reverse Causality Checks (Wide). Socio-Political Origins, Epistemic Origins and Policy Consequences

Note: Summary basic sample properties across data sources. Note *N* corresponds to the number of non-missing cases on that dataset's measure of anti-intellectualism. In the panel studies, this corresponds to the number of non-missing cases on that variable in the survey's final wave. Actual model outputs for *N* may vary based on the availability of other cross-ectional and time-varying measures.

GSS Time Series Studies (1974–2018)

The General Social Survey (GSS) Time Series Study is a biannual (formerly yearly) cross-sectional and nationally representative public-opinion survey fielded by the National Opinion Research Center (NORC). Over the six decades that the study has been administered, the GSS has asked Americans to provide their opinions and self-report behaviors on hundreds of socially and politically relevant phenomena. Additional information about this widely used survey can be found in NORC's public GSS data files.

I chose to make use of GSS data for several reasons. First and perhaps most importantly for the investigation that I hope to offer in this book, the survey regularly asks the question featured earlier in this chapter that pertains to Americans' confidence in the scientific community. This serves as an indicator of anti-intellectual attitude endorsement, which has the added benefit of having been well studied in past research (Motta, 2018a; see also Merkley, 2020) as an indicator of anti-intellectualism.

Second, this survey also contains measures of partisan identification, political ideology, limited-government views, and religious service attendance variables necessary to study differences *between people* in the acceptance of anti-intellectual attitudes. This is true in nearly all survey administration periods. Consequently, the GSS is ideal for studying several of the predictions from the theoretical model that I laid out in Chapter 2.

Finally, the GSS Time Series Study has the major advantage of being both nationally representative, temporally expansive, and (when pooled) massive with respect to its sample size (e.g., over forty thousand respondents answered the question used to measure anti-intellectualism). However, due to the cross-sectional nature of the data, an important limitation is that the GSS Time Series offers only correlational tests of my theoretical expectations.

This means that while the GSS is well suited for studying the prevalence and between-person correlates of anti-intellectual attitude acceptance, it cannot study (1) how factors that change over time influence anti-intellectual attitudes (e.g., dynamic inputs; path b in Figure 2.1) or (2) provide tests that assess the possibility of reverse causality. To address those limitations, I next turn to a related series of *panel studies* from the GSS.

GSS Panel Studies (2006–2010, 2008–2012, 2010–2014)

Longitudinal studies (panels) are surveys that re-interview the same respondents over several periods of time. Panels are extremely valuable resources because they allow me to observe within-respondent *change* in anti-intellectualism over time. As I hope will become obvious throughout this book, this property of panel studies allows me to overcome the limitations of the GSS Time Series Study discussed earlier because of its cross-sectional structuring.

Fortunately, during the administration of its time series studies in 2006, 2008, and 2010, the GSS randomly selected a subsample of participants in its cross-sectional studies to be recontacted in future biannual waves. This allowed the GSS to form three, three-wave, and nationally representative panel studies (i.e., surveys that interview the same people multiple times). All panel surveys were conducted face to face with an in-person interviewer. Additional technical information about how respondents were recruited into each sample can be found in NORC's public data downloads.

Important for my purposes in this book is that all three panel studies contained series of questions about Americans' attitudes toward science and technology. This includes not only the items used to measure trust in the scientific community—which, as mentioned earlier, I use as a measure of anti-intellectual attitude endorsement—but also assessments of both interest in and knowledge about science. This makes the panel studies suitable for testing the hypothesized dynamic inputs that explain change in anti-intellectualism within-respondents over time.

Specifically, because these data measure responses within respondents and over time, they are well suited to detect time varying effects via fixed and random effects panel analyses when the data are *long* or *stacked* (i.e., containing multiple observations or rows per individual panelist). I discuss in more detail why this approach is advantageous in the technical compendium for this chapter (see the appendix for more information). Additionally, these data are well suited to test for reverse causality via cross-lagged regression modeling—e.g., to assess the possibility that anti-intellectualism is not the result but the *cause* of socio-political factors that I expect to breed expert negativity—when the data are *wide* (i.e., a single observation per respondent, with different variables or columns denoting responses to the same questions at different time points). Again, I will discuss the advantages of wide data for assessing reverse causality in this chapter's technical compendium.

Moreover, the GSS panel studies are advantageous because they also featured a variety of questions related to Americans' preferences about the role that experts play in the policymaking process. These include (but are not limited to) the extent to which Americans think that climate scientists, medical doctors, and economists ought to have a say in major policy issues related to their fields of expertise. This enables me to pose rigorous time-varying tests of the Bidirectionality Thesis.

Before moving on, it is also important to note that as subsets of the GSS Time Series Study, all items are also available in the cross-sectional data described earlier. Consequently, one might ask why I do not use the GSS Time Series to *also* provide tests of the theoretical model's dynamic inputs or to test the Bidirectionality Thesis. Here there are both conceptual and empirical challenges at play.

First, conceptually, studying dynamic inputs cross-sectionally allows me to say whether hypothesized inputs are correlated with anti-intellectualism. But they nevertheless fail to provide a sense of whether those factors explain change in anti-intellectualism over time. While that information may nevertheless be useful, a larger empirical limitation is at play.

Second, and more practically, it is important to note that the GSS regularly administers its studies with multiple ballots. This often means that the survey randomly assigns respondents to answer questions about just one of several thematic topics. Consequently, the questions used to measure inputs like science interest/ knowledge and outputs related to experts' policymaking role are available in (1) a limited series of GSS survey years and (2) shown to just a subset of respondents. Consequently, attempting to include these variables in analyses from the cross-sectional studies severely reduces the study's sample size and—of course—its temporal range (as the panel studies were fielded in only the mid-to-late 2000s).

This balloting issue poses an important challenge for the GSS panel studies as well. Because questions about science and technology are not administered to all respondents, the number of respondents answering questions used to test the dynamic inputs and bidirectional outputs of anti-intellectualism can be quite small. Moreover, as these studies are administered longitudinally, sample attrition—i.e., the inability to recontact panelists in future study waves—further reduces sample size.

To address these limitations, I assembled a single pooled GSS panel. This means that I combined all Wave 1 respondents across the panels beginning 2006, 2008, and 2010 into a single collection of first-wave respondents. I did the same for the second and third waves, adjusting the date references accordingly. Readers interested in learning more about this strategy, and the viability of its technical assumptions it makes, can find more information in the technical compendium for this chapter.

To further resolve the issues listed here, I next turn to a panel study that both leverages the advantages of a longitudinal survey design while offering an alternative (and less conceptually limiting) measure of anti-intellectualism.

CSPP Panel Study (2016)

The 2016 CSPP panel study is a four-wave panel administered in the lead-up to (and aftermath of) the 2016 US general election administered by the Center for the Study of Political Psychology (CSPP) at the University of Minnesota. As I helped to oversee data collection administration for this study during my time in graduate school, I will refer to it as "our" panel at times throughout this book.

Respondents were initially recruited into our panel from Survey Sampling International's (SSI, now Dynata) large online opt-in sampling frame. At the time we fielded this study, SSI employed demographic quota sampling procedures to solicit participation in the survey in a way that targeted national representativeness with respect to respondents' race, gender, age, household income, and educational attainment. As detailed methodological information about these data—unlike the GSS and (as I describe later) the American National Election Study (ANES)—are not readily available online, I offer comparisons of unweighted and weighted sample summary statistics in the appendix (Table S3.1).

The CSPP panel included the question referenced earlier in this chapter from Oliver and Rahn's *expert mistrust* sub-scale of their (2016) populism measure, which asked survey respondents to report the extent to which they would rather place their trust in ordinary people over experts and intellectuals. This question has been used to measure anti-intellectualism in past research (Merkley, 2020; Merkley & Loewen, 2021), including previously published work from the CSPP panel (Motta, 2018a). This question was featured in the panel's first (July 2016) and second (September 2020) survey waves.

Here it is important to note that while Oliver and Rahn's work included multiple indicators of expert mistrust in their original (2016) work, just a single-item measure is available in the CSPP study. Correspondingly, for the sake of both standardization and to reflect previous methodological practice offered in past work, I make use of only this single-item measure throughout the book.

Because the CSPP panel survey primarily pertained to politics, it offers the ability to measure the socio-political factors necessary to assess the relationship between anti-intellectualism and its hypothesized static inputs. It is also suitable for testing for the possibility of reverse causality with respect to the potential causes of anti-intellectual attitude endorsement (e.g., by rigorously testing the possibility that partisan identification is also shaped by anti-intellectualism). Unfortunately, though, the CSPP data do not contain science knowledge or interest measures used to test expectations about the model's dynamic inputs.

These data are also advantageous because they include a measure of the extent to which panelists hold populist attitudes. As I noted previously, there is room for conceptual debate regarding whether anti-intellectualism can be thought about as a component of populism more generally. While resolving this debate is outside the purview of this book, I at least try to ensure that any effects of anti-intellectualism I might observe are *distinct* from those of populist sentiments more generally in the CSPP data.

To be clear, documenting independent effects of anti-intellectualism does not necessarily negate the possibility that it may be a subcomponent of populism more generally. Nor does it rule out the possibility that populism might also exert an influence on the outcomes studied in this book. However, by accounting for populist attitude endorsement in the models used to study anti-intellectualism and its effects, I hope to further underscore both the methodological soundness and empirical robustness of the effects documented throughout this book.

Still, the CSPP panel data are not without some important limitations. Unlike the GSS panel, for example, the CSPP study contains the variables necessary to test the theoretical model outlined in Chapter 2 in just two (versus three) survey waves. The CSPP study also features far less spacing between waves than the GSS (several months versus two years). If anti-intellectual and other attitudes change only slowly over time—i.e., over the course of years and election cycles, as opposed to months or within an election cycle—it may therefore be difficult to assess the temporal dynamics of anti-intellectual attitudes in the CSPP data.

Moreover, unlike the GSS studies that I discussed earlier, these data are not formally nationally representative. Although SSI (now Dynata) employed quota-sampling procedures aimed at producing a sample that matched the US population on race, gender, age, household income, and educational attainment, responses were nevertheless drawn from an online opt-in sampling frame. This means that although I can both observe and correct for observed differences between the sample and the US adult population (i.e., via post-stratification weighting), I cannot ensure that the sample does not deviate from the population in unobserved ways.

Fortunately, though, I primarily use the CSPP panel study to study *change* in anti-intellectualism in relation to social, political, and policy factors. This means that the modeling approach I employ (described in detail shortly) primarily focuses on measuring *within-panelist* change and testing for reverse causality. As the former set of tests are not concerned with differences *between* panelists, systematic differences between the sample and the population are unlikely to affect the inferences I draw from CSPP data.

Readers interested in learning more about these procedures, including information about how I use post-stratification weights in this study (i.e., efforts to correct for deviations between the sample and population in non-representativeness), can find additional information about them in this chapter's technical compendium in the appendix.

Finally, as a general rule—and with respect to the representativeness of the CSPP panel—it is important to note that I treat these data as a *supplement* for other data resources that I draw on in this book. In the chapters that follow, I never make claims based on data that are not nationally representative that I don't also provide in a nationally representative context. As I document throughout the book, I find similar patterns of results irrespective of formal national representativeness, the application of post-stratification weights, and many other differences in the construction of each survey.

Fortunately, and consistent with this objective, I have the opportunity to contextualize results drawn from the CSPP panel study using formally nationally representative data that also administered versions of the *trust experts* measure of anti-intellectual attitude endorsement. In what follows, I discuss how I draw on two recent studies from the American National Election Studies (ANES) to accomplish this objective.

ANES Pilot Study (2019) and 2020 Time Series Study

The 2019 ANES Time Series Pilot Survey was designed to pre-test several series of items slated for inclusion on the 2020 ANES. The pilot study was administered online in December 2019 via YouGov, who used propensity score-matching procedures to ensure that they drew a nationally representative sample from their online opt-in sampling frame. You can find additional technical information about sampling and recruitment in ANES public data files.

The corresponding 2020 ANES is a nationally representative two-wave survey (Pre-Election: August–November 2020; Post Election: December 2020). Unlike the 2019 ANES pilot, the 2020 ANES used address-based sampling to achieve national representativeness (i.e., by sending web survey recruitment links to a random sample of US households and then providing respondents with screening instructions to randomly select a member from that household to complete the study).

Due to the challenging nature of conducting survey research during a global pandemic, the ANES—which in recent years is typically conducted face to face, with supplementary online subsamples—featured a more-complex design. Specifically, the 2020 ANES is a mixed-mode survey, including online only, online + phone, and online + phone + video subsamples. The 2020 ANES also featured an internet-based recontact effort to resurvey panelists from the ANES 2016 web survey and included a unique cross-section recruited to answer items for the 2020 GSS (which, at the time I began writing this book, had not yet been released). Again, additional information about sampling and recruitment from this widely used study can be found in the ANES public data files.

In addition to asking a question about Americans' trust in experts that is similar to the item featured in the CSPP panel, the ANES studies contains the sociopolitical inputs necessary to assess both the causes and the potential policy consequences of anti-intellectual attitude endorsement (e.g., questions about climate and health policy, misinformation about the COVID-19 pandemic, and much more). Note that despite the fact that the 2020 ANES is administered as a panel study, the anti-intellectualism item is administered only once (in its post-election wave). This means that I treat both the 2019 and 2020 ANES as cross-sectional studies (see Table 3.1).

Note, however, that the 2019 pilot and 2020 studies feature versions of the *experts* question that differed slightly from the example (derived from the CSPP panel) provided earlier in this chapter. Specifically, the 2019 ANES pilot asked respondents a single question that—in contrast to the original Oliver and Rahn measure—was not administered using an agree-disagree series of response options. Instead, the question asked respondents to report the extent to which they trusted ordinary people more than experts or vice versa. Specifically, the question asked:

When it comes to public policy decisions, whom do you tend to trust more, ordinary people or experts?

<1> Trust ordinary people much more
<2> Trust ordinary people somewhat more
<3> Trust both the same
<4> Trust experts somewhat more
<5> Trust experts much more

The 2020 ANES asked a similar question structured in a similar format. However, unlike the pilot, the 2020 ANES administered this question in two stages: first asking respondents whether they trusted ordinary people more than experts (or vice versa) and then asking them to report the extent to which they do so (much versus somewhat more). Despite this administrative difference, the resulting scale looks analogous to that of the 2019 ANES pilot.

More generally, and as I alluded to earlier, ANES data have the important advantage of being nationally representative. However, like the GSS Time Series Studies, they have the drawback of not being able to assess change in anti-intellectualism over time, and they provide insights from just two years of data collection. Correspondingly, it is important to supplement these studies with other correlational efforts to study anti-intellectualism and its policy-relevant effects, especially throughout the early stages of the COVID-19 pandemic. In a series of surveys I fielded from mid 2020 to early 2021, I aimed to do precisely this. I discuss those studies in turn.

Science and Policy Rolling Cross-Sectional Study (2020–2021)

Throughout the first year of the COVID-19 pandemic, I fielded a series of six bimonthly and cross-sectional surveys (from April 2020 to February 2021), which I call the Science Policy Rolling Cross-Sectional Study (SciPol, for short). Although the study asks questions about a variety of topics (e.g., climate change, moral values, political attitudes and identities), it primarily focuses on attitudes and self-reported behaviors related to public health. As detailed methodological information about these data (unlike the GSS and ANES) are not readily available online, I again provide weighted and unweighted sample demographics in the appendix for this chapter. I fielded the SciPol study via Lucid Theorem, which is an online opt-in quota-sampling service. Like the Dynata sample used to build the CSPP panel study, Lucid uses quota sampling to target demographic representativeness on respondents' age, race, gender, household income, educational attainment, geographic region, and partisan identification. As a rolling cross-sectional study, SciPol is something of a hybrid between panel and cross-sectional studies. Although I did not recontact respondents to participate in future waves, the study administered many of the same questions across multiple time points (fielded bimonthly from April 2020 through February 2021).

As I discuss in more detail shortly, an important advantage of SciPol is that it administers *both* the Oliver and Rahn *experts* question (albeit with seven Likert-style agree-disagree scale points rather than five) and a question that measures trust in the scientific community (constructed similarly to that of the GSS, with the addition of a *trust a little* scale point in-between *somewhat* and *not at all*).

Consequently, SciPol enables me to assess the coherence between these two measures and to justify both their empirical and conceptual relatedness. Moreover, SciPol features a variety of questions regarding misinformation about the COVID-19 pandemic, compliance with evidence-based health recommendations, and support for pandemic-related health policies not featured in the other datasets. It also features the socio-political items necessary to test the model's hypothesized static inputs.

Nevertheless, the study (like the CSPP panel) is also limited in the sense that it is not nationally representative. I therefore again apply survey weights (see the technical compendium in the appendix for additional information about the use of survey weights) and urge caution when attempting to generalize results to the general population. As always, I encourage the reader to avoid drawing inferences about proportions and effect sizes to the general population.

Validating the Two Micro-Level Indicators of Anti-Intellectualism

Now that I have provided a description of the two approaches I take to measure anti-intellectualism in the surveys featured throughout this book—as well as important methodological information regarding how each survey asked Americans these questions—it's time to consider the extent to which the two measures can be considered *valid* indicators of anti-intellectualism.

If Americans tend to think about the groups referenced in each question in complementary ways (content validity), earn similar scores on each one (convergent validity), and express the types of negative views toward experts that we would expect to be associated with anti-intellectual attitude endorsement across each measure (predictive validity), then I believe I will have solid evidence in favor of the idea that each measurement approach is well validated.

Doing this, however, requires that I make use of data that asks each set of questions in the *same survey*. This allows me to assess whether people who are classified as highly anti-intellectual on one measure are categorized in the same way on the other. It also allows me to assess the degree to which each measure is correlated with several different manifestations of anti-intellectualism in contemporary American public life in a way that is not confounded by survey administration decisions. In other words, because both sets of items are measured in the same study, it cannot possibly be the case that sample size/composition, sampling methods, question wording, and dozens of other survey-level idiosyncrasies are instead responsible for any effects I might observe.

Fortunately, as noted earlier, the SciPol study included both the more-general and more-narrow approaches I take to measuring anti-intellectual attitude endorsement in this book. This makes it possible for me to take on the validation procedures discussed earlier. At times, I also include data from supplemental studies (i.e., not used throughout the rest of this book and not listed in Table 3.1) to further substantiate the measures' validity.

In what follows, I consider the extent to which each of the two approaches I take to measuring anti-intellectual attitude endorsement can be thought about as having strong levels of content, convergent, and predictive validity.

Coping with Satisficing: A (Brief) Methodological Aside

Before assessing the extent to which these two conceptually related questions might also be empirically similar to one another, one important methodological detail about these analyses is worth noting. In this chapter, I exclude respondents who may have engaged in what survey methodologists call *satisficing* behavior (Simon, 1956; Krosnick, 1991). Even in a short and relatively straightforward survey like those that I make use of in this book, some respondents may cope with both the opportunity costs (i.e., time allocated to survey taking, when respondents could have been doing something else) and cognitive demands (e.g., the potentially taxing process of mapping one's abstract thoughts onto available survey response options; see Tourangeau, 2000) of the survey environment by failing to engage fully with survey questions and instructions.

As my goal in what follows is to validate two measures of anti-intellectual attitude endorsement, the possibility of satisficing poses a particularly important methodological challenge. This is especially true with respect to the Oliver and Rahn *experts* question, which is administered using Likert scales with agree-disagree formats. Unfortunately, the types of strategies that satisficers take to reduce a survey's cognitive and temporal demands are often especially problematic for questions administered in this format. Consequently, I make a special effort in this chapter to address the potentially deleterious effects of satisficing on my ability to draw valid inferences from the validation analyses.

Conceivably, one reason why satisficing may uniquely impact the *experts* question has to do with the question's *agree-disagree* format. One way respondents might cope with the survey's cognitive demands is by simply indicating that they agree with all questions formulated in an agree-disagree format. This is known as acquiescence bias. Because the *experts* question features response options administered via an agree-disagree format, we might worry that some satisficing respondents simply agree with the prompt in order to advance onward in the survey.

Alternatively, satisficers might reduce the survey's cognitive and time burdens by simply selecting middle responses (*neither agree nor disagree*) to attitude questions administered on Likert scales. This too implies that some individuals may hold positive or negative feelings toward experts but fail to categorize their opinions as such in the survey.

Satisficing therefore poses a unique burden on the types of analyses I present in this chapter. Specifically, mis-categorization on the *experts* question attributable to satisficing could therefore make it more difficult to assess its empirical similarity with the *trust scientists* item. For example, one could imagine a situation where someone who holds negative views toward the scientific community (GSS item) might also hold negative views toward experts more generally (ANES item) but fail to register their opinions as such on the latter question. This would make it appear as if the two items have less in common than we otherwise might assume that they do in the absence of satisficing.

Because this is the only chapter where I directly compare scores on *both* measures of anti-intellectualism employed throughout this book, I make a special effort to account for the possibility of satisficing behavior.

To do this, I construct a commonly used indicator of respondents' motivation to carefully complete the survey (Gummer & Robmann, 2015)—which is thought to be correlated with other indicators of satisficing behavior (Roberts et al., 2019)—by identifying and removing all respondents from the analysis who completed each survey reported below in less than seven minutes (half of each survey's anticipated completion time).

Overall, low respondent motivation to carefully complete the survey was relatively uncommon (but far from rare) in both sets of surveys that I employ in this chapter. In the SciPol dataset, 17 percent (N = 1,143 out of N = 6,499 responses) finished the survey in under half of the anticipated completion time. Similarly, in the supplemental Lucid survey, I find that about one-fifth (20 percent, N = 94 out of 478 respondents) may have been motivated to engage in potential satisficing behavior.

Of course, I recognize that some readers may be uncomfortable with omitting somewhere between one-sixth and one-fifth of survey responses that may have engaged in satisficing behavior. Consequently, in the appendix I provide an alternate version of all analyses with the inclusion of potential satisficers. As I discuss in this chapter, the results are highly substantively similar across methodological strategies, albeit with somewhat lower levels of statistical precision when including satisficers in these analyses.

Content Validation, Part 1: Americans' Definitions of Expertise and How Scientists Contribute to It

With an understanding of how I operationalize anti-intellectualism in each public-opinion dataset in place, readers may have several questions about the extent to which Americans might bring different attitudes to mind when answering questions about experts and intellectuals (the more-general approach) versus the scientific community (the more-narrow approach). To that end, I begin by providing a sense of the extent to which each measure is *content valid* (i.e., that the two are, despite their substantive differences, nevertheless measuring similar quantities).

In other words, I am to answer the following question: when Americans are asked to define the term *expert*, what comes to mind?

Survey respondents might think about the extent to which individuals considered to be experts in their field have formal training or education in a particular area, their superior knowledge of a subject (compared to those who we might consider to be non-experts), or their competencies at carrying out complicated subject-related tasks. They might also take it upon themselves to provide *examples* of whom they consider to be an expert.

If attitudes toward the scientific community are on American's minds when thinking about expertise more generally, we should expect that many choose to offer up scientists as examples of who are considered experts. This should be true even without additional prodding asking respondents *whether or not* they consider scientists to be experts, which, presumably, many might.

Indeed, in a small public-opinion survey that I carried out several years before writing this book, I found that most survey respondents do think about experts in this way. Back in the fall of 2017, when I was first beginning to think about the measurement of anti-intellectual attitudes and their theoretical underpinnings, I asked a small sample of N = 250 participants on Amazon's online opt-in

Mechanical Turk platform (MTurk; see the appendix for additional information about this study) to answer the following question:

> We'd like to know a bit more about how people think about experts. When you hear the term "expert," what comes to mind?
>
> Some potential topics to write about include: (1) What are some examples of experts? (2) How do we know that someone is an expert? (3) What role should experts play in making social and political decisions?

Respondents could write as much or as little as they wanted when replying to this question. After collecting the data, I churned through these qualitative, open-ended data to assess different themes emerging in respondents' definitions of what it means to be an *expert*. Note that all raw qualitative data is available in the online supplementary materials associated with this book.

As we might expect, nearly all respondents (81 percent) who chose to provide a substantive answer to this open-ended question (35 percent, $N = 87$) defined experts as individuals who exhibit superior knowledge, skills, or other competencies in a particular area of specialization. One, for example, made the point that experts are people who can make credible claims to superior knowledge on a particular subject by writing: "Experts are people who know about something very well, either through experience, training, knowledge, and a combination of these."

Others mentioned formal education and training in their definition. One, for example, defined experts as "professors and people with doctorate degrees are experts in their fields" (i.e., directly listing advanced academic degrees as being a requisite component of expertise). Others mentioned that experts typically go through "many years of school training" or "went to college."

For the sake of comparison, I also fielded a multiple-answer (i.e., *closed*) question in this survey, where I asked respondents to indicate whether a series of adjectives that could potentially define expertise happens to come to mind when thinking about experts. Note that for reasons that will become obvious shortly, I specifically omitted terms related to science and scientists in this task to avoid potentially prompting respondents, who otherwise might not have done so, to list that as a consideration in the open-ended qualitative data described earlier.

Respondents' open-ended definitions of *expertise* strongly matched the adjectives they selected to describe experts in this multiple-answer question. Specifically, 96 percent of respondents characterized experts as *knowledgeable*, and 94 percent described them as *experienced*. More than two-thirds (71 percent) opted to include *formally trained/educated* in their conceptualization of expertise, as well.

In general, then, the picture emerging from both the open-ended and multiple-answer data suggests that nearly all respondents in this pilot study view experts as people who can make legitimate claims to superior knowledge about some area of specialization.

Additionally, and perhaps most importantly for my purposes in this chapter, many respondents *spontaneously chose* to mention scientists as examples of experts. Specifically, 22 percent of respondents who attempted to provide a substantive answer to this question mentioned scientists directly as examples of expertise.

Some mentioned examples of science popularizers, like Neil deGrasse Tyson. Others listed "someone who works with DNA advancements," while another simply referred to the term *scientist*.

Although 22 percent is far from a majority of responses, it is important to bear in mind that I *did not require* respondents to provide examples of whom they consider to be an expert. Nor did I directly ask *whether or not* scientists ought to be considered experts. This means that more than one in five Americans spontaneously chose to include scientists in their definition of expertise with virtually no prodding.

For purposes of comparison, recall that I found—via the close-ended multiple-answer data—that just over 70 percent of respondents felt as if formal training/education is part of what it means to be an expert. This theme, however, appeared in just 24 percent of the open-ended qualitative responses, rivaling mentions of scientists as an example of what it means to be an expert.

What this potentially implies, therefore, is that more Americans might be inclined to define expertise as pertaining to science or scientific authority if asked whether that term was applicable in a close-ended format. Although I cannot test that proposition directly in these data, this analysis further underscores why it is so noteworthy that over one in five Americans spontaneously chose to list scientific exemplars when defining what it means to be an expert. While experts and scientists are substantively distinct categories, they nevertheless overlap both conceptually (see Chapter 1) and empirically.

Content Validation, Part 2: How Anti-Intellectual Thought Underpins Evaluations of Scientists

Moving on, some might ask whether how Americans think about intellectuals— which is included in the more-general approach I take to measuring anti-intellectual attitude endorsement (i.e., the question references experts and intellectuals)—differs substantively from how they evaluate members of the scientific community.

Specifically, some might express concern that Americans' conceptualizations of the former are focused more on perceived class and status-based differences between intellectuals and everyday people in comparison to those of the scientific community. Recall that as I discussed in Chapter 1, a perceived misalignment in the valuation of intellectual pursuits over the everyday concerns of most people was a central part of Hofstadter's understanding of anti-intellectualism and has continued to motivate social science research on Americans' attitudes toward expertise to this day (Rutjens & Heine, 2016). In other words, negative feelings toward intellectuals may arise disproportionately from the dislike of experts' perceived status-seeking behaviors and other class-based suspicions.

This, too, is a testable hypothesis. Turning again to the MTurk pilot study referenced earlier, I asked respondents a series of questions related to their distrust of scientists and college professors.

We might, for several reasons, consider the latter group to be prototypical example of someone considered to be an intellectual. In addition to the fact that college professors often have many years of advanced academic training in their field of specialization (i.e., showcasing their commitment to intellectual pursuits), scholars often use terms related to academics and intellectuals synonymously (Peters, 2018). Demonstrative of the high degree of similarity between the two terms, sociologist Paul Lazarsfeld and Wagner Thielens' seminal work on the social and political opinions of American intellectuals (Lazarsfeld & Thielens, 1957; see also Gross & Simmons, 2007) drew its conclusions about perceived McCarthy era threats to intellectual freedom—and how professors coped with them in the classroom—on the basis of surveys with social-science PhDs and other academics.

With that in mind, Table 3.2 compares Americans attitudes toward scientists and college professors in two domains. First the table investigates the extent to which survey respondents reported viewing either of the aforementioned groups as *elitist* (i.e., on the basis of perceived class asymmetries between themselves and each group). The results show that although the proportion of respondents rejecting this term in application to scientists is slightly higher (45 percent) than that of intellectuals (40 percent), many Americans hold negative or mixed feelings toward both groups (see the table caption for additional information on the wording and coding of these responses). Moreover, and further demonstrative of overlap between the two groups, I find that 77 percent of respondents who characterized scientists as elitist also did the same for intellectuals (row A3). Similarly, 66 percent of those who characterized intellectuals as elitist did the same for scientists (row A4).

I find a similar pattern of effects when asking Americans questions about whether the motivations of scientists or college professors align with the concerns of everyday people.

Table 3.2 **Evidence of Anti-Intellectual Thought in Americans' Characterization of Scientists and Experts.**

Prompt	Percentage
(A) Elitism Evaluations (Scientists and Experts)	
(1) Disagree: "Most SCIENTISTS are Elitist"	45%
(2) Disagree: "Most COLLEGE PROFESSORS are Elitist"	40%
(3) Disagree: Prompt 2 // Prompt 1	77%
(4) Disagree: Prompt 1 // Prompt 2	66%
(B) Important Problems vs. Self-Interest (Scientists and Experts)	
(1) Disagree: "COLLEGE PROFESSORS care less about solving important problems than advancing their own personal interests."	49%
(2) Disagree: "SCIENTISTS care less about solving important problems than advancing their own personal interests."	65%
(3) Disagree: Prompt 2 // Prompt 1	86%
(4) Disagree: Prompt 1 // Prompt 2	66%

Note: Pilot study data collected via Amazon's Mechanical Turk on September 28, 2017. N = 250. Respondents were asked (A) to report the extent to which they agreed or disagreed with the statement "Most [SCIENTISTS / COLLEGE PROFESSORS] are elitists" (on a five-point Likert scale, with those indicating neither agree nor disagree treated as *not disagreeing* with the statement); (B) the extent to which they agreed or disagreed with the statement "College professors care less about solving important problems than advancing their own personal interests" (measured and coded analogously to A); and (C1) whether or not the phrase "formally trained/educated" comes to mind when respondents "hear the term 'expert.'" Respondents were also asked to write a short passage answering the question "When you hear the term 'expert,' what comes to mind?" Note that throughout the table, the operator // refers to frequency of the quantity listed to its left, given responses to the quantity on its right. Raw data used to calculate these percentages can be found in the book's online supplementary materials.

The results suggest that more than half (65 percent) of Americans disagree with the idea that scientists "care less about solving important problems than advancing their own personal interests," while slightly under half (49 percent) say the same of college professors. Again, demonstrative of substantial overlap between evaluations of the two groups, I find that 86 percent of those who disagreed with this statement in application to scientists felt the same way about college professors. A similarly high percentage (66 percent) of those who rejected the term for college professors did the same for scientists.

Taken together, these analyses further underscore the conceptual and empirical similarity between how Americans think of at least one prototypically intellectual group and how they think about the scientific community. Americans hold a fair amount of suspicion toward both groups, with a high degree of consonance between evaluations of each one.

Convergent Validation: Assessing the Empirical Overlap between the Two Measures

As the findings in the preceding section show, Americans think about scientists (specifically) and experts (more generally) in similar ways. Figure 3.1 provides a first pass at assessing the coherence of these two questions. It does this by displaying the percentage of people agreeing (pooled across ordinal response options), neither agreeing nor disagreeing, or disagreeing (again pooled across response options) with the Oliver and Rahn style of question (referred to as the ANES version, on the y-axis), plotted over levels of trust indicated in response to the GSS-style question (on the x-axis). Note that for consonance with the GSS, the middle *trust somewhat* and *trust a little* response options are collapsed into a single *somewhat* category.

The results indicate a strong degree of correspondence between the two measures. For example, among those who greatly trust the scientific community—as

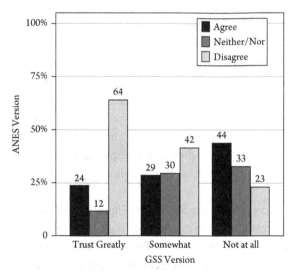

Figure 3.1 The Correspondence Between GSS and ANES Style Measures of Anti-Intellectualism (SciPol 2020-2021)

measured by the GSS-style question—a majority (64 percent) disagree with the Oliver and Rahn/ANES-style prompt, while under a quarter (24 percent) agree with it. Likewise, for those who place low levels of trust in the scientific community on the GSS-style item, a plurality (44 percent) express agreement with the Oliver and Rahn question, while an additional 33 percent fall somewhere in the middle. Intuitively, people who hold neutral feelings toward the scientific community on the GSS-style question, as we might expect, hold a roughly equal mix of opinions across response options on the ANES-style question.

Additionally, as noted earlier, I replicate Figure 3.1 with the inclusion of potential satisficers in the supplementary materials. There I report an analogous—albeit slightly more muted—pattern of effects. Even when satisficers are included in the analysis, I find that 59 percent of respondents who disagree with the *experts* question also express high levels of trust in the scientific community, while 41 percent of those who agree with the former express low levels of trust in the latter.

To further assess the correspondence between the GSS-style and ANES-style questions, I fielded a supplemental Lucid survey in May 2021 (N = 478) where I (1) readministered both the GSS-style and ANES-style questions (enabling me to replicate Figure 3.1) and (2) asked respondents to provide affective ratings regarding how they feel about several different types of scientific, medical, economic, and other experts using 101 *feeling thermometer* scales. Feeling thermometer scales allow respondents to indicate how coldly (toward 0 degrees), warmly (toward 100 degrees), or neutral (approximately 50 degrees) they feel about each target (i.e., high-profile experts, groups of expert, expert institutions, etc.) that I asked them to evaluate. You can find summary statistics for this supplementary study in the appendix.

The latter task enables me to compare each of the two measures' *predictive* validity. If the GSS measure, despite its limited substantive focus, is a suitable proxy for the broader ANES anti-intellectualism measure, it should bear similarly strong and statistically significant associations with negative affect toward many different types of experts (i.e., not just those who are scientific experts) in multivariate models. These models are structured analogously to the models offered in later chapters (see the caption accompanying Figure 3.3 for additional information).

Figure 3.2 offers a direct replication of Figure 3.1. There I again find that a majority (60 percent) of people who hold high levels of trust in the scientific community also disagree with the Oliver and Rahn–style ANES question. Correspondingly, I find that 50 percent of people who place no trust at all in the scientific community on the GSS-style question express agreement with the ANES item. As was the case in Figure 3.1, those indicating more-moderate levels of trust held a roughly equal mix of opinions on the ANES question.

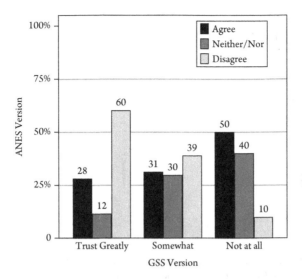

Figure 3.2 The Correspondence Between GSS and ANES Style Measures of Anti-Intellectualism (2021 Supplemental Lucid Study)

These results further document a strong empirical overlap between the two measures.

As I did for Figure 3.1, I replicate the results presented in Figure 3.2 with the inclusion of potential satisficers and present the results in the appendix. There I find that 49 percent of respondents who disagree with the *experts* question also place high levels of trust in the scientific community, while 47 percent of those who agree with the former place low levels of trust in the latter. While these supplemental results recover the pattern of effects presented in Figure 3.2, they are somewhat more muted than those that I presented earlier when replicating Figure 3.1.

This more-muted pattern of effects may be due to elevated levels of acquiescence bias among satisficers. As I show in the appendix, the proportion of respondents who *agree* with the *expert* item and also *trust* the scientific community is 10 percentage points higher (38 percent versus 28 percent) when satisficers are included (versus excluded) in this analysis. In other words, it may be the case that respondents who truly hold negative views toward experts avoid reporting those views on the Likert-style question in order to reduce the survey's time and cognitive burden. Nevertheless, the two sets of analyses converge on a similar set of findings and further underscore the empirical similarities between the two items.

Finally, Figure 3.3 assesses the predictive validity of the GSS and ANES items. Again, if both are capturing anti-intellectual attitude endorsement, they should

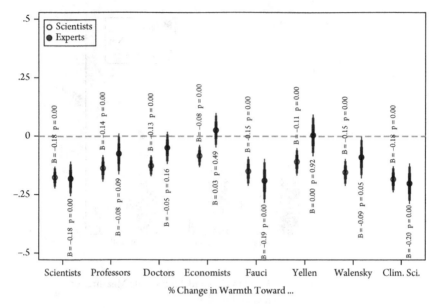

Figure 3.3 Predictive Validation of the GSS and ANES Style Measures of Anti-Intellectualism (2021 Supplemental Lucid Study)

be negatively and significantly associated with a broad range of expert *targets* (i.e., people and institutions) on the feeling thermometer question (displayed on the figure's x-axis). Moreover, if the two are similarly well suited to proxy anti-intellectual attitude endorsement, I should observe few differences in the direction, size, or statistical significance of these effects across the two items.

The results again offer strong support for the idea that the GSS-style item is a suitable indicator of anti-intellectual attitude endorsement. They also provide strong evidence in favor of the interchangeability of the two items. Figure 3.3 suggests that the GSS item is both negatively and significantly associated with negative feelings toward all targets. This includes feelings toward a wide range of expert targets, including the scientific community (e.g., Drs. Anthony Fauci [President Biden's chief medical advisor] and Rochelle Walensky [CDC director]; climate scientists), economists (e.g., Treasury Secretary Janet Yellen), and more-general references to academic and other forms of experts (e.g., professors).

The ANES item is also associated with significantly more-negative affect toward the aforementioned targets in five out of eight tests. Two tests—i.e., those pertaining to economic experts—were positively signed, although neither effect is statistically distinguishable from zero. A third test (*doctors*) was correctly signed but narrowly missed attaining conventional levels of two-tailed significance. In the remaining five tests, the ANES item performed similarly to the GSS item, as demonstrated by the figure's negatively signed coefficient estimates and overlapping 95 percent confidence intervals.

Again I provide a replication of Figure 3.3 in the supplemental materials, where I include responses from those who may have engaged in satisficing behavior. There I report a highly similar pattern of effects to those presented in the main text, albeit with (unsurprisingly) lower levels of statistical precision. All instances in which the *scientists* items indicated statistically significant levels of negative affect toward each person/group listed in Figure 3.3 retain their directionality and significance when satisficers are included in the model. This is true for the *experts* item too, except in the case of evaluations of CDC Director Rochelle Walensky, where—although correctly signed ($\beta = 0.04$)—the effects fall short of attaining conventional levels of two-tailed significance ($p = 0.31$).

Overall, the predictive validation analyses in Figure 3.3 suggest that both the ANES (*experts*) and GSS (*scientists*) style of questions are suitable measures of anti-intellectualism. Moreover, and inconsistent with concerns that the more-narrow focus of the GSS item might make it unsuitable to detect negative attitudes toward expertise outside of domains pertaining to science and scientific research, I find that the *trust in the scientific community* question is negatively and significantly associated with a broad range of attitudes toward scientific experts. If anything, the GSS item may slightly *out*-perform the ANES item, although I again stress that the pattern of effects is highly similar across measures.

Still, despite the interchangeability of the two measures, I recognize that it would nevertheless be ideal to employ the same approach to measuring anti-intellectualism in each of the surveys studied in this project. Unfortunately, this is not possible. Absent the ability to pursue full measurement standardization, however, the next best thing I can do is to at least document not only that available measures are conceptually appropriate indicators of the underlying construct I hope to study (anti-intellectualism) but also that they closely track with one another. I believe that the results presented thus far strongly make that case.

Nevertheless, I want to briefly note that when making use of the SciPol data throughout this book (which offers a choice between the GSS and ANES items), I generally prefer to use the Oliver and Rahn *experts* question. This question has the advantage of featuring more response-option scale points than the GSS question (seven in SciPol, as opposed to three in the standard-issue GSS item). This allows me to calculate effects of anti-intellectualism on policy-relevant science with higher levels of granularity than the GSS item otherwise would. Moreover, the Oliver and Rahn style of question has the benefit of being more conceptually inclusive of many forms of expertise (i.e., the *eye of the beholder* approach referenced earlier in this book). Thus, while both measures are conceptually and empirically suitable stand-ins for one another, this move allows me to offer a parsimonious presentation of results with added levels of operational granularity.

Conclusion

In this book, I study the prevalence, origins, and policy consequences of anti-intellectual attitude endorsement using a variety of different indicators of anti-intellectualism measured across several different data sources and using many different modeling techniques. In this chapter, I described what each of those methods will look like and contrasted their relative strengths and weaknesses. Perhaps most importantly, I also offered a demonstration that the two micro-level survey measures of anti-intellectualism that I rely on throughout this book are (1) both conceptually and empirically related to one another and (2) appear to be equally valid indicators of anti-intellectual attitude endorsement.

None of these approaches, of course, is perfect on its own. Instead, I hope that by documenting similar patterns of results *across* approaches I can draw empirically sound and methodologically pluralistic conclusions about the nature and impact of anti-intellectualism in the United States. In the following chapters, I offer data-driven assessments of each of these objectives.

Perhaps the most fundamental question we can ask about the nature of anti-intellectual attitude endorsement in the United States pertains to its prevalence. Just how many Americans hold negative views toward scientists and other experts? I take up this task in Chapter 4.

Anti-Scientific Americans: The Prevalence, Origins, and Political Consequences of Anti-Intellectualism in the US.
Matthew Motta, Oxford University Press. © Oxford University Press 2024. DOI: 10.1093/9780197788844.003.0003

4

The Prevalence of Anti-Intellectual Attitudes

According to popular press coverage of the Trump presidency and Americans' response to the COVID-19 pandemic, anti-intellectualism is seemingly everywhere. Some have argued, for example, that anti-intellectual attitudes pervade the American public not because expert negativity is unique to the age of Donald Trump and face-mask burnings but that it has been with us since the nation's founding and "never went away" (Masciotra, 2020). Others have likened the Republican Party, and those who identify with it, as a "modern version of the nineteenth-century Know-Nothing Party" (Bartlett, 2020). Some have even suggested that the appeal of anti-expert politicians like Donald Trump is the result of "at least a plurality of Americans" embracing his "anti-intellectual bias" (Grier, 2016).

Claims like these raise an important question: *how many Americans can be thought about as holding anti-intellectual attitudes?* Throughout this chapter, I aim to provide a new, historically expansive, and data-driven answer to that question.

Of course, I am not the first to ask this important question. In his seminal 1963 book on anti-intellectualism, Richard Hofstadter provided rich anecdotal evidence of expert animosity among both elite political actors and the American public more generally. What Hofstadter did not do, however, was offer a standardized assessment of just *how many* Americans express some degree of negativity toward experts.

Instead, Hofstadter forcefully implies that anti-intellectualism pervades American public life. For example, he concludes his 1963 book by writing:

> The evidence is abundant, and it is nearly unanimous in its testimony to a popular culture that has been proudly convinced of its ability to get along indeed, to get along better without the benefits of formal knowledge, even without applied science. The possession and use of such knowledge was always considered to be of doubtful value; and in any

case it was regarded as the prerogative of specialized segments of the population that were resented for their privileges and refinements."

—Hofstadter, 1963, 272

Hofstadter's remarks clearly indicate that he felt as if anti-intellectualism pervades American public life—i.e., that "popular culture" is "proudly convinced" of its ability to survive without experts. And he also seems to think that this has been the case for quite some time. As Hofstadter puts it, that specialized knowledge was "always considered" to lack merit. Whether or not available public-opinion data support these strong claims, however, is an open question. Quantitatively assessing the prevalence of anti-intellectualism in opinion surveys of the American public is an important exercise because it can help us better contextualize the consequences of anti-intellectual attitude endorsement. As I document throughout this book, anti-intellectualism has powerful political and policy consequences. People who hold anti-intellectual views are more likely to take issue with the role that experts play in the policymaking process, embrace misinformation about matters of expert and scientific consensus, and oppose evidenced-informed policies. Moreover, politicians tend to respond to fluctuations in anti-intellectualism by consulting experts less frequently in congressional hearings and scaling back legislative activity on technical issues that might demand expert input.

Consequently, documenting the degree to which anti-intellectualism pervades the American public provides a critical context for understanding its pernicious effects. If few Americans hold negative views toward experts, even a strong association between anti-intellectualism and policy-relevant outcomes may not be all that substantively important. In this case, anti-intellectualism would motivate the rejection of expert-backed policies (e.g., climate-change mitigation) or policy-relevant behavior (e.g., vaccine rejection), but the extent to which it does so would be limited to a relatively small number of people. This would (perhaps) cast doubt on the degree to which anti-intellectualism might pose a challenge to evidence-based policymaking.

However, if many Americans report holding negative feelings toward experts, the policy consequences of anti-intellectual attitude endorsement may be more troubling. In this case, a substantial segment of the American public would not only hold negative views toward experts but also *take action* on those feelings.

Of course, what exactly constitutes a *substantial* footing for anti-intellectualism in the American public is, to some extent, subjective. It is also a matter of considerable debate in previous work on the prevalence of negative views toward scientists in the United States.

For the remainder of this chapter, I aim to resolve this uncertainty by outlining the contours of scholarly debate about the prevalence of negative feelings toward experts. Herein, I provide reason to suspect that anti-intellectualism is indeed a pervasive presence in American public life. I then offer a pluralistic assessment of the prevalence of anti-intellectualism in the US public.

Aggregating opinion estimates across hundreds of opinion polls, I find that just over one-third of Americans can be thought about as holding anti-intellectual attitudes at any particular time. These views fluctuate over time and reach distinguishable peaks immediately preceding the presidential candidacies of major anti-intellectual figures (George Wallace in 1968, Donald Trump in 2016). I conclude by briefly discussing why the prevalence of anti-intellectual attitudes has problematic social and political implications. This helps me better contextualize the findings I present throughout the remainder of this book.

Macro Anti-Intellectualism Database (1944–2021)

I assess the prevalence of negative attitudes toward experts via a unique dataset that measures public anti-intellectual attitude endorsement in the aggregate (i.e., across the entire US population) and over time. Throughout the book, I refer to these data as the macro anti-intellectualism database (MAID).

MAID is a database that measures fluctuations, at the quarterly level, in anti-intellectual attitude endorsement as a matter of aggregated opinion. I created MAID using polling toplines from Roper's iPoll service that featured Americans' responses to nearly five hundred opinion polls conducted since 1944. MAID also includes measures of quarterly legislative activity (congressional hearings) on science-relevant topics related to the economy, climate, and health (i.e., the focuses of Chapter 8) from the Policy Agendas Project (John, 2006), including both the project's general policy topic and subtopic coding schemes. MAID also includes event history counts of congressional testimonies from economists (Maher et al., 2020), which serve a similar role in my analyses.

Additionally, the database includes Stimson's (Stimson, 2018) widely used indicators of Americans' quarterly policy mood (i.e., Americans' policy orientations for larger or smaller government intervention, across a variety of different issues) and an indicator macro-partisanship (i.e., the percentage of Americans identifying with the Democratic versus Republican parties over time). Finally, MAID includes average levels of consumer sentiment—i.e., an average of how positively (versus negatively) Americans rate current economic conditions— conducted weekly by Gallup. These too are aggregated at the quarterly level.

Collectively, the indicators available in MAID data are advantageous for several reasons. First, MAID is useful because it allows me to take a methodologically pluralistic approach to assessing the prevalence of anti-intellectual attitude endorsement in the United States across hundreds of different potential survey-based indicators. Whereas the micro-level analyses featured throughout this book make use of just two indicators, the macro-level analyses average opinion estimates across many different ways that pollsters have asked the public, over the years, to provide their opinions about experts.

Although I could, theoretically, aggregate the GSS, ANES, CSPP, and SciPol studies to study these trends in a similar way, that approach would necessarily be limited by the fact that neither of the two items can perfectly or completely capture what it means to dislike and distrust scientists and other experts. That approach would also be limited by the comparatively fewer opportunities to observe change in anti-intellectual attitude endorsement across studies. MAID therefore affords a more-pluralistic and temporally expansive approach because it allows many different types of questions—asked in many different formats—to contribute to an estimate of expert sentiment.

Second, and perhaps even more importantly, MAID also allows me to assess the effect of anti-intellectual attitudes on *actual legislative behavior* in response to changes in anti-intellectualism and to control for the potential influences of other factors that could influence legislative activity (e.g., partisanship, policy mood, and consumer sentiment). In contrast to the micro-level data, which can provide insight into the correlates of individual-level policy stances, MAID allows me to observe whether Congress becomes more or less deferential to scientists, academics, economists, and other experts in quarters where anti-intellectual attitude endorsement is comparatively greater. Because the data are time varying, MAID further allows me to test for (and rule out) the possibility that changes in legislative activity cause people to develop more anti-intellectual attitudes over time.

Finally, these data are advantageous because they offer an opportunity to observe fluctuations in anti-intellectualism prior to the administration of the GSS Time Series Study. This allows me to broaden the book's temporal focus. In so doing, I am able to, for example, provide preliminary insights into how changes in public sentiment toward experts coincide with the candidacy of noted anti-intellectual presidential candidates like George Wallace and Donald Trump. Assessments like these are nearly impossible in the micro-level data, even in the long-running GSS surveys, which began collecting data in 1972 and (necessarily) asked questions about Wallace's candidacy only in retrospect.

I constructed the quarterly indicator of anti-intellectual attitudes that I used to build MAID by pulling US national polling toplines from the Roper Center's iPoll database. I began by first identifying a universe of potential polling questions to include. To do this, I performed a Boolean search for the following terms: scientist* OR expert* OR intellectual* OR academic*. Note that the asterisk following each term indicates a wild character (to allow the search function to include both singular and plural terms in the results list). This procedure yielded N = 2,647 unique polling questions.

Pursuant with the conceptualization of anti-intellectualism that I introduced in Chapter 1, I then selected questions for inclusion into a quarterly, weighted, running average across polls if they met the following criteria:

- Target: The subject being evaluated in each question is a *person* (e.g., academics, climate scientists).
- Origin: The study must feature a US-based national sample.
- Scope: The question must ask respondents to render an affective appraisal about the target being evaluated (e.g., whether scientists care more about advancing their own interests over those of the American public).

This winnowing process produced 495 unique polling questions suitable for inclusion in the quarterly average. I determined which response options corresponded to anti-intellectual attitude endorsement by determining whether each one indicated (1) directionally negative views toward experts (e.g., strong distrust) or (2) uncertainty regarding whether respondents feel positively toward them (e.g., *don't know* or middle responses to attitude questions). The quarterly average denotes the percentage of Americans falling into either of those two categories.

For illustrative purposes, I provide here examples of the types of questions featured in the index. To do this, I pulled a random selection of three questions from the raw datafile used to construct MAID. Sample questions, with response options used to calculate the average indicated by asterisks, include the following:

Switching gears now, below is a short list of institutions. How often do you trust each of them to do the right thing? Scientists

<1> All the time
<2> Most of the time
<3> Some of the time *
<4> Never *

Source: Harvard Institute of Politics (GfK). 3/18/2015

The following statements describe what most experts today are saying about some health and nutrition issues. Please tell me if you think the experts will or will not have completely different ideas about each within the next five years.

The statement is ... that moderate alcohol use can promote good health.

Do you think the experts will or will not have a completely different idea about this?

<1> Will have a different idea*
<2> Will not have a different idea
<3> Don't Know *

Source: *Heart & Soul Magazine* (Princeton Research). 1/15–28/1996

Now I'd like to read you some statements about scientists. Please tell me if you agree or disagree with each one. If you feel especially strongly about a statement, please say that you strongly agree or strongly disagree. Okay?

Most scientists want to work on things that will make life better for the average person. Do you strongly agree, agree, disagree, or strongly disagree?

<1> Strongly agree
<2> Agree
<3> Disagree *
<4> Strongly disagree *
<5> DK/NA *

Source: National Science Foundation. 10/1/1979

The questions presented above demonstrate the substantive breadth of items included in the final quarterly average. Whereas the first item is a fairly straightforward question pertaining to respondents' general trust in scientists (similar to the items featured in the GSS studies), the third item asks respondents to render a *specific* affective appraisal about scientists' motivations for conducting scientific research.

The second question adds a somewhat different dimension to the measure by asking respondents to weigh in on the common stereotype (Jamieson et al., 2019) that experts have a difficult time achieving consensus about policy-relevant scientific recommendations (a view which previous research suggests is correlated with Americans' more general levels of trust in scientists and other experts; e.g., Suldovsky & Akin, 2023; Chinn et al., 2018; van Stekelenburg et al., 2021). Also note the use of the phrase *completely* as a modifier for *different* in the second question, which may imply a negative affective and subjective characterization of scientific experts.

Of course, the procedure by which I assembled the aggregate quarterly indicator of anti-intellectual attitude endorsement is not perfect. It cannot account for the possibility that I may have failed to include relevant items in the calculation of the quarterly anti-intellectualism average. It also cannot account for the possibility that I have included items that others might not interpret as being indicators of anti-intellectualism. Moreover, this approach necessarily deals with data that do not use standardized response options or sampling frames/methods and are not (necessarily) administered at the same time. Differences between questions may therefore reflect systematic differences in question construction as opposed to change in anti-intellectual attitudes.

These are important limitations. Nevertheless, my hope is that by applying a standardized coding scheme and aggregating across *many* surveys and polling questions, potentially unobserved differences between questions with respect to their ability to measure anti-intellectualism produce random (and not systematic) error in its quarterly assessment. In other words, these random errors should *cancel out* in the aggregate.

Additionally, at least when assessing the policy consequences of anti-intellectual attitude endorsement, it is important to remember that I will assess related quantities at the micro level as well. Finding that anti-intellectualism influences both public preferences for experts to play a less-pronounced role in the policymaking process—and opposition to expert-backed policies and other recommendations—would help lend additional conceptual plausibility to any effects I might observe of changes in public anti-intellectual sentiment on congressional deference to experts (i.e., by suggesting a public *demand* for their elected officials to curtail expert influence).

For the sake of replication and transparency, I have made all of the raw polling topline data—including decisions about inclusion and how each response option was coded—publicly available at the following web page: https://osf. io/ajz96/.

The Problem with Prevalence

Before turning to the objectives outlined at the outset of this chapter, I want to briefly expand on an issue that I hope is apparent in my discussion of how I plan to aggregate polling data to assess anti-intellectual attitude endorsement. *Measuring the prevalence of anti-intellectual attitudes in the United States is not easy.*

This is true not only due to the limited supply of data and available polling questions that ask people to render affective evaluations of scientific experts, or the conceptual thorniness of identifying *who counts* as an expert, but also due to the nature of prevalence assessments themselves.

Asking questions about *how many* Americans harbor negative views toward experts necessarily assumes the existence of a dichotomy. Some people should be classified as anti-intellectuals while others should not be. This assumption is necessary to calculate the percentage of US adults who hold anti-intellectual views and—in so doing—to provide an answer to the *how many* question.

The problem, though, is that—at least in theory (and as I discussed briefly in Chapter 3)—anti-intellectualism is not dichotomous. People can express anti-intellectual attitude endorsement to varying degrees. Some people may hold uniformly negative attitudes, while others hold a more-mixed balance of positive and negative feelings. These issues are not necessarily problematic when studying social and psychological influences that might lead to incremental change in the *degree* to which people express anti-intellectual attitudes. Nor are they a problem when studying how higher (versus lower) levels of anti-intellectualism might influence relevant policy outcomes.

However, these issues pose an important measurement problem for assessing the prevalence of anti-intellectual opinions. How can we best classify people who hold either a mix of positive and negative views, or neither positive nor negative attitudes, toward experts?

The aggregated estimates of anti-intellectual attitude endorsement available in MAID have the important benefit of assessing anti-intellectual attitude endorsement across a variety of different polling questions. As I reviewed in Chapter 3, this makes it possible to include many indicators of what it means to hold negative views toward experts when calculating the proportion of Americans who hold anti-intellectual views.

There is, however, a catch. Differences in the construction of response options across questions imply that some questions may not feature *middle options*. These include response options capturing whether people self-report holding mixed views about the degree to which they trust experts or if they fall somewhere in the middle of scales that ask respondents to rate their favorability toward that group. The questions also vary in the extent to which they offer respondents the opportunity to indicate that they *don't know* (DK) the answer to a question. These responses could be indicative of attitudinal ambivalence (i.e., feeling *both ways* about an issue), a lack of familiarity with the subject being presented in the question, or an attempt to simply cope with the survey's cognitive demands by advancing through the survey without offering a substantive response.

This puts me in a tricky position with respect to measuring the prevalence of anti-intellectual attitude endorsement. How can I best classify people who hold mixed feelings about experts? And what about those who report to hold no feelings at all toward scientists, academics, and other experts?

Unfortunately, I must make *some* decision—however imperfect—about how to code middle and DK responses when assessing aggregated anti-intellectual attitude endorsement in MAID data. Consequently, throughout the remainder of this chapter, I opt to calculate average levels of anti-intellectual attitude endorsement that treat both middle and DK responses as *indicative* of holding anti-intellectual attitudes.

This coding decision, although imperfect, is nevertheless necessary. I also believe that it is a justifiable one. My reasoning for doing so is twofold.

First, I consider middle responses to be indicative of anti-intellectual attitude endorsement because they imply that people hold at least some negative feelings toward experts. People who select middle responses, of course, hold a mix of positive views as well. But it is the presence of negative affect—albeit to a lesser degree than those who distrust and dislike experts outright—that is indicative of the concept I am trying to measure in this book. Consequently, I opt to consider these individuals as endorsing anti-intellectual attitudes.

Second, I consider the particularly thorny issue of DK responding. I consider DK responses to be indicative of anti-intellectual attitude endorsement for a similar reason as that which I outlined earlier. Not rendering an opinion about experts again implies a *lack* of positive feelings. Not trusting or liking experts is, of course, not the same thing as actively distrusting or disliking those individuals. We can, after all, say that DK responses imply a lack of negative judgments as well. Still, these respondents were put in a position, in each survey, to report the extent to which they support scientists and experts. Ultimately, they opted not to do so. Correspondingly, I consider DK answers to be indicative of anti-intellectual attitude endorsement.

Some might argue that a simpler solution would be to simply exclude DK responses from the calculation of the quarterly anti-intellectualism average. This is an attractive solution at some level, not only because of the thorny issues outlined earlier but also because DK responding (1) does not necessarily indicate a lack of familiarity with the concept (Lupia, 2016; i.e., because people who fail to render a substantive response may nevertheless have *some* unmeasured feelings about scientists and other experts), (2) may reflect individual differences in the tendency to offer opinions of *any* variety in public-opinion research, which often map onto existing gender (Atkeson & Rapoport, 2003; Dolan & Hansen, 2020) and socioeconomic (Berinsky, 2002, 2013) inequalities in American public life, and (3) may be more indicative of attitudinal certainty than the lack of an opinion about an issue (Graham, 2021).

As noted earlier, however, the issue with ignoring DK responses is that the questions summarized in the MAID data necessarily vary (sometimes quite significantly) in construction. Some questions expressly offer respondents the opportunity to indicate a DK response. Others accept that answer only if offered or solicited by the respondent. And many do not offer that option at all. Removing DK responses from the calculation of a national average implies blending tallies that add up to different quantities (i.e., not 100 percent), which would make the resulting national average almost impossible to interpret.

Luckily, though, for my purposes in this book, the overwhelming majority of Americans tend to register opinions about experts in public-opinion research.

As discussed in Chapter 2, levels of opinionation about scientists, academics, and other experts (i.e., the extent to which Americans report feeling either positively or negatively toward that group) tend to be quite high. For example, in the nationally representative GSS data that I use when testing this book's micro-level predictions, less than 5 percent of respondents since 1974 have failed to provide a substantive answer to the *trust in scientists* question. In the (also nationally representative) 2020 ANES, just under 1 percent did the same on the *trust ordinary people over experts* question.

More generally, and as I noted in Chapter 3, it is important to remember that the problem of DK and middle responding is unique, at least in this book, to assessing the *prevalence* of anti-intellectual attitude endorsement. As discussed in Chapter 3, I embrace a series of modeling strategies that allow me to treat anti-intellectualism as a continuum when assessing its origins and policy consequences. These modeling strategies allow me to exclude DK responses from the estimation of both the causes and effects of anti-intellectual attitude endorsement and to account for gradation therein. Moreover, I will test later in this book (Chapter 8) whether the quarterly estimates of anti-intellectualism I derive from the MAID data are associated with how Congress responds to change in anti-intellectual attitude endorsement over time. Evidence that Congress curtails expert influence in the policymaking process during periods of increased anti-intellectual attitude endorsement further helps to substantiate the quarterly average is indeed reflective of Americans displeasure with experts.

Finally, in addition to my conceptual rationale for opting to not exclude DK responses, I provide a preliminary micro-level test of the possibility that those who provide DK responses to the anti-intellectualism items may nevertheless hold mixed or negative views toward experts. Recognizing that (1) people who supply DK responses may indeed have substantive opinions about the matter at hand (Lupia, 2016) but lack the confidence necessary to map those opinions onto available response options (Graham, 2021) and/or (2) that, as noted earlier, DK responses are (at the very least) *not* indicative of holding positive feelings toward scientists and experts, I consider the possibility that people who are unsure as to how to respond to either of the anti-intellectualism items may nevertheless hold some degree of negative feelings toward experts.

To do this, I turned to the 2020 ANES dataset described in Chapter 3. The ANES is useful for studying this question not only because of its large sample size (N = 8,280). This facilitates the study of DK responding because, as noted earlier, relatively few people provide DK responses to these questions. It also has the benefit of being nationally representative, and it (critically) included *both* a version of the *experts* question used to measure anti-intellectualism throughout this book (see Chapter 3) *and* an alternative measure of Americans' affective attitudes toward (in this case) the scientific community. In addition to the *experts* question, respondents were asked to evaluate *scientists* using a 101 point feeling thermometer scale measuring affective warmth (100) and coldness (0) toward the scientific community. These are constructed similarly to those measures I employed throughout Chapter 3 when validating my approach to measuring anti-intellectualism.

In the ANES, just 46 respondents (0.62 percent of valid Wave 2 responses) either refused or offered a DK response to the item I use to assess anti-intellectual attitude endorsement. Fortunately, however, all 46 answered the feeling thermometer question. This allows me to assess the potential informational content of DK responses (by assessing the extent to which DK respondents' affective feelings toward scientists might match those of respondents who both answer the question and express anti-intellectual sentiments).

If DK respondents' affective attitudes toward scientists are similar to those of people who expressly endorse anti-intellectual attitudes, I will have not just conceptual but *empirical* evidence in favor of treating DK responses as indicative of failing to hold positive views toward scientists and experts in the MAID data. This is precisely what I find.

Consistent with my theoretical expectations, I find that average scientist feeling thermometer ratings for respondents who place the highest level of trust in ordinary people over experts was 69 degrees [95 percent CI: 66, 71]. Similarly, I find that average scores on the feeling thermometer were identical for DK respondents (69 degrees [62, 76]), albeit with less statistical precision due to their relatively small number. These quantities, as the overlapping confidence intervals suggest, are not statistically differentiable from one another.

These analyses, of course, are not perfect. For one, while the ANES accepted DK and refusal responses, it did not offer a *hard* (explicit) DK option (unlike some questions in the MAID database). Correspondingly, the proportion of people willing to provide a substantive answer to the item used to assess anti-intellectual attitude endorsement in the ANES might be higher than we would otherwise expect with the offering of a hard DK option (although see Graham, 2021 for an example of efforts to gauge the substantive content of DK responses using similar questions on the ANES). Moreover, the survey affords just one possibility to provide an alternate measure of respondents' affective impressions of experts, which is limited in application to the scientific community.

Still, this analysis provides additional support for my decision to treat DK responses as indicative of failing to hold positive attitudes toward scientists and experts (and, therefore, coding this group as expressing anti-intellectual attitudes). While some people choose to forego answering questions designed to assess anti-intellectual attitude endorsement, these people may have quite a bit in common with those who hold negative feelings toward experts.

Ultimately, while the *problem with prevalence* presents important conceptual and empirical challenges to estimating anti-intellectual attitude endorsement, this issue is primarily isolated to Chapter 4. Moreover, while these challenges force me to make difficult decisions when estimating the prevalence of anti-intellectual attitude endorsement, it is important to remember the *benefits* of the MAID database, which allow me to offer a novel, pluralistic, and temporally expansive glimpse into the prevalence of anti-intellectual attitude endorsement over the course of the past century. With these benefits and limitations in mind, I next discuss whether Hofstadter's characterization of anti-intellectualism as a pervasive problem is supported by the available data.

A Pervasive Problem or an Overhyped Myth?

Political elites' willingness to both denigrate experts and challenge their policy influence—particularly on the ideological right—has received a fair amount of attention in the popular press in recent years. Consequently, some journalists have referred to the contemporary Republican Party as wielding a brand of "murderous anti-intellectualism" (Bartlett, 2020), a reference to the possibility that political ideology has motivated the rejection of expert-backed public health recommendations designed to limit viral spread during the COVID-19 pandemic (see Grossman et al., 2020; Gadarian, Goodman, & Pepinsky, 2021 for documentation of a link between political ideology and governments' pandemic responses, as well as Americans' attitudes toward those responses). Other commentators have referred to the GOP as a modern-day incarnation of the Know Nothing Party (Blake, 2021). More-systematic efforts to study how GOP elites talk about and interact with scientific experts have documented broad levels of expert mistrust and denigration on the ideological right (Mooney, 2006).

Examples used to support this point of view abound. During a congressional hearing in the spring of 2021, for example, Representative Jim Jordan (R-OH) made headlines after he accused chief Biden administration medical advisor Dr. Anthony Fauci of issuing public health guidelines without respect for Americans' individual liberties to ignore public health ordinances. At one point, Jordan sarcastically remarked, "Well, that's obvious," in response to Fauci suggesting that he viewed infectious disease risks as a matter of public health and not one of individual freedoms. Fauci replied to these accusations by saying, "You're making this a personal thing, and it isn't" (Weixel, 2021).

Recognizing the personal nature of these accusations, we might therefore classify Jordan's claims as evidence of anti-intellectual rhetoric, per the definition of *anti-intellectualism* I outlined in Chapter 1. Indeed, some political observers were quick to suggest that "reason and logic were lost on Jordan" (Levin, 2021), while others labeled the representative as "anti-science" (Cole, 2021).

These anecdotes tell us something important about how political elites feel toward experts. However, referring to a major US political party as a modern-day incarnation of the Know Nothing Party, and drawing attention to the anti-intellectual rhetoric of some of its most high-profile members, may lead some to assume that anti-intellectualism is prevalent not just among GOP elites but also among the US public as well.

This, of course, is not necessarily the case. The apparent prevalence of anti-intellectual attitude endorsement among political elites does not necessarily imply that the public feels the same way. In fact, the number of Americans who hold anti-intellectual has for several years been a matter of scholarly and popular debate.

Some argue that the prevalence of negative feelings toward scientists, medical doctors, and other experts may be overstated. Proponents of this view (see Glazer, 2021 for a review) typically point to polling data suggesting that a near-majority (typically, between 40 and 50 percent) of Americans place a great deal of trust in the medical and scientific communities to act in the best interests of the American public. Proponents of this view also note that a majority of Americans place at least *some* level of trust in scientists and other experts and that these trends have held fairly steady since the early 1970s (Besley, 2018; Funk, Kennedy, & Johnson, 2020; Carter, 2020).

Likewise, most Americans report that they trust subject-area experts—like environmental scientists on issues related to the climate and medical doctors and nutrition scientists on issues related to public health—to provide them with accurate information about matters related to their field of expertise (Funk et al., 2019; Mitchell et al., 2020). Perhaps somewhat surprisingly, even as Centers for Disease Control (CDC) public health recommendations became highly politically polarizing throughout the duration of the COVID-19 pandemic, a majority of Americans (including a slight majority of Republicans) nevertheless reported holding favorable attitudes toward medical scientists, the CDC, and Dr. Anthony Fauci (Sanger-Katz, 2020).

Still, it can simultaneously be true that the prevalence of anti-intellectualism in the American public may be problematically high *despite* the observation of comparatively high levels of trust in scientific experts. This could be the case for at least three reasons.

First, although it is certainly true that a majority of Americans place at least some level of trust in experts to provide them with accurate information—especially on subjects related to their field of expertise—many nevertheless harbor negative sentiments toward experts in other highly personal respects. For example, a recent Pew Center study (Funk & Hefferson, 2019) found that over two-fifths (43 percent) of Americans describe research scientists as *socially awkward* and as feeling *superior to others*. An additional 32 percent reported that scientists *don't pay attention to moral values of society*, a finding backed by social-science research on how the moralization of science (in general) spills over to influence feelings toward scientists as people (Rutjens & Heine, 2016).

These findings present an important context to bear in mind when assessing whether negative views toward experts might be overstated. The same Pew poll as the one discussed earlier found that just 35 percent of Americans placed a *great deal* of confidence in the scientific community, with the remainder holding more-mixed evaluations. Fifty-one percent indicated a *fair amount* of confidence, with the remainder expressing *not too much* (11 percent) or *no confidence at all* (2 percent). This means that the number of Americans harboring negative stereotypes toward scientific researchers was *roughly equal to or greater than* the percentage placing high levels of trust in the scientific community. Findings like this raise the possibility that while near-majorities of Americans place high levels of trust in scientists, similar numbers also harbor negative feelings toward the scientific community.

Still, relying on a single polling question, or set of related polling questions about the same subject, when making claims about the prevalence of anti-expert attitudes might lead us to draw conclusions that mask its manifestation in other important areas. This could be problematic not only for accurately estimating the prevalence of anti-intellectualism in the American public but also because negative feelings could—as I document later—influence Americans' support for the role that experts play in the policymaking process. Consequently, throughout this book I attempt to offer a pluralistic assessment of both the prevalence and policy relevance of anti-intellectual attitudes using as many survey-based indicators as I have available.

Second, disagreements about the prevalence of anti-intellectual attitude endorsement depend at least in part on how it is that we define *prevalence* itself. Even if a majority of Americans hold generally positive views toward scientists, doctors, and other experts, the size of the minority holding more-negative views is—as alluded to previously—also important to consider. Opinion polls, like the Pew Research Center study cited earlier (Funk & Hefferson, 2019), suggest that 81 percent of Americans place at least some level of trust in the scientific community. This means that in addition to the 51 percent who place only a *fair amount* (as opposed to a *great deal*) of trust in this group, nearly one in five Americans (19 percent) actively express *distrust* in the scientific community. If the roughly one-fifth of Americans who distrust the scientific community also choose to donate to political candidates who support policies that undermine experts' policy recommendations, or refuse vaccines for their children, a view held by a minority of the American public could nevertheless have major social and political consequences.

The Prevalence of Anti-Intellectual Attitudes   105

What this debate implies is that, ultimately, what constitutes a *substantial minority* is a matter of subjective opinion. My goal is not to select a critical threshold at which we might consider anti-intellectualism to be pervasive. Instead, my hope is to draw attention to the idea that anti-intellectualism is not necessarily rare or unimportant simply because it is a minority opinion. As I document later in this book, even opinions held by a minority of the public can nevertheless have a tremendous impact on politics and policymaking in the United States.

Third, and finally, it is important to point out that *aggregate* assessments of negative attitudes toward experts might mask comparatively larger subgroup differences. Take, for example, a well-known (Glazer, 2021) finding from the National Science Foundation's regularly administered Science & Engineering Survey suggesting that most Americans report placing at least some level of trust in the scientific community and that these views have held relatively constant since the mid-1970s (Besley, 2018).

At face value, one might reasonably conclude public opinion about scientific experts is both generally positive and relatively slow to change. However, this assessment would miss an important level of sub-national nuance. Trust in the scientific community has declined steadily on the ideological right since the mid-1990s, while ticking up slightly on the ideological left (Gauchat, 2012; Motta, 2018a; Glazer, 2021). In the aggregate, these effects mostly *cancel out*, making it appear as if there has been only a slight downtick in trust toward the scientific community in recent years. The aggregated trends thereby mask an important sub-population trend lurking beneath the surface.

Detecting ideological subgroup differences is important because it may help resolve the puzzle I raised at the beginning of this section. How can it be the case that anti-intellectualism appears to be common among GOP elites but relatively rare in the public more generally? Is anti-intellectualism only a phenomenon that we observe among political elites?

Refined subgroup analyses suggest that anti-intellectualism has found a footing among conservatives in the *public* as well. This raises the possibility that Americans are taking cues from elite actors. For example, Merkley & Stecula, 2020 find that Republicans in the public became increasingly distrusting of climate science in response to pro-climate messaging from Democratic elites—who are especially likely to appeal to scientific experts (Merkley & Stecula, 2018)—and, to a lesser degree, anti-climate messaging from GOP elites (see Zaller, 1992 for a broader demonstration of this point). This type of work also raises the possibility that GOP politicians are adjusting their rhetoric in response to shifts in public opinion among their constituents. For example, Oliver & Rahn (2016) find that elites are more likely to embrace populist and anti-intellectual attitudes when Americans feel poorly represented by the government in Washington, DC.

How, then, can researchers best assess the prevalence of anti-intellectual attitudes in American public life? What my review of recent work on this subject implies is that we need to embrace a pluralistic approach to measuring and tracking anti-intellectual opinion over time (i.e., to assess whether *many* different indicators of anti-intellectualism, measured across many different surveys, point to similar conclusions about its prevalence).

This is precisely what I hope to do for the remainder of this chapter. If measured based on responses to a variety of different questions designed to measure negative feelings toward experts suggest that a certain percentage of the American public holds anti-intellectual attitudes, I believe that I will be on firm analytical ground to draw conclusions about both its prevalence and relevance. I take up this possibility in the pages that follow.

A Pluralistic Prevalence Assessment

I begin this pluralistic assessment of the degree to which Americans hold anti-intellectual attitudes by assessing public responses across 495 surveys conducted between 1944 and 2021. I described the process by which I assembled these data (MAID) at length in Chapter 3 and encourage those interested in learning more about the database to consult my discussion there for additional information.

As a brief review, MAID is a database that calculates quarterly averages of the number of Americans who endorse anti-intellectual views, based on responses to hundreds of different survey questions aggregated across nearly five hundred opinion polls. All questions used to calculate the quarterly averages ask respondents to provide (1) an affective evaluation (e.g., trust/distrust, like/dislike, confidence/lack of confidence) of (2) academics, scientists, and other experts (i.e., as opposed to views about the scientific method or expertise more generally) across (3) both general (e.g., scientists) and more-specialized (e.g., medical doctors, climate scientists) dimensions. A full list of all questions included— and those not included—in the database, their response options, and the percentage of respondents endorsing each available response option is available for download at https://osf.io/ajz96/.

Figure 4.1 presents quarterly averages of the percentage of Americans expressing anti-intellectual attitudes over time. Each gray point on the figure denotes the average percentage of people who express anti-intellectual views in each quarter. For reference, the points are scaled in size (*weighted*) according to the total number of polling questions included in the average in that quarter.

I account for the fact that some quarters produce more polls than others, including quarters that contain no available survey questions (and therefore no

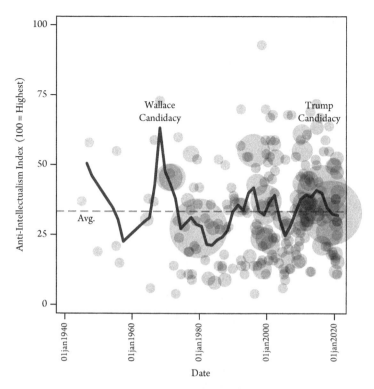

Figure 4.1 The Prevalence of Anti-Intellectualism in MAID (1944–2021)

quarterly estimate), by using locally weighted regression to produce a running-average estimate of anti-intellectual attitude endorsement. I adjust (weight) the running average to account for differences in the total number of polls aggregated in each quarter. I present the running trend line as a dark black line in the figure.

Figure 4.1 offers several important insights about the number of Americans who hold anti-intellectual attitudes. Focusing first on the movement of the black trend line over time, the results suggest that on average (M = 33.46 percent [31.28, 35.63] throughout the series) somewhere between one-quarter and one-third of Americans hold anti-intellectual views at any given point in time.

While anti-intellectualism certainly fluctuates *within* those boundaries over time, deviations outside of the one-quarter to one-third threshold have been uncommon since the early 1980s. This is likely due to the fact that polling questions about the topics used to measure anti-intellectualism have become comparatively more frequent in recent decades. Correspondingly, the number of Americans expressing negative attitudes toward experts is more volatile at the beginning of the series (i.e., the mid-1940s to the early 1980s). As the size and spacing of the grayed circles indicate, this is likely due to the relative sparsity of surveys asking the types of questions necessary to measure anti-intellectual attitude endorsement.

In addition to providing insight into the broad acceptability of expert dislike and distrust in the United States, Figure 4.1 offers insights into how fluctuations in anti-intellectual attitude endorsement might influence the acceptability of anti-intellectual thought in the US government. As noted earlier, I test this possibility more systematically in Chapter 8, where I investigate legislative responsiveness to change in public anti-intellectual attitude endorsement (i.e., Congress' unwillingness to involve experts in the policymaking process). For now, though, I want to point to two important political moments that, at least anecdotally, seem to take place following an uptick in anti-intellectual attitude endorsement.

First, survey data from the 1960s point to an anecdotal uptick in anti-intellectualism immediately following the decision of former Alabama Governor George Wallace to run as the American Independent Party's nominee for president in 1968. Although Wallace's first bid for president (as a Democrat in 1964) occurred following the publication of Hofstadter's 1963 book, it seems (very) likely that Hofstadter would have classified Wallace among the prototypical anti-intellectuals of his day.

Wallace often used anti-intellectual rhetoric on the campaign trail to drum up support for his campaign. During his first run for the Democratic nomination in 1964, for example, Wallace attempted to appeal to Democrats outside of Alabama by highlighting his opposition to the role of the growing influence of government bureaucrats. Wallace accused these individuals of being "pointy-headed" intellectuals who were out of touch, notably claiming that they "had their heads in the clouds" when it came to addressing the concerns of ordinary people (Pearson, 1998; Lim, 2008).

Wallace significantly intensified his use of anti-intellectual rhetoric during his run for president in 1968. At a campaign event in Warren, Michigan, for example, Wallace was met with cheers when he referred to members of the press as "parasites" and "pointy-headed intellectuals." In what some might classify as an eerie forebearer of Donald Trump's campaign rhetoric half a century later, Wallace made attacking the press, and their intellectual *bona fides*, a regular component of his stump speech repertoire. Some reports even suggested that attendees at the Warren event derided journalists covering the rally and threatened them with physical violence by hurling rocks in their direction (Enright, 2016).

Turning back to the results presented in Figure 4.1, the figure documents a clear uptick in public anti-intellectual sentiment in the quarters immediately preceding 1968, the year in which Wallace ran for president a second time. Although data are sparse in MAID's first twenty years of reporting (making it difficult to engage in formal, statistical hypothesis testing), smoothed quarterly anti-intellectualism estimates had been on the rise for several years prior to Wallace's candidacy in 1968. Notably, the proportion of the public endorsing anti-intellectual views ticked up from about 41 percent in the third quarter of 1966 (there were no polls included in the average in 1967) to about 63 percent in the third quarter of 1968.

This anecdotal evidence, of course, does not constitute a causal relationship between increasing public endorsement of anti-intellectual attitudes and the candidacy of anti-intellectual politicians. However, it may imply that increased anti-intellectual attitude endorsement creates a *demand* for elites who share public skepticism about the role that experts play in American political life to seek elected office. Correspondingly, as I have shown in past research, people who endorsed anti-intellectual attitudes in the early 1970s were significantly more likely to report voting for Wallace in the 1968 election (Motta, 2018a).

Similarly, the figure presents an analogous (albeit more modest) pattern in the lead-up to Donald Trump's candidacy. The former president is often likened to a modern-day George Wallace (Elliott, 2016; Enright, 2016; Lowndes, 2018). Scholars and journalists draw this comparison not only due to Trump's penchant for stoking fears about threats of violence from racial minorities and immigrants (Hooghe & Dassonneville, 2018; Newman, Shah, & Collingwood, 2018) but also because of his willingness to denigrate experts on the campaign trail. Donald Trump routinely referred to climate scientists as hoaxsters, sewed doubt about CDC-recommended vaccine scheduling guidelines, and aligned himself with the Brexit movement's skepticism of EU economists and bureaucrats (Motta, 2018a).

Perhaps no quote from the former president better exemplifies the link between Trump's 2016 campaign and Wallace's 1968 campaign than the following defense he offered regarding his willingness to rely on foreign policy advisors to inform his campaign's stance on issues related to Chinese military aggression. As Trump put it:

> Let me tell you, I do have experts, but I know what's happening. And look at the experts we've had, okay? Look at the experts. All of these people have had experts.
>
> You know, I've always wanted to say this – I've never said this before with all the talking we all do—all of these experts, "Oh we need an expert . . . The experts are terrible."
>
> —Donald Trump, *campaign event in LaCrosse, Wisconsin. 4/3/2016*

Trump's comments, while somewhat meandering, nevertheless make clear that he viewed even his own chosen expert advisors as, in his own words, *terrible*. These remarks fit in well with Wallace's remarks half a century earlier. In fact,

California's American Independent Party—a rebranded, local offshoot of Wallace's American Independence Party (which he founded)—endorsed Donald Trump for president in 2016 and listed him as the party's nominee (Mejia Davis, 2016). Perhaps that's why Charlie Snider, a former advisor on Governor Wallace's 1968 campaign referred to Donald Trump's 2016 campaign as a replay of 1968. As Snider put it, Trump was, quite simply, "a modern-day George Wallace" (Elliott, 2016).

Correspondingly, the data in Figure 2.1 again document an uptick in anti-intellectualism prior to Trump's announcement of his intentions to run for president in June 2015. During President Obama's first years in office (2009–2012), average levels of anti-intellectual attitude endorsement were just about 37 percent (M = 36.69 [31.93, 41.44]). By the end of his second term, however, and the announcement of Trump's candidacy, average levels of public anti-intellectual attitude endorsement rose to nearly 50 percent (M = 49.72 [38.99, 61.45].

Given the comparatively greater number of quarterly estimates available at this point in the time series, it is possible—in this case—to offer a preliminary investigation into whether aggregated levels of anti-intellectualism were significantly different from one another between these two periods. Here I document a statistically significant ($t_{(43)}$ = –2.44, p = 0.01; N = 45 quarters) uptick of about 13 percentage points on the eve of Donald Trump's presidential run. While the data necessary to carry out this analysis is less sparse than those presented when documenting a rise in anti-intellectualism on the eve of Wallace's candidacy—thereby enabling me to perform the reasonably well-powered, albeit preliminary, statistical tests cited earlier—it is nevertheless anecdotal. These findings align well with past research suggesting that people who express more anti-intellectual views were indeed more likely to support both George Wallace in 1968 and Donald Trump in 2016 (Motta, 2018a). Taken together, the data presented for both Wallace's and Trump's candidacies provide additional evidence of candidates offering a *supply* of anti-intellectual rhetoric to meet what appears to be rising *demand*.

Conclusion

The findings presented in this chapter suggest that anti-intellectual attitude endorsement in the United States is pervasive. Across hundreds of opinion polls from the mid-1940s to present, I find that approximately one-third of Americans can be classified as holding anti-intellectual views at any given point in time.

The data also offer a preliminary glimpse into the political *importance* of public anti-intellectual attitude endorsement. Anti-intellectualism, at the macro level, is not static. On the eve of the candidacies of two of the most widely recognized anti-intellectual presidential candidates of the past century, I document both a significant uptick—both anecdotally and statistically—in the mainstream acceptability of negative feelings toward scientists and other experts. These results help lay an empirical foundation for my conceptual expectation that policymakers are both aware of and responsive to changes in public anti-intellectual sentiment. I take up this matter more systematically in Chapter 8.

Of course, I recognize that these findings are, to some extent, unsatisfying. Assessing the prevalence of anti-intellectual attitude endorsement necessarily required me to make difficult—but, I hope, conceptually justified—decisions about how to classify responses from hundreds of different polls and polling questions. Classification *itself* is also problematic to some extent. As I argued earlier in this book, anti-intellectualism is likely best thought about not as a binary classification but as a continuum. While many people might reject holding positive feelings toward scientists and other experts, there is plenty of room for gradation among members of that group (ranging from those who hold steadfastly negative views to those who hold a mix of positive and negative feelings).

Although these limitations are important, it is nevertheless worthwhile to remember that assessing the prevalence of anti-intellectualism is just one part of the story I hope to tell in this book. While the results presented in this chapter help us better understand the scope of expert negativity in the United States, they tell us less about *why* some people are more likely to hold these views than others and *how* the prevalence of anti-intellectual attitudes might shape politics and public policy. For the remainder of this book, I offer a data-driven assessment of both the origins and policy consequences of anti-intellectual attitude endorsement.

Anti-Scientific Americans:The Prevalence, Origins, and Political Consequences of Anti-Intellectualism in the US.
Matthew Motta, Oxford University Press. © Oxford University Press 2024. DOI: 10.1093/9780197788844.003.0004

‖ 5 ‖

Origin Story Part I: Explaining Between-Person Differences in Anti-Intellectual Attitude Endorsement

At the outset of the COVID-19 pandemic in the spring of 2020, Pastor Curt Landry implored his online following of over forty-five thousand YouTube subscribers to place their trust in the public health advice of then-President Donald Trump over that of infectious disease expert Dr. Anthony Fauci (Landry, 2020). In addition to claiming that COVID-19 vaccines (then still in development) would likely ascend "from the pit of hell," he argued that although he is by his own admission "not a doctor" he felt that "in the order of spiritual alignment, Donald J. Trump is the Cyrus above [Dr. Fauci]." (Cyrus is a reference to an ancient Achaemenid king who, according to some religious doctrine, was divinely chosen to release the Jewish people from Babylonian subjugation.)

Consequently, Landry suggested that his followers "need to agree" with "what [Donald Trump] is saying." At the time, what the former president was saying was often at odds with the best available scientific evidence from health and medical experts. For example, he suggested that the COVID-19 virus was no more dangerous than seasonal influenza, floated the possibility that ingesting common household cleaning products might help stave off viral infection, and suggested that the country would be ready to curb social-distancing guidelines by Easter 2020 (in defiance of public health recommendations from the CDC) (Dyer, 2020; Rutledge, 2020; Yamey & Gonsalves, 2020).

Pastor Landry's comments, of course, are just one example of how deference to medical, scientific, and other experts—even in times of crisis—has become politically and socially polarizing. Correspondingly, Landry's comments raise two important questions. First, how did we get to a point where deference to expertise has become politically and socially contentious? Second, do Americans who share Landry's political and social outlooks express similar levels of distrust in experts?

In this chapter, I provide new answers to both of these important questions.

The prevalence of anti-intellectual attitude endorsement in the American mass public helps set the stage as to why it is so important to offer a rigorous investigation of the political and social underpinnings of negative attitudes toward experts. As I demonstrated in Chapter 4, about one-third of the American public can be thought about as endorsing anti-intellectual views at any given time since the mid-1940s. The prevalence of negative attitudes toward experts is problematic because—as I demonstrate later in this book—anti-intellectual attitude endorsement in the American public could have important consequences for American politics and public policy.

Connecting investigations of the prevalence of anti-intellectualism to its potential policy impact are questions about the social, political, and psychological origins of anti-intellectual attitude endorsement. Why are some Americans more likely to express negative feelings toward scientists and other experts? Under what conditions might some people be willing to update their anti-expert attitudes? The answer to these questions can help us better understand how anti-intellectual attitude endorsement maps onto contemporary sources of political and social division in the United States and thereby provide a useful context for understanding its policy effects.

Unfortunately, aggregated assessments of the prevalence of anti-intellectual attitude endorsement—like those that I offered in the previous chapter—can only take us so far in studying where anti-intellectual attitudes come from and how they might impact public policy. On the basis of aggregated opinion data alone, we might assume that anti-intellectualism is something of a *constant* in American public life. Although anti-intellectualism in the aggregate both ebbs and flows over time—and while I offered evidence that these changes tend to coincide with important political events—shifts in public opinion are generally modest.

Viewing anti-intellectualism as a constant—or a set of beliefs that are always with us and in relatively great number—might also lead us to assume that Americans are similar in their propensities to harbor negative feelings toward experts. As the nation has experienced major technological advances like the advent of personal computing, the rise to prominence of the Christian Right, and changes in the political balance of power in Washington, DC, anti-intellectual attitude endorsement in the aggregate has continued to bounce around its central tendency of about 33 percent.

While this view has some merit, it might obscure important socio-political differences and temporal changes going on beneath the surface—i.e., the composition of who holds anti-intellectual attitudes at a disaggregated (micro) level. In this chapter, I show that Americans are not equal in their propensities to harbor negative feelings toward scientific experts. I find that religious preferences and political identities, for example, play a powerful explaining why some people are more likely to accept these views than others.

Moreover, I make the case that anti-intellectual attitude endorsement has become highly politically polarized at the micro level, despite the consistent prevalence of aggregated anti-intellectual opinion. As Democrats have become more likely to hold positive views toward scientists and experts over time, those changes have been offset by Republicans' tendencies to hold more-negative views.

However, and in contrast to previous work in this area, I also show that partisan polarization in anti-intellectual attitude endorsement is a fairly recent phenomenon. Previously, some scholars have argued that anti-intellectual attitude endorsement became politically contentious during the Reagan administration in the mid-1980s. Others claim that polarization has increased gradually over time. In this chapter, I provide new evidence that polarization is a fairly recent phenomenon, arising as a reaction to the presidency of Barack Obama and the ascendency of Tea Party politics.

Of course, I am not the first to attempt to study the *origin story* of anti-intellectual attitude endorsement. Few, however, have attempted to track its social and political building blocks over time. Fewer still have attempted to study whether insights gleaned from one approach to operationalizing anti-intellectual attitude endorsement can be applied to others. Past work also lacks conceptually expansive tests of the many factors that could potentially shape anti-intellectual attitude endorsement, derived from a single theoretical infrastructure, and that rule out the possibility that those effects might function *in reverse*.

In this chapter, I aim to provide a series of tests that accomplish all of these goals. Specifically, I offer a series of novel tests of the *static-inputs* stage of the group-centric model presented in Chapter 2. Here I consider the differences *between* Americans in their propensities to accept anti-intellectual attitudes and study how those dynamics have changed over time. These analyses set the stage for Chapter 6, where I study how individuals come to change their views toward scientists and experts over time (i.e., the theoretical model's dynamic inputs).

In what follows, I provide an analytical strategy for testing the static inputs that shape anti-intellectual attitude endorsement, discuss the data and methods necessary to carry out these tests, and present the results of that effort.

Analytical Strategy: Detecting Between-Person Differences in Anti-Intellectual Attitude Endorsement

To test the *between-person* predictions from the group-centric model outlined in Chapter 2 (path a in Figure 2.1), I perform a series of multivariate tests that regress anti-intellectualism, as an ordered scale, on each of the model's hypothesized static inputs plus a series of demographic controls. Recognizing the difficulties associated with dichotomizing anti-intellectual attitude endorsement in Chapter 4, these models allow me to assess (via ordered logistic regression) how each of the model's potential static inputs might lead to incremental change in the *degree* to which people hold anti-intellectual attitudes (i.e., as opposed to whether people hold or do not hold some negative attitudes toward experts).

As I am primarily concerned with explaining change between people across individual differences in partisan identity, ideology, limited-government attitudes, and religiosity, I rely on cross-sectional data from the GSS, ANES, SciPol, and CSPP panel studies when conducting these tests. While cross-sectional data are incapable of allowing me to quantify within-person change in anti-intellectual attitude endorsement (as they only interview respondents at a single point in time)—a task I take up in Chapter 6 using panel data—they are nevertheless well suited to help me explain why some people are more likely to hold anti-intellectual attitudes than others.

Still, while the theoretical expectations I test in this chapter are not time varying, I need to take into account at least two important temporal elements. The first concerns the stability, or what we might call the *dynamic reliability*, of the model's inputs. When outlining my theoretical expectations in Chapter 2, I suggested that socio-political inputs like partisanship, ideology, limited-government views, and religiosity are slow to change over time. Their dynamic stability helps explain why we should expect each of these factors to lead to change in the degree to which people hold anti-intellectual attitudes (and not vice versa).

Consequently, before constructing the ordered logistic regression models mentioned earlier, I first turn to the GSS and CSPP panel data (discussed at length in Chapter 3) to assess the stability of each model input. To do this, I treat the panel data as a repeated cross-sectional design. In other words, I treat observations of the same variable at different time points as separate variables (i.e., columns in a data matrix). This allows me to assess the correspondence between panelists' scores on each variable across panel waves.

For interval measures (e.g., limited-government attitudes), I present Pearson correlation coefficients (ρ) that assess the strength of the association between continuous variables over time. For ordinal measures (e.g., partisanship), I cross-tabulate each variable and calculate Goodman and Kruskall's gamma (γ) coefficient, which is often used as a measure of the strength of association between ordinal variables (Chen & Kianifard, 1999). As both ρ and γ coefficients are scaled identically (and range from 0 to 1, with 1 indicating high levels of temporal stability), I would expect to observe coefficients that are both positive and in excess of about 0.60, which would be indicative of at least moderately high levels of temporal stability.

Additionally, and as implied in my earlier comments, the models I construct in this chapter make the potentially strong assumption that a *reverse* causal story is not true. In other words, anti-intellectualism should not explain between-person change in each of the model's hypothesized static inputs. To assess whether this assumption is a good one, I construct a series of cross-lagged panel regression models (Kearney, 2017) that regress, in one set of models, anti-intellectualism in each panel's final wave on itself (measured in the study's first wave), plus first-wave indicators of each hypothesized static input. I then repeat this process by swapping the anti-intellectualism outcome variable for each hypothesized static indicator of anti-intellectualism and control for first-wave estimates of anti-intellectual attitude endorsement.

If my theoretical expectations are correct, the static inputs should continue to exert a positive and statistically significant influence on anti-intellectual attitude endorsement in former set of cross-lagged models, which—in comparison to the ordered logistic regression models outlined above—are comparatively more statistically conservative (i.e., because they regress anti-intellectualism on itself, which we would expect to be highly correlated over time and thereby providing less opportunity for other factors to exert an influence). Additionally, in the latter set of models, I should *fail* to see that each of the hypothesized static inputs is associated with anti-intellectualism. Together these results would imply that the socio-political inputs collectively explain between-person change in the degree to which people endorse anti-intellectual attitudes but are not themselves shaped by anti-intellectualism.

Additionally, the cross-sectional ordered logistic regression models make the important assumption that I have attempted to account for all potential factors *aside* from the model's hypothesized static inputs that could alternatively explain between-person change in anti-intellectual attitude endorsement. Correspondingly, I account for respondents' levels of educational attainment in all models, in addition to a wide variety of other demographic factors (e.g., respondents' racial and gender identities, household income, and age). It is particularly important to account for educational attainment in these models because people who themselves have advanced degrees may be more likely to have had contact with academic experts in the past—like a favorite professor or a research lab manager—and therefore be more likely to hold feelings toward this group. Moreover, people with college and advanced degrees may be more likely to view themselves as experts in a particular scientific, academic, or other technical field and therefore be more likely to empathize with experts as a social group.

Additionally, as discussed in Chapter 1, some researchers consider anti-intellectualism to be a component of more general populist (i.e., anti-elite) sentiments. The 2016 CSPP study contained a short-form measure of Oliver &

Origin Story Part I: Anti-Intellectual Attitude Endorsement 117

Rahn's (2016) scale used to capture the measure's anti-elite and national-affiliation subcomponents (which I reviewed in more detail in Chapter 1).

Finally, recall that—later in this book—I will test whether epistemic motives and abilities (i.e., science knowledge and interest) explain *within-person* change in anti-intellectual attitude endorsement. Unfortunately, while the questions used to measure these scales are available in some GSS cross-sectional waves (see Chapter 3), they are not offered uniformly throughout. Accounting for these factors in only those cross-sectional waves where the measures are offered would therefore lead me to make nonstandardized comparisons across the series or (alternatively) severely limit the temporal scope of this investigation. I therefore reserve my discussion of science interest and knowledge for Chapter 6.

Measures and Data

The primary outcome variables in all analyses presented in this chapter are the measures of anti-intellectualism available in GSS (the *trust in the scientific community* question) and the ANES, CSPP, and SciPol datasets (the "trust in ordinary people over experts" question) that I reviewed in detail in Chapter 3. The key explanatory variables are measures of four socio-political and cultural factors—partisan identification, ideology, limited-government attitudes, and religiosity—which serve as potential determinants (the model's *static inputs*) of between-person differences in anti-intellectual attitude endorsement. I discuss each of these measures in turn.

Before doing so, however, I want to briefly note that throughout all micro-level analyses offered in this book I standardize all variables to range from 0 to 1 for both consistency and ease of interpretation. This means that continuous and interval variables take on values ranging between 0 (the observed minimum) to 1 (the observed maximum), while all dichotomous variables take on values of either 0 or 1. Summary statistics for all variables included in these analyses in the appendix.

First I measure *partisan identification* using a standard seven-point measure of whether respondents identify as either Strong Democrats (Republicans), Democrats (Republicans), lean toward the Democratic (Republican) Party, or identify as Independents with no particular partisan lean. As is common in political-science research, most studies that I draw on here administer this question as a series of two-branched questions (Krosnick & Berent, 1993). To do this, each survey—aside from the GSS, which administers the question as a single, ordered, seven-point scale—first asks respondents whether they identify as Democrats, Republicans, or Independents. They then follow up to ask whether Democrats and Republicans strongly identify with their preferred party label, and they ask Independents whether they lean toward one of the two parties (or just simply identify as an Independent). The resulting seven-point scale is scored to range from 1 (self-identifying as a strong Democrat) to 7 (self-identifying as a strong Republican) and recoded to range from 0 to 1. I exclude respondents from analysis if they do not identify as Democrats, Republicans, or Independents.

Similarly, *symbolic ideology* is a seven-point scale measuring respondents' self-identification with liberal and conservative ideological labels (Ellis & Stimson, 2012). Respondents can indicate that they identify as extremely liberal (conservative), liberal (conservative), slightly liberal (conservative), or moderate. In all studies aside from the 2019 ANES Pilot Survey, the variable is scored such that a value of 1 corresponds to self-identifying as extremely conservative, and 7 corresponds to identifying as extremely liberal (again recoded to range from 0 to 1). Note, however, that the 2019 ANES Pilot Survey referred to the *slightly* options associated with each label as *closer to* liberals/conservatives and the (unmodified) liberal/conservative placements as *somewhat* liberal/conservative.

Another notable difference in the measurement of symbolic ideology across studies concerns whether surveys offer *don't know* (DK) options. In the GSS and 2020 ANES studies (but not in the SciPol or CSPP studies), respondents could indicate that they *don't know* (GSS) or *haven't thought much about* (ANES 2020) their symbolic ideological leanings. In the GSS, I treat DK responses as missing data and exclude those respondents from analysis. However, the 2020 ANES followed up with respondents by administering the ideology item as a branched question, first asking respondents to place themselves on the seven-point scale and then asking those who failed to do so whether they would identify as liberal or conservative if they *had to choose*. Again, as is conventional in political-science research (e.g., Ellis & Stimson, 2012; Kinder & Kalmoe, 2017), I treat respondents who select either of these answers as being *slightly* liberal or conservative on the seven-point scale.

Next I measure *limited-government* values in the GSS, 2020 ANES, and CSPP studies as an intervalized variable taking on a value of 0 if respondents believe that the size and scope of government ought to be more expansive and 1 if they think that it ought to be more limited. Unfortunately, the 2020–2021 SciPol study did not ask questions pertaining to limited-government orientations. As I lack a single standardized measure of limited-government values in each survey, my measures of limited-government attitudes take on a handful of different forms.

First, in the GSS studies, respondents were asked whether they think that the government is spending *too little, about the right amount,* or *too much* on a variety of programs. Programs provided in all cross-sectional waves of the GSS measure limited-government attitudes in application to spending on environmental issues, health care, solving problems in major cities, drug enforcement, education, race relations, foreign aid, and welfare. I indexed (averaged) these items together into a single itemized indicator of limited-government attitudes

$(a_{p\ ooled} = 0.63)$. A full list of policies included in this measure is available in the appendix.

I employed an analogous procedure in the 2020 ANES, which featured a similar set of questions as those available in the GSS. These items, however, varied slightly from those available in the GSS in both their substantive focus and response-option measurement. Programs provided in the 2020 ANES include spending on Social Security, education, border security, crime, welfare, infrastructure, aid to the poor, and protecting the environment. Additionally, whereas the GSS offered response options on three-point categorical scales, the 2020 ANES administered these items as branched questions. The first leg of the branch was identical to the response options offered in the GSS. The ANES then followed up to ask those indicating that spending should be increased or decreased whether they think spending should be increased/decreased *a lot* or *a little*. The result is a five-point scale ranging from 1 (*increase a lot*) to 5 (*decrease a lot*) and recoded to range from 0 to 1. Despite these minor differences in item administration, the resulting index again produced acceptable levels of internal consistency ($a = 0.67$). As was the case for the GSS items, a full list of policies included in this measure is available in the appendix.

A few additional caveats about the GSS and ANES measures bear mentioning. First, I exclude spending items in the GSS and ANES that are expressly related to science and scientific research from this scale (e.g., spending on the space program, scientific research). I make these exclusions to allow the scale to measure Americans' preferred policy influence for scientists and experts. Because I expect this more-specific *expert policy role* measure to be *co-constitutive* with anti-intellectualism (as discussed in Chapter 2), I omit related policy questions from the calculation of the limited-government scale (because they could lead to overestimating its effect on anti-intellectual attitude endorsement).

Relatedly, and out of an abundance of caution, I also exclude items related to environmental protection from the calculation of limited-government attitudes. Some respondents might view environmental issues as falling within the domain of scientific research, which would therefore introduce a high degree of conceptual overlap with anti-expert attitudes. This would be particularly problematic in the GSS, which features the trust in scientists anti-intellectualism proxy. Additionally, I exclude items from the scale that are not positively intercorrelated with the remaining scale items, potentially due to partisan asymmetries in selective support for increased government intervention in those areas. These items include the border and crime funding items available in the ANES. Also note that in some cross-sectional waves, the GSS administered the limited-government items as split-ballot questions with alternate question wordings. To preserve a sufficiently large sample size within each survey wave, I pool questions across ballots.

While the ANES and GSS measures of limited-government attitudes are relatively similar in construction, I take a somewhat different approach to measuring limited-government views in the 2016 CSPP panel study. In that study, I make use of a single survey item that asks respondents *directly* whether the federal government should *provide fewer services, even in areas such as health and education in order to reduce spending* or whether it should *provide more services even if it means an increase in spending*. Response options were offered on a seven-point scale ranging from 1 (fewer services) to 7 (more services), reverse coded, and scored to range from 0 to 1.

Finally, I measure *religiosity* by asking respondents in the GSS, ANES, and CSPP studies how often they attend religious services. In all the studies, respondents were asked to self-report how often they attend religious services. In the GSS, respondents offered answers on an eight-point scale ranging from 0 (*never*) to 8 (*more than once per week*) The ANES and CSPP studies asked a similar question, with the ANES employing a six-point scale that ranged from 1 (*more than once per week*) to 6 (*never*) and the CSPP study employing a seven-point measure ranging from 1 (*never*) to 7 (*more than once a week*). In all cases, responses were scored to range from 0 to 1, such that a score of 0 indicates the least frequent levels of religious service attendance and 1 indicates the highest.

An important advantage of asking about religious services—as opposed to prayer, church, or measures of sacred text orthodoxy and dogmatism—is that the item is *nondenominational in focus*. Consequently, this measure allows me to isolate the effects of being more (versus less) religious, irrespective of respondents' preferred religious traditions.

Finally, note that all models control for a series of self-reported demographic factors that could potentially influence how Americans view scientists and experts. All models control for binary indicators of whether or not respondents self-identify as women (1) versus men (0), Black and Non-Hispanic (1) versus all other racial categories (0; although note that because an ethnicity indicator was not available in all survey waves, the GSS models only compare Black to not Black respondents, without accounting for whether respondents are Hispanic), Hispanic or Latinx (1) versus Not Hispanic (0), and age categories (18–24, which serves as an analytical baseline in multivariate models, followed by 24–44, 45–64, and 65+). I also control for respondents' educational attainment, a binary indicator of whether respondents have a Bachelor's degree. All models include measures of respondents' household income, measured categorically (a full list of available response options by survey is available in the appendix) and rescaled to range from 0 to 1 (such that a score of 0 indicates the lowest observed income levels and 1 indicates the highest).

Model Input Stability Assessment

A key assumption of my theoretical model is that individual differences in partisan identity and ideology, limited government, and religious preferences are unchanging over time. Correspondingly, prior to assessing whether each one explains between-person differences in anti-intellectual attitude endorsement, it is important that I first demonstrate that each of these factors do not *themselves* change much over time. Their dynamic reliability should then enable each potential socio-political influence on views toward scientific experts to explain change in the comparatively more-malleable anti-intellectual attitude endorsement outcome variables without themselves being changed in response to increased or decreased anti-intellectual attitude endorsement.

Table 5.1 offers a test of this assumption across the GSS and CSPP panel studies. Each row in the table presents the Goodman and Kruskall's gamma coefficients (γ, for ordinal variables) and Pearson correlation coefficients (ρ, for continuous variables) discussed earlier in this chapter as an indicator of dynamic reliability for each model input (partisan identification, ideology, limited-government attitudes, and religiosity) as well as its output (anti-intellectual attitude endorsement). Based on data availability, and to allow for multiple comparisons of temporal consistency, I calculate these quantities in the survey's first

Table 5.1 **The Stability of Model Inputs and Outputs (06–10, 08–12, and 10–14 GSS Panel Studies)**

Variable	GSS Stability (Wave 1–2)	GSS Stability (Wave 1–3)	CSPP Stability (Wave 1–2)
Party ID	$\gamma = 0.82$	$\gamma = 0.79$	$\gamma = 0.93$
Religiosity	$\gamma = 0.74$	$\gamma = 0.70$	—
Science Knowledge	$\rho = 0.67$	$\rho = 0.67$	—
Ideology	$\gamma = 0.65$	$\gamma = 0.64$	$\gamma = 0.87$
Science Interest	$\gamma = 0.60$	$\gamma = 0.54$	—
Limited Government	$\rho = 0.62$	$\rho = 0.59$	$\gamma = 0.55$
Anti-Intellectualism	$\gamma = 0.63$	$\gamma = 0.63$	$\gamma = 0.52$

Note: Goodman and Kruskall's gamma coefficients (γ) presented for comparisons of ordinal variables. Pearson correlation coefficients (ρ) presented for interval variables. Entries around or exceeding 0.60 can be thought about as exhibiting moderately high levels of temporal stability, while entries at or exceeding 0.80 can be thought about as expressing very high levels of stability.

and second waves (for both CSPP and the GSS) and between both the first and second and the first and third waves (for the GSS only). For comparison, and because I will reference these quantities later in Chapter 6, I also include measures of science knowledge and interest. As I discussed earlier (in Chapter 2), science knowledge and interest ought to be comparatively more prone to change over time than the other model inputs and therefore better suited to explain within-person change in anti-intellectual attitude endorsement.

Table 5.1 offers fairly strong support for the theoretical model's most basic time-varying assumptions. First, in both the GSS and CSPP studies, partisan identification is highly stable, ranging from $\gamma = 0.70$ over the span of four years between the GSS's first and third waves, to $\gamma = 0.93$ in the three months between the CSPP study's first and second waves. I find similar results for religiosity and, to a lesser degree, symbolic ideology. Whereas the ideology measure reaches only middling levels of stability in the GSS panel (observed between two to four years), it is highly stable in the CSPP study (observed over the course of three months). While a more-substantive exploration into the temporal dynamics of symbolic ideology is beyond the scope of this book, these results may imply that ideological self-placements are highly stable when observed in the short term but comparatively less stable when observed over the span of several years.

Additionally, and somewhat unexpectedly, I find that limited-government attitudes attain only middling levels of temporal stability in both the CSPP and GSS panel studies. While not observing high levels of temporal stability in the CSPP study may seem concerning—given the panel's comparatively short duration—this may be the result of methodological artifact. Because the CSPP study makes use of only a single item indicator of limited-government attitudes, the assessment of temporal reliability may be prone to random measurement error (Ansolabehere, Rodden, & Snyder, 2008) and therefore more likely to exhibit change over time. Nevertheless, this potential assumption violation of the theoretical model makes it all the more important to test for a reverse causal relationship between each of the model's hypothesized static inputs and anti-intellectual attitude endorsement. I perform these tests later in this chapter.

Moreover, and as I discuss in more detail in Chapter 6, both science knowledge and (particularly) science interest are less temporally stable than partisan identity, religiosity, and short-term symbolic ideological placements. This makes each one comparatively better suited to detect within-person change in anti-intellectual attitude endorsement. Of course, given the fact that even the theoretical model's hypothesized static inputs do change somewhat over time, it will be important to also account for the time-varying influence of those factors when studying within-person change (a task I take up again in Chapter 6).

Finally, and importantly, Table 5.1 presents evidence that anti-intellectual attitude endorsement is comparatively more prone to change over time than each of the model's hypothesized static inputs. Of all the factors listed in Table 5.1, anti-intellectualism has the single lowest inter-wave reliability, observed in-between the first and second waves of the CSPP panel study ($\gamma = 0.52$). This is particularly notable given the panel's shorter duration than the GSS, where I also observe only moderate levels of dynamic reliability, which we might otherwise expect to produce comparatively higher levels of stability.

Overall then, the results presented in Table 5.1 largely support the model's theoretical assumptions. Anti-intellectual attitudes are comparatively more malleable than the model's hypothesized static inputs, which are themselves relatively stable over time. However, the potential for assumption violations underscores the importance of the tests devised to detect reverse causal effects presented at the end of this chapter. With the model's core theoretical assumption standing on firm empirical ground, I next present a series of tests designed to study between-person differences in anti-intellectual attitude endorsement.

Results

Having demonstrated that partisan identification, symbolic ideology, religiosity, and (to some degree) limited-government attitudes are highly temporally stable over time, I next assess the effects of individual differences in each of these socio-political factors on between-person differences in the acceptance of anti-intellectual attitudes. Each figure shown here illustrates the results of the ordered logistic regression models discussed earlier. I estimated these models across every GSS cross-sectional wave (odd-numbered figures) and the ANES, CSPP, and SciPol studies (even-numbered figures), for each of the I expected to produce between-person change in anti-intellectual attitude endorsement. Full model output used to produce each of these figures is included in the factors appendix.

All figures can be interpreted as follows. The black dots in each figure are ordered logistic regression parameter estimates. Dots *above* the dashed red line indicate a positive effect of partisanship (GOP identification), ideology (conservatism), limited-government (versus expanded-government) attitudes, and/or high (versus low) religiosity on anti-intellectual attitude endorsement. When the 95 percent confidence intervals extending out from each one (with 90 percent and 68 percent CIs overlaid) intersect with the dashed red line, I can rule out the possibility of a statistically significant effect of each static input on anti-intellectual attitude endorsement.

Because ordered logistic regression coefficients are somewhat obscure indicators of effect size, I then interpret the substantive magnitude of these quantities (presented in text) by calculating the predicted probability that individuals endorse anti-intellectual attitudes from cross-sectional results that are representative of the broader trend documented in each figure (e.g., the probability that Republicans versus Democrats harbor strong levels of distrust toward the scientific community). For reference, parameter estimates (β) and their corresponding p values are printed directly in the figure next to each estimate.

After discussing the effects of each of the theoretical model's hypothesized static inputs (Figures 5.1–5.8), I then provide a series of tests designed to test the Tea Party's influence (Figures 5.9–5.10) on the partisan polarization of anti-intellectual attitude endorsement. For the sake of completeness, I consider other potential forms of polarization as well (i.e., for individual differences in ideology, limited-government attitudes, and religiosity). I conclude by rendering a judgment on the degree to which the results presented in this chapter support the theoretical model's empirical expectations.

Partisan Identity

If my theoretical predictions are correct, partisan identification with the GOP should be associated with increased anti-intellectual attitude endorsement. As I outlined in Chapter 2, Republican elites' willingness to denigrate scientific and other forms of expertise as a political strategy and their pursuit of policies that defy expert consensus in a variety of policy areas may have "trickled down" into public consciousness. This would thereby facilitate the polarization of anti-intellectual attitude endorsement along party lines.

Figure 5.1 offers an initial test of this possibility by presenting a multidecade analysis of the effects of partisan identity on anti-intellectual attitude endorsement dating back to 1974. The results present three important findings.

First, partisan identification with the GOP is both positively (as indicated by the black dots above the dashed line) and significantly (as indicated by the non-intersecting 95 percent confidence intervals) associated with anti-intellectual attitude endorsement in most GSS survey waves dating back to 2010. The effect of GOP identification attains conventional levels of two-tailed significance at the $p < 0.05$ level in 2012 and 2018 and approaches conventional levels of significance at the $p < 0.10$ level in 2010 ($p = 0.06$) and 2016 ($p = 0.08$). The effects of partisan identification fail to approach conventional levels of significance in just one cross-sectional wave since 2010 (in 2014, where $p = 0.15$).

The effect of GOP identification on anti-intellectual attitude endorsement is also substantively strong. The most-recent GSS wave (2018) offers a representative example, producing estimates that were similar in both substantive size and

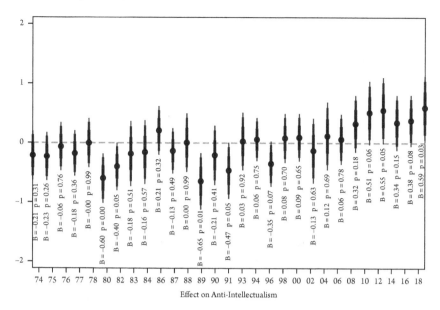

Figure 5.1 The Effect of Partisan Identification on Micro-Level Anti-Intellectual Attitude Endorsement Over Time (GSS Cross-Sectional Studies: 1974–2018)

significance to other post-2010 GSS cross-sections. In that wave, I find that GOP identification is associated with a 4 percentage point increase in the probability of holding the strongest measured levels of distrust in the scientific community (from 5 percent among those who self-identify as a strong Republican to 9 percent for those who identify as a strong Democrat).

Second, and as is perhaps implied by the previously mentioned analyses, I find that partisan polarization of anti-intellectual attitude endorsement appears to be a *fairly recent phenomenon*. Early on in the series (1974–1978), I observe little influence of self-reported partisanship on anti-intellectual attitude endorsement. Interestingly, and contrary to some past work that posits the Reagan administration as a key political moment linking partisanship to anti-intellectual attitude endorsement (Mooney, 2006), I find that partisan identification with the GOP is associated with significantly *lower* levels of anti-intellectual attitude endorsement at the beginning of the Reagan administration (1980–1982) and at the beginning of the George H. W. Bush administration (1989, 1991).

More generally, though, for most of the 1980s and 1990s partisanship bears no statistically discernible influence on anti-intellectual attitude endorsement. The same is true of most of the mid-2000s, again contrary to accounts suggesting that the George W. Bush administration's anti-science policy maneuvers may have tightened the link between partisanship and anti-intellectualism in the public.

Instead, I find that the *first* time period in which GOP identification has a significant effect on harboring distrust toward the scientific community is in

2010. As I discuss (and test) later in this chapter, this provides preliminary evidence that the Tea Party may have been instrumental in linking Republican partisan identification to anti-intellectual attitude endorsement.

This leads to my third and final point regarding the results presented in Figure 5.1. The fact that partisan identification bears little association with anti-intellectual attitude endorsement for most of the series (and even at times suggests a *negative* relationship between GOP identification and anti-intellectualism during the Reagan and first Bush administrations) suggests that its effects are not monotonic or linear over time. Contrary to both bivariate and multivariate accounts suggesting a gradual increase in anti-intellectual attitude endorsement over time on the ideological right (e.g., Gauchat, 2012, who documents these effects across multiple estimation strategies), I find that consistent partisan polarization in anti-intellectual attitude endorsement is a recent phenomenon.

Differences between the results offered here and Gauchat's work may arise for a few different reasons. One possibility is that differences in estimation strategy lead us to draw different conclusions about the time-varying effect of partisan identity on anti-intellectual attitude endorsement. However, I think perhaps a more obvious explanation is that the results presented in this book incorporate more data from the post–Tea Party era (which as I show later in this chapter represents a key opportunity for Americans to link their partisan identities to anti-intellectual attitudes). Correspondingly, my data might perhaps just simply have a greater *capacity* to detect sharp time-varying effects such as those that may be attributable to the Tea Party movement.

Figure 5.2 offers additional evidence consistent with the findings presented above. In this figure, I shift away from the GSS *trust in scientists* question in favor of Oliver and Rahn's *trust ordinary people versus experts* measure of anti-intellectualism. On balance, I find that GOP identification is positively associated with increased anti-intellectual attitude endorsement in nearly every survey dating from 2016 to 2021 (with the exception of the 12/20 SciPol study) and meets conventional levels of two-tailed significance in all but three tests: the second wave of the CSPP panel study in 2016 ($p = 0.51$) and the December 2020 and February 2021 waves of the SciPol study ($p = 0.21$ and $p = 0.79$, respectively).

Again, these effects are substantively large. Treating the nationally representative 2020 ANES as representative both in terms of substantive size and statistical significance of the other results presented in Figure 5.2, I find that GOP identification is associated with a 5 percentage point increase in the likelihood that respondents strongly value the expertise of ordinary people over experts (from 6 percent for strong Democrats to 11 percent for strong Republicans).

Overall the results suggest that anti-intellectual attitude endorsement is indeed polarized along partisan lines, such that self-identified Republicans are significantly more likely to express negativity toward scientists and experts.

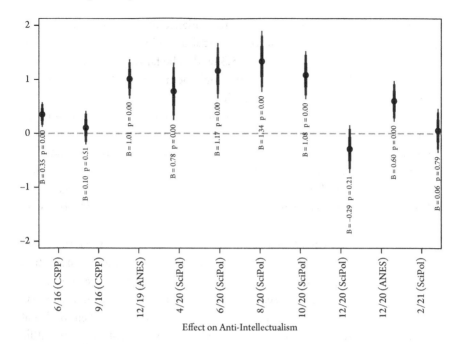

Figure 5.2 The Effect of Partisan Identification on Micro-Level Anti-Intellectual Attitude Endorsement Over Time (CSPP 2016; ANES 2019–2020; SciPol RXC 2020–2021)

However, the results provide preliminary evidence that these polarizing effects are both recent and did not emerge gradually.

One could argue, of course, that the pattern of results displayed so far are superficial. Party labels come to stand for different *ideas* over time. Perhaps, then, the symbolic ideological affiliations or operational preferences for limited government that have come to define contemporary support for the GOP (Bafumi & Shapiro, 2009) exhibit more consistent patterns of polarization over time. I test this possibility in the sections that follow.

Ideology

Next I assess the effect of Americans' symbolic ideological orientations on anti-intellectual attitude endorsement. Recall that given the tight link between symbolic identification with conservative (versus liberal) ideological labels and identification with the GOP, I expect ideological conservatism to be associated with increased anti-intellectual attitude endorsement.

I test this possibility by presenting a series of figures identical in construction to those in the previous section. In both the GSS (Figure 5.3) and CSPP, ANES, and SciPol studies (Figure 5.4), I find a similar—albeit somewhat weaker—pattern of effects to those presented for partisan identification.

For most of the GSS series, I find little evidence of an association between ideological conservatism and anti-intellectual attitude endorsement. The parameter estimates presented in Figure 5.3 tend to be fairly close to the zero line throughout the 1970s to the mid-2000s, only occasionally attaining statistical significance in 1989 and 1996. In both of those cases, increased ideological conservatism is associated with increased distrust in the scientific community.

In more recent years, however, I again find some evidence that—like partisan identification—symbolic identification with conservative ideological labels is associated with increased anti-intellectual attitude endorsement. However, this effect attains statistical significance at the $p < 0.05$ level in just two years (2014, 2018) and approaches conventional levels of significance at the $p < 0.10$ level in 2016 ($p = 0.09$).

Similar to the approach I took in the previous section, I treat the results from the 2018 GSS survey as indicative of the recent uptick in ideological polarization in anti-intellectual attitude endorsement in order to offer a more-substantive interpretation of the results presented in Figure 5.3. I find that symbolic conservatism is associated with a 5 percentage point increase in the likelihood that respondents express the strongest measured levels of distrust in the scientific community (from 4 percent for the most liberal respondents to 9 percent for the most conservative).

In the remaining studies summarized in Figure 5.4, I again find a similar (but weaker) pattern of effects compared to what I observed for partisan identification.

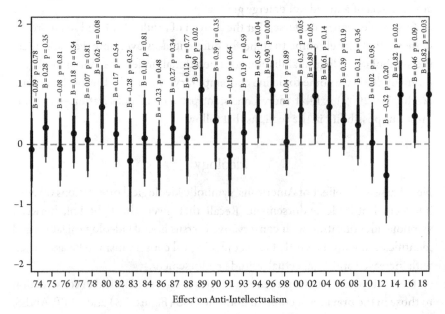

Figure 5.3 The Effect of Ideology on Micro-Level Anti-Intellectual Attitude Endorsement Over Time (GSS Cross-Sectional Studies: 1974–2018)

Origin Story Part I: Anti-Intellectual Attitude Endorsement 129

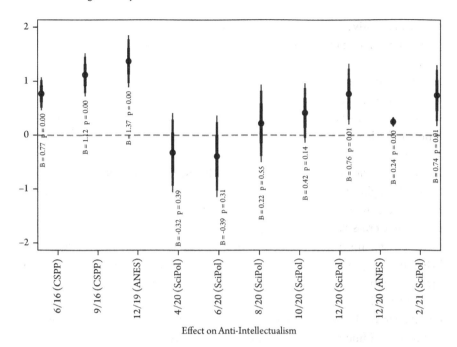

Figure 5.4 The Effect of Ideology on Micro-Level Anti-Intellectual Attitude Endorsement Over Time (CSPP 2016; ANES 2019–2020; SciPol RXC 2020–2021)

Increased ideological conservatism is again associated with increased anti-intellectual attitude endorsement in all but two studies (the 4/20 and 6/20 SciPol surveys), significantly so at the p < 0.05 level in six out of ten. Treating the 2/21 SciPol study as indicative of the more-general trend, I find that symbolic conservatism is associated with a 6 percentage point increase in the probability of expressing the strongest measured levels of distrust in the scientific community (from 7 percent for the most liberal respondents to 13 percent for the most conservative).

Overall the results suggest that symbolic ideological attachments are, to some extent, associated with anti-intellectual attitude endorsement above and beyond the effects of partisan identification. I find that conservatives (versus liberals) are more likely to harbor negative attitudes toward scientific experts, but again caution that I tend to observe this effect strongly and consistently only during and following the Obama presidency. These findings again provide preliminary evidence that the political polarization of anti-intellectual attitude endorsement is a fairly recent phenomenon.

Limited-Government Attitudes

Next I test for the influence of limited-government attitudes on anti-intellectual attitude endorsement. As I outlined in Chapter 2, people who see less of a role for government intervention in daily life may also be more likely to harbor some degree of negative feelings toward experts, given the important role that experts play in formulating public policy (a dynamic I explore in much more detail later in this book).

Again, the figures presented in this section are analogous to those presented for the GSS (Figure 5.5) and all other studies (Figure 5.6) referenced in the previous sections. Recall, however, that a measure of limited-government attitudes is not available in the SciPol study.

In Figure 5.5, I find little evidence in support of the idea that limited-government orientations are associated with anti-intellectual attitude endorsement. Throughout the GSS time series, I find that limited-government attitudes are significantly associated with increased anti-intellectual attitude endorsement in just three cross-sectional waves (1990, 2006, and 2018). Typically, the parameter estimates hover just above or just below the dashed horizontal zero line. While limited-government attitudes appear to be more consistently positive in their association with anti-intellectual attitude endorsement following the election of Barack Obama in 2008 and the rise of the Tea Party shortly thereafter, I hesitate to read a temporal pattern into (primarily) nonsignificant findings.

Likewise, I find only limited evidence of an effect of limited-government attitudes in the 2016 CSPP studies and 2020 ANES study presented in Figure 5.6. Limited-government attitudes are positively and significantly associated with anti-intellectual attitude endorsement in the 2020 ANES and second wave of the 2016 CSPP study. However, these views bear no statistically discernible

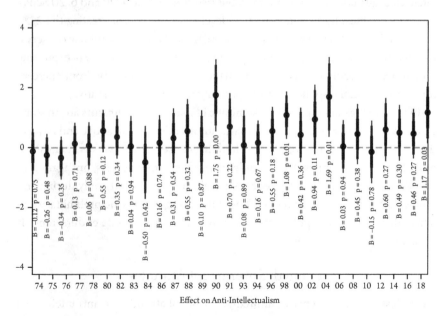

Figure 5.5 The Effect of Limited Government Attitudes on Micro-Level Anti-Intellectual Attitude Endorsement Over Time (GSS Cross-Sectional Studies: 1974–2018)

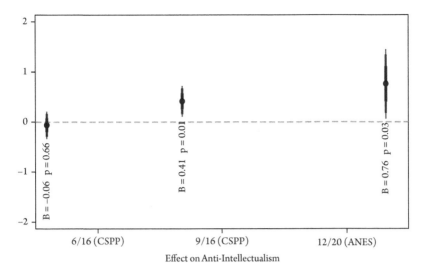

Figure 5.6 The Effect of Limited Government Attitudes on Micro-Level Anti-Intellectual Attitude Endorsement Over Time (CSPP 2016; ANES 2019–2020; SciPol RXC 2020–2021)

association with anti-intellectual attitude endorsement in the first wave of the 2016 CSPP study. Taken together, the results present a murky relationship between general preferences for limited-government intervention in people's lives, and anti-intellectual attitude endorsement.

Religiosity

Having surveyed the effects of three classes of political attitudes on anti-intellectual attitude endorsement, I next assess the effect of Americans' religious orientations on anti-intellectual attitude endorsement. As I outlined in Chapter 2, people who attend religious services more often may be more likely to value the advice of religious leaders and sacred texts over the expertise of academics, scientists, and other professionals.

I test these expectations in Figure 5.7 (GSS) and Figure 5.8 (CSPP and ANES), which are again structured analogously to those in the previous sections. Recall, however, that the religiosity questions were not administered in the 2020–2021 SciPol study.

Turning first to Figure 5.7, I find a similar pattern of effects to those I reported previously for partisan identification. For most of the series, religiosity bears no consistent relationship with anti-intellectual attitude endorsement. In fact, for most of the 1970s through 1990s, more-religious people were typically *less* likely to endorse anti-intellectual attitudes. These effects even attained conventional levels of statistical significance at several points in the 1980s and early 1990s.

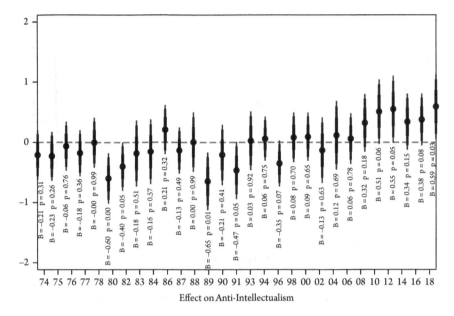

Figure 5.7 The Effect of Religiosity on Micro-Level Anti-Intellectual Attitude Endorsement Over Time (GSS Cross-Sectional Studies: 1974–2018)

However, as was the case with partisan identification, the effect of religiosity on anti-intellectual attitude endorsement only becomes consistently positive over the course of the early-to-mid 2000s. In the years following the election of Barack Obama in 2008, and the subsequent rise of the Tea Party, religiosity is positively and significantly associated with increased anti-intellectual attitude endorsement in all but one cross-sectional survey (the 2014 GSS, p = 0.15). This effect exceeds conventional levels of two-tailed significance in 2012 and 2018 and approaches conventional levels of significance in 2010 and 2016.

Taking the 2018 GSS wave as indicative of the broader trend, I find that although religiosity is not meaningfully associated with holding high levels of distrust in the scientific community—corresponding to a change in predicted probabilities of less than 1 percentage point—it is associated with a somewhat greater 2 percentage point decrease in the probability of holding *high* levels of trust for the least (43 percent) versus the most religious (45 percent). These results are, of course, both more conceptually nuanced and much smaller in substantive magnitude than those presented elsewhere in this chapter. Consequently, these results may indicate that political polarization of anti-intellectual attitude endorsement is stronger than polarization along religious lines.

The results presented in Figure 5.7 are less consistent. Whereas increased religiosity is positively and significantly associated with anti-intellectual attitude endorsement in both waves of the CSPP study, I find that the effect of religiosity

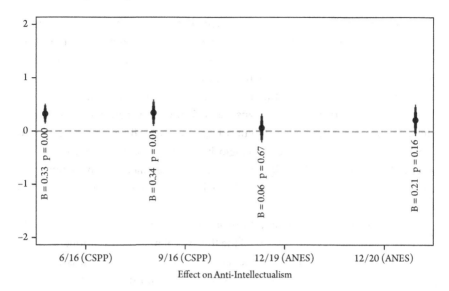

Figure 5.8 The Effect of Religiosity on Micro-Level Anti-Intellectual Attitude Endorsement Over Time (CSPP 2016; ANES 2019–2020; SciPol RXC 2020–2021)

in the 2019 and 2020 ANES—while positive—fails to attain conventional levels of significance. Although I again hesitate to offer post hoc explanations for effects that fail to attain statistical significance, it could be the case that questions pertaining to scientific expertise in particular (i.e., the items featured in the GSS) are more likely to engender attitude polarization along religious lines—i.e., because issues related to science (e.g., teaching evolution in public schools, human agency over climate change, vaccine regulations) are more likely to pose a conflict with matters of faith or religious teachings.

Overall the results in Figures 5.7 and 5.8 provide some evidence consistent with the idea that more-religious individuals are also more likely to hold anti-intellectual attitudes. Further, and similar to the effects of partisan identification, anti-intellectual attitude endorsement appears to have become polarized along religious lines only in recent years. However, these effects are weaker than the effects of partisan identification with the GOP and therefore offer only limited support for my theoretical expectations.

Reverse Causality Assessment

So far, I have presented evidence that anti-intellectual attitude endorsement has recently become polarized along partisan lines. Specifically, I find that Republicans (in the public) have become significantly more likely to express anti-intellectual attitudes in the past decade. I also offer similar, albeit more mixed, evidence suggesting that the same is true of ideological conservatives and people who regularly attend religious services. Before formally assessing whether the rise of the Tea Party might be responsible for the recent political polarization I observed earlier in this chapter, I first want to consider the possibility that effects presented thus far might be reverse causal.

It is important to rule out the possibility that anti-intellectualism is driving people to self-identify as Republicans versus Democrats, conservatives (versus liberals), shaping limited-government orientations, or influencing the extent to which people express high levels of religiosity. Finding a reverse pattern of effects would obscure the relationship between anti-intellectualism and its hypothesized socio-political origins, making it unclear which set of factors influences change in the other.

Luckily, there is good theoretical reason to reject a reverse causal account. As I discussed earlier, a key assumption of the theoretical model I test throughout this chapter is that Americans' partisan and ideological identities—as well as their religious preferences—are both highly stable over time and fundamental to understanding one's sense of self. Consequently, it should be the case that anti-intellectual attitudes (1) tend to move in *response* to changes in socio-political factors like partisan identity (however rare those changes might be) and (2) do not themselves explain change in Americans social and political identities. Whether those theoretical expectations can be empirically verified, however, is an open question.

Table 5.2 offers an assessment of this claim by summarizing the results of the cross-lagged modeling approach described earlier in this chapter. Here, I rely on panel data from the pooled GSS panel studies and 2016 CSPP panel study (described at length in Chapter 3). Full cross-lagged model output can be found in the appendix.

The table can be interpreted as follows. The first column summarizes the directionality of the test being evaluated. Looking first at the top half of the table, I test whether lagged values of each of the socio-political inputs studied in this chapter are associated with current levels of anti-intellectualism, controlling for anti-intellectualism in the past. Here parameter estimates that are both positive (see β columns) and statistically significant (see p columns) indicate support for my empirical expectations. They are, in other words, an additional test of the hypotheses studied in this chapter using time-varying data. The performance of each test across datasets in relation to those expectations is summarized in the table's final column.

Conversely, the bottom half of the table assesses the effect of lagged anti-intellectualism on present levels of each of the socio-political inputs studied in this chapter, controlling for past attitudes and behavior. If my expectations are correct, lagged anti-intellectualism should bear *no statistically significant influence* on change in each of these factors. Again, these results are summarized in the table's final column. These are the tests that assess the possibility of reverse causality.

Table 5.2 **Reverse Causality Test Summary**

Test	β	GSSp	Estimator	β	CSPPp	Estimator	Theory Supported? (GSS, CSPP)
AI ← PID	0.55	< 0.05	Ordered	0.00	n.s.	Ordered	Y, N
AI ← Ideo.	−0.18	n.s.	Ordered	0.67	< 0.05	Ordered	N, Y
AI ← Lim. Gov.	−0.13	n.s.	Ordered	0.50	< 0.05	Ordered	N, Y
AI ← Rel.	0.29	< 0.10	Ordered	0.32	< 0.05	Ordered	Y, Y
Summary							Y (5), N (3)
AI → PID	0.12	n.s.	Ordered	0.16	n.s.	Ordered	Y, Y
AI → Ideo.	0.08	n.s.	Ordered	0.18	n.s.	Ordered	Y, Y
AI → Lim. Gov.	0.03	< 0.05	OLS	0.29	n.s.	Ordered	N, Y
AI → Rel.	0.05	< 0.05	Ordered	–	–	–	N, N/A
Summary							Y (5), N (2)

Note: Please see the text for information about how to interpret each column presented in this table. *Ordered* estimators refer to ordered logistic regression, whereas *OLS* refers to ordinary least squares.

The results presented in Table 5.2 support my expectation that the effects of the hypothesized socio-political influences on anti-intellectual attitude endorsement are not reverse causal. Of the eight tests summarized in the top half of the table, five recover the effects observed earlier in this chapter. Lagged partisanship in the GSS study, lagged ideology and limited-government attitudes in the CSPP study, and lagged religiosity in both panel studies are associated with increased anti-intellectual attitude endorsement over time.

Critically, turning next to the bottom half of the table, I find that anti-intellectual attitude endorsement exhibits a reverse-causal effect in just two out of seven tests. Specifically, lagged anti-intellectualism is significantly associated with increased religiosity and limited-government attitudes in the GSS panels (which, as noted earlier, was only weakly related to anti-intellectual attitude endorsement). Most importantly, I find *no evidence* that lagged anti-intellectualism is associated with increased Republican partisan self-identification or conservative symbolic ideological self-placement.

On balance, then, the panel data provide much stronger support for the idea that anti-intellectual attitudes are shaped by the socio-political factors studied throughout this chapter and less evidence in favor of the idea that anti-intellectual attitudes lead to change in each of these factors. The results also present robust evidence that the area where I observe the strongest rise in polarization—partisan self-identification with the GOP—is unlikely to be reverse causal. Consequently, the results do not appear to be contaminated by concerns about reverse causality.

"Taxed Enough by Academics?" Attitude Polarization and the Rise of the Tea Party

To this point, I have shown that anti-intellectual attitudes have become highly polarized along partisan lines in recent years and have provided evidence that these effects are not reverse causal. I conclude by offering a series of tests assessing whether the rise of the Tea Party, as I suggested in Chapter 2, may be responsible for this polarization.

I test this expectation in two ways. First, in the GSS cross-sectional studies, I pool responses collected from survey waves conducted prior to the presidency of Barack Obama (1974–2008) and those following his election (2010–2018). I then interact these temporal indicators with each socio-political factor hypothesized to increase anti-intellectual attitude endorsement.

If the Tea Party's reaction to the Obama presidency's expert-backed policies—and his personal intellectual *bona fides*—is indeed responsible for contemporary political and social polarization of anti-intellectual attitude endorsement, I would expect to find that the effects of ideology, limited-government attitudes, religiosity, and especially—given the results reported earlier in this chapter—partisan identification on anti-intellectual attitude endorsement are significantly *stronger* in the post-Obama period than in the pre-Obama period.

The results are presented in Figure 5.9. The dashed line in the figure presents the predicted likelihood that respondents report holding *hardly any trust* in the scientific community across the previously mentioned measures of limited-government attitudes, symbolic ideological conservatism, partisan identification with the GOP, and religiosity in the *post-Obama* period. The solid gray line does the same for all GSS waves conducted before Obama's presidency. If my theoretical expectations are correct, conservatives, Republicans, highly religious individuals, and people who strongly value limited-government intervention should all be more likely to hold negative views toward experts in the post-Obama period (dashed line) compared to the pre-Obama period (solid line). Models control for all other factors included in the GSS models discussed earlier in this chapter and are available in full in the appendix.

The models used to construct Figure 5.9 suggest that the effects of partisan identification ($\beta = 0.62$, $p < 0.01$), symbolic ideology ($\beta = 0.54$, $p < 0.01$), limited-government attitudes ($\beta = 0.68$, $p < 0.01$), and religious service attendance ($\beta = 0.38$, $p < 0.01$) on anti-intellectual attitude endorsement are all significantly stronger in the post-Obama period relative to the pre-Obama period. Furthermore, these effects are often substantively meaningful. For example, whereas the likelihood that strong Republicans held the strongest measured levels of distrust toward the scientific community was 6 percent in the pre-Obama period, and the likelihood that they did so in the post-Obama period rose to 9 percent (a statistically significant difference of 3 percentage points).

Because comparatively few Americans harbor the strongest levels of distrust toward the scientific community, it is also worthwhile to assess these predicted quantities at other points on the ordered anti-intellectualism scale. Again turning to partisan identification as an example, and flipping the reference point on the anti-intellectualism outcome variable used to produce the probabilities in Figure 5.9 to its most-positive response option, I find that the likelihood that strong Republicans held high levels of trust in the scientific community was 45 percent in the pre-Obama period but just 35 percent in the post-Obama period (a statistically significant decrease of 10 percentage points).

Together the results suggest that anti-intellectual attitude endorsement became more socially and politically polarized following the election of Barack Obama in 2008. These tests do not, however, *directly* demonstrate whether the Tea Party is responsible for these effects.

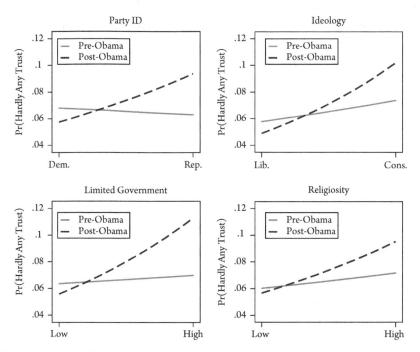

Figure 5.9 The Effect of Partisanship, Ideology, Limited Government Attitudes, and Religiosity in Pre/Post Obama Periods (GSS Time Series Study)

At best, the GSS analyses are indirect tests of the Tea Party's influence. While my theoretical expectations lead me to suspect that the Tea Party is the driver of polarization in the post-Obama period, any number of intervening factors taking place in that time period could alternatively be responsible for these effects.

One might argue, for example, that increasing internet access and social media permeation—which also took place in the mid-2000s with the rise of social networking platforms like Facebook and Twitter—made it easier for Americans to both consume and share information that enabled them to feel as if they themselves are experts on a wide variety of policy issues. This could thereby sour Americans' views on the need for expertise more generally (Nichols, 2017).

Consequently, I provide a second test of the effects of the Tea Party on the political polarization of anti-intellectual attitude endorsement in the 2016 CSPP panel study. There I regress the survey's anti-intellectualism measure on an indicator of whether self-identified Republicans—the Tea Party's primary base of political support (Abramowitz, 2012; Skocpol & Williamson, 2016)—also self-identified as members of the Tea Party near the end of Obama's presidency. Given the strong evidence of partisan polarization (as opposed to other forms of attitude polarization) documented earlier in this chapter, finding that Tea Party Republicans are more likely than all other Republicans to hold anti-intellectual attitudes would again provide suggestive evidence that the Tea Party movement helped politically polarize anti-intellectual attitude endorsement on the ideological right.

The results are presented in Figure 5.10, which plots the predicted probability of strongly agreeing with the statement that, for self-identified Republicans,

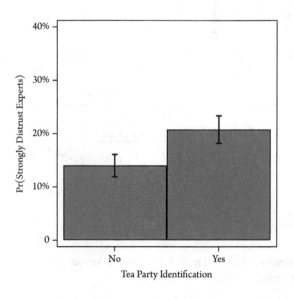

Figure 5.10 The Effect of Tea Party Identification on Anti-Intellectual Attitude Endorsement for Self-Identified Republicans

Origin Story Part I: Anti-Intellectual Attitude Endorsement 139

respondents would rather place their trust in ordinary people over experts and intellectuals across Tea Party identification. The model used to produce this figure (provided in full in the appendix) suggests that Tea Party affiliation is positively and significantly associated with increased anti-intellectualism ($\beta = 0.50$, $p < 0.01$). Whereas the likelihood that Tea Party–identifying Republicans hold the highest observed levels of anti-intellectual attitude endorsement is 21 percent, that number is just 14 percent for non-identifiers (a statistically significant difference of 6 percentage points across groups).

Taken together, the results from the GSS and CSPP studies provide evidence in favor of the view that the polarization of anti-intellectual attitude endorsement is a relatively recent phenomenon and one potentially attributable to the rise of the Tea Party. Most polarization in anti-intellectual attitude endorsement appears to occur in the post-Obama period (GSS), and GOP self-identifiers who also hold positive feelings toward the Tea Party tend to be significantly more likely than those who do not to harbor negative attitudes toward experts and intellectuals (CSPP).

Conclusion

Collectively, the results presented in this chapter suggest that anti-intellectual attitude endorsement is highly politically and socially contentious. In line with my theoretical expectations, self-identified Republicans are more likely to hold negative views toward scientists and experts. This, however, is primarily true *only* in recent years. I find similar—albeit substantively weaker—patterns for people who hold symbolically conservative ideological positions, regularly attend religious services, and (to a lesser degree) support limited-government intervention in people's lives. Panel data further document the robustness of these effects by showing that they are most likely not reverse causal.

Perhaps most importantly, the studies presented in this chapter show that anti-intellectual attitude endorsement became politically polarized following the election of Barack Obama. This finding is somewhat inconsistent with accounts positing polarization taking place in the late 1980s or that it increased gradually over time. Polarization in anti-intellectual attitude endorsement appears to be less of the result of a gradual process, or a reaction to the presidencies of Ronald Reagan and George Bush, and more likely due to an embrace of the Tea Party's anti-expert rhetoric following the presidency of Barack Obama.

On balance, then, the results presented in this chapter offer strong support for the *static inputs* portion of my theoretical model. They also advance our understanding of the degree to which the rise of the Tea Party had a negative effect on

140 ANTI-SCIENTIFIC AMERICANS

American political life and the polarization of attitudes that—in the not too recent past—were far less likely to be politically contentious.

I have yet to discuss, however, whether anti-intellectual attitude endorsement—which appears to fluctuate at both the macro (Chapter 4) and individual level (Chapter 5)—might be influenced by factors that are more likely to change over time.

This is an important test to carry out. If I can demonstrate that some more-mutable influences (e.g., what people know about science and interest in scientific topics) are associated with decreased anti-intellectual attitude endorsement, they may offer potential pathways for developing strategies to improve public faith in scientists and experts. In other words, educational interventions and strategic communication efforts aimed at moving (e.g., temporarily increasing science knowledge/interest) or stabilizing (e.g., promoting long-term gains in science knowledge/interest) the potential *dynamic* influences on anti-intellectual attitude endorsement could produce temporary or long-term declines in hostility toward scientists and experts.

To do this, of course, I must first document that anti-intellectualism is indeed subject to the dynamic influences I proposed in Chapter 2. I take up this possibility next in Chapter 6.

Anti-Scientific Americans: The Prevalence, Origins, and Political Consequences of Anti-Intellectualism in the US.
Matthew Motta, Oxford University Press. © Oxford University Press 2024. DOI: 10.1093/9780197788844.003.0005

6

Origin Story Part II: Change in Anti-Intellectual Attitude Endorsement

Americans' attitudes toward experts have become both socially and (especially) politically contentious in recent years. This is problematic for many reasons. Perhaps the most obvious consequence of the results presented in Chapter 5 is the possibility of social and political asymmetries in the extent to which Americans are willing to exhibit deference to scientists and other experts. If negative feelings toward experts in turn influence misinformation acceptance and opposition to policy-relevant science, they may help explain not only why it is so difficult to achieve consensus about the best way to combat pressing challenges related to the environment, public health, and other issues that might require the input of scientists and other experts, but also why we often disagree about the very nature of reality itself.

Another potential downside to the results presented in the previous chapter is the dynamic stability of the social and political factors that are responsible for division in the public's views of scientists and experts. For most Americans, partisan, ideological, and religious preferences are highly stable over time. Correspondingly, these attitudes tend to be highly resistant to change. It is therefore difficult to imagine a path whereby anti-intellectual attitude endorsement might become de-polarized. How, for example, might we be able to decouple the tight link between partisan identity and negativity toward scientists and experts?

There is, however, a potential solution to this pessimistic outlook. If I can identify factors that both (1) reduce anti-intellectual attitude endorsement and (2) are comparatively more likely to exhibit change over time than Americans' partisan and religious preferences, it may be possible to devise educational and communications-based interventions that engender positive feelings toward scientists and experts.

Chapter 2 described two individual differences that I think are particularly likely to satisfy both of the above conditions. Specifically, what people know about basic scientific facts (*science knowledge*) and people's levels of interest in scientific topics (*science interest*) both hold promise, at least in theory, as factors that could help mitigate anti-intellectual attitude endorsement. As I reviewed earlier, both factors have been associated with holding more positive views toward science.

Moreover, as documented in Table 5.1, both science knowledge and interest are comparatively more likely to exhibit change over time than Americans' less-mutable partisan identities and other socio-political commitments. Correspondingly, it could be the case that individual differences in knowledge and interest not only shape public views toward scientists but—given the link between views of the scientific community and "experts" more generally that I documented in Chapter 3—other types of experts as well.

However, before I can point to efforts to elevate science knowledge or stimulate science interest as potential ways to reduce anti-intellectual attitude endorsement—a task which I take on in more detail in Chapter 9—I must first resolve two areas of uncertainty in previous work. First, although it is clear that science knowledge and interest are associated with more positive views toward science *in general*, it is less clear whether each/both of these factors are associated with positive affect toward scientists *as people* (as opposed to, say, support for funding scientific research and support for other policies not directly related toward views of scientists). It could be the case, for example, that people who are knowledgeable about science are willing to accept scientific facts as true—as implied by their elevated understanding of basic scientific concepts—without necessarily translating those views into positive feelings toward scientists.

Second, few have attempted to determine whether the correlation between science knowledge/interest and positive views toward science might be reverse causal. It could be the case that both factors are influenced by anti-intellectual attitude endorsement, without themselves generating more positive feelings toward scientists and experts. Evidence of reverse causality would correspondingly imply that efforts to stimulate science interest or increase science knowledge may have little impact on anti-intellectual attitude endorsement, as anti-intellectualism would instead play a role in shaping what it is that people know or care to know about science.

In this chapter, I offer new answers to both of these unanswered questions. I begin by outlining an analytical strategy by which I can test the within-person predictions of the affect-based theoretical model outlined in Chapter 2, as well as its corresponding data and measures. Given the time-varying nature of my theoretical expectations, I primarily make use of panel data throughout this chapter.

I then build an empirical case suggesting that people who become more interested in scientific topics over time tend to also become more likely to also hold positive feelings toward scientific experts. I further find that these effects are not reverse causal. Interestingly, and consistent with research casting some amount of doubt on the benefits of science knowledge with respect to pro-science views, I find that people who come to learn more about basic scientific facts over time are neither more nor less likely to hold positive views toward the scientific community.

Finally, I offer a series of exploratory analyses that investigate whether the effects of science interest might be enhanced among Americans currently in the process of completing a college education. The process of completing a college degree represents a period of exposure to new people and ideas, including those related to science and scientific research. Correspondingly, the college experience not only may strengthen both science knowledge and interest but also may provide people with the opportunity to better *connect* their knowledge and curiosity to feelings toward individuals who produce scientific research (e.g., by attending lectures from scientific researchers, befriending peers who study science-related issues, or by enrolling in science-related courses themselves). I conclude by providing evidence that the link between science interest and positive feelings toward scientific experts is at least temporarily elevated for people currently enrolled in college.

Analytical Strategy

The primary statistical tools that I use to test for the effects of science knowledge and interest on anti-intellectual attitude endorsement are a series of fixed-effects regression models. As a reminder, I described the technical details and assumptions underlying this modeling approach in Chapter 3.

Briefly, fixed-effects models calculate the extent to which time-varying factors—like science knowledge and interest (see Table 5.1)—are associated with *within-person change* in another time-varying outcome variable (in this case, anti-intellectual attitude endorsement). Because these models estimate within-person change, the effects I observe are unlikely to be influenced by unobserved differences *between* survey respondents. Fixed-effects models are therefore a powerful and highly statistically conservative way to test for the effects of science knowledge and interest on anti-intellectual attitude endorsement. To further guard against the possibility of detecting spurious effects, I include time-varying estimates of each of the socio-political factors studied in Chapter 5 (i.e., partisan identification, symbolic ideology, limited-government attitudes, and religiosity) in the fixed-effects models.

Despite this advantage, however, fixed-effects models do not necessarily rule out the possibility of reverse causality. In other words, they cannot determine whether anti-intellectualism might also shape the extent to which people are knowledgeable about and/or interested in scientific topics. Consequently, I use the cross-lagged modeling approach that I described in Chapter 3, and employed in Chapter 5, to ensure that neither interest nor knowledge is itself the product of change in anti-intellectual attitude endorsement.

Finally, while the theoretical expectations I outlined in Chapter 2 are general in scope—in that I expect them to apply to the entire adult population—I nevertheless consider the possibility that they might be stronger in application for some groups in society relative to others. For example, as I alluded to earlier in this chapter, it could be the case that post-secondary educational experiences may represent a key moment in exposure to science-related information. Consequently, the effects of knowledge/interest may be heightened among respondents enrolled in colleges and universities throughout the duration of the panel studies I rely on in this book.

I test this possibility by constructing fixed-effects models that *subset* the longitudinal data into three sub-populations: (1) people who completed a college degree prior to enrolling in the General Social Survey (GSS) study, (2) people who completed a college degree throughout their time enrolled in each panel study—measured via change in degree attainment throughout the panel (as none of the panel studies directly ask questions about whether people are currently enrolled in college), and (3) all remaining panelists. I then compare whether the magnitude of the fixed effect is substantively/statistically stronger in the *current enrollees* sub-population in comparison to the latter.

Data and Measures

Given the time-varying nature of my theoretical expectations, I again rely on panel data when testing whether science knowledge/interest are associated with within-person change in anti-intellectual attitude endorsement. Because both factors are not measured in the Center for the Study of Political Psychology (CSPP) panel, I limit my analytical focus to just the three (pooled) GSS panel studies.

I measure science knowledge using a series of eleven questions originally developed by Jon Miller (Miller, 1998) and featured in the National Science Board's regular Science & Engineering Indicators report (National Science Board, 2018). These items ask respondents to answer questions about basic scientific facts such as whether antibiotics kill viruses as well as bacteria (they do not), if the earth has a hot core (it does), or if electrons are smaller than atoms (they are subatomic particles). Most questions are administered as binary choice (i.e., true/false) items, with the exception of one question pertaining to how long it takes the earth to orbit the sun (one year), which featured three discrete response options. All questions and their available responses are provided in the appendix. I score responses to each question as correct if respondents offer an accurate answer and as incorrect if they either offer an incorrect answer or fail to give a substantive response. You can find additional information about the science-knowledge scale in the appendix.

Next, I measure science interest using a series of three questions that asked respondents to report their interest in (1) new scientific discoveries, (2) technologies, and (3) space exploration. Respondents could reply that they were either very interested, moderately interested, or not at all interested in those topics. I averaged responses into an intervalized scale—scored such that higher values indicate higher levels of interest and recoded to range from 0 to 1—pursuant with a procedure I have used to measure science interest using the same data in previous research (Motta, 2018b).

All other variables included in the models, including the anti-intellectualism outcome variable, are identical to those measures I relied on in Chapter 5 and are again scored to range from 0 to 1.

Results

Figure 6.1 offers the most straightforward test of the effects of science knowledge and interest on anti-intellectual attitude endorsement. There I present the results of a fixed-effects panel regression model regressing change in anti-intellectual attitude endorsement on change in science knowledge, interest, and all other controls discussed previously. Parameter estimates are presented as black circles, with 95 percent confidence intervals extending out from each one (again, with 90 percent and 68 percent confidence intervals overlaid). Circles falling to the left of the dashed zero line, and whose confidence intervals do not intersect with it, have a negative and statistically significant effect on anti-intellectual attitude endorsement.

The figure suggests that just one input into the model—gains in science interest over time—is both negatively and significantly associated with anti-intellectual attitude endorsement ($\beta = -0.13, < 0.01$). Because all variables are keyed to range from 0 to 1 in a linear model framework, the parameter estimate for science interest can be interpreted as the percentage point change in anti-intellectual attitude endorsement—i.e., a 13 percentage point decline—for those who become the most interested in science over time, compared to those who become the most disinterested over the duration of the panel. Correspondingly, linear predictions derived from this model suggest that whereas predicted scores on the anti-intellectualism scale are 0.40 for people who become highly disinterested over time, that same quantity is just 0.27 for people becoming highly interested over time.

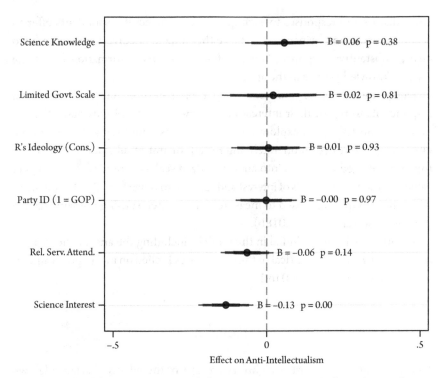

Figure 6.1 The Effect of Science Knowledge & Interest on Anti-Intellectual Attitude Endorsement

Interestingly, I find no statistically discernible effect of gains in science knowledge on anti-intellectual attitude endorsement. As discussed in Chapter 2, several recent studies have noted some amount of both conceptual and empirical ambiguity with respect to the relationship between the knowledge of scientific facts and positive views toward science. Consequently, the findings presented in Figure 6.1 are consistent with the broader pattern of results emerging from past research.

Some, however, might raise concerns that the effects of science knowledge are "crowded out" by the inclusion of other time-varying factors in the model (i.e., the political and social controls listed in the figure). Additionally, some might also note the possibility of conceptual overlap between science knowledge and interest—e.g., due to the possibility that knowledge may be a necessary precondition for interest in scientific topics or that interest facilitates gains in knowledge—which might further raise the possibility of crowding out the effects of science interest.

Consequently, I address this possibility by re-estimating a model that includes science knowledge (alone) as an independent variable and drops all other potential predictors. Even in this highly favorable case, I again observe no statistically discernible effects of change in science knowledge on anti-intellectual attitude endorsement ($\beta = 0.09$, $p = 0.15$).

Finally, and consistent with the idea that partisan identity, political ideology, limited-government attitudes, and religiosity are better suited to explain change *between* people with respect to anti-intellectual attitude endorsement (Chapter 5) than they are to explain individual-level change, I find no time-varying effect of any of these factors on within-subject change in anti-intellectual attitude endorsement.

Reverse Causality Assessment

While the above analyses document an association between increased science interest over time and decreased anti-intellectual attitude endorsement, it is important to also demonstrate that these effects are not reverse causal. Some might argue that people may become more likely to express an interest in science over time if they come to hold more positive views toward scientists. For example, someone exposed to science documentaries and television programs that feature charismatic "science popularizers" may become more likely to take an interest in scientific topics. Of course, this conceptual alternative is muddied to some degree by the possibility that—in high-choice media environments (Prior, 2007)—people who are not interested in science may never seek out this type of programming. Nevertheless, this reverse causal account would call into question whether science interest actually influences anti-intellectual attitude endorsement (as the effects could flow in the opposite direction) and cast doubt on the effectiveness of efforts to elevate science interest as a means by which to improve trust in scientists and experts (as discussed in more detail in Chapter 9).

I test the possibility that the effects detected in this chapter may function in reverse by using the now-familiar cross-lagged regression modeling techniques first described in Chapter 3 and then implemented in Chapter 5. The results are presented in Table 6.1.

Table 6.1 **Reverse Causality Test Summary**

Test	β	p	Supported?
AI ← Science Knowledge	−0.16	< 0.05	Y
AI ← Science Interest	−0.10	< 0.05	Y
AI → Science Knowledge	0.02	n.s.	Y
AI → Science Interest	−0.01	n.s.	Y

Note: OLS coefficients presented from cross-lagged regression models. Please refer to Chapter 5 for additional information about how to interpret results from these models.

Table 6.1 presents strong support for my theoretical expectations. First, as the table's bottom two rows demonstrate, past levels of anti-intellectual attitude endorsement have no statistically discernible effect on current levels of science knowledge or interest—controlling for past levels of science knowledge and interest (p = n.s. in both cases). This casts doubt on the possibility that anti-intellectual attitudes influence individuals' knowledge about or interest in science.

The table also recovers the pattern of effects documented in the fixed-effects models. Past levels of science interest have a negative and statistically significant (β = −0.16, p < 0.05) effect on current anti-intellectual attitude endorsement—controlling for past anti-intellectual attitude endorsement (row 1). Surprisingly, given the pattern of effects documented in Figure 6.1, the same is true of science knowledge as well (β = −0.10, p < 0.05; row 2), albeit to a lesser degree.

The difference in results for science knowledge between Figure 6.1 and Table 6.1 may have to do with a fairly technical difference between fixed-effect (Figure 6.1) and cross-lagged (Table 6.1) regression models. Whereas the former offers a highly conservative test of within-person change—and correspondingly negates the possibility that unobserved differences between subjects might explain away the effects we observe—the same is not necessarily true of cross-lagged panel models, which (as described in Chapter 3) make use of repeated cross-sectional data. Correspondingly, unobserved influences cannot be treated as completely "ignorable" in cross-lagged models (Kearney, 2017).

This means that the effect of science knowledge on anti-intellectual attitude endorsement is, at best, empirically murky. The pattern of effects documented in Table 6.1 may be spurious due to omitted variable bias, or modeling misspecification. What is more important, however, is that I (1) find no evidence of a reverse causal effect for either science knowledge or interest and (2) I recover the anticipated pattern of effects for the lone significant within-subject influence on anti-intellectual attitude endorsement (science interest). Collectively, these results imply that increased science interest has a strong effect on decreased anti-intellectual attitude endorsement and that this pattern of effects is unlikely to function in reverse.

Exploring the Effects of Expert Contact in Higher-Educational Settings

Finally, as noted earlier in this chapter, higher-educational experiences may represent a key moment in many Americans' exposure to engaging with scientific topics and with information about the basic workings of science and the scientific method. It may also represent an opportunity for people to indulge their curiosity about scientific topics through the courses they take, conversations they have with peers, and other college/university events they might choose to attend (or in which they might otherwise be exposed even if disinterested in scientific topics, such as a "general education" science course). Indeed, although

Origin Story Part II: Change in Anti-Intellectual Attitude Endorsement 149

testing for a relationship between educational attainment and anti-intellectual attitude endorsement was not my primary goal in Chapter 5, I present evidence in the appendix materials showing that people who have earned a college degree tend to be less likely to hold anti-intellectual attitudes throughout most of the GSS time series, as well as the contemporary American National Election Study (ANES), Center for the Study of Political Psychology (CSPP), and SciPol studies.

Correspondingly, college may offer individuals an opportunity to align their interest in science with their attitudes toward those involved in scientific research. This could potentially imply that the effects of science interest on anti-intellectual attitude endorsement are more pronounced during this time.

Table 6.2 tests this possibility by re-estimating the models summarized in Figure 6.1 and restricting analysis to three GSS three subsamples: (1) people who were in college at the time of the study, and—for reference—(2) those who have never attended college, and (3) those who earned a college degree prior to participating in each GSS study. The former group is, necessarily, also the smallest (N = 219, or about 10 percent of the N = 2,203 panelists included in this study). This provides me with comparatively low statistical power to detect an effect of change in science interest on anti-intellectual attitude endorsement.

Despite subsample size limitations, however, I nevertheless detect a negative and statistically significant relationship between increased science interest and anti-intellectual attitude endorsement among GSS panelists currently receiving a college education. I find this to be the case across the remaining two subsamples as well, and I detect no evidence of an effect of science knowledge on anti-intellectual attitude endorsement.

For non-college-educated people and past bachelor degree earners, the effects of science interest are relatively similar in substantive magnitude. In each case, moving from the minimum to maximum value is associated with a 16 and 15 percentage point decline, respectively (Non-College: $\beta = -0.16$; Bachelor Earners: $\beta = -0.15$). However, for individuals currently attending college, the effects are substantially more pronounced. In the final row in Table 6.2, I find that increases in science interest among current college students are associated with over a 40 percentage point decline—from a predicted score on the anti-intellectualism scale of 0.56 at low levels of curiosity to just 0.15 at high levels of curiosity—in anti-intellectual attitude endorsement ($\beta = -0.41$, p < 0.05).

This effect is nearly three times the substantive size of those for non-college-educated people and individuals who already have college degrees. However, given the subsample's comparatively small size, I caution that effects are highly variable [95 percent CI: −0.76, −0.07]. Unsurprisingly, they are therefore not statistically differentiable from those of individuals who earned a college degree in the past [95 percent CI: −0.30, −0.03] or those who have never attended college [95 percent CI: −0.22, −0.08].

Table 6.2 **The Effect of Science Knowledge and Interest on Anti-Intellectual Attitude Endorsement, by College Completion Status (GSS Panel Studies)**

	$\beta_{Sci.Interest}$	p	$\beta_{Sci.Knowledge}$	p
Not College Grads	−0.15	< 0.01	0.09	0.12
College Grads	−0.16	0.02	−0.09	0.46
Current College Enrollees	−0.41	0.02	0.25	0.25

Note: Fixed-effect linear model coefficients presented. Because the subsamples featured in these models are comparatively smaller than those presented in Figure 6.1, and therefore have less statistical power to detect effects, I omit controls for change in partisan identification, ideology, limited-government attitudes, and religiosity. It is also important to note that none of the controls provided in Figure 6.1 were found to exert a significant influence on change in anti-intellectual attitude endorsement, which further underscores their suitability to be omitted from analysis. Note also that because all variables are keyed to range from 0 to 1 in a linear modeling framework, parameter estimates can be interpreted as the percentage point change in anti-intellectual attitude endorsement moving from the minimum to maximum value of each covariate in the model. Please see the main text for supplemental values (linear predictions) that further explicate the substantive magnitude of these effects. Full model output can be found in the appendix.

Still, the results provide preliminary support for the idea that higher-educational experiences represent a period in which Americans more strongly connect their interest in scientific topics to their views toward scientific professionals. These effects may be short-lived, however, as the effects of interest among past degree earners appear no different from those of people who have never earned a college degree. More generally, though, the results provide strong evidence that science interest has both powerful and crosscutting effects on anti-intellectual attitude endorsement, both in the general population and across educational subgroups.

Conclusion

The results presented in this chapter suggest that people who exhibit a greater interest in science over time tend to also become more likely to hold positive views toward scientists. These effects are especially pronounced for people currently enrolled in college and do not appear to be reverse causal. I also document little influence of gains in knowledge about science with respect to decreased anti-intellectual attitude endorsement.

Of course, it is important to caveat that I was able to test these time-varying expectations only in the GSS, which includes just the "trust in scientists" measure of anti-intellectual attitude endorsement. Although this measure is both highly correlated with views toward experts more generally and tends to exhibit similar levels of predictive validity (as demonstrated in Chapter 3), it could nevertheless be the case that interest in scientific topics may be more strongly associated with views toward the scientific community—which are more directly related to the subject of individuals' interests—than it is toward other types of experts. As I discuss in Chapter 9, additional efforts to explore (1) the effect of science interest on attitudes toward other types of experts and (2) how interest in other technical subjects might influence anti-intellectual attitude endorsement are therefore worthwhile endeavors for future research.

This important caveat aside, I believe that the findings presented in this chapter could have important implications for how science communicators and educators might attempt to address negative feelings toward the scientific community. As documented in Chapter 5, interest in scientific topics is malleable. When science interest increases, it tends to have a positive influence on how Americans view scientific experts.

Correspondingly, as I discuss in more detail in Chapter 9, efforts to boost science interest (especially in young adulthood) may prove effective at engendering support for the scientific community. In contrast, efforts aimed at attempting to increase knowledge about basic scientific facts—which past research suggests are a prevalent science communication priority among members of the scientific community (Besley & Tanner, 2011; Besley et al., 2016)—may be comparatively less effective at doing the same.

By increasing positive feelings toward the scientific community and other experts, efforts to increase science interest could serve as the basis for a communications strategy aimed at (ultimately) boosting support for evidenced based public policy. Of course, this hinges on documenting that positive views toward scientists are indeed associated with support for policies informed by scientific research and expert opinion. I spend the remainder of this book assessing how it is that anti-intellectualism shapes and is shaped by Americans' policy preferences.

Anti-Scientific Americans: The Prevalence, Origins, and Political Consequences of Anti-Intellectualism in the US.
Matthew Motta, Oxford University Press. © Oxford University Press 2024. DOI: 10.1093/9780197788844.003.0006

7

The Bidirectionality Thesis: Hofstadter's Forgotten Prediction

The possibility that anti-intellectualism and opposition to the role that experts play in the policymaking process might be mutually reinforcing was essential to Hofstadter's understanding of anti-intellectualism and its pernicious impact on American public life. As I discussed in Chapter 2, Hofstadter believed that negative attitudes toward scientists and experts had the potential to undercut their social and policy influence. At the same time, however, Hofstadter saw experts' influence over both government decisions and in Americans' increasingly complex daily lives more generally as facilitating negativity toward those who could credibly make claims to superior knowledge about complex, politically relevant issues.

Hofstadter, in other words, theorized that experts' policy influence and negative feelings toward that group are two mutually reinforcing phenomena. Americans' collective dependence on experts facilitates negativity, which in turn drives efforts to reduce experts' influence in daily life. Whether Hofstadter's theoretical expectations are borne out empirically, however, is an open question.

As I reviewed in Chapter 2, studies of the relationship between anti-intellectualism and support for evidence-based policies, as well as the role that experts play in the policymaking process itself, are typically one-directional. Often scholars (myself included) have assumed that anti-intellectualism shapes policy orientations and that those effects do not function in reverse (Motta, 2018a; Merkley, 2020; Callaghan et al., 2021; Motta et al., 2021). The precious few studies that do assess the possibility of a reverse causal relationship are, necessarily, limited in policy focus (Merkley & Loewen, 2021).

In this chapter, I offer a series of tests devised to assess the plausibility of what I described earlier as the Bidirectionality Thesis. As I discuss shortly, these tests are quite general with respect to their policy focus. This enables me to offer a conceptually expansive assessment of the theory's plausibility.

Before doing so, however, it is important to point out that although the possibility of bidirectionality has received limited attention in previous work, we can nevertheless spot glimpses of its relevance to contemporary American politics.

Comments, for example, from Republican governor of Florida Ron DeSantis about Dr. Anthony Fauci (chief medical advisor to the Biden administration) regarding his involvement in the COVID-19 pandemic exemplify the bidirectional nature of anti-intellectualism and aversion to the role that experts play in the policymaking process.

Even before the onset of the pandemic, DeSantis had a somewhat contentious relationship with scientific experts. For example, shortly after winning election to the governor's office in 2019, DeSantis made headlines for refusing to answer questions about whether he agrees with climate scientists about the likelihood the climate change is caused by human activities (Gross, 2019). Although DeSantis appointed the state's first chief science officer—who was tasked with, among other objectives, proposing and developing evidence-based environmental policies (Sun Sentinel Editorial Board, 2019)—the officer played only a modest role in shaping the state's environmental policy decisions. Ultimately, the director resigned the post midway through DeSantis' term (Bruggers & Green, 2021).

DeSantis' conflictual relationship with scientific experts became increasingly contentious throughout the COVID-19 pandemic. DeSantis, for example, often questioned what he deemed to be Dr. Fauci's political and self-serving motives. Taking pride in Florida's decision to choose "freedom over Fauci-ism" (Stone, 2021)—a reference to the state's willingness to prematurely break with CDC guidelines regarding the enforcement mask wearing and physical distancing recommendations—DeSantis attacked Fauci's public-facing role as a communicator of the Biden administration's public health recommendations.

At the heart of DeSantis' concerns was the highly prominent role that Dr. Fauci played in the process of formulating and communicating public health advice from the federal government. Speaking about the number of interviews that Fauci does with the popular press—which DeSantis described as being "about himself and his own image"—the governor expressed concern that "to elevate anybody [i.e., Fauci] like that is problematic." DeSantis went so far as to question whether Fauci may have played a role in the supposed lab leak of the COVID-19 virus from a lab in Wuhan, China (Gancarski, 2021)—a theory alleging that Dr. Fauci supported gain-of-function research that could result in the virus' spread to serve his own material interests.

Although DeSantis did not levy these conspiratorial allegations outright, those who hold similar views have ascribed several potential objectives to

Dr. Fauci for allegedly facilitating or initiating the spread of a deadly global pandemic. These include gaining public notoriety, advancing his alleged political ambitions, or even profiting from life-saving vaccine technology that could slow or stop the spread of the virus (Enserink & Cohen, 2020; Kim, 2021). Notably, Fauci is listed on a Department of Health and Human Services patent for HIV vaccine technology, which some conspiracy theorists cite as evidence of the possibility that he is working to either develop a vaccine for COVID-19 or spread the virus further (Funke, 2020).

At the same time, DeSantis's distrust of scientific experts and displeasure with the role that they play in the policymaking process also helped formulate his administration's response to the COVID-19 pandemic in Florida. DeSantis, for example, chose to assemble a team of pandemic advisors that included pseudoscientific personalities like Dr. Scott Atlas (Fleshler, 2021), a Stanford radiologist (and a former Trump administration advisor) with no experience in infectious disease research, who claimed that herd-immunity thresholds were just a fraction of what leading health experts projected (Rummler, 2020), advocated in favor of easing public health guidelines in order to (ironic, given the fears about Fauci noted earlier) facilitate viral spread (Romo, 2020), and even encouraged Michigan residents to "rise up" in opposition to health policies that limited interaction in public spaces (which coincided with a foiled plot to kidnap Governor Gretchen Whitmer and mount an armed insurrection on the state capitol; Bogel-Burroughs, Dawn, & Gray, 2020).

Taken together, DeSantis's denigration of Dr. Fauci as a person and his aversion to the role that Fauci played in the policymaking process highlight the mutually reinforcing nature of anti-intellectualism and aversion to expert policy influence. The governor's views of Fauci as self-serving seemingly helped to motivate his decisions to break with CDC guidelines, consult non-expert authorities, and object to the influence that Fauci ought to have in the process of formulating and communicating sound policy. At the same time, disapproval of Fauci's elevated role in the policymaking process helped motivate accusations of conspiratorial intent (i.e., that Fauci could further his own self-promotional and material interests by supporting risky viral research that could facilitate a global pandemic).

The DeSantis example is, of course, just one case. It lends some anecdotal plausibility to Hofstadter's bidirectional predictions. Yet it is unclear whether anti-intellectualism and aversion to the role that experts play in the policymaking process are indeed mutually reinforcing for the American public more generally. In what follows, I offer a series of tests designed to assess this possibility and present new longitudinal evidence that anti-intellectualism and expert policy role aversions are, indeed, co-constitutive.

Testing the Bidirectionality Thesis

Given the time-varying nature of the Bidirectionality Thesis, I again make use of panel data when testing my theoretical expectations. I do this using two now-familiar inferential approaches: fixed effects and cross-lagged panel regression modeling.

First, I provide results from two sets of fixed effects models: one regressing anti-intellectualism on preferences about the role that experts play in the policymaking process (plus all time-varying controls included in the fixed effect models presented in Chapter 6) and one doing the reverse. The first set of models enables me to determine whether people who experience change in *either* anti-intellectualism or expert policy role opposition become more likely to hold negative views toward the role that experts play in the policymaking process (in one set of models). The second set of models allows me to determine whether increased opposition to the role that experts play in the policymaking process might be associated with increased anti-intellectualism. If the Bidirectionality Thesis holds empirical muster, it should be the case that both anti-intellectualism and expert policy orientations are associated with within-person change in one another.

I further probe the bidirectionality of the relationship between anti-intellectualism and expert policy role preferences using cross-lagged regression modeling. This approach has the benefit of enabling me to test whether the co-constitutive effects I expect to observe might be stronger between two time periods (e.g., a *short-run* effect between Waves 1 and 2 in the GSS data) or across longer time intervals (e.g., between Waves 1 and 3 in the GSS).

Another important benefit of the cross-lagged approach has to do with a quirk in the GSS of measuring Americans' preferences regarding experts' role in the policymaking process. As I discuss in more technical detail in this chapter, measuring expert policy role orientations across the GSS panel studies is no easy task. These challenges make it particularly important to test for potential temporal asymmetries.

Specifically, as I discuss in more detail shortly, I measure expert policy role orientations using the same sets of items and latent variable scaling procedures across all study waves. However, missing data patterns—featured as part of the GSS instrumentation design—imply that some respondents answered subsets of the full item list more often than others throughout the duration of the panel. Correspondingly, testing for periodic effects via cross-lagged modeling helps me further ensure that differences observed across time are not merely the result of changes in measurement (i.e., missing data) resulting from the studies' longitudinal designs.

Data and Measures

Data

Data used to test the Bidirectionality Thesis come from the pooled GSS panel surveys (see Chapter 3 for additional information). As the GSS panels contain both a measure of anti-intellectualism and a series of items that I could use to build an indicator of expert policy role orientations (which I describe in detail in this chapter), the study is ideal for testing this often-neglected prediction from Hofstadter's work. Unfortunately, while the CSPP panel study contained a time-varying measure of anti-intellectual attitude endorsement, it did not feature time-varying items pertaining to opinions about experts' role in the policymaking process. I therefore limit analysis to just the GSS panel.

Measuring General Expert Policy Role Orientations

Measuring Americans' general preferences regarding the role that scientists and other experts play in the policymaking process is essential to testing the bidirectionality thesis. Fortunately, the GSS panel studies inquire about public support for funding scientific research and preferences regarding the influence of various experts in policy decisions. These experts include climate scientists, medical doctors, and economists, who play pivotal roles in policy matters aligned with their expertise, such as environmental policy, stem cell research, and unemployment, respectively. A full list of questions used to build the expert policy role (EPR) scale and their availability across panel waves can be found in Table 7.1.

Table 7.1 **Summary of Items Included in the EPR Scale**

Question	Availability
General Science Funding. Even if it brings no immediate benefits, scientific research that advances the frontiers of knowledge is necessary and should be supported by the federal government. [1] Strongly agree [2] Agree [3] Disagree [4] Strongly disagree	2006 (B, C) 2008 (All) 2010 (A, C) 2012 (B, C) 2014 (B, C)

Question	Availability
Science Research Funding. Are we spending too much, too little, or about the right amount on supporting scientific research? [1] Too little [2] About right [3] Too much	All waves and panels
Best Interests. When making policy recommendations about global warming, on a scale of 1 to 5, to what extent do you think the following groups would support what is best for the country as a whole versus what serves their own narrow interests? Item A. Environmental scientists Item B. Economists Item C. Medical researchers	2006 (B, C) 2010 (A, C)
Policy Influence: Environmental Scientists. How much influence should each of the following groups have in deciding what to do about global warming? [Environmental Scientists] [1] A great deal of influence [2] A fair amount of influence [3] A little influence [4] None at all	2006 (B, C) 2010 (A, C)
Policy Influence: Medical Researchers. How much influence should each of the following groups have in deciding about government funding for stem cell research? [Medical Researchers] [1] A great deal of influence [2] A fair amount of influence [3] A little influence [4] None at all	2006 (B, C) 2010 (A, C)
Policy Influence: Economists. How much influence should each of the following groups have in deciding whether to reduce federal income taxes? [Economists] [1] A great deal of influence [2] A fair amount of influence [3] A little influence [4] None at all	2006 (B, C) 2010 (A, C)

I measure Americans' general preferences regarding the role that experts play in the policymaking process (hereafter EPR) by combining responses to each question listed in Table 7.1 into a single scale. I do this using a technique known as graded response modeling (GRM). GRM is an application of item response theory (IRT) suitable for data measured at the ordinal level. I scored the resulting scale to range from 0 to 1, such that a score of 1 denotes expressing strong opposition to the role that experts ought to play in the policymaking process.

Although I provide a more detailed summary of how GRM works in the appendix, I want to briefly summarize this procedure and explain why it is advantageous for measuring EPR orientations. GRM operates by assessing how respondents' scores at each level of the variables input into the model—i.e., the different response options corresponding with the questions listed in Table 1— influence placement on a latent scale measuring EPR preferences. Measuring EPR orientations via GRM is therefore advantageous for two reasons.

First, GRM estimates placement on the latent scale separately for respondents who select each option across items. Technically, it does this by including multiple parameter estimates in the model for each question, as opposed to one single estimate. Consequently, this technique does not need to assume that all variables are measured using the same response options, as we might otherwise assume if combining responses together via, for example, a simple averaging process.

Additionally, and in contrast to methods that simply average across constituent scale items, GRM does not make the often conceptually untenable assumption that each question included in the model is equally influential in determining respondents' placement on the latent scale (Treier & Jackman, 2008; Treier & Hillygus, 2009). This is especially advantageous for measuring EPR attitudes because some of the questions included in Table 7.1 may be more conceptually related to the latent concept I am trying to measure than others. For example, the *expert influence* questions may be better conceptual indicators of Americans' preferred role that experts play in the policymaking process than questions about science funding.

Moreover, the GRM model is well suited to address an important limitation of the GSS data. As I've noted in previous chapters, the GSS administers dozens of modules about a variety of socially relevant topics. To avoid overburdening respondents, and thus prevent panel attrition, the GSS randomly assigns each respondent to complete some modules but not others. Collections of models randomly presented to some respondents (and not others) are known as *ballots*. Each GSS panel study assigned respondents to receive one of three ballots (A, B, and C), which were held constant throughout the duration of each panel.

Unfortunately, these procedures imply that most respondents saw only a subset of the items presented in Table 7.1. While one question (the second question listed in the table) was administered to all respondents throughout the study, the remainder were administered on a more-infrequent basis. For example, in the 2006 panel, only respondents assigned to ballots B and C had the opportunity to answer any of the *influence* items. No respondents were administered those items in 2008, and those respondents assigned to ballots A and C were given the opportunity to answer those questions in 2010. This somewhat-complicated setup implies that one-third (ballot C) of 2006 GSS panelists were administered these items at more than one point in time, while one-third of 2006 panelists answered those questions for the first time in 2010.

Fortunately, the GRM procedure is able to estimate respondents' placement on the latent expert policy orientations scale as long as they answered at least one of the questions summarized in the table. However, we might have reason to doubt the scale's ability to capture the underlying EPR concept if, for most people, scores on the latent scale are based on responses to just a single question across waves. We might further expect the distribution of the latent variable to systematically differ across waves based on item availability.

Figure 7.1 assesses that possibility. While it is too onerous to visualize the (many) different missing data patterns respondents could experience across items and waves, it is at least possible to convey the total number of respondents who had one or more substantive responses recorded in the process used to generate the resulting EPR scale (see the top row in Figure 7.1) and the distribution of scale points from the EPR scale across waves (see the bottom row in Figure 7.1).

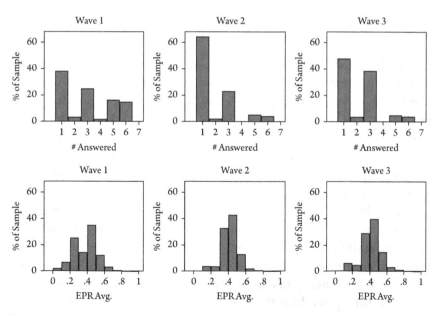

Figure 7.1 Missing Data Assessment and Distributional Summary for EPR Index.

Figure 7.1 suggests that in both Waves 1 and 3 across the pooled GSS panel studies scores on the latent EPR orientation scale are based on more than one substantive response for a majority of respondents. This, however, is not the case in Wave 2, where a slight majority contribute just one substantive response to their placement on the latent scale. Importantly, however, the histograms provided in the bottom half of the figure suggest that the distribution of EPR attitudes are highly similar across panel waves, even in Wave 2, where comparatively fewer respondents' positioning was determined by two or more items. Of course, high rates of missing data across items are certainly not ideal. Still, the results presented in Figure 7.1 suggest that the EPR scale is at least based on multiple-item responses for a majority of respondents in Waves 1 and 3. Moreover, while missing data rates are comparatively higher in Wave 2, little evidence suggests that the resulting EPR scale has a systematically different response distribution than in waves where comparatively more responses are available across items. Nevertheless, these differences underscore the importance of documenting similar effects across different combinations of panel waves, a task I take up later in this chapter.

Collectively, the results presented thus far suggest that the EPR scale appears to be both conceptually appropriate and methodologically sufficient for assessing public attitudes toward the role that experts play in the policymaking process. With that in mind, I next report the results of a series of tests designed to test Hofstadter's often-overlooked theoretical predictions.

Results

First I offer an initial pass at testing the Bidirectionality Thesis by assessing the effects of anti-intellectualism on EPR opposition and vice versa using fixed effect panel regression modeling. Figure 7.2 plots the results of these models as linear predictions—i.e., the predicted value of the policy role opposition scale across levels of anti-intellectualism (leftmost panel) and the predicted score on the anti-intellectualism indicator across the policy role opposition scale. Ninety-five percent confidence intervals extend out from each one. Full model output is available in the appendix.

The results provide strong evidence in favor of the bidirectional relationship between anti-intellectual attitude endorsement and opposition to the role that experts play in the policymaking process (EPR). Turning first to the leftmost panel, I find that people who become more likely to hold anti-intellectual views over time are positively and significantly more likely to express increased opposition to the role that experts play in the policymaking process ($\beta = 0.05$, $p < 0.05$). The

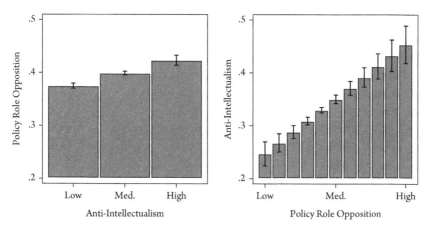

Figure 7.2 The Co-Constitutive Effects of Change Anti-Intellectualism and Science Policy Opposition, (Panel Fixed Effects; Pooled GSS Panel Data)

linear predictions presented in Figure 7.2 suggest that whereas the predicted value of the policy role opposition scale is just 0.37 for those expressing the highest levels of trust in the scientific community, that quantity increases to 0.42 for people expressing the highest levels of distrust (a 5 percentage point increase).

I find an analogous relationship when considering change in EPR opposition (the rightmost panel in Figure 7.2). People who come to hold more negative views toward the role that experts play in the policymaking process are again positively and significantly more likely to embrace anti-intellectual sentiments ($\beta = 0.21$, $p < 0.05$). Whereas predicted scores on the three-point anti-intellectualism scale (which, recall, is scored to range from 0 to 1) are just under 0.25 for people scoring lowest on the EPR measure, that quantity increases to 0.45 for those scoring highest (an approximately 21 percentage point increase).

Before moving on, the careful reader might note something of an asymmetry in the supposed bidirectionality of the relationships studied in this chapter. Specifically, the effects of policy role opposition appear to be larger when anti-intellectualism is the outcome variable compared to when it is treated as an independent variable.

I want to strongly caution readers *against* interpreting this as evidence that anti-intellectualism plays less of a role in shaping policy orientations than policy orientations do in shaping anti-intellectual attitude endorsement. It is important to remember that due to data limitations the EPR scale is a multi-item index with many scale points, whereas the anti-intellectualism item is a single trichotomous measure. The EPR scale therefore gives me greater opportunity to observe incremental attitudinal change than does the three-point anti-intellectualism item.

It may therefore be somewhat easier to observe change in the former (compared to the latter) over time, implying that differences in item construction may thus enhance the EPR scale's explanatory power.

Consequently, any evidence suggesting that the directionality of the relationship between anti-intellectualism and EPR preferences might be stronger in one direction than another should be treated as *highly preliminary* and potentially the result of a fairly arcane methodological artifact. Therefore, these differences, while worth documenting here and potentially exploring in future research, do not necessarily imply an asymmetry in the bidirectionality of the relationship between anti-intellectualism and EPR orientations.

Next I provide an alternate test of the Bidirectionality Thesis using cross-lagged regression models. Recall that a benefit of these tests is that they allow me to detect whether differences in the measurement of EPR preferences over time might lead to asymmetric temporal effects between survey waves. The results are presented in Table 7.1.

The table again provides strong support for the Bidirectionality Thesis. As I noted in Figure 7.1., I again find that lagged anti-intellectualism is positively and significantly associated with increased opposition to the role that experts play in the policymaking process between Wave 1 and both Waves 2 and 3 (in both cases, $\beta = 0.05$, $p < 0.05$). As all variables are scored to range from 0 to 1, these results imply that movement from the minimum to maximum value on the anti-intellectualism indicator is associated with a 5 percentage point increase in expert policy role opposition.

Furthermore, I again find an analogous pattern to the results reported in Figure 7.1 regarding the influence of EPR orientations on anti-intellectualism. Across both Waves 2 ($\beta = 0.15$, $p < 0.05$) and 3 ($\beta = 0.17$, $p < 0.05$), I find that EPR views are positively and significantly associated with increased anti-intellectualism. The results suggest that opposition to the role that experts play in the policymaking process is associated with between a 15 and 17 percentage point increase in anti-intellectual attitude acceptance.

Importantly, as documented by the overlapping confidence intervals in Table 7.2, the results further suggest no significant difference in effect size or direction across survey waves. Consequently, despite limitations in the measurement of EPR orientations across pooled GSS panel waves that I discussed earlier, I find no evidence that these differences impact the conclusions we can draw about the viability of the Bidirectionality Thesis.

Table 7.2 **The Co-Constitutive Effects of Change In Anti-Intellectualism and Science Policy Opposition (Pooled GSS Panels, Cross-Lagged Regression Models)**

DV =	Wave 2		Wave 3	
	AI → EPR	AI ← EPR	AI → EPR	AI ← EPR
Anti-Intellectualism	0.05*	0.30*	0.05*	0.33*
	[0.03,0.07]	[0.25,0.35]	[0.03,0.07]	[0.27,0.38]
Sci. Policy. Opposition	0.11*	0.15*	0.18*	0.17*
	[0.08,0.15]	[0.06,0.25]	[0.13,0.23]	[0.06,0.27]
Party ID (1 = GOP)	0.03*	0.02	0.01	0.06*
	[0.01,0.04]	[−0.03,0.07]	[−0.01,0.03]	[0.00,0.11]
Ideo. (1 = Conservative)	0.03*	0.05	0.02	−0.01
	[0.01,0.05]	[−0.01,0.12]	[−0.01,0.05]	[−0.08,0.06]
Limited-Govt. Index	0.08*	0.00	0.08*	−0.04
	[0.04,0.12]	[−0.09,0.10]	[0.03,0.12]	[−0.15,0.06]
Female	0.01*	0.03*	0.01+	0.03*
	[0.00,0.02]	[0.01,0.06]	[−0.00,0.02]	[0.01,0.06]
College Educ.	−0.03*	−0.06*	−0.03*	−0.06*
	[−0.04,−0.02]	[−0.09,−0.04]	[−0.04,−0.02]	[−0.09,−0.03]
Race = Black	0.02*	0.06*	0.01	0.10*
	[0.01,0.04]	[0.02,0.10]	[−0.01,0.03]	[0.05,0.15]
Race = Other	0.01	0.03	−0.01	−0.01
	[−0.00,0.03]	[−0.02,0.07]	[−0.03,0.02]	[−0.06,0.05]
Rel. Service Attendance	0.02*	0.06*	0.04*	0.04+
	[0.00,0.04]	[0.03,0.10]	[0.02,0.05]	[−0.00,0.08]
β_0	0.28*	0.11*	0.26*	0.13*
	[0.26,0.30]	[0.06,0.16]	[0.23,0.29]	[0.07,0.19]
N	2819	2751	2346	2292

Note: Cross-lagged panel regression models present OLS coefficients with 95% confidence intervals in brackets. AI stands for anti-intellectualism, and EPR stands for experts policy role orientations. All covariates are measured in Wave 1. Note that in a slight departure from previous cross-lagged analyses presented elsewhere in this book, I *am interested* in comparing the substantive magnitude of effects across models (as noted in the text). I therefore use an OLS estimator to assess change in both outcome variables across different combinations of survey waves.

Conclusion

The results presented in this chapter suggest that Hofstadter's often-overlooked predictions about the bidirectional relationship between anti-intellectualism and EPR preferences may, in fact, be correct. People who come to hold negative views toward experts also tend to become more likely to think that experts ought to play less of a role in the policymaking process. Simultaneously, people concerned about experts' influence over public policy tend to become more likely to hold negative feelings toward experts.

Of course, these findings are not without some important limitations. As was the case in Chapter 6, which also made use of GSS panel data, these findings are necessarily based on a single measure of anti-intellectual attitude endorsement (i.e., Americans' distrust in the scientific community). This is an important caveat. While I again note that views toward the scientific community tend to be highly correlated with views toward experts more generally, future research should study the Bidirectionality Thesis in application to a broader class of people who can credibly claim superior knowledge in technical and policy-relevant fields.

I also recognize, of course, that these results are to some extent unsatisfying. They imply that any insights we might glean about the policy relevance of anti-intellectual attitude endorsement may also function in reverse. Consequently, studies that assess the *effects* of anti-intellectualism on policy-relevant outcomes that pertain to expert influence in the policymaking process—including the extent to which policymakers ought to defer to scientific and other experts when formulating public policy, the rejection of expert-backed policy recommendations, and even the acceptance of policy-relevant misinformation (all of which I take up in the next chapter)—may also be the *result* of Americans' displeasure with experts' influence in these areas.

I view these dynamics not as a limitation of previous work but as an opportunity to better our understanding of what anti-intellectualism is and why it matters for American politics. In the next chapter, for example, I investigate the relationship between anti-intellectual attitude endorsement and policy-relevant outcomes in several different areas (economic policy, public health, and climate change). The results presented here in Chapter 7 offer an important context for the results I will present. They suggest that any relationship I document between anti-intellectualism and the dozens of outcomes studied in that chapter may, in fact, be mutually reinforcing. As I note in the book's conclusion, this presents an opportunity to conduct longitudinal research—of the type I used in this chapter—to better assess the complex temporal dynamics of Hofstadter's predictions with respect to *specific* (as opposed to general) policy orientations.

With this in mind, I conclude this book's study of anti-intellectualism and its political relevance by studying its relationship with misinformation acceptance, evidence-based policy rejection, and other policy-relevant outcomes across a wide range of salient policy considerations.

Anti-Scientific Americans: The Prevalence, Origins, and Political Consequences of Anti-Intellectualism in the US. Matthew Motta, Oxford University Press. © Oxford University Press 2024. DOI: 10.1093/9780197788844.003.0007

8

Anti-Intellectualism and Its Pernicious Policy Consequences

So far in this book, I have shown that anti-intellectualism is pervasive. I also explored why some people are more likely to hold anti-intellectual attitudes than others and provided evidence that it both shapes and is shaped by Americans' feelings toward the role that experts play in the policymaking process.

What I have yet to do, however, is document that anti-intellectualism—as both an individual and macro-level phenomenon—has a tangible and far-reaching impact on US public policy. Understanding the prevalence and origins of anti-intellectualism is certainly important in its own right. But for anti-intellectualism to be *politically consequential*, it must also have some impact on the way that Americans think about public policy or influence the way that legislators in Washington, DC, make relevant policy decisions.

In this chapter, I offer a wide-ranging investigation into the policy consequences of anti-intellectual attitude endorsement. I begin at the micro level by assessing the extent to which people who endorse anti-intellectual attitudes reject evidence-based solutions to pressing policy problems or who endorse policy-relevant misinformation. Across three domains that span a diverse range of highly salient policy debates—including issues related to environmental, health, and economic policy—I find that anti-intellectual attitude endorsement is broadly associated with both the rejection of evidence-based policy and the acceptance of policy-relevant misinformation.

I then turn to the macro level by studying the extent to which fluctuations in (aggregated) public anti-intellectual attitude endorsement might create an incentive for policymakers to limit experts' influence in each of the aforementioned policy areas. I find that in periods when anti-intellectualism is comparatively high, Congress tends to invite fewer experts to testify in legislative hearings.

Collectively, the results suggest that anti-intellectualism has pernicious effects on public policy in the United States. Anti-intellectualism (at the micro level) reduces the demand for policies guided by the best available evidence and input from subject-area experts, which may (at the macro level) provide an incentive for Congress to curtail experts' influence in the policymaking process.

Before assessing the pernicious policy effects of anti-intellectualism, however, one important caveat bears mentioning. As I documented in Chapter 7, the relationship between anti-intellectualism and expert policy role orientations (as a generalized phenomenon) is bidirectional. Inasmuch as feelings (at the micro level) about the role that experts play in the policymaking process are associated with support for the types of *specific* policies they endorse, these effects may also be mutually reinforcing. Unfortunately, that's not something I can test in this chapter because of a dearth of rich longitudinal data assessing Americans' policy preferences over time.

Still, this limitation does not necessarily imply that anti-intellectualism fails to motivate policy orientations. On the contrary, it simply cautions us to be cognizant of the possibility that policy attitudes might also, in turn, reinforce the negative attitudes toward subject-area experts. As I note in this chapter's conclusion, the possibility of bidirectionality challenges us to think about and investigate the complex interrelationships between negative views toward experts and policy orientations in future research.

With that caveat in mind, I proceed by discussing how I investigate the relationship between anti-intellectualism and policy-relevant opinions at the micro level. I then report the results of that investigation across environmental, economic, and public health domains (including the US response to the COVID-19 pandemic). I conclude by doing the same at the macro level.

After making the case that the (micro-level) link between anti-intellectualism and expert-backed policy opposition might create an incentive for elites to curtail experts' policy influence, I propose and validate two indicators of legislative deference to experts in the policymaking process across each of the aforementioned subject areas. I then test for a relationship between fluctuations in aggregate anti-intellectual attitude endorsement and expert deference in Congress. I conclude by discussing the far-reaching consequences of anti-intellectualism and its pernicious policy consequences for US democracy in the twenty-first century.

Anti-Intellectualism and the Rejection of Evidence-Based Policy

I study the relationship between anti-intellectual attitude endorsement (at the individual level) and opposition to expert-backed policy and policy-relevant information using data from the cross-sectional, micro-level studies presented throughout this book. In addition to capturing public sentiments toward scientists and other experts, these studies regularly included questions about support

168 ANTI-SCIENTIFIC AMERICANS

for expert-recommended policies and the acceptance of policy-relevant misinformation in each of the three subject areas I study in this chapter (environmental, economic, and public health policy). As I summarized each of these datasets in detail in Chapter 3, I encourage the reader to consult Table 3.1 for additional information about these studies.

Table 8.1 presents a full list of the questions that I use to assess policy support in each of the aforementioned domains and the dataset with which each one is associated. Here it is important to note that *all* cross-sectional studies that I rely on in this chapter featured the Oliver and Rahn–style *trust in experts* question. This allows me to take both a conceptually inclusive (with respect to how survey respondents are asked to conceptualize expert negativity) and standardized approach (i.e., by relying on the same indicators across surveys) when assessing the policy consequences of anti-intellectual attitude endorsement.

I determine whether anti-intellectual attitude endorsement is associated with economic, public health, and/or environmental policy attitudes by constructing a series of multivariate regression models that regress each policy-relevant outcome presented in Table 8.1 on that survey's measure of anti-intellectualism, as well as the standard set of social, political, and demographic controls included

Table 8.1 **Question Wording for Micro-Level Policy Items**

Domain	Outcome	Wording
Climate Beliefs (Binary)	Global Warming	Which of these two statements do you think is most likely to be true? * [1] World temperatures have risen on average over the last 100 years. [2] World temperatures have not risen on average over the last 100 years. [2] (ANES 2019)
Climate Beliefs (Binary)	Anthropogenic	Which of these three statements about the Earth's temperature comes closest to your view? * [1] The Earth is getting warmer mostly because of human activity such as burning fossil fuels [2] 2 The Earth is getting warmer mostly because of natural patterns in the Earth's environment [3] There is no solid evidence that the Earth is getting warmer [4] Not sure. (2020-21 SciPol)

Domain	Outcome	Wording
Climate Beliefs (Ordinal)	Concern	Q1. To what degree, if at all, are you concerned about the effects climate change might have on daily life for you and your family? Q2. To what degree, if at all, are you concerned about the effects climate change might have on daily life for the average person living in the United States? * [1] Very concerned [2] Somewhat concerned [3] Not too concerned [4] Not concerned at all. (2020-21 SciPol)
Climate Beliefs (Ordinal)	Concern	How important is the issue of climate change to you personally? [1] Not at all important [2] A little important [3] Moderately important [4] Very important * [5] Extremely important (ANES 2020)
Climate Policy (Ordinal)	Envi. Protection	The environment. Are we spending too much, too little, or about the right amount on the environment? [1] Too much * [2] Too little [3] About the right amount
Climate Policy (Ordinal)	Biz. Regulations	Q1. Do you favor, oppose, or neither favor nor oppose increased government regulation on businesses that produce a great deal of greenhouse emissions linked to climate change? * [1] Favor [2] Oppose [3] Neither favor nor oppose; Q2. Do you [favor/oppose] that [a great deal, a moderate amount, or a little/a little, a moderate amount, or a great deal]? (ANES 2020)
Climate Policy (Ordinal)	Biz. Regulations	Increased government regulation on businesses that produce a great deal of greenhouse emissions linked to climate change. * [1] Favor strongly [2] Favor somewhat [3] Neither favor nor oppose [4] Oppose somewhat [5] Oppose strongly (ANES 2019)

(*Continued*)

Table 8.1 **Continued**

Domain	Outcome	Wording
Climate Policy (Ordinal)	Fuel Efficiency	Higher fuel efficiency standards for cars and trucks. * [1] Favor strongly [2] Favor somewhat [3] Neither favor nor oppose [4] Oppose somewhat [5] Oppose strongly (ANES 2019)
Climate Policy (Ordinal)	Power Plant Emissions	Policymakers have considered several proposals to reduce the effects of global climate change. Please tell us the extent to which you support or oppose each of the following proposals: Restrictions on power plant emissions. * [1] Support strongly [2] Support somewhat [3] Neither support nor oppose [4] Oppose somewhat [5] Oppose strongly (SciPol 2020-21)
Climate Policy (Ordinal)	International Agree- ment	…An international agreement to limit carbon emissions. * [1] Support strongly [2] Support somewhat [3] Neither support nor oppose [4] Oppose somewhat [5] Oppose strongly (SciPol 2020-21)
Climate Policy	Carbon Tax Credits	…Corporate tax incentives to encourage businesses to reduce their carbon footprint, O that is the amount of greenhouse gas emissions caused by their actions. * [1] Support strongly [2] Support somewhat [3] Neither support nor oppose [4] Oppose somewhat [5] Oppose strongly (SciPol 2020-21)
Climate Policy (Ordinal)	Fuel Efficiency	…Tougher fuel efficiency standards for automobiles and trucks. * [1] Support strongly [2] Support somewhat [3] Neither support nor oppose [4] Oppose somewhat [5] Oppose strongly (SciPol 2020-21)

Anti-Intellectualism and Its Pernicious Policy Consequences 171

Domain	Outcome	Wording
Climate Policy (Ordinal)	Infrastructure	…A policy in which the Federal government creates jobs and invests in low-income communities building energy efficient infrastructure, replacing lead water pipes, and updating America's energy grids. * [1] Support strongly [2] Support somewhat [3] Neither support nor oppose [4] Oppose somewhat [5] Oppose strongly (SciPol 2020-21)
Climate Policy (Ordinal)	Insurance	…A policy in which cities and towns can apply for Federal funding to prepare for flooding, fires, drought, and other potential consequences of climate change. * [1] Support strongly [2] Support somewhat [3] Neither support nor oppose [4] Oppose somewhat [5] Oppose strongly (SciPol 2020-21)
Economic Mis-information (Binary)	Recession 2020	Would you say that over the past twelve months, the state of the economy in the United States has [gotten much better, gotten somewhat better, stayed about the same, gotten somewhat worse, or gotten much worse/gotten much worse, gotten somewhat worse, stayed about the same, gotten somewhat better, or gotten much better]? [1] Gotten much better [2] Gotten somewhat better [3] Stayed about the same * [4] Gotten somewhat worse * [5] Gotten much worse. (ANES 2020).
Economic Policy (Ordinal)	Immigration	Do you [agree strongly, agree somewhat, neither agree nor disagree, disagree somewhat, or disagree strongly /disagree strongly, disagree somewhat, neither agree nor disagree, agree somewhat, or agree strongly] with the following

(*Continued*)

172 ANTI-SCIENTIFIC AMERICANS

Table 8.1 **Continued**

Domain	Outcome	Wording
		statement? 'Immigrants are generally good for America's economy. * [1] Agree strongly [2] Agree somewhat [3] Neither agree nor disagree [4] Disagree somewhat [5] Disagree strongly. (ANES 2020).
Health Misinfo. (Binary)	Flu Vaccine	Which of the following statements comes closest to your views on the seasonal influenza vaccine or flu shot? * [1] The flu shot cannot cause you to become sick with influenza [2] The flu shot cannot cause you to become sick influenza, but normal reactions to the vaccine may resemble flu-like symptoms [3] The flu shot can cause you to become sick with influenza [4] I am not sure
Health Misinfo. (Binary)	COVID Origins	Please tell us which of the following statements about the novel coronavirus (COVID-19) you agree with the most. [1] The novel coronavirus (COVID-19) was created in a lab, on purpose [2] The novel coronavirus (COVID-19) was created in a lab, by accident * [3] The novel coronavirus (COVID-19) came about naturally [4] I am not sure
Health Misinfo. (Ordinal)	MMR Safety	Can vaccines administered to children at young ages cause them to become autistic? [1] They definitely can [2] They probably can [3] They probably cannot * [4] They definitely cannot
Health Misinfo. (Binary)	5G	Which of the following statements comes closest to your views on 5G cellular networks? [1] Radio waves emitted from 5G cellular networks can cause people to get sick by weakening peoples' immune systems [2] Radio waves emitted from 5G cellular networks can cause people to experience symptoms resembling the flu and other diseases

Domain	Outcome	Wording
Health Misinfo. (Binary)	COVID Origins	* [3] Radio waves emitted from 5G cellular networks cannot cause people to get sick, or feel sick [4] I am not sure Which of these two statements do you think is most likely to be true? [1] The novel coronavirus (COVID-19) was developed intentionally in a lab. * [2] The novel coronavirus (COVID-19) was not developed intentionally in a lab. (ANES 2020)
Health Misinfo. (Binary)	Hydroxy. as a COVID Treatment	Which of these two statements do you think is most likely to be true? [1] There is clear scientific evidence that the anti-malarial drug hydroxychloroquine is a safe and effective treatment for COVID-19. * [2] There is not clear scientific evidence that the anti-malarial drug hydroxychloroquine is a safe and effective treatment for COVID-19. (ANES 2020)
Health Behavior (Binary)	Flu Vaccine Uptake	Did you receive the seasonal influenza vaccine (flu shot), this year? (Fall 2019 - Winter 2020). * [1] Yes [2] No [3] Not sure (SciPol 2020-21)
Health Behavior (Ordinal)	COVID Vaccine Uptake	When a vaccine for the novel coronavirus (COVID-19) becomes widely available, how likely are you to request to be vaccinated? * [1] Very likely [2] Somewhat likely [3] Not too likely [4] Not likely at all (SciPol 2020-21)
Health Policy (Binary)	Vaccine Exemptions	Which of the following statements comes closest to your view about vaccination requirements for healthy children, under the age of 7? * [1] Children should receive all CDC recommended vaccines, without exception. [2] Children should receive all CDC recommended vaccines, unless parents seek exemption on religious grounds. [3] Children should receive all CDC recommended vaccines, unless

(*Continued*)

Table 8.1 **Continued**

Domain	Outcome	Wording
		parents seek exemption for any personal beliefs (including moral concerns). [4] Children should not be required to receive all CDC recommended vaccines. (SciPol 2020-21)
Health Policy (Binary)	Vaccine Mandates	Do you favor, oppose, or neither favor nor oppose requiring children to be vaccinated in order to attend public schools? * [1] Favor [2] Oppose [3] Neither favor nor oppose (ANES 2020)
Health Policy (Ordinal)	Sci. Importance for Pandemic	In general, how important should science be for making government decisions about COVID-19? [1] Not at all important [2] A little important [3] Moderately important [4] Very important * [5] Extremely important (ANES 2020)
Health Policy (Binary)	COVID Restrictions	Do you think the limits your state placed on public activity because of the COVID-19 pandemic were … [1] Far too strict [2] Somewhat too strict * [3] About right * [4] Not quite strict enough * [5] Not nearly strict enough (ANES 2020)
Health Policy (Ordinal)	COVID Restrictions	Please tell us the degree to which you think that each of the following actions was necessary to prevent the spread of the novel coronavirus (COVID-19). Closing schools and universities. * [1] Definitely necessary [2] Probably necessary [3] Probably not necessary [4] Definitely not necessary. (SciPol 2020-2021)
Health Policy (Ordinal)	COVID Restrictions	… Prohibiting people from ordering in at restaurants and bars. [1] Definitely necessary [2] Probably necessary [3] Probably not necessary [4] Definitely not necessary. (SciPol 2020-2021)

Domain	Outcome	Wording
Health Policy (Ordinal)	COVID Restrictions	...Prohibiting public gatherings of more than ten people [1] Definitely necessary [2] Probably necessary [3] Probably not necessary [4] Definitely not necessary. (SciPol 2020-2021)
Health Policy (Ordinal)	COVID Restrictions	... 'Shelter in Place' orders [1] Definitely necessary [2] Probably necessary [3] Probably not necessary [4] Definitely not necessary. (SciPol 2020-2021)
Health Policy (Binary)	COVID Behavior	In the PAST MONTH, have you taken any of the following actions as a result of the coronavirus (COVID-19) outbreak? Please select all that apply. Worn a mask when out in public. Note: coded as "yes" if selected. (SciPol 2020-2021)
Health Policy (Binary)	COVID Behavior	...Avoided dining-in at restaurants or bars (SciPol 2020-2021)
Health Policy (Binary)	COVID Behavior	...Stayed at least six feet away from others in public spaces (SciPol 2020-2021)
Health Policy (Binary)	COVID Behavior	...Changed travel plans (SciPol 2020-2021)

Note: Full question wording and response option list for all outcome variables presented in Figures 8.1 through 8.6. All variables are coded such that agreement with expert consensus or support for evidence-based policies take on higher values (1 for dichotomous items; the maximum on ordered or continuous scales). For reference, starred answers reflect the response options that are indicative of agreement (dichotomous items) or the directionality of agreement with expert consensus (ordered and continuous items).

in previous chapters. For reference, full model output can be found in the appendix.

I summarize these results by presenting a series of bar charts that plot linear predictions (for continuous outcome variables estimated via OLS) and predicted probabilities (for dichotomous and ordered outcome variables estimated via logistic and ordered logistic regression models, respectively) on each outcome variable. The purpose of these figures is to provide both an intuitive and standardized way to visualize of the substantive effects of anti-intellectualism observed across the dozens of models for each of the three policy domains studied in this chapter. For standardization purposes, all outcome variables are scored such that if my theoretical predictions are correct, anti-intellectualism should be associated with *decreases* in each one, indicating opposition to expert-backed policy and other evidence-based positions.

Climate Science

I begin my investigation into the policy-relevant consequences of anti-intellectual attitude endorsement by assessing the relationship between expert negative attitudes toward experts and policy-relevant climate-change beliefs, including misinformation about the sources of climate change and a lack of concern about its effects. Strong majorities of both climate scientists (Cook et al., 2016) and the scientific community more generally (Funk, Rainie, & Page, 2015) believe that climate change is caused by human (as opposed to natural) activities and that climate change poses a number of social, economic, and environmental threats to everyday life in the United States and beyond (IPCC, 2018). Understanding whether Americans share scientists' beliefs about the origins and severity of climate change is important because both are thought to motivate support for climate-change adaptation and mitigation policy (Marquart-Pyatt et al., 2011; Ehret et al., 2018).

Figure 8.1 summarizes the results of four tests from the ANES (2019, 2020) and SciPol studies that assess the relationship between anti-intellectualism and (1) beliefs in human-caused climate change and (2) concern about its impact on human life. In three out of four cases, I find that people who hold more anti-intellectual attitudes are significantly less likely to believe that climate change is anthropogenic (caused by humans) and express lower levels of concern about its effects (at the $p < 0.05$ level, two-tailed).

The figure also offers additional insights into the substantive magnitude of these effects. With the exception of climate-change concern in the SciPol study, people who hold highly anti-intellectual attitudes (compared to those who do not) are 13 percent less likely to accept that the planet is warming (ANES, 2019, top-left panel). They're also 28 percent more likely to express skepticism about its human origins (SciPol, top-right panel) and score 17 percentage points lower on interval scales measuring concern about its effects in the 2020 ANES (bottom-left panel).

I observe an analogous relationship when turning to the effect of anti-intellectual attitude endorsement on Americans' policy priorities concerning environmental protection and climate change. Many climate scientists see

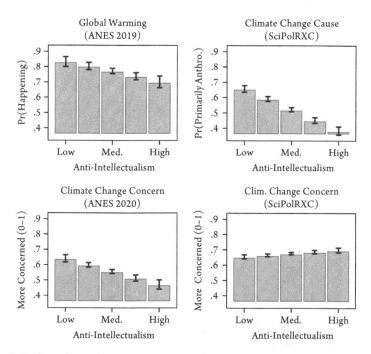

Figure 8.1 The Relationship Between Anti-Intellectualism on Climate Change Beliefs

human-caused emissions from manufacturing industries and transportation—among dozens of other human-caused factors—as important drivers of greenhouse gas emissions (Rosa & Dietz, 2012) and point to policies regulating the actions of businesses (e.g., formal restrictions on power plant emissions), governments (e.g., international agreements to reduce carbon emissions within and across nations), and ordinary people (e.g., limiting the ability to purchase of fuel-inefficient automobiles) as key to decreasing humans' carbon footprint (for a review, see Hughes & Lipscy, 2013).

Figure 8.2 summarizes the association between anti-intellectualism and opposition to efforts to both protect the environment and curtail fossil-fuel emissions in the 2019 and 2020 ANES (i.e., climate-change mitigation policies; see Table 8.1 for additional information). Here, I again find that anti-intellectualism is negatively and significantly associated with pro–climate policy stances in all four models. People who hold the most negative views toward experts (compared to those who express the most positive views) are 18 percent less likely to favor increased environmental protection efforts (top left) and score 13 percentage points lower on scales measuring support for environmental regulations on businesses in general (top right). People who express strong anti-intellectual sentiments are also 27 percent less likely to strongly support taking action to regulate corporate polluters (bottom left) and 26 percent less likely to

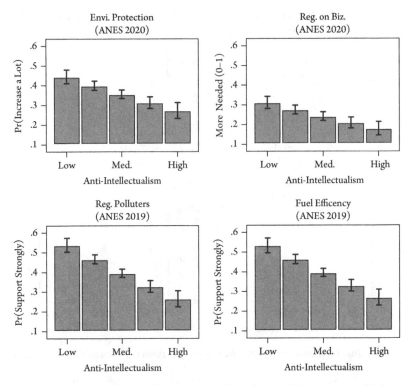

Figure 8.2 The Relationship Between Anti-Intellectualism and Environmental Policy Importance / Climate Change Mitigation Attitudes (2019 & 2020 ANES)

favor increasing fuel-efficiency standards for automobiles available to consumers in the United States.

I find an analogous pattern of results when studying support for climate regulations in the SciPol studies, presented in Figure 8.3. In four out of six tests, I find that anti-intellectualism is negatively and significantly associated with increased opposition to pro-climate policies. Specifically, people who strongly endorse anti-intellectual attitudes are 14 percent less likely (in all cases) to strongly support restrictions on power-plant carbon emissions, maintaining an international agreement (like the Paris Climate Accord) to limit carbon emissions, and setting higher fuel-efficiency standards for US automobiles. They are also 16 percent less likely to support plans that adapt to the challenges of a changing climate by making energy-efficient updates to existing infrastructure. I find no evidence, however, of an association between anti-intellectualism and support for policies that allow localities to apply for preventive funds to preempt and adapt to the effects of climate change or tax incentives for businesses that try to reduce their carbon footprint.

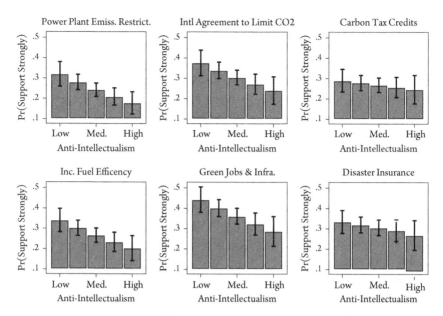

Figure 8.3 The Relationship Between Anti-Intellectualism on Climate Change Mitigation & Adaptation Policy

Here it is important to remember that because climate change is a highly politically contentious issue (McCright & Dunlap, 2011; Brulle, Carmichael, & Jenkins, 2012; Fisher, Waggle, & Leifeld, 2013), I control for Americans' partisanship and ideology in all multivariate models used to produce the figures shown earlier. Correspondingly, the results present the effects of anti-intellectualism *after accounting* for the influence of partisan and ideological disagreement on views toward climate change.

Collectively, then, the correlational results presented thus far suggest that people who hold anti-intellectual attitudes are less likely to take seriously climate science consensus on the severity and reality of climate change and less supportive of evidence-based policy recommendations designed to combat the effects of climate change. Although climate change could have far-reaching social, economic, and environmental consequences for most people, some Americans appear to allow their negative feelings toward experts and their anti-intellectual proclivities to supersede efforts to protect the planet from excessive levels of global warming.

Public Health

Next I study the association between anti-intellectualism and health policy orientations, both throughout and prior to the COVID-19 pandemic. I begin by focusing first on the acceptance of misinformation about a wide variety of health-related topics, including vaccine safety and the origins of the COVID-19 pandemic.

Medical researchers and public health experts—as well as the scientific community more generally (Funk, Rainie, & Page, 2015)—agree that childhood vaccines like MMR and elective adulthood vaccines like the seasonal influenza shot are both safe and provide significant protective health benefits (Van der Linden, Clarke, & Maibach, 2015). Yet, many Americans hold views at odds with scientific consensus. For example, although many Americans believe that the seasonal influenza can cause people to develop the flu (Nyhan & Reifler, 2015), public health authorities have long cast doubt on this possibility by noting that the shot does not contain a live virus and therefore cannot infect people with influenza (CDC, 2021). Scientific consensus (Ashraf, 2001; Hviid et al., 2019) also casts doubt on the widely held belief that the MMR vaccine can cause children to develop autism (Nyhan et al., 2014; Motta, Callaghan, & Sylvester, 2018).

Another and arguably more controversial issue concerns the origins of the COVID-19 pandemic. Intelligence reports suggesting that several members of the Institute of Virology in Wuhan, China, came down with a flu-like illness just weeks before the spread of COVID-19 in China (Maxmen & Mallapaty, 2021) led some US government scientists and intelligence experts to welcome an investigation into the origins of the virus (Bloom et al., 2021). As its precise origins are not yet known, some scientists have indicated that they are open to the possibility that the virus escaped from the lab in Wuhan. What many scientists agree on, however, is the implausibility of conspiracy theories (Miller, 2020; Uscinski et al., 2020) alleging that the virus was *deliberately* manufactured (Maxmen & Mallapaty, 2021), given discrepancies between its genetic code and what scientists would otherwise expect to observe in a bioweapon (Andersen et al., 2020).

The acceptance of misinformation about vaccine safety, the origins of the COVID-19 virus, and other health issues can have important policy and public health consequences. People who are misinformed about vaccines, for example, tend to be less likely to intend to vaccine themselves or their children (Callaghan et al., 2019; Lindholt et al., 2021) against vaccine-preventable disease and are more likely to oppose policies that encourage vaccination and other pro-social health behavior (Joslyn & Sylvester, 2019; Motta, Callaghan, & Sylvester, 2018; Stecula et al., 2020). Moreover, people who fear that COVID-19 was lab made are more likely to think that the pandemic's risks are exaggerated (Motta, Stecula, & Farhart, 2020) and may correspondingly be less likely to take action to protect themselves and others (Callaghan et al., 2020).

Figure 8.4 reviews the relationship between anti-intellectualism and the acceptance of several forms of public health misinformation and the rejection of scientific evidence. Across all six outcomes presented in the figure (again, see Table 8.1 for additional information about each question), I document a negative and statistically significant effect of anti-intellectual attitude endorsement on the acceptance of views informed by the best available science.

Compared to those who express the lowest levels of anti-intellectual attitude endorsement, people who hold strong anti-intellectual attitudes are 14 percent less likely to believe that the flu vaccine cannot cause the flu and 46 percent less likely to believe that the MMR vaccine does not cause autism in the SciPol studies (note that I document a similar pattern of effects in the ANES in previous research, which is not presented in this figure; for additional information, see Motta, 2021a). They are also considerably less likely to reject conspiracy theories suggesting that the COVID-19 virus originated or was deliberately spread from a lab in both the SciPol (a 15 percent decrease) and ANES surveys (a 23 percent decrease).

People who hold negative attitudes toward experts are also less likely—by a factor of 14 percent—to reject the idea popularized by former President Trump and re-circulated by other prominent political elites on the ideological right (Mahase, 2020; Enders et al., 2020) that the anti-malarial drug hydroxychloroquine can treat COVID-19 or prevent people from infection—a claim disputed by many observational (e.g., Skipper et al., 2020; Geleris et al., 2020) and experimental (e.g., Self et al., 2020) scientific studies. Demonstrative of the broad reach of anti-intellectual attitude endorsement on health-related misinformation acceptance, I find (in analyses not presented in Figure 8.4) that people who

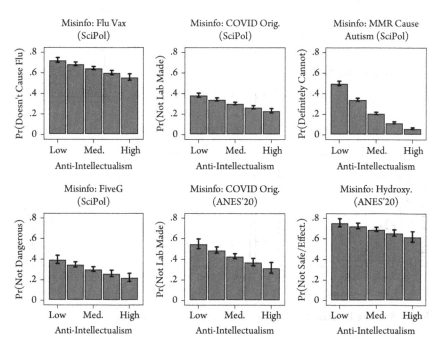

Figure 8.4 The Relationship Between Anti-Intellectualism on Public Health Misinformation

hold anti-intellectual attitudes are even 18 percent less likely to reject a conspiracy theory popular on alternative health social networking pages (Bruns, Harrington, & Hurcombe, 2020) suggesting that 5G cellular towers pose no direct harm to human health (Douglas, 2021).

Perhaps unsurprisingly, given the policy and behavioral implications of misinformation acceptance, I also present evidence in Figure 8.5 and Figure 8.6 that anti-intellectualism is associated with significantly lower levels of support for expert-recommended policies and health behaviors. First, and somewhat encouragingly, I find that when it comes to *personal* decisions about whether to vaccinate, people who hold strongly anti-intellectual attitudes were neither more nor less likely than those who do not intend to vaccinate against seasonal influenza prior to the start of the fall 2020 vaccination season (i.e., in spring through summer 2020). Unfortunately, though, even in the face of a global pandemic that killed more than one million Americans, I find that people who strongly endorsed anti-intellectual attitudes in the pandemic's early stages (spring through summer 2020) were 7 percent less likely to report that they were very likely to vaccinate against COVID-19 as soon as a vaccine became available to them.

The effects of anti-intellectualism are even stronger when focusing on vaccine-related issues that concern *other people*. Specifically, Figure 8.5 suggests

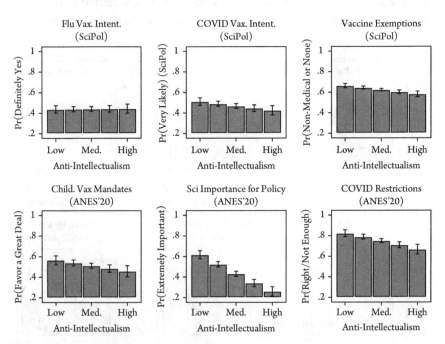

Figure 8.5 The Relationship Between Anti-Intellectualism on Health Behavior & Policy Attitudes

that people who endorse anti-intellectual views are much more likely than those who hold more favorable views toward experts to oppose expert-backed vaccine policy. For example, compared to those who hold the least anti-intellectual attitudes, people who hold strongly negative views toward experts are 12 percent less likely to support restricting parents' ability to pursue nonmedical exemptions for vaccinating their children in order to attend public schools and 11 percent less likely to support mandates that require vaccination.

The potential policy impact of anti-intellectual attitude endorsement extends beyond vaccine uptake. Throughout the COVID-19 pandemic, people who held highly anti-intellectual views were 36 percent less likely to think that scientific research should play a major role in shaping the government's pandemic response and 15 percent less likely to think that public health recommendations—such as stay-at-home orders and mask-wearing and physical-distancing requirements in public spaces—were either sufficient or not expansive enough to ensure public safety (meaning that they were comparatively more likely to think that these regulations were overly stringent).

Concerning the COVID-19 pandemic specifically, I also assess whether Americans' willingness to take non-vaccination-related action to protect themselves and others from the spread of COVID-19 vary across levels of anti-intellectual attitude endorsement. Initially, at the outset of the pandemic, the scientific community expressed uncertainty about the effectiveness of some protective behaviors—like mask wearing—as a way to reduce the spread of the pandemic. Shortly thereafter, however, scientific studies (Howard et al., 2021) underscored the personal and community health benefits of mask wearing. Both US and international public health experts echoed these findings by recommending that most people engage in acts of physical distancing and mask wearing in public spaces (CDC, 2020; see also Pearce, 2020; Qian & Jiang, 2020).

As Figure 8.6 demonstrates, however, that people who express strong anti-intellectual attitudes did not heed this call. In the early stages of the pandemic, people who held anti-intellectual attitudes were (based on self-reporting) significantly less likely to wear masks in public places (by a factor of 29 percent), avoid dining in at restaurants (30 percent), change travel plans (30 percent), and practice physical distancing (16 percent). They were also less likely to view various government actions as *definitely necessary* to contain the spread of COVID-19, including state and local governments' efforts to close schools (by a factor of 11 percent) and restaurants (5 percent) and restrictions on large gatherings (by a factor of 14 percent) and the implementation of stay-at-home orders (4 percent).

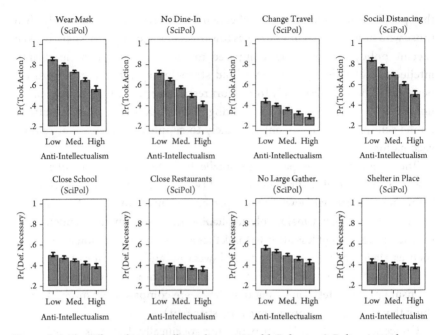

Figure 8.6 The Effect of Anti-Intellectualism on Health Behavior & Policy Attitudes

Again, given the politically polarizing nature of government responsiveness to the COVID-19 pandemic (Gollust, Nagler, & Fowler, 2020; Grossman et al., 2020; Gadarian, Goodman, & Pepinsky, 2021) and perennial bouts of partisan disagreement about both vaccine safety (Joslyn & Sylvester, 2019; Motta, 2021a) and the necessity of placing limits on Americans' choices to not vaccinate themselves or their children (Amin et al., 2017), it is important to point out that all models used to calculate the quantities presented above account for Americans' partisan and ideological leanings, as well as all other controls presented elsewhere in this book. Collectively, the findings presented here suggest that even in the face of a global pandemic, negative attitudes toward scientists and other experts motivated some Americans to accept health-related misinformation, reject evidenced-based policy, and take actions that endangered both themselves and other people.

Economics

Next, I assess the relationship between anti-intellectual attitude endorsement and the rejection of evidence-based economic policy and other policy-relevant information. Whether Americans hold factually accurate beliefs about the state of the economy or the impact of expert-recommended policies is important because either could motivate public opposition to efforts to improve the functioning of the US economy. Documenting an effect of anti-intellectualism on economic issues would be an especially powerful testament to its policy relevance because it would suggest that negative views toward experts is associated with views of policy-relevant expertise outside of the medical and physical sciences studied throughout this chapter thus far (i.e, climate science, medicine, and public health).

One important area where economists and the public hold substantially different policy views, for example, is with respect to the economic benefits of immigration (Lapinski et al., 1997; Segovia & Defever, 2010). Economists have long argued that immigration has a number of desirable benefits for the economy (Borjas, 2018). In 2018, economists summarized some of these benefits in an open letter to Congress, following the Trump administration's wave of anti-immigration executive actions taken throughout the first two years of his presidency (such as attempting to limit immigration from Muslim-majority countries; Collingwood, Lajevardi, & Oskooii, 2018). In the letter, nearly 1,500 economists—including several Nobel laureates—argued that expanded immigration offers an opportunity to replace retiring cohorts in the labor force, diversify workforce skills, and start new and innovative businesses (Smith et al., 2017).

The left-side panel in Figure 8.7 summarizes the effect of anti-intellectualism on beliefs regarding whether immigration is beneficial for the US economy. These figures and modeling procedures are structured analogously to those in the previous sections and assessed in the 2020 ANES.

Here I again find that anti-intellectual attitude endorsement is negatively associated with the acceptance of policy-relevant expertise. Americans who hold anti-intellectual attitudes are significantly less likely to view immigration as being helpful to

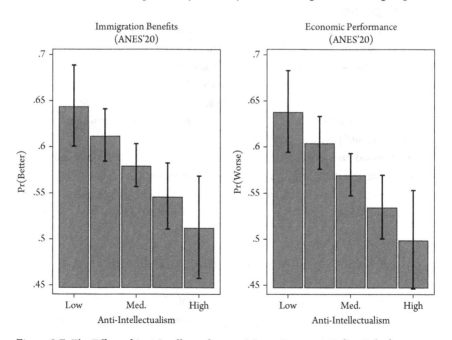

Figure 8.7 The Effect of Anti-Intellectualism on Macro-Economic Policy Beliefs

the US economy. Specifically, Americans who hold the most anti-intellectual attitudes are 13 percent less likely to indicate that immigration has positive economic benefits as compared to those who hold the most positive attitudes toward experts. It is again important to remember that although Americans' views on immigration are highly politically polarized (e.g., Sides, Tesler, & Vavreck 2016; Lajevardi & Abrajano, 2019), the estimates of the effect of anti-intellectualism that I observe here *account* for the effects of partisanship and ideology on immigration attitudes.

The right-side panel in Figure 8.7 summarizes the association between anti-intellectual attitude endorsement and beliefs that the macro economy performed better in 2020 (measured in December 2020) than in the previous year—a proposition that according to economic experts is incorrect. Perhaps unsurprisingly given the pattern of results presented earlier, anti-intellectualism is negatively and significantly associated with believing that the economy performed worse in 2020 than it did in the previous year.

Compared to those who hold the most positive views toward experts, people expressing highly anti-intellectual attitudes are 14 percent less likely to believe that the economy worsened in 2020. Again, recognizing that retrospective evaluations of economic performance are often biased by partisanship and ideology—i.e., that Republicans may report holding positive views about the economy in order to express their support for Donald Trump, who presided as president over the economy during that time (Sides, Tesler, & Vavreck, 2016, 2019; Schaffner & Roche, 2016; Bullock & Lenz, 2019)—it is important to point out that the models used to estimate these effects account for the influence of partisanship and ideology on economic evaluations.

Taken together, I have provided evidence thus far that anti-intellectual attitude endorsement is associated with the rejection of policy-relevant expertise in not just natural-science fields—i.e., medicine (as it pertains to public health) and climate science—but in policy domains relevant to social-science expertise as well (i.e., the performance of the macro economy). The idea that anti-intellectualism influences economic policy orientations further underscores its wide-ranging and pernicious policy effects.

These broad and negative micro-level effects may be *particularly* harmful if public dislike and distrust of scientists and other experts provides policymakers with an incentive to curtail experts' influence in the policymaking process. I conclude this chapter by devising several tests designed to assess that possibility.

Elite Responsiveness to Public Anti-Intellectualism

The above analyses clearly demonstrate that Americans who hold anti-intellectual views are more likely to reject experts' preferred approaches to solving salient policy problems. Thy are also more likely to reject expert-backed evidence that informs those policies. Next I consider the possibility that the policy implications of (micro-level) anti-intellectual attitude endorsement might give political elites at the macro level an incentive to *respond* to those concerns by curtailing experts' influence in the policymaking process. As I discussed in Chapter 2, rational and election-seeking political elites may—contingent on recognizing the prevalence or policy impact of negative views toward experts in the mass public—take action to limit experts' policy influence in an effort to appease potential voters.

Whether politicians are aware of public fluctuations in anti-intellectual attitude endorsement, and whether they might take action on those changes, is—of course—an open question. Before I put this proposition to the test, however, there is at least some anecdotal reason to suspect that they might.

Former President Donald Trump's relationship with government research scientists exemplifies the possibility of elite recognition and responsiveness to public anti-intellectual attitude endorsement. As noted in Chapter 4, Donald Trump's announcement of his intentions to run for president in 2016 aligned with a swell in anti-intellectual sentiment. Correspondingly, I have shown in past research (Motta, 2018a) that Americans who endorsed anti-intellectual attitudes in the lead-up to the 2016 election were more likely to vote for Donald Trump. Given the link between anti-intellectual attitude endorsement and opposition to evidence-based policy documented throughout this chapter, we might suspect that the Trump administration viewed itself as having a mandate to interfere with the influence that experts have in American political life.

And interfere, they did.

In June 2019, for example, the Trump White House made headlines for taking action to forbid Dr. Rod Schoonover—a State Department intelligence analyst and professor at Georgetown University—from testifying before Congress about the national security risks of climate change (Friedman, 2019; UCUSA, 2019). Although Schoonover was ultimately allowed to speak, the White House struck passages from his testimony that cited studies from other government departments (e.g., NASA and NOAA) portraying climate change as the result of human activities.

The administration's primary concern with Schoonover's testimony was the fact that it drew too much on scientific research to support its conclusions. Per a White House legislative affairs staffer, the testimony ought to have been redacted because it focused "heavily on the science" and did not "reflect the ... administration's position" (UCUSA, 2019). The administration's position to which this staffer was referring was likely its America First Energy Plan, which was a series of policy priorities that eschewed environmental regulations informed by scientific research—i.e., those that the administration deemed to be at odds with the interests of ordinary people—in favor of fossil-fuel production and a revitalization of the coal industry (Vakhshouri, 2017). What this episode suggests is that the Trump administration may have been responding to what it interpreted as a public rejection of climate science in favor of policies that might stimulate economic growth.

Relatedly, the Trump administration received substantial attention for its decision to nominate former Governor Rick Perry (R-TX) to direct the Department of Energy. During the 2012 Republican primary, Rick Perry (then seeking the presidency) famously suggested that he would abolish the Department of Energy if elected to the presidency (MaGill, 2016), despite forgetting the agency's name during a debate response that would go on to achieve widespread attention in popular media. Perry's chief gripe with the agency was its irrelevance to the concerns of everyday Americans, quipping that he was "more concerned about Iran" (i.e., the possibility of nuclear conflict) than the changing "temperature of New York" (Gillman, 2014).

Ironically, despite the fact that Perry's gubernatorial reelection campaign included a team of social scientists—which some members of the campaign referred to as *eggheads*, harkening back (whether consciously or not) to Hofstadter's documentation of attacks on Adlai Stevenson's intellectual credentials (Mazure, 2011)—his tenure at the Department of Energy was characterized by efforts to forbid department scientists from sharing the results of their research and to curtail their influence over federal energy-oversight policy (Carter et al., 2019). Here too we observe evidence of the Trump administration taking action to limit the influence of scientific researchers in order to better serve what it assumed to be the public's policy preferences.

Ultimately, whether political elites feel as if public anti-intellectual sentiments give them an electoral incentive to curtail the influence of scientists and other experts in the policymaking process is an open question. It is also, to some extent, and unknowable one. Absent the ability to ask members of the executive and legislative branch whether they feel an electoral pressure to allow anti-intellectual sentiments to guide their policymaking choices, the next best way to answer this question is to determine if policymakers are more likely to take action that undermines the role that experts play in the policymaking process in periods when public anti-intellectual sentiment is comparatively high. This would be demonstrative of a degree of policy responsiveness to changes in public opinion toward experts. In the remainder of this chapter, I present a series of empirical tests devised to assess this possibility.

Measuring Expert Influence in the Policymaking Process

Before assessing how fluctuations in anti-intellectual attitude endorsement at the macro level might influence Congress's consultation with experts throughout the policymaking process, I first propose two ways to operationalize expert policy influence.

One way, and arguably one of the most intuitive ways, to measure expert influence is via expert testimony in congressional hearings.

Policymaking is difficult. Legislators are routinely asked to propose and formulate policies on highly technical matters with which they may not have any formal training or experience. Consequently, legislators rely on both lobbyists and interest groups (Smith, 1995; Hall & Deardorff, 2006; Heaney, 2006; Schnakenberg, 2017) and on testimony in congressional and committee hearings (Diermeier & Feddersen, 2000; Shafran, Jones, & Dye, 2020) to provide them with relevant information to help guide their legislative actions on highly complex issues.

Counts of expert testimony in congressional hearings (Maher et al., 2020) allow me to directly measure the number of times that Congress felt the need to consult with experts in a particular policy area over time. If my theoretical expectations are correct, experts' appearances in congressional hearings should temporarily wane following increases in public anti-intellectual sentiment. This could indicate that Congress is, on some level, both aware of and responsive to changes in the public's preferences for the role that experts play in the policymaking process. This aligns with prior research showing that Congress tends to defer to public opinion when determining the policy scope of committee-related actions (Jones & Baumgartner, 2004; Bevan, Jennings, & Pickup, 2019).

Unfortunately, assembling counts of expert appearances in congressional hearings is a difficult task. Doing this involves searching through hearing transcripts for references to different types of experts—who may not always be referenced by their title or field of expertise—and cross-validating those references with information about those individuals' educational backgrounds. Fortunately, some social scientists (Maher et al., 2020) have already done the hard computational work of assembling these data for one of the expert groups I study in this chapter (economists).

For climate scientists and public health experts, however, this data is neither readily available nor easily attainable. Correspondingly, I propose an alternative *proxy* measure for assessing experts' congressional testimony: the number of hearings held on issues related to economics, climate change, and public health. While there are many potential subjects on which Congress might solicit expert advice, I chose these three areas due to their direct correspondence with three substantive policy areas studied in the micro-level analyses presented throughout this chapter. I measure all of these quantities via the Policy Agendas Project's Congressional Hearings Database (John, 2006; Bevan, 2019), which codes every hearing held from 1946 to present into one of twenty-three different policy domains and then divides each one of those into dozens of other subdomains.

My rationale for turning to congressional hearings is simple. If Congress is choosing to hold more fact-finding efforts (hearings) to guide policymaking decisions with external evidence (i.e., information from individuals outside of Congress), they may be more likely to turn to experts in each of the aforementioned policy areas.

Of course, holding hearings on (say) climate change does not *necessarily* imply that Congress is consulting with climate scientists to inform their legislative activity. Some members of Congress, in periods when parties hostile to expert-informed points of view are charged with leading legislative committees, may even choose to hold hearings that feature testimony from non-expert sources aiming to discredit scientific and scholarly evidence. For example, Republican-led committees have in recent years invited testimony from a select and minority group of scientists who represent the view that climate change is not caused by human activity (Nuccitelli, 2015; see also Perna, Orosz, & Kent, 2019 for a more general investigation of how experts can be used selectively to bolster partisan legislative objectives).

Correspondingly, it is important that I validate the use of legislative hearings as a proxy for expert testimony using both more-direct and other alternative indicators of legislative deference to policy experts. I take up that task in Figure 8.8.

First, in the leftmost panel, I assess the degree to which the number of congressional hearings on macroeconomic issues (measured via the Policy Agendas Project) is correlated with *direct observations* of economists' appearances in congressional testimony, both measured at the quarterly level (i.e., up to eight times within each Congress). I find that dating back to 1947 these two quantities are tightly associated with one another ($r = 0.73$). This indicates that in periods when Congress holds more hearings on economic issues, economists are correspondingly more likely to testify before Congress. Consequently, the hearing proxy measure appears to be capable of serving as an imperfect, yet reliable, stand-in for expert influence measured via congressional testimony appearances.

Next, to ensure that these effects are not peculiar to economists specifically, I perform a similar validation exercise for hearings related to the environment and health (again captured in the Policy Agendas Project coding). Lacking direct observation of climate scientists' or health policy experts' legislative appearances, however, I instead searched the Congressional Record for references to climate scientists—search term: (climate OR envi*) AND scientist*—and health policy experts—search term: health policy—within congressional hearings. I caution here that the latter search term is necessarily somewhat broader than the first because I lack a particular word/phrase that directly refers to health policy expertise.

If the hearings proxy is a valid indicator of expert influence, raw counts of references to some (but certainly not all) of the types of experts we might expect

Anti-Intellectualism and Its Pernicious Policy Consequences 191

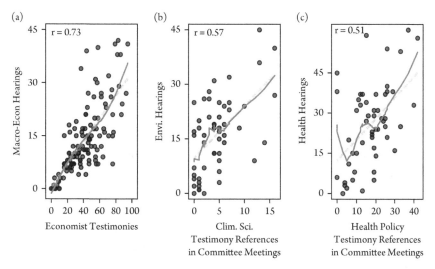

Figure 8.8 Validating the Use of Hearing Count Data as a Proxy for Expert Testimony

to provide evidence-based testimony on climate and public health issues should be highly correlated with references to each one in congressional hearing record proceedings.

The middle and rightmost panels in Figure 8.8 again provide strong evidence in favor of the use of congressional hearing counts as a proxy for expert influence. Note that due to data-limitation restrictions when searching the Congressional Record, I can only assess this relationship from the 107th Congress (2001–2003) onward. Still, in both cases, hearings are positively correlated with references to experts in the Congressional Record (r = 0.57 for climate scientists, and r = 0.51 for health policy experts). This means that in periods when Congress tends to hold more hearings about each issue, we tend to see more references to subject-matter experts in the Congressional Record. Consequently, legislative hearings again appear to be a valid stand-in for congressional consultation with experts in each field.

Collectively, the results of this validation exercise suggest that when Congress holds more hearings about the climate, economy, and public health, they tend to be more likely to involve experts in the policymaking process. Hearings can therefore serve as an imperfect, yet suitable, proxy for a more-direct indicator (expert testimony) of the core concept I am trying to measure: congressional deference to experts when formulating legislation.

In the discussion that follows, I conclude this book's empirical investigation into the policy consequences of anti-intellectual attitude endorsement by assessing how changes in the public's endorsement of anti-intellectual attitudes might influence the extent to which Congress involves experts in the policymaking process.

Climate Science

First I assess the extent to which Congress responds to fluctuations in public anti-intellectual attitude endorsement on issues related to climate science. As suggested in Figure 8.8, I rely on the congressional hearing proxy for expert influence in this investigation.

Figure 8.9 summarizes the results of two different modeling strategies designed to test my expectations. The first set comprises fixed effects models (dark circles). This modeling approach enables me to assess the effect of fluctuations in public anti-intellectualism, measured quarterly, on the number of hearings held *within* Congresses (implying a maximum of eight observations per Congress, assessed across twenty-seven Congresses; N = 120). Studying within-Congress variation in responsiveness to anti-intellectual sentiment is useful because it may help shed light on the electoral pressures legislators encounter when faced with the prospect of reelection at the end of the term (Mayhew, 1974; Fenno, 1977; Abramowitz, 2001).

Because the measure of expert influence is a count variable (i.e., the number of hearings held on environmental issues, per the Policy Agendas

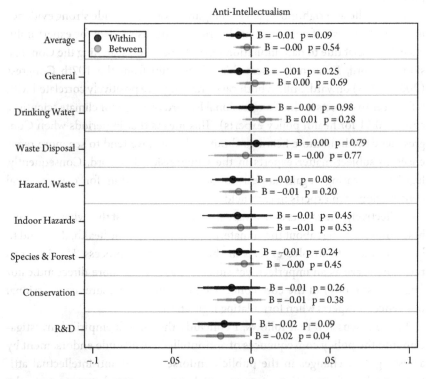

Figure 8.9 The Effect of Change in Macro Anti-Intellectualism on Environmental Hearing Counts

Project), I rely on a negative binomial application of fixed effect panel regression modeling. This modeling approach is more appropriate than conventional fixed effects modeling techniques for assessing change in count data over time.

Similarly, I calculate an analogous series of results *between* Congresses using a negative binomial application of random effects panel regression modeling (light circles). Here an important and somewhat technical caveat is worth mentioning. Because assumptions about the "ignorability" of unobserved confounders do not hold in random effects models—and in the negative binomial case, even in the fixed effects models that I use to calculate within-Congress change (Allison & Waterman, 2002)—I must attempt to control for several factors that could alternatively explain why Congress might take more legislative action in a particular quarter.

Correspondingly, both the fixed and random effects models include several control variables as covariates. First, because the public may express less demand for legislative activity when preferences for limited-government increase, I control for a quarterly indicator of Americans' policy mood (i.e., an indicator of Americans' desired role for government intervention across a variety of policy issues; Stimson, 2018) and macro partisanship (i.e., the proportion of the public identifying as Democrats versus Republicans; MacKuen, Erikson, & Stimson, 1989).

I also control for consumer sentiment, which is an opinion-based measure of Americans' satisfaction with the performance of the macro economy. My rationale for doing so is that public concern about the performance of the economy could inspire Congress to take legislative action to improve macroeconomic performance (most relevant to economic models that I test later in this chapter) or to correspondingly deprioritize legislating in other areas (most relevant to the climate and health models). Furthermore, recall that because I expect Congress to *respond* to changes in anti-intellectual sentiment, I include measures of anti-intellectualism (and all the aforementioned covariates) in the model that are assessed one quarter prior to each observation. In statistical parlance, we can say that these quantities are *lagged* by one quarter. Full model output for all results presented throughout this chapter is available in the appendix.

Finally, it is important to remember that the Policy Agendas Project codes each hearing on the basis of not only its broad policy domain (e.g., environmental issues) but also specific issue areas (e.g., conservation policy). Correspondingly, I include both an averaged measure of the effect of anti-intellectualism on (in this case) experts' environmental policy influence across all policy areas—which I list first in the figure—followed by tests for the possibility of issue-specific heterogeneity across each subdomain.

Figure 8.9 provides evidence in favor of the view that Congress is indeed aware of and responds to changes in public anti-intellectual sentiment with respect to experts' influence on climate policy. I focus first on *within-Congress* effects (dark circles). Across all policy areas (averaged), change in anti-intellectualism within Congresses is negatively ($\beta = -0.01$) and significantly (at the $p < 0.10$ level, two-tailed) associated with decreased hearing counts on environmental issues. As the results of negative binomial regression models are difficult to assess on their own, supplementary analyses suggest that a two standard-deviation shift in anti-intellectual attitude endorsement leads Congress to hold approximately one less hearing on environmental issues per quarter—from 4.17 hearings (on average) in quarters when anti-intellectualism is low to 2.66 in quarters when anti-intellectualism is comparatively high.

I document similar negative and statistically significant within-Congress effects in two sub-issue area domains: hazardous waste disposal hearings ($\beta = -0.01$, $p < 0.10$) and research and development (R&D) for environmental issues ($\beta = -0.02$, $p < 0.10$). Failing to detect similar effects across related subjects may be due to the fact that while the fixed effect regression parameter estimates were negatively signed (and of a similar magnitude) in virtually every subdomain model, the number of hearings held in each area is (necessarily) much smaller than that of the cumulative average. This could therefore increase the estimates' standard errors and reduce the likelihood of documenting a statistically significant effect.

Additionally, I find a less-consistent pattern of effects *between* Congresses (light circles). In these tests, I observe evidence of Congress responding to fluctuations in anti-intellectual attitude endorsement for just issues related to environmental research and development policy ($\beta = -0.02$, $p < 0.10$). Arguably, this may be the policy area in which we might expect Congress to be most likely take action to limit experts' influence, because R&D directly pertains to the funding of expert research. Finding a similar pattern of effects for R&D policy across the fixed and random effects is particularly interesting because it helps further underscore the idea that Congress is reacting to changes in public anti-intellectual sentiment with respect to deference toward expert research. Still, as the random effect models fail to detect evidence of responsiveness across the full series of issue domains, I prefer to treat that interpretation of the results as largely preliminary.

Collectively, the results are consistent with the view that members of Congress are aware of and responsive to fluctuations in public anti-intellectual sentiment and react to those changes by curtailing experts' influence in the policymaking process. This particularly seems to be the case when assessing legislative behavior within (as opposed to across) Congresses. In the discussion that follows, I assess whether the same pattern holds when looking at experts' legislative influence over issues related to the economy and public health.

Economics

Next I study the link between change in public anti-intellectual sentiments and experts' involvement in the policymaking process on macro-economic issues. Because I have both direct (i.e., testimony counts) and proxy (i.e., congressional hearings) measures of expert influence available on this issue, I employ both measures in this empirical exercise.

I begin in Figure 8.10 by plotting the correspondence between counts of economists' testimonies before Congress as a function of lagged quarterly anti-intellectual attitude endorsement in the mass public. I summarize the results of the fixed and random effect negative binomial regression models (analogous to those presented in the previous section) in text at the top of the figure.

Descriptively, the results document a clear correspondence between anti-intellectual sentiments (dashed line) and congressional limits on expert influence (solid line) on macroeconomic issues. In quarters when anti-intellectualism increases, we tend to see a corresponding decline in expert testimony (and vice versa). For example, the late 1970s to early 1990s experienced a period of heightened legislative deference to economic experts precipitated by a corresponding decline in public anti-intellectual sentiment.

Statistically, the results further suggest evidence of congressional responsiveness to anti-intellectual flare-ups in public opinion. Both within ($\beta =$, $p < 0.05$) and

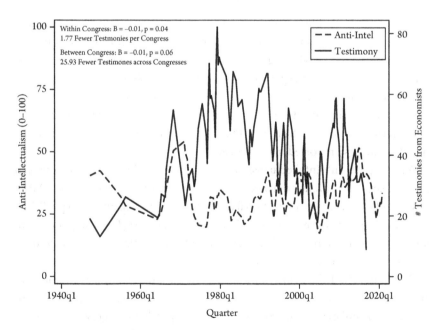

Figure 8.10 The Effect of Change in Macro Anti-Intellectualism on Testimony from Economists in Congressional Hearings

between ($\beta =$, p < 0.05) Congresses, I find that Congress invites fewer economists to participate in the policymaking process when levels of anti-intellectual public sentiment are comparatively high. Within Congresses, these changes correspond to nearly two fewer testimonies per quarter, from 4.71 to 2.94 (a difference of 1.77 testimonies) given a two standard-deviation shift in anti-intellectual attitude prevalence. Between Congresses, I find that a two standard-deviation shift is associated with 25.93 fewer testimonies (from 76.88 to 50.95 per Congress) on average.

In analyses provided in the appendix, I also replicate Figure 8.10 using the committee hearing proxy for expert influence. There I find that (as anticipated) anti-intellectualism is negatively associated with hearing counts on macroeconomic issues. However, these effects fail to attain statistical significance in both the fixed and random effects models. Given the results documented in Figure 8.10, the lack of an effect is somewhat surprising. Still it is important to recognize that these supplemental tests are based on an imperfect proxy for expert influence and are nevertheless correctly signed both within and across Congresses.

Collectively, then, the results broadly support the idea that Congress is responsive to increases in public anti-intellectual sentiments. When the public comes to hold more-negative views toward scientists and experts, Congress tends to respond by limiting their influence in the legislative process.

Public Health

Finally I explore the link between changes in public anti-intellectual sentiment and congressional deference to public health experts on health-related issues. As was the case when studying legislative activity on environmental issues, I again lack a direct measure of expert involvement in the policymaking process and turn to the committee hearing proxy measure discussed earlier.

In the appendix, I create an analogous version of Figure 8.9 that focuses on health-related committee hearings. There I find a more mixed pattern of effects than the findings I reported in the previous two sections.

While lagged anti-intellectualism is associated with decreases in hearings in general (i.e., when averaged across domains) within Congresses ($\beta = -0.01$), these results fail to attain conventional levels of two-tailed significance ($p = 0.18$). I also find little evidence of an effect between Congresses ($\beta = 0.00$ p = n.s.). In both the fixed and random effects cases, I find similar, albeit statistically insignificant, effects across subdomain issue areas.

Consequently, it does not appear to be the case that Congress responds to changes in anti-intellectual sentiment by curtailing the influence of public health experts in the policymaking process. This may imply that Congress is somewhat selective with respect to the areas in which it decides to reduce experts' policy influence. It could be the case, for example, that Congress views expert influence as being more expendable (so to speak) on policies regarding the environment (whose most-dangerous harms may take decades to materialize) versus public health crises (which may have more immediate consequences). Whether this is the case is a fascinating question and one that social scientists ought to explore in future research.

Robustness Checks

In addition to the results presented thus far, I also provide a series of tests designed to assess the robustness of the effects documented earlier. First, if Congress is indeed *responding* to changes in anti-intellectual sentiments by curtailing experts' policy influence, it should be the case that (lagged) changes in expert testimony or committee hearings are not associated with current levels of aggregated anti-intellectual attitude endorsement. This would imply that the public comes to hold more-negative views toward experts when experts are counted on less in the policymaking process (a prediction inconsistent with Hofstader's theorizing and the pattern of effects I documented in the preceding chapter).

Consequently, I provide a series of robustness checks in this chapter's appendix where I swap the temporal ordering of experts' policy influence and public anti-intellectual sentiments. There I find no evidence that this relationship might function in reverse on climate or economic issues (I omit public health from this analysis because those results failed to attain statistical significance in the results presented earlier), which further strengthens the plausibility of the results presented throughout this chapter.

Conclusion

Anti-intellectualism has both a profound and pernicious impact on policymaking in the United States. In this chapter, I showed that people who hold negative feelings toward experts are more likely to reject evidence-based policies, accept policy-relevant misinformation, and take behavioral actions that spurn expert policy guidance. I also showed that the impact of anti-intellectualism on the rejection of expert-recommended policy might further create an incentive for policymakers in Washington, DC, to take action to curtail experts' legislative influence. Indeed, as I show in the latter half of this chapter, Congress tends to respond to increases in public anti-intellectual sentiments by expressing less deference toward experts in the policymaking process.

Taken together, the results presented throughout this book suggest that anti-intellectualism is pervasive and has the potential to diminish the extent to which the United States pursues evidence-based policies on important political issues. Correspondingly, we might then ask whether something can be done to *decrease* the prevalence of anti-intellectualism in the American public and thereby bolster support for policies informed by expert opinion and research.

I conclude this book by discussing the importance of attempting to reduce anti-intellectual attitude endorsement. Pointing to findings presented throughout this book and to previous political and science communication research, I outline a research agenda for scholars interested in taking these critical next steps. I also explore how the findings from this book might be applied cross-nationally, both to better understand the far-ranging policy impact of anti-intellectual attitudes and to explore ways to mitigate its pernicious political influence.

Anti-Scientific Americans: The Prevalence, Origins, and Political Consequences of Anti-Intellectualism in the US. Matthew Motta, Oxford University Press. © Oxford University Press 2024. DOI: 10.1093/9780197788844.003.0008

9

What's Next, Doc?

One week after assuming the presidency on January 20, 2021, President Biden issued a memorandum regarding the restoration of trust in evidence-based policymaking. In the memo, Biden claimed that his administration placed a strong priority on making "evidence-based decisions guided by the best available science and data" (Biden, 2021).

The memo went on to claim:

> Improper political interference in the work of Federal scientists or other scientists who support the work of the Federal Government and in the communication of scientific facts undermines the welfare of the Nation, contributes to systemic inequities and injustices, and violates the trust that the public places in government to best serve its collective interests."
>
> Biden Administration Briefing Room Memo 1/27/2021

At first glance, the Biden administration's defense of policy-relevant research and those who produce it may seem fairly uncontroversial and routine. So too might its corresponding executive order requiring federal agencies to report the degree to which government scientists and other researchers are able to produce and share insights from their work without political interference.

After all, the Obama administration conducted audits like this one on more than one occasion. Typically, when the Obama administration did this, they tended to document generally strong levels of compliance with regulations promoting the free exchange of scientific research and other data (Malakoff, 2021). It may not therefore be immediately obvious why the Biden administration's memo or executive order would be a newsworthy political headline.

The context in which the Biden administration made these comments, however, is crucial. As discussed throughout this book, it represents a major point of departure from the actions of Biden's predecessor, Donald Trump. In addition to ignoring and publicly challenging the advice of his administration's own policy experts, former President Trump forbid researchers from sharing the results of their research and derided scientific and other forms of expertise. The Trump administration, in other words, regularly interfered in the process that experts play in crafting evidence-based policy.

In fact, a similar audit of data transparency and ethics in government organizations conducted in 2019 (during the Trump administration) found that of nine federal research agencies subjected to auditing, five did not regularly follow established protocols for preserving scientific integrity. Two of the nine agencies failed to adopt these protocols *at all* (AIP, 2021). Put simply, the Trump administration fell short of Obama-era expectations with respect to protecting scientific integrity. Perhaps tellingly, a similar rationale may have motivated the Obama administration's effort to take executive actions similar to Biden's (Malakoff, 2021), potentially inspired by allegations of interference from the George W. Bush administration regarding government scientists' abilities to share the results of climate research (Revkin, 2006).

The fact that the Biden administration felt the need to make protecting the integrity of evidence-based policymaking one of the president's first actions in office speaks to the importance of research—and those who produce it—in American political life. Government depends on the advice of experts to inform innovative solutions to pressing policy challenges.

Unfortunately, as I have documented throughout this book, many Americans do not feel the same way. And that may be undermining support for evidence-based public policy.

In *Anti-Scientific Americans* I have demonstrated that anti-intellectualism is both a pervasive and politically consequential phenomenon. After conceptualizing anti-intellectualism as negativity expressed toward people who can credibly claim superior knowledge in highly specialized subject areas, I proposed a new theoretical model for investigating its socio-political origins and policy consequences.

This model made a series of theoretical predictions about how a diverse range of static (partisan identity, ideology, limited-government values, and religiosity) and dynamic (science knowledge and interest) individual-level factors might shape anti-intellectual attitude endorsement. Perhaps even more importantly, the model's Bidirectionality Thesis drew on Hofstadter's often-forgotten theoretical insights to suggest that anti-intellectualism and opposition to the role that experts play in the policymaking process are *mutually reinforcing*.

In testing the model's core predictions, I have presented evidence that nearly one in three Americans can be thought about as holding at least some degree of negativity toward experts at any given time. Correspondingly, macro-level fluctuations in anti-intellectual attitude endorsement tend to precipitate the rise to prominence of major anti-intellectual figures in American public life.

I have also shown that anti-intellectual attitude endorsement, as an individual-level phenomenon, has become highly polarized along partisan, ideological, and religious lines in recent years. Contrary to prior research on the subject, however, I demonstrated that there was a time in the not-too-distant past when Republicans and Democrats alike held similar views toward scientists and experts. The Tea Party, I argue, played a key role in facilitating the recent partisan polarization in anti-intellectual attitude endorsement that we observe today.

Moreover, I have explored the micro dynamics of anti-intellectual attitude endorsement at length in this book. I found that people who become more interested in scientific topics (but not necessarily more knowledgeable) tend to be more likely to reject anti-intellectual attitudes over time, even if they once held negative views toward experts in the recent past. This effect is particularly strong for people currently receiving a college education, where they may be (perhaps for the first time) exposed to scientists and other experts in a highly personal way.

Applying an often-overlooked prediction from Hofstadter's pioneering work on anti-intellectualism to contemporary American public life, I went on to show that views about the role that experts ought to play in the policymaking process and negative attitudes toward scientists and other experts are *co-constituitive*. Consistent with Hofstadter's bidirectional insights, people who fear that experts play too much of a role in the public and political sphere are more likely to harbor negative attitudes toward those individuals. The reverse is also true. People who hold negative views toward experts are more likely to prefer that these individuals play less of a role in the policymaking process. These findings offered an important conceptual background for investigating the myriad effects of anti-intellectualism in American political life.

I concluded the book by showcasing the strong and pernicious effects of anti-intellectual attitude endorsement on American politics and policy, as both a micro- and macro-level phenomenon. People who express stronger anti-intellectual attitudes are less likely to heed public health guidance to protect themselves and others from communicable disease. Moreover, they are more prone to oppose climate and health policies guided by expert voices and evidence, they tend to hold positions about the state of the macro economy and the nature and severity of climate change, and they endorse misinformation/conspiracy theories about public health that defy expert consensus. Alarmingly, studying anti-intellectualism as a macro-level phenomenon, I go on to show that anti-intellectual attitude endorsement appears to create an incentive for Congress to curtail the extent to which it defers to economic, environmental, and health policy experts in the policymaking process, shutting out expert voices to cater to public opinion.

This book, of course, is not meant to be the final word on either the state or consequences of anti-intellectualism in the United States. In many ways, the book raises more questions than it answers.

If anti-intellectualism is so pervasive and pernicious, for example, what can be done to *improve* public sentiment toward experts in the future? We might also consider how American anti-intellectualism compares to negative feelings toward experts in cross-national contexts. Are the causes and consequences of anti-intellectualism that I identified in this book a uniquely American phenomenon? Or might they be transportable to other contexts? Moreover, recent political events may lead us to question whether the expression of anti-intellectual attitudes is necessarily one that overtly denigrates scientists and other experts. Might more subtle but (perhaps) equally pernicious forms of anti-intellectual attitude endorsement play a role in shaping US politics and policy?

For the remainder of this book, I attempt to provide some preliminary answers to these important questions. I also aim to provide a road map by which researchers might attempt to answer each one in future research. It is unlikely, of course, that we will ever obtain complete answers to these important questions. Finding all the answers, however, may not be necessary. As long as researchers continue to try to understand what anti-intellectualism is and why it matters, I believe that we will be able to make significant progress in devising strategies that restore public trust in scientists and other experts and thereby mitigate its pernicious policy effects.

I review several of these basic points in the pages that follow.

Just Asking Questions: Emerging Strains of Anti-Intellectualism

Throughout this book, I conceptualized anti-intellectualism as the dislike and distrust of people who can credibly claim expertise in scientific, medical, academic, and other highly specialized areas. Implied in both this definition and how it is that I operationalized anti-intellectual attitude endorsement in public opinion surveys is the idea that anti-intellectualism is in large part *overt* in nature. Some Americans do not like or trust experts and are more than happy to tell public opinion researchers (like me) about it when asked.

I want to briefly consider, however, the possibility that other, more-subtle variants of anti-intellectualism might either already exist or are starting to develop. What this might imply is that anti-intellectualism does not *necessarily* need to be overt in order to have pernicious policy effects. In fact, more subtle forms of anti-intellectual attitude endorsement may be even more worrisome than the trends documented in this book if they are both politically impactful and hard to detect.

A more subtle, yet equally politically impactful form of anti-intellectualism might look something like this.

In early 2021, Republican lawmakers across the United States introduced a series of proposals to place restrictions on educators' abilities to teach critical race theory (CRT) in primary, secondary, and post-secondary classrooms (Harris, 2021). These proposals came on the heels of former President Trump's efforts to ban the teaching of CRT in government offices by banning government contractors from issuing racial-sensitivity training (Cineas, 2020). The move was later reversed by President Biden (Guynn, 2021) and ignited a widely publicized political debate about the matter.

Although efforts to ban CRT lacked a cohesive definition of what exactly critical race theory is and what the nature of the offense of it being taught in educational settings might be, the measures collectively sent a clear message. Republicans were concerned that teaching young people that America's legacy of slavery can still be felt to this day—a central insight from critical approaches to studying the codification of racism in the United States (Gray, 2021)—could engender support for political causes (e.g., reparations) that stand in opposition to the GOP's policy platform as it is presently constructed. Seemingly tied up in these considerations was the suspicion that high school teachers and college professors had some type of political incentive to import a theory once confined to specialized academic debate into mainstream classroom environments. This suspicion was held not only by Republican elites but also among Republicans in the mass public (Safarpour et al., 2024).

The movement to ban CRT provided some notable points of departure from previous attacks on secondary and higher education from the Trump administration. And of particular relevance to this book, it differed somewhat in the way it expressed negativity toward *educators themselves*. While the comments of some supporters of the movement to ban CRT were reminiscent of the types of anti-intellectual rhetoric discussed throughout this book (i.e., overt and personal attacks on those responsible for educating American youth), others were somewhat more subtle.

Reminiscent of the types of anti-intellectual rhetoric documented throughout this book are President Trump's reactions to an incident in which a campus recruiter for Turning Point USA (TPUSA). TPUSA is a political interest group devoted to promoting conservative voices on college campuses that was attacked by protesters on campus at UC Berkeley (AP, 2019). The former president, troubled by the incident, signed an executive order that would bar universities who fail to uphold his administration's conceptualization of free speech standards from receiving federal research grants.

After signing the order, Trump directly attacked universities, and those who work at them, by claiming that "even as universities have received billions and billions of dollars from taxpayers, many have become increasingly hostile to free speech and to the First Amendment" (AP, 2019). He rekindled this attack weeks later on the social media platform X, formerly known as Twitter, and doubled down on his vow to defund colleges that he viewed as hostile to conservative voices by suggesting that "our children must be Educated [sic], not Indoctrinated [sic]."

The former president's attack on both higher education and educators themselves, as well as his ensuing effort to defund colleges and universities, was met with deep concern from the academic community, who feared that it might lead to government censorship of the free exchange of ideas in university settings. Trump's words, however, were met with enthusiasm from TPUSA. TPUSA maintains a *professor watchlist*, an online database where students can report evidence of supposed political bias in classrooms and that provides information about how to contact the offending individuals (Mele, 2016). The professor watchlist has been thought to play a role in facilitating attacks and online harassment of college professors across the country (Lawson, 2021).

Trump's overtly anti-intellectual rhetoric and alignment with groups who promote anti-intellectual causes differ from those of other key players in the CRT debate. Certainly, there were some who embraced a Trump-style approach to taking on CRT. For example, some well-financed conservative activists have taken action to advocate for tenure denial for academics who take a critical approach to studying race, and in the process have rekindled McCarthy-era attacks by labeling some academics as cultural Marxists (Kamola, 2021). Other examples include Florida Governor Ron DeSantis, who took executive action to defund Florida educational institutions that teach CRT (Ceballos, 2021). In language that strongly echoes that of former President Trump (discussed earlier), DeSantis directly questioned college professors' political motivations in the process by saying:

> I mean, they will attack cops with this type of ideology in schools, and meanwhile, they have like 87% of the kids that aren't even literate in some of these schools. So it shows you they're not trying to educate; they're trying to indoctrinate.
>
> Ron DeSantis (R-FL) on Fox News (6/16/2021), reprinted in
> Gancarski, 2021

Other attacks on CRT and those who allegedly profess it, however, were more subtle. For example, in his response to President Joe Biden's first joint address to Congress, Representative Tim Scott (R-SC) focused less on questioning educators' trustworthiness and potential political motives and more on attacking the principles of CRT itself. For example, he claimed:

> From colleges to corporations to our culture, people are making money and gaining power by pretending we haven't made any progress.

You know this stuff is wrong. Hear me clearly: America is not a racist country.

> Tim Scott (R-SC) rebuttal to President Biden's joint address to Congress (4/28/2021)

Why would educators teach a theory that, in Scott's view, is so self-evidently flawed? A hidden political agenda? A lack of expertise and ability to discern political fact from fiction? While these are reasonable questions to ask, given Scott's comments, the representative does not directly answer these question in his rebuttal to Joe Biden.

Arguably, Scott is brandishing a more subtle form of anti-intellectualism. Rather than expressly denigrate educators outright, he is instead simply raising questions about the acceptability of what is being taught in the classroom. While his comments may imply accusations of nefarious intent or intellectual short-comings, they do not say so outright.

Still, despite their subtlety, comments like Scott's—if the public were to accept them—could create an appetite for limits on what teachers and profes-sors are permitted to say in the classroom. And as I've shown throughout this book, the public's feelings toward experts can play an important role in guiding how politicians in Washington, DC, make policy decisions. Less-overt forms of anti-intellectualism could therefore have enormous political consequences if they (say) foster support for academic censorship.

Going forward, more work should be done to (1) measure more-subtle forms of anti-intellectual thinking and rhetoric in other policy applications and (2) to devise ways to detect evidence that the public holds those views in opinion sur-veys. In addition to assessing how views about (for example) CRT map onto anti-intellectual attitude endorsement, researchers could also ask questions about CRT itself (e.g., the extent to which it can be used to accomplish political objectives). Views that CRT does not belong inside the classroom, due to fears of undue bias, may stand in for related fears about educators' political agendas that survey respondents are unable or unwilling to vocalize.

Beyond CRT, researchers ought to consider how more-subtle forms of anti-intellectual thought might pervade American political discourse more generally. In theory, the ways in which political elites—and potentially members of the mass public—cast doubt on experts' financial, academic, and other motivations without *expressly* denigrating those individuals could shape political discourse on any number of issues where policymakers solicit expert input. For example, some might raise questions about the rigor or appropriateness of academic peer review to the selectively credit (or discredit) policy-relevant academic studies that advance one's political goals. Whatever form this research may take, I look forward to both producing and reading this work in the years to come.

Toward a Unified Approach for Improving Trust in Experts

Throughout this book, I have shown that anti-intellectualism has both a powerful and pernicious effect on policymaking in the United States. I also showed that it is relatively common, with approximately one-third of Americans endorsing anti-intellectual attitudes. Correspondingly, efforts to improve public sentiments toward scientists, doctors, academics, and other experts could not only reduce the popularity anti-intellectual views in the mass public but also bolster support for expert-backed and evidence-based policies.

Suggesting that it is worthwhile to try to reduce anti-intellectual attitude endorsement is, of course, fairly easy. Envisioning what those efforts might actually look like, however, is quite difficult. Here I want to take up that challenge.

Restoring Faith in Experts: A Unified Approach

Previous research from studies in political and science communication represents something of a patchwork effort to improve attitudes toward science, scientific experts, and evidence-informed policies. Conceptually, this makes a lot of sense. As I showed in this book, people do not come to hold negative views about experts for any *one* reason; many socio-political factors underlie anti-intellectualism. The same is true of the myriad factors thought to influence anti-science views more generally.

Correspondingly, it may seem unlikely that any one communication strategy will be effective at engendering support for experts. Communication efforts that make an effort to understand why people hold views that are hostile to policies or positions backed by experts are often most effective when they attempt to (1) understand why people hold the positions that they do and (2) present alternative information in a way that affirms those beliefs (Lupia, 2016; often referred to in social psychological research as *message matching*; Snyder & DeBono, 1985; Rothman, Desmarais, & Lenne, 2020).

For example, self-identified Republicans—who are more likely than Democrats to believe that changes in the planet's climate are not the result of human activity or a serious threat to human life (McCright & Dunlap, 2010; Brulle, Carmichael, & Jenkins, 2012)—are more likely to accept scientific consensus about the dangers and reality of climate change when fellow Republicans (Benegal & Scruggs, 2018) or groups with ideologically conservative reputations (Bolsen et al., 2014; Motta et al., 2020) encourage them to do so. They also tend to be more receptive to arguments that portray environmental protection as advancing traditional conservative moral values (Graham, Haidt, & Nosek, 2009), such as preserving the planet's environmental purity (Scharmer & Snyder,

2021). Relatedly, people who see childhood vaccination as a violation of bodily sanctity are more likely to think that vaccines are safe if presented with information highlighting the bodily transgressions exacted on children by diseases like measles, mumps, and rubella (Lunz-Trujillo et al., 2021).

Because people come to hold anti-intellectual views for many different reasons, some might argue that a single communication strategy aimed at boosting trust in experts may therefore be inefficient. Communicators must devise many different messages that appeal to many different subgroups in the mass public. These messages may also be ineffective if some people are *mis-targeted* with messages that don't functionally "match" the reasons that underlie their skepticism, thereby increasing the possibility of backlash to those messages (Hersh & Schaffner, 2013).

Of course, it is certainly possible to design effective messages that can be more readily presented to broader populations. For example, fact checks and warning labels presented in response to misinformation exposure (e.g., Bode & Vraga, 2015, 2021; Pennycook & Rand, 2019; Clayton et al., 2020; Walter et al., 2020) or in anticipation of it (e.g., Compton, 2013; van der Linden et al., 2017; van der Linden, Roozenbeek, & Compton, 2020) have been shown to reduce the acceptance of untrue claims about political and science-relevant topics.

However, corrective messages are often limited in their ability to shape behavioral intentions (Chan et al., 2017; Nyhan et al., 2014, 2020), which casts some doubt on their ability to improve support for compliance with expert-recommended health, environmental, and other behaviors. More broadly, even if fact-checking methods are effective at correcting misinformation, it is less clear how they could be applied *outside* of the domain of misinformation endorsement (i.e., in this case, improving attitudes toward experts the policies they prefer).

We might therefore ask whether it is possible to move beyond a patchwork approach to strategically communicating the benefits of expertise and instead present a more-unified approach to reducing anti-intellectual attitude endorsement in the United States. I think that some of the insights I shared in this book represent a potential path forward toward achieving this goal.

In Chapter 6, I found that people who come to take a greater interest in scientific topics also tend to become more likely to trust experts over time. I showed that these effects were especially pronounced for individuals currently in the process of earning a college degree, a period in which, as I argued earlier, we might expect people to be particularly receptive to taking an interest in scientific topics. I also noted that one reason why we might see these effects is that people who are more curious about science tend to be more cognitively open to entertaining ideas that challenge their previously held beliefs and partisan commitments (Kahan et al., 2017; Motta et al., 2019).

Correspondingly, it is perhaps unsurprising that people who become more interested in scientific topics over time are more likely to hold positive views toward experts, even if they did not in the past, or subscribe to political or social world views that might otherwise challenge deference to expert authorities.

Can science curiosity be leveraged into a more-universal communication strategy for improving public trust in scientists and other experts? It's certainly possible. I think that to do so, however, requires satisfying three criteria, all of which are presently open questions for future research to take up.

These unanswered questions include:

1. **Demonstrating that science curiosity can function as both a lasting trait and a temporary state.** Perhaps we can increase science curiosity (as a temporary state) through strategic communication strategies. For some, their science curiosity may be a more or less stable trait held throughout their lifetime (i.e., some people are just more interested in and curious about science than others). For others, we might be able to move levels of science curiosity as a temporary state. To do so, we must convince people to take an interest in science, after which they will therefore (if my expectations are correct) hold more positive views toward experts. While I have presented evidence here and elsewhere (Motta, 2018b, 2019) that interest in scientific topics is at least somewhat malleable, whether it might shift in response to *particular* communication efforts to elevate curiosity is an open question.

2. **Demonstrating that short-term effects can lead to long-term change.** For efforts to enhance science curiosity to function as a universal framework for improving trust in experts, it should also be the case that short-term gains in curiosity (i.e., in response to strategic communication interventions) can inspire lasting increases in science curiosity. This ensures that any effort to improve public trust in experts is truly universal in nature (i.e., imparting positive views not just in response to one particular message but for months and years to come).

3. **Demonstrating that curiosity affects evaluations of many different experts.** As discussed in this book, I have found that increased interest in scientific topics is associated with more positive feelings toward scientists, which is itself highly correlated with views toward expertise more generally. Whether science interest has similar effects on other types of experts is, presently, an open question. One could imagine a situation, for example, in which curiosity about scientific topics is effective at engendering support for scientists and medical experts, but less effective at bolstering positive feelings toward economists, academics in non-STEM fields, and others. It may therefore also be helpful to not only explore how elevated levels of science curiosity impact views toward a variety of experts but also to assess how other

forms of *curiosity itself* might do the same. For example, does boosting curiosity about finance, investing, and the economy more generally lead people to develop more-positive views toward economists? Here there is much work to be done.

With these objectives in mind, we might then ask what an effective effort to increase curiosity—and thereby engender positive feelings toward experts—might actually look like in practice. As noted earlier, although several important and unanswered questions remain, I think that this book offers some insight into what an effective strategy might be.

Past research has demonstrated that science interest is highly malleable at young ages (Motta, 2018b) and has underscored the importance of early-life educational experiences at piquing curiosity about science (Miller, 1988). Moreover, as I documented in Chapter 6, the effects of change in science curiosity have a comparatively stronger effect on holding positive attitudes toward experts during one's college years. Correspondingly, one potentially fruitful path forward might be to devise interventions aimed at boosting interest among teenagers and college-age adults. Doing so offers an opportunity to establish interest in scientific topics before people come to hold durable views regarding their feelings about scientific experts and those factors (political, religious, and otherwise; as reviewed in Chapter 2) thought to influence anti-intellectual attitude endorsement.

One way to structure interventions suitable for young adulthood could be as follows. Past research on curiosity suggests that making people aware of deficits in their knowledge about a particular topic can whet their appetite for more information about that subject (Loewenstein, 1994; Arnone & Small, 1995; Golman & Loewenstein, 2015). Correspondingly, presenting young adults with engaging science content—e.g., videos that draw attention to areas of uncertainty in scientific research or common misconceptions about science and that discuss what researchers are doing to address them—might increase their interest in consuming more information about that topic and related scientific concepts. One could imagine, for example, partnering with secondary schools or universities to regularly present students with short, engaging videos that introduce them to deficits in their knowledge about a variety of science-related topics. The hope would be that persistent exposure to knowledge deficits across a pluralistic set of issues that cross many different fields of inquiry could inspire both short-term and (eventually) long-term change in curiosity.

These efforts, of course, would need to be capable of presenting areas of scientific uncertainty in both arousing and approachable formats. This would help ensure that as many people as possible come to understand the limits of their own knowledge and feel the need to acquire more information about those subjects. However, these efforts might be limited in their effectiveness to those who express a strong need to resolve epistemic uncertainty by acquiring more information (Arceneaux & Vander Wilden, 2017). This includes those who have what psychologists refer to as a *strong need for cognition* (i.e., the tendency to enjoy using information and intellect to solve problems; Cacioppo & Petty, 1982) or the need for *cognitive closure* (i.e., the drive to obtain answers to unanswered questions to reduce cognitive uncertainty; Webster & Kruglanski, 1994).

Whether a more-universal approach to reducing anti-intellectual attitude endorsement is plausible is an open question. My goal in this chapter is not necessarily to endorse a particular path forward. Instead, I hope that this discussion presents a series of testable strategies and an agenda for future research for increasing trust in scientists and other experts. In my view, what is most important is not only what these efforts might look like but also that scholars continue to think about how it might be possible to establish lasting gains in positive feelings toward scientists and other experts.

A Brief Note on System-Level Reforms

Before moving on, it is important to mention that individual-level changes in how Americans think about science and scientific expertise are not the only mechanism by which anti-intellectual attitude endorsement might be reduced. Although the linkage might not be obvious (at first), broad system-level changes in American governmental and economic institutions might also play a role in restoring trust in experts.

Consider, for example, unprecedently high levels of wealth inequality in the United States (Piketty & Saez, 2014). As the wealthy accumulate comparatively greater levels of wealth, everyday people may have reason to feel as if they have gotten the "short end of the stick"—i.e., that their economic concerns bear little reflection on government policy (Inglehart & Norris, 2017). This dynamic, Inglehart and Norris argue, in turn provides Americans with an incentive to back populist movements and candidates (such as Donald Trump) who express broad distrust in government and expert authorities, particularly during times of economic uncertainty (Oliver & Rahn, 2016). These movements and candidates promise to empower ordinary people by returning control of the government into their hands. In this way, wealth inequality may (albeit indirectly) foster support for populist worldviews that are in turn associated with expert dislike and distrust.

Beyond the case of Donald Trump (as highlighted throughout this book), perhaps no one exemplifies this dynamic more clearly than 2024 presidential candidate and anti-vaccine activist Robert F. Kennedy Jr. (RFK Jr.).

While it might seem odd to refer to a member of one of America's most prominent political families as a populist—although I suppose the same could be said of a multibillionaire former president—RFK Jr.'s efforts to challenge Joe Biden in the 2024 Democratic primaries were characterized by blanket distrust in government authorities (Goldberg, 2023). Although he is perhaps best known as a vaccine skeptic who casts doubt on the intentions of the pharmaceutical industry and medical experts, Kennedy's campaign routinely suggested that government, military, and other institutions have nefarious intentions at odds with the interests of ordinary people.

In a 2023 stump speech, for example, RFK Jr. directly tied his disdain for American intervention in international conflicts to domestic wealth inequality, arguing that:

> We have a decaying economic infrastructure. We have a demoralized people and despairing people. We have toxins in our air and our soil and our water. We have deteriorating mental and physical health.
>
> RFK Jr., June 22, 2023

RFK Jr.'s campaign vowed to upend the *status quo* by claiming that a Kennedy presidency could "restore America to the awesome vitality of the original Kennedy era." As *New York Times* opinion columnist Michelle Goldberg (2023) put it, this language can be thought of as representing a "more eloquent version of Make America Great Again." In this way, RFK Jr.'s candidacy aimed to link economic inequality as a reason to distrust many institutions—including scientific experts—in order to motivate his efforts to upend conventional politics in Washington, DC. Thus policy efforts to increase economic mobility may have the perhaps-unintended consequence of reducing populist angst and restoring Americans trust in government, economic, and expert institutions. Although we might not think of student loan forgiveness programs, progressive taxation, universal basic income, or efforts to expand the social safety net as having important consequences for anti-intellectual attitude endorsement in the United States, it is quite possible that this might be the case. Correspondingly, I urge researchers and policy practitioners to consider in the future how efforts to mitigate economic inequality might influence Americans' faith in experts.

Is American Anti-Intellectualism Exceptional?

Another set of questions worth investigating in future research involves American exceptionalism with respect to anti-intellectual attitude endorsement on the global stage. Are Americans more likely to hold anti-intellectual attitudes than people in similarly economically developed democracies? Do negative attitudes toward experts map onto existing political divides more clearly in the United States—with a highly polarized two-party system—than it does in multiparty systems? And if so, does anti-intellectual attitude endorsement map less clearly onto support for politically contentious evidence-based policies in political systems where expert negativity may be less polarized by partisanship and ideology?

Past research offers some preliminary insights into some of these questions. For example, efforts to study anti-intellectualism in Canada suggests that. Although support for evidence-based policies and health recommendations in the wake of the COVID-19 pandemic was less polarized by partisanship in a democracy with multiple viable parties in parliament (Pickup, Stecula, & Van Der Linden, 2020), anti-intellectual attitude endorsement was nevertheless strongly associated with the tendency to spurn mask-wearing recommendations and to forego seeking out pandemic-related information from health experts (Merkley & Loewen, 2021). This work suggests that the policy relevance of anti-intellectual attitude endorsement may persist in countries even where the dislike and distrust of experts has not become tightly entangled with partisan identification.

Data from the Wellcome Global Monitor (WGM)—a massive, globally representative survey administered by the Gallup organization in partnership with Wellcome Global Trust—also offers some insights into the dynamics of expert distrust on the global stage. Their 2018 survey asked respondents in 144 countries a series of questions about their trust in scientific and medical experts, as well as their beliefs about the importance of science in everyday life, attitudes toward vaccination, and perceived knowledge about scientific topics. Findings from this survey have found, for example, that positive feelings toward the scientific community are associated with positive views toward vaccination across a variety of national contexts (Sturgis, Brunton-Smith, & Jackson, 2021) and that negative feelings toward medical doctors tend to exacerbate the effect of misinformation accessibility on vaccine skepticism (Lunz-Trujillo & Motta, 2021).

Data from WGM further suggest that the United States is *not* exceptional with respect to harboring negative feelings toward medical doctors and scientific experts. Included in WGM's publicly available datafile, for example, is a four-point intervalized index measuring cross-national trust in the scientific community in academic, industry, and other domains (Gallup, 2019, p 52). Data from the report suggest that cross-nationally few people (fewer than one in five) place high levels of trust in the scientific community. Much of Europe and Oceania have high levels of trust in the scientific community, with high-income countries expressing comparatively high levels of trust (although note that this does not necessarily translate into the acceptance of expert consensus about issues such as vaccine safety and efficacy in wealthier countries; see Lunz-Trujillo & Motta, 2021).

To provide a clearer sense of where the United States ranks among peer high-income countries, I disaggregate the report's regional-level trends in Figure 9.1 among countries deemed to be *high income* by the World Bank (N = 45 countries, N = 44,618 survey respondents). I do this by mean standardizing the study's four-point *trust in scientists* scale, meaning that a score of zero indicates that respondents' views from a particular country tend to match those of the *global* average. Higher scores indicate higher-than-average levels of trust, whereas lower scores denote lower levels of trust. This enables me to draw comparisons between both the United States and its economic peers and between the group of high-income countries collectively and the views of people in other parts of the world.

The results suggest that the United States is *not* exceptional with respect to how it feels about scientists. As Figure 9.1 indicates (see the arrow for reference), Americans score somewhat higher on the *trust in scientists* scale than the high-income global average, but somewhat less highly than those of other wealthy nations. Out of the forty-five countries represented in this figure, the United

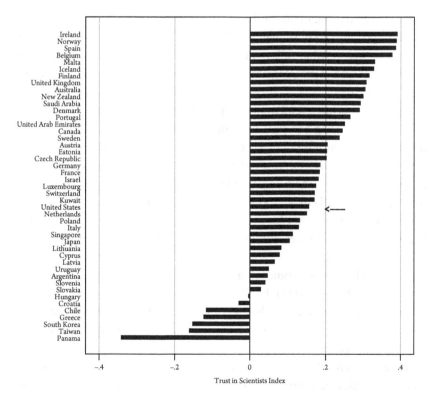

Figure 9.1 Trust in the Scientific Community Across High Income Countries

States ranks twenty-sixth. Democracies in Northern (e.g., Iceland, Norway) and Western (e.g., Ireland, Belgium), and Southern Europe (e.g., Spain, Malta) score particularly highly on this scale compared to the global average. In fact, democracies in Europe comprise the top eight scores on this measure. More generally, high-income countries—with just a handful of exceptions (e.g., Eastern European countries such as Croatia and Hungary and East Asian countries like South Korea and Taiwan)—tend to score more highly than the global average on this measure.

What these results collectively suggest is that inasmuch as there is an opportunity to observe anti-intellectualism in the United States, there appears to be ample opportunity to do so cross-nationally as well (at least in the high-income countries referenced in this chapter). Future research ought to therefore investigate differences in the socio-political foundations of anti-intellectualism cross-nationally explore its policy consequences in a variety of different political systems.

Limitations and Directions for Future Research

As I have noted throughout this book, my efforts to understand the prevalence, origins, and policy consequences of anti-intellectual attitude endorsement are not perfect. In what follows, I discuss what some of these limitations are and how we can best interpret the book's central findings in response to these concerns.

Before I do so, however, I want to begin with a more general point. I *do not* see this book as offering the *final word* on what anti-intellectualism is, where it comes from, or why it is politically problematic. Instead, I see it as the beginning of a broader scholarly conversation devoted to studying each of these topics in greater detail. In fact, the data presented throughout this book suggest that—if anti-intellectualism is indeed a pervasive and problematic presence in contemporary American political life—it is incumbent on the scholarly community to *continually* devise novel and innovative efforts to survey its prevalence and problematic effects.

With that being said, I now discuss several potential limitations of the analyses presented throughout this book.

First, as I discussed at length in Chapter 3, my individual-level measures of anti-intellectual attitude endorsement are not perfect. While I believe that both are well-validated indicators of the concept I hope to measure, they nevertheless offer a just one complementary pair of ways to operationalize anti-intellectualism. Future research may benefit from considering how the American public thinks about many different types of scientific, academic, medical, technical, and other forms of expertise beyond those studied in this book to develop more-holistic assessments of anti-intellectual attitude endorsement.

Similarly, as I discussed in Chapter 4, my efforts to survey the prevalence of anti-intellectual attitude endorsement over time are based on a wide variety of survey questions that vary (at times dramatically) in both frequency and composition over time. The heterogeneity of these questions, as I discussed earlier, can be viewed as a major strength (i.e., because they provide an estimate of anti-intellectual attitude endorsement based on many different ways to gauge negative views toward experts in the American public). As noted above, Chapter 4 overcomes a potential limitation of my more-standardized, yet more-limited, approach to studying anti-intellectualism at the micro level. However, the lack of macro-level standardization over time implies that my cross-sectional quarterly estimates of anti-intellectual attitude endorsement in any one year are not *perfectly* comparable to those of other time points.

Unfortunately, I cannot go back in time to the mid-1940s and warn public-opinion researchers that they ought to ask a variety of standardized questions that gauge anti-intellectualism systematically over time. ("They might be useful one day!") Still, failing to investigate this important topic would be unfortunate, in my view, because it would make it difficult to contextualize the historical roots of modern anti-intellectual attitude endorsement. Instead, I simply caution that the findings presented throughout Chapter 4 are based on aggregated assessments of anti-intellectual attitude endorsement—and used to assess the impact of anti-intellectualism on legislative behavior in Chapter 8—that reflect my best efforts to approximate anti-intellectual attitude endorsement over time. *They are not gospel.*

While I cannot change the past, scholars can take proactive action now to avoid experiencing similar methodological issues in the future. Going forward, researchers should attempt to regularly survey the public via a standardized set of items—perhaps even some of those presented throughout this book—that aim to measure the prevalence and policy consequences of anti-intellectual attitude endorsement.

Finally, it is important to recognize my assessment of the policy consequences of anti-intellectual attitude endorsement is, necessarily, limited in substantive scope. In Chapter 8, I investigated how anti-intellectualism shapes support for expert-backed policies—and the role that experts play in the policymaking process—in just a handful of policy areas. As I noted in Chapter 8, this is not an exhaustive investigation. Far from it!

It very well could be the case that anti-intellectual attitude endorsement influences the rejection of policy-relevant expertise in policy domains that pertain to technical expertise (e.g., nuclear and alternate energy viability, genetically modified food safety, high school and college curricula, etc.) beyond those studied in this book. Scholars should therefore continue to explore the potentially far-reaching policy consequences of anti-intellectualism in future survey research on the topic. I look forward to both consuming and producing this research in the coming years.

It's Personal: Concluding Reflections on the State of Anti-Intellectual Attitude Endorsement in the United States

Now that I have discussed the limitations of this research and directions for future work, I want to offer a few brief concluding remarks about the state of anti-intellectualism in contemporary US politics.

In December 2021, Rob Standridge, a Republican Oklahoma state senator, introduced a series of bills in the state legislature that would—among other things—allow parents to report whether their children were being exposed to "the study of sex, sexual preferences, sexual activity, sexual perversion, sex-based classifications, sexual identity, or gender identity or books that are of a sexual nature" (Kilwans, 2021). To incentivize parent participation, the law—if passed—would offer parents a bounty in exchange for their participation.

Parents could earn up to $10,000 per day that the offending book remained in the classroom, library, or other educational setting. Educators failing to remove the offending texts within thirty days could be dismissed from their job and unable to work in educational settings for two years.

This bill did not become law. But as an educator living in Oklahoma at the time, I worried that it might. Was I worried about nothing? Book-banning bills, after all, may seem as if they lie at the fringes of American politics.

Unfortunately, they do not.

In early 2022, the newly elected governor of Virginia, Glenn Youngkin (also a Republican), established a web page that would allow parents to submit evidence of their children being exposed to *divisive* topics in the classroom, including critical race theory (Villareal, 2022). Similarly, after state legislator Matt Kruse (R-TX) took extra-legislative action to assemble a list of books that he personally found to contain potentially divisive content, he asked school districts to report whether they had any copies of those books in their libraries and classrooms (Chappell, 2022). These efforts came on the heels of broader politically motivated efforts to strip college and university professors who teach about politically and socially contentious subjects in the classroom of tenure protections (Heyward, 2021).

Book bans like the one proposed by Standridge are likely motivated by the types of negative feelings toward experts that underlie anti-intellectual attitude endorsement. As the legislator noted in an interview with *Newsweek*, he felt as if schools should be institutions for math, science, and (ironically) reading. Standridge felt as if educators were, as he put it, trying to "indoctrinate" students and, in so doing, could not be trusted to carry out these essential functions without legislative oversight (Kilwans, 2021).

I know that some may consider it a bit unorthodox to introduce analyses of new data in a book's final passage. However, when given the opportunity to apply recently collected data in service of studying the claims I made earlier, I felt compelled to offer at least a preliminary investigation of whether or not anti-intellectualism might influence Americans' suspicions about college and university professors' political motives.

To study whether anti-intellectualism underlies perceptions of political bias in higher-education settings, I fielded a short public-opinion survey in December 2021 (just before Standridge filed his legislative package proposals in the Oklahoma state legislature) in which I asked 2,007 respondents whether colleges and universities in the United States tend to respect the views of politically liberal students more than those of conservative students, respect the views of conservative students more than those of liberal students, or respect the views of both groups mostly equally.

In that survey, I found that 39 percent of respondents believe that colleges and universities are disproportionately amenable to liberal viewpoints. Critically, in multivariate models structured analogously to those presented in Chapter 8, I found that increased anti-intellectual attitude endorsement is associated with a 19 percent increase—from 29 percent at low levels of anti-intellectual attitude endorsement to 48 percent at high levels—in the likelihood that survey respondents selected this option.

What these preliminary findings suggest is that public opinion about perceptions of liberal bias in educational settings may very well be motivated by the exact same type of anti-intellectual sentiments that underlie the rejection of human-caused climate change, unwillingness to take up evidence-based health behaviors, and susceptibility to accepting misinformation in a variety of politically relevant domains. These findings are, of course, correlational. It could very well be the case that perceptions of political bias also fuel anti-intellectual attitude endorsement (i.e., exhibiting the type of bidirectional relationship I study throughout this book).

Still, the idea that anti-intellectualism underlies (at least in part) the perception of political bias in the classroom may have important policy consequences for the future of higher education in the United States. Bills such as SB 1142 in Oklahoma did not directly target books like the one you are reading right now.

But they very well could have.

Concern about political indoctrination could lead to the censorship of academic writing deemed to be politically incongruous with the goals and values of those who hold political power. Consequently, I believe that the persistent (and pernicious) policy impact of anti-intellectualism in American public life further underscores the need for scholars continue to continue to innovate in this area. It's important to monitor the prevalence of anti-intellectualism, study its politically relevant impacts, and devise new efforts to improve public trust in expert communities.

I look forward to these efforts and to the insights they might bring.

Anti-Scientific Americans: The Prevalence, Origins, and Political Consequences of Anti-Intellectualism in the US. Matthew Motta, Oxford University Press. © Oxford University Press 2024. DOI: 10.1093/9780197788844.003.0009

APPENDIX MATERIALS FOR "ANTI-SCIENTIFIC AMERICANS: THE PREVALENCE, ORIGINS, AND POLITICAL CONSEQUENCES OF ANTI-INTELLECTUALISM IN THE US"

MATTHEW MOTTA, PHD. ASSISTANT PROFESSOR

Dept. of Health Law, Policy, & Management Boston University School of Public Health mmotta@bu.edu

CONTENTS

Supplementary Materials for Chapter 3   221

TECHNICAL COMPENDIUM TO CHAPTER THREE   221

   Estimation Strategy   221

   Notes on Sample Pooling: GSS Panel Study   225

   Notes on the Use of Panel Weights in Non representative Data: CSPP Panel Study   226

TABLE A3.1. COMPARISON OF WEIGHTED AND UNWEIGHTED SAMPLE SUMMARY STATISTICS, 2016 CSPP PANEL SURVEY   228

TABLE A3.2. COMPARISON OF WEIGHTED AND UNWEIGHTED SAMPLE SUMMARY STATISTICS, 2020–2021 SCIPOL ROLLING CROSS-SECTIONAL SURVEY   229

TABLE A3.3. MODELS USED TO BUILD FIGURE 3.3 (ANES MODELS)   232

TABLE A3.4. MODELS USED TO BUILD FIGURE 3.3 (GSS MODELS)   234

TABLE A3.5. SUMMARY STATISTICS FOR SUPPLEMENTAL LUCID STUDY (2021)   236

FIGURE S3.1. REPLICATION OF FIGURE 3.1 WITH THE INCLUSION OF POTENTIAL SATISFICERS   237

FIGURE S3.2. REPLICATION OF FIGURE 3.2 WITH THE INCLUSION OF POTENTIAL SATISFICERS   237

FIGURE S3.3. REPLICATION OF FIGURE 3.3 WITH THE INCLUSION OF POTENTIAL SATISFICERS   238

Supplementary Materials for Chapter 4   238

TABLE A4.1. SAMPLE SUMMARY STATISTICS FOR MAID DATABASE   238

Supplementary Materials for Chapter 5   239

VARIABLE MEASUREMENT   239

GSS Cross-Section   239
2016 CSPP   242
2019 ANES   243
2020 ANES   246
2020–2021 SciPol   249

TABLE A5.1A. MODELS USED TO PRODUCE FIGURES 5.1, 5.3, 5.5, AND 5.7   251

TABLE A5.1B. MODELS USED TO PRODUCE FIGURES 5.1, 5.3, 5.5, AND 5.7   253

TABLE A5.1C. MODELS USED TO PRODUCE FIGURES 5.1, 5.3, 5.5, AND 5.7   255

TABLE A5.2. MODELS USED TO PRODUCE FIGURES 5.2, 5.4, 5.7, AND 5.9   257

TABLE A5.3. MODELS USED TO PRODUCE TABLE 5.1 (REVERSE CAUSALITY TEST SUMMARY)   260

TABLE A5.4. MODELS USED TO PRODUCE FIGURE 5.9 (TEA PARTY, GSS)   263

TABLE A5.5. MODELS USED TO PRODUCE FIGURE 5.10 (TEA PARTY, CSPP)   264

TABLE A5.6. SUMMARY STATISTICS FOR GSS, ANES, CSPP, AND SCIPOL SURVEYS   265

Supplementary Materials for Chapter 6   268

SCIENCE KNOWLEDGE TEST (QUESTION WORDING AND CODING PROTOCOL)   268

TABLE A6.1. FULL MODEL OUTPUT USED TO PRODUCE FIGURE 6.1   270

TABLE A6.2. FULL MODEL OUTPUT USED TO PRODUCE TABLE 6.1   270

TABLE A6.3. FULL MODEL OUTPUT USED TO PRODUCE TABLE 6.2   271

Supplementary Materials for Chapter 7   272

FIGURE S7.1. EXPERT POLICY ROLE ORIENTATIONS: GRADED RESPONSE MODEL (IRT) DIAGNOSTICS AND SUMMARY   272

TABLE S7.1. FULL MODEL OUTPUT USED TO PRODUCE FIGURE 7.2   274

Supplementary Materials for Chapter 8   274

TABLE S8.1. FULL MODEL OUTPUT USED TO PRODUCE FIGURE 8.1   274

TABLE S8.2. FULL MODEL OUTPUT USED TO PRODUCE FIGURE 8.2   276

TABLE S8.3. FULL MODEL OUTPUT USED TO PRODUCE FIGURE 8.3   278

TABLE S8.4. FULL MODEL OUTPUT USED TO PRODUCE FIGURE 8.4   280

TABLE S8.5. FULL MODEL OUTPUT USED TO PRODUCE FIGURE 8.5   283

TABLE S8.6. FULL MODEL OUTPUT USED TO PRODUCE FIGURE 8.5   287

TABLE S8.7. FULL MODEL OUTPUT USED TO PRODUCE FIGURE 8.7   290

TABLE S8.8A. FULL MODEL OUTPUT USED TO PRODUCE FIGURE 8.8
(FIXED EFFECTS)   291

TABLE S8.8B. FULL MODEL OUTPUT USED TO PRODUCE FIGURE 8.8
(RANDOM EFFECTS)   292

TABLE S8.9A. FULL MODEL OUTPUT USED TO PRODUCE FIGURE 8.9
(FIXED FX)   293

TABLE S8.9B. FULL MODEL OUTPUT USED TO PRODUCE FIGURE 8.9
(RANDOM FX)   294

TABLE S8.10A. FULL MODEL OUTPUT USED TO REPLICATE FIGURE 8.8,
FOR HEALTH-RELATED HEARINGS (FIXED FX)   295

TABLE S8.10B. FULL MODEL OUTPUT USED TO REPLICATE FIGURE 8.8,
FOR HEALTH-RELATED HEARINGS (RANDOM FX)   296

TABLE S8.11. REVERSE CAUSALITY CHECKS FOR FIGURES 8.8 AND 8.9   297

Supplementary Materials for Chapter 3

Technical Compendium to Chapter Three

Estimation Strategy

Throughout Chapter 3, I discussed at length the different forms of data that
I draw on throughout this book and the book's corresponding measures of anti-
intellectualism. In this compendium, I briefly review how I *use* these data to put
my theoretical expectations to the empirical test.

Turning back to the theoretical model depicted in Figure 2.1, I first assess the
correlates of anti-intellectualism thought to explain between-person differences
in negative views toward scientists and experts (path a in the figure) in Chapter 5.
To do this, I rely on ordered logistic regression modeling. Because each of the
two anti-intellectualism outcome variables are ordered scales, this modeling
approach is more appropriate than ordinary least squares (OLS) regression
because ordered logistic models are flexible enough to measure separate model
intercepts for each value on the ordered scale. This is advantageous not only because the model is more conceptually appropriate for ordered data (e.g., see
Long 1997) but also because it allows me to calculate quantities (predicted
probabilities) that do not assume *equal spacing* between scale points. More formally, this approach allows me to assume that the effect (β) of each static input
variable thought to produce change in anti-intellectualism (X, Static Inputs) on

anti-intellectualism (Y, AI) is constant across scale points (j), as exemplified in the following equation:

$$AI_j = \beta_0 + \beta \, Static \, Inputs + \beta \, Controls \tag{1}$$

Additionally, this modeling approach implies that I am treating anti-intellectualism *not* as a binary outcome variable—i.e., whether someone can be considered anti-intellectual or not—but instead as a continuum. In other words, I am not classifying people as anti-intellectuals. Instead, I consider people who hold very negative attitudes toward experts to be comparatively more anti-intellectual than people who hold only slightly or more-neutral attitudes. This approach is advantageous because it allows me to both exploit full variation on the anti- intellectualism outcome variables and avoid making conceptually thorny and (somewhat) arbitrary decisions about who to classify as anti-intellectual versus not. In other words, these models "let the data do the talking" by estimating the correlates of anti-intellectual attitude endorsement.

I employ a similar approach when attempting to assess reverse causality. Specifically, in the longitudinal datasets, I *cross lag* the ordered logistic regression models. This means that I regress anti-intellectualism measured in the panel studies' final waves (t) as a function of those same attitudes measured in its first wave (t−1), including each of the potential static inputs as covariates (also measured previously at t−1). To assess the possibility of reverse causality, I then *flip* the temporal ordering of anti-intellectualism and its potential static inputs.

More formally I estimate:

$$AI_t = \beta_0 + \beta \, AI_{t-1} + \beta \, Static \, Inputs_{t-1} + \beta \, Controls_{t-1} \tag{2}$$

And compare those results to:

$$Static_t = \beta_0 + \beta \, Static_{t-1} + \beta \, AI_{t-1} + \beta \, Controls_{t-1} \, \forall \, Static \tag{3}$$

If my theoretical expectations are correct, each of the static inputs entered into these models (measured in the past) should explain (i.e., bear a statistically significant association) differences in the most recent levels of anti-intellectual attitude endorsement (Equation 3.2), while anti-intellectualism (measured in the past) should not be associated with change in the hypothesized static inputs (Equation 3.3).

Before moving on, I want to briefly point out cross-lagged models are typically constructed using OLS regression (Kenny, 1975; Kearney, 2017). This enables researchers to directly compare the substantive magnitude of effect sizes in either the hypothesized causal or reverse causal direction so long as all variables are measured on similar scales.

However, as noted earlier, OLS regression is less conceptually appropriate and empirically less desirable for my purposes in this book than ordered logistic regression modeling. Consequently, I estimate the cross-lagged models using ordered logistic regression when anti-intellectualism is the outcome variable and whatever estimator is most appropriate for each static input. This means that while effect sizes are not directly comparable (as is often the case when interpreting coefficients from maximum likelihood models), it is at least possible to determine the direction (negative, positive) and statistical significance of the reverse causality tests. As I am less concerned with the magnitude of potential reverse causal effects—and instead consider a relationship to be spurious if anti-intellectualism is significantly associated with each of the static inputs into the model—this, in my view, is an empirically justifiable approach.

Note also that the panel data are *wide* when estimating the cross-lagged models. This means that columns in the dataset are each variable measured at a different point in time, with one row per survey respondent. When wide, the data record one measure of anti-intellectualism, per respondent, and per longitudinal wave (i.e., there are several columns, or variables, denoting anti-intellectual attitude scores per wave). It is helpful to contrast the wide structure from *long* or *stacked* structuring of the panel data—a single column per variable with multiple observations per respondent—which is necessary to estimate the models I discuss below.

Next I test for a relationship between the anti-intellectualism and its hypothesized dynamic inputs (path b in Figure 2.1) using fixed effects regression modeling. Fixed effects models allow me to estimate how change in science knowledge and interest might lead to change in anti-intellectualism, controlling for the influence of other time varying factors (in this case, each of the hypothesized static inputs: partisanship, political ideology, religiosity, and limited government attitudes).

Fixed effects models estimate change *within survey respondents* over time. Consequently, because they are not concerned with estimating between-person effects, results from these models cannot be attributed to unobserved differences between survey respondents (Allison, 2009). This property of fixed effects modeling is desirable because it allows me to estimate the effect of science knowledge and interest independently of potentially unobserved between-person confounds that may result from model specification choices (i.e., the factors I choose to include and/or exclude from the model). These models have the added benefit of providing an alternate, time-varying, and within-person test of the *static inputs* expectations from the theoretical model (i.e., by assessing whether change in each one—which I suspect is rare—leads to change in anti-intellectualism) and allowing me to directly estimate the stability of each one prior to conducting the correlational analyses described earlier.

More formally, I estimate the effect of change in anti-intellectualism over time (t through T) for each respondent (i through N) as follows:

$$AI_{it} = \beta_0 + \beta \, Dynamic_{it} + \beta \, Controls_{it}, \quad i = 1...N, t = 1...T. \tag{4}$$

Unfortunately, however, it is difficult to apply fixed effects modeling techniques in ordered logistic regression setups. The primary reason for this difficulty is that it is impossible to preserve the ordered nature of the outcome data when differencing each entry into the model (Baetschmann, Staub, & Winkelmann, 2011). Consequently, I rely on ordinary least square applications of fixed effects modeling when testing each dynamic hypothesis. Moreover, as was the case when testing path a from Figure 2.1, I again turn to cross-lagged models to assess the possibility of reverse causality regarding the hypothesized dynamic inputs (e.g., to assess whether changes in anti-intellectualism are associated with change in science knowledge).

Finally, I test expectations related to the bidirectionality of anti-intellectualism and expert policy role attitudes using a combination of both time-varying approaches reviewed above (i.e., fixed effects regression modeling, cross-lagged modeling). First, because I have a measure of both anti-intellectualism and a general indicator of opposition to the role that scientists play in the policymaking process (Chapter 7) available in the GSS panel study (see Table 3.1), I can estimate both fixed effects and cross-lagged models. This allows me to assess how anti-intellectualism might lead to within-person change in policy orientations (fixed effects) and to assess the possibility of reverse causality (cross-lagged).

Beyond testing the hypothesized bidirectional relationship between expert policy attitudes and anti-intellectualism in Chapter 7, I also offer an exploration into a wide variety of specific politically relevant consequences anti-intellectualism might have for both Americans' policy preferences on expert-backed issues and positions and on Congress's willingness to defer to expertise in the policymaking process.

When testing the former—i.e., the effect of anti-intellectualism on Americans' policy orientations, policy-relevant misinformation endorsement, self-reported behavior, and other outcomes—I rely on a combination of either logistic, ordered logistic, or OLS regression modeling, depending on the measurement of the outcome variable. As most studies containing outcomes relevant to specific policy orientations tend to do so in just a single survey wave (as I review in Chapter 8), my goal is simply to assess whether a correlation exists between anti-intellectualism and policy-relevant positions, controlling for other factors that could potentially influence policy orientations.

When assessing the latter—i.e., the effects of anti-intellectualism on legislative deference to experts in the aggregate—I again turn both fixed effects and random effects panel regression modeling. Random effects models are similar to fixed effects models in construction, but instead estimate effects *between* subjects (in this case, legislative activity across Congresses and over time). Because data are calculated at the quarterly level, I treat each Congress as a panel unit and estimate the effects of anti-intellectualism both within (fixed effects) and between (random effects) Congresses. Because random effects models do not share with fixed effects models the assumption of ignorability between subjects (i.e., because they are models that aim to draw inferences between observations), I account for several time-varying factors that could alternatively explain differences in deference to experts both within and across Congress (i.e., policy mood, macro partisanship, and consumer sentiment; discussed in detail earlier in this chapter).

Note that because the hearing and testimony aggregations that I use to measure legislative activity are count data, it would be most appropriate to estimate negative binomial fixed and random effect regression models. However, as Allison and Waterman (2002) demonstrate, assumptions of between-panelist effect independence does not hold in negative binomial fixed effect models. Consequently, I again make use of an OLS application of fixed effects modeling with estimating these effects.

Notes on Sample Pooling: GSS Panel Study

As a brief but important technical note, pooling longitudinal survey ballots together in the way outlined in Chapter 3 makes the assumption that attitudes toward the scientific community are not systematically different across the initial years of survey contact. In other words, levels of anti-intellectual attitude endorsement in the general public should be relatively similar across panel waves. If this assumption is not met, the panel studies may *underestimate* the likelihood of detecting the effects described earlier, implying that the relationship between anti-intellectualism and its hypothesized causes or consequences applies in some time periods and not others.

The assumption of temporal intransigence may seem to be a fairly safe one given the panels' relatively short duration. Still, it is important to note that one of the initial contact periods (the 2010–2014 panel) takes place following the rise the Tea Party, which I expect to exacerbate partisan polarization in anti-intellectual attitude endorsement. Fortunately, the cross-sectional data described earlier allow me to test the viability of intransigence across the population. I find that initial levels of anti-intellectual attitude endorsement (which I discuss in more detail later on in this chapter) are generally quite similar across time points, ranging from 32 percent [95 percent CI: 29, 34] in 2006, 32 percent again in 2008 [30, 34], and 31 percent in 2010 [29, 33]. As implied by the overlapping 95 percent confidence intervals across waves, none of these differences are significantly different from one another statistically. Correspondingly, the assumption of intransigence seems to be well supported by the available data. And in the unlikely event that this assumption were to be violated, it is also important to keep in mind that doing so would make it more *difficult* for me to find evidence consistent with my theoretical expectations—not easier.

One final (and more general) limitation of the GSS panel study is that it provides just a single measure of anti-intellectual attitudes: trust/distrust in the scientific community. As I show later in this chapter, this measure is strongly associated with other measures of anti-intellectualism and is similarly correlated with other attitudes that we might expect to be associated with anti-intellectualism (e.g., distrust in specific experts and institutions). Still, it is nevertheless conceptually limited with respect to who it identifies as an expert.

Notes on the Use of Panel Weights in Non representative Data: CSPP Panel Study

As I alluded to in the main text, one major benefit of the CSPP panel study is that its longitudinal structure allows me to devise tests of reverse causality. As noted earlier, I primarily do this via cross-lagged regression modeling procedures that are correlational in nature and are primarily concerned with drawing comparisons about the direction and statistical significance of effects they might detect. Because the goal of cross-lagged modeling is to ascertain *whether an observed relationship may function in reverse*—and not necessarily documenting the precise size of that effect in the population—differences between the sample and population are unlikely to negatively influence findings from those tests as well.

Appendix Materials

One final (and important) point bears mentioning. As data from the CSPP panel study are not formally nationally representative, some might ask whether it is worthwhile to apply survey weights when attempting to draw conclusions from this study. If my primary goal were to use this study to generalize *proportions* from this survey to the general population (e.g., the percentage of people in the sample who endorse anti-intellectual attitudes), applying post-stratification weights would be essential. Indeed, the study includes weights that (1) correct for differences between the sample and population on race, age, gender, and educational attainment and (2) adjust for the possibility of asymmetric non-response across demographic groups in the study's second wave.

This, however, is not the primary reason I make use of the CSPP data. As outlined above, I use the CSPP study throughout this book to (1) provide correlational tests of the theoretical model's socio-political inputs and to (2) construct time-varying tests reverse causality assessments. Panel weights are, correspondingly, not necessarily required to do that.

In fact, some might even see it as inappropriate to weight the CSPP data for these purposes. Recently, several scholars have noted important challenges with weighting data drawn from nonprobability samples of the American public like the CSPP panel. Because these studies lack of a sampling frame where respondents have a known and/or equal probability of selection into the sample, we cannot be sure that unobserved resource-based or behavioral factors might not have influenced self-selection into the sampling frame (Pasek, 2016; MacInnis et al., 2018). Sampling weights might therefore not adequately support assertions that can be generalized to the entire US population. Additionally, they may information about how to adjust respondents' probability of being included in the sampling frame on the basis of their observed demographic characteristics. More technically, this means that any weighting strategy we might employ must make the, likely incorrect, assumption of equal probability of selection into the sampling frame.

Consequently, I opt to apply post-stratification weights selectively. As a general rule, I do not apply survey weights making correlational or within-subject time-varying claims from the CSPP and other opt-in studies used throughout this book. I do, however, apply post-stratification weights where available in the nationally representative probability sample studies (ANES, GSS) to provide the most accurate and statistically conservative test of my theoretical expectations. Consequently, I urge caution when attempting to generalize sample means, effect sizes, and point estimates to the US adult population, particularly from online opt-in panel studies like the CSPP panel study.

Table A3.1 **Comparison of Weighted and Unweighted Sample Summary Statistics, 2016 CSPP Panel Survey**

Variable	CSPP Data (Raw)	CSPP Data (Weighted)	Benchmark	Benchmark Source
		Wave 1 (Recruitment)		
Female	62%	53%	51%	CPS
College Degree	45%	31%	31%	CPS
Black	14%	15%	13%	CPS
White	64%	67%	62%	CPS
Hispanic	17%	17%	18%	CPS
Democrat	42%	39%	34%	ANES (Wgt.)
Republican	32%	33%	28%	ANES (Wgt.)
Independent	25%	27%	32%	ANES (Wgt.)
Mean Age	51	44	47	ANES (Wgt.)
Median Income	$50 – 74,999	$50 – 74,999	$55 – 59,999	ANES (Wgt.)
		Wave 2 (Remaining)		
Female	62%	54%	51%	CPS
College Degree	44%	33%	31%	CPS
Black	14%	11%	13%	CPS
White	67%	73%	62%	CPS
Hispanic	14%	13%	18%	CPS
Democrat	43%	41%	34%	ANES (Wgt.)
Republican	32%	32%	28%	ANES (Wgt.)
Independent	25%	26%	32%	ANES (Wgt.)
Mean Age	54	47	47	ANES (Wgt.)
Median Income	$50 – 74,999	$50 – 74,999	$55 – 59,999	ANES (Wgt.)

Note: Comparison of CSPP panel to known population benchmarks. CPS = Current Population Survey (US census, 2018; five-year averages). ANES = American National Election Study (2016). We prefer to rely on CPS, given its sample size and representativeness, but make use of weighted ANES data whenever it was not possible to use CPS (e.g., CPS does not ask questions about party ID). Weights in column two adjust for gender, education, race, age, and income.

Appendix Materials

Table A3.2 Comparison of Weighted and Unweighted Sample Summary Statistics, 2020–2021 SciPol Rolling Cross-Sectional Survey

Variable	SciPol Data (Raw)	SciPol Data (Weighted)	Benchmark	Benchmark Source
Wave 1				
Female	50%	52%	51%	CPS
College Degree	43%	34%	31%	CPS
Black	11%	14%	13%	CPS
White	68%	60%	62%	CPS
Hispanic	12%	17%	18%	CPS
Democrat	37%	34%	34%	ANES (Wgt.)
Republican	34%	35%	28%	ANES (Wgt.)
Independent	23%	23%	32%	ANES (Wgt.)
Mean Age	45	46	47	ANES (Wgt.)
Median Income	$45 – 49,999	$65 – 69,999	$55 – 59,999	ANES (Wgt.)
Wave 2				
Female	51%	51%	51%	CPS
College Degree	45%	34%	31%	CPS
Black	11%	14%	13%	CPS
White	68%	64%	62%	CPS
Hispanic	12%	16%	18%	CPS
Democrat	40%	41%	34%	ANES (Wgt.)
Republican	35%	36%	28%	ANES (Wgt.)
Independent	23%	23%	32%	ANES (Wgt.)
Mean Age	45	47	47	ANES (Wgt.)
Median Income	$40 – 44,999	$60 – 64,999	$55 – 59,999	ANES (Wgt.)

(*Continued*)

Table A3.2 **Continued**

Variable	SciPol Data (Raw)	SciPol Data (Weighted)	Benchmark	Benchmark Source
		Wave 3		
Female	51%	50%	51%	CPS
College Degree	38%	33%	31%	CPS
Black	11%	12%	13%	CPS
White	68%	64%	62%	CPS
Hispanic	12%	16%	18%	CPS
Democrat	36%	36%	34%	ANES (Wgt.)
Republican	36%	32%	28%	ANES (Wgt.)
Independent	24%	23%	32%	ANES (Wgt.)
Mean Age	45	47	47	ANES (Wgt.)
Median Income	$40 – 44,999	$60 – 64,999	$55 – 59,999	ANES (Wgt.)
		Wave 4		
Female	51%	51%	51%	CPS
College Degree	51%	33%	31%	CPS
Black	10%	11%	13%	CPS
White	66%	64%	62%	CPS
Hispanic	14%	17%	18%	CPS
Democrat	36%	37%	34%	ANES (Wgt.)
Republican	38%	43%	28%	ANES (Wgt.)
Independent	21%	21%	32%	ANES (Wgt.)
Mean Age	45	46	47	ANES (Wgt.)
Median Income	$50 – 54,999	$70 – 74,999	$55 – 59,999	ANES (Wgt.)

Appendix Materials

Variable	SciPol Data (Raw)	SciPol Data (Weighted)	Benchmark	Benchmark Source
Wave 5				
Female	53%	51%	51%	CPS
College Degree	54%	36%	31%	CPS
Black	10%	11%	13%	CPS
White	70%	60%	62%	CPS
Hispanic	13%	21%	18%	CPS
Democrat	49%	46%	34%	ANES (Wgt.)
Republican	26%	27%	28%	ANES (Wgt.)
Independent	22%	26%	32%	ANES (Wgt.)
Mean Age	43	46	47	ANES (Wgt.)
Median Income	$45 – 49,999	$65 – 69,999	$55 – 59,999	ANES (Wgt.)
Wave 6				
Female	52%	50%	51%	CPS
College Degree	48%	34%	31%	CPS
Black	10%	12%	13%	CPS
White	70%	62%	62%	CPS
Hispanic	11%	18%	18%	CPS
Democrat	41%	41%	34%	ANES (Wgt.)
Republican	28%	31%	28%	ANES (Wgt.)
Independent	24%	28%	32%	ANES (Wgt.)
Mean Age	46	47	47	ANES (Wgt.)
Median Income	$50 – 54,999	$60 – 64,999	$55 – 59,999	ANES (Wgt.)

Note: Comparison of SciPol RXC to known population benchmarks. CPS = Current Population Survey (US census, 2018; five-year averages). ANES = American National Election Study (2016). We prefer to rely on CPS, given its sample size and representativeness, but make use of weighted ANES data whenever it was not possible to use CPS (e.g., CPS does not ask questions about party ID). Weights in column two adjust for gender, education, race, age, and income.

Table A3.3 **Models Used to Build Figure 3.3 (ANES Models)**

	Sci.	Profs.	Drs.	Econ.	Fauci	Yellen	Walensky	Clim. Sci.
Anti-Intel. (Expert Version)	-0.18* [-0.25,-0.11]	-0.08+ [-0.16,0.01]	-0.05 [-0.12,0.02]	0.03 [-0.05,0.10]	-0.19* [-0.28,-0.10]	0.00 [-0.09,0.09]	-0.09* [-0.18,-0.00]	-0.20* [-0.29,-0.12]
College Educ.	0.06* [0.01,0.11]	0.04 [-0.02,0.10]	0.01 [-0.04,0.05]	0.07* [0.02,0.12]	0.07* [0.01,0.14]	0.08* [0.01,0.14]	0.10* [0.04,0.16]	0.05 [-0.01,0.10]
Ideo. (1 = Conservative)	-0.12* [-0.21,-0.03]	-0.18* [-0.29,-0.07]	-0.06 [-0.15,0.03]	-0.02 [-0.11,0.07]	-0.27* [-0.39,-0.15]	-0.19* [-0.30,-0.07]	-0.18* [-0.29,-0.06]	-0.23* [-0.34,-0.12]
Party ID (1 = GOP)	-0.12* [-0.19,-0.05]	-0.21* [-0.29,-0.12]	-0.06+ [-0.12,0.01]	-0.13* [-0.20,-0.06]	-0.35* [-0.44,-0.26]	-0.28* [-0.37,-0.20]	-0.30* [-0.38,-0.21]	-0.18* [-0.26,-0.09]
Rel. Service Attendance	-0.02 [-0.09,0.04]	-0.02 [-0.09,0.06]	0.04 [-0.02,0.10]	0.03 [-0.04,0.09]	0.09* [0.00,0.17]	0.08+ [-0.00,0.16]	0.08+ [-0.00,0.16]	-0.01 [-0.09,0.06]
Race = Black	-0.08+ [-0.17,0.01]	-0.04 [-0.15,0.07]	-0.09* [-0.17,-0.00]	0.02 [-0.08,0.11]	-0.02 [-0.13,0.10]	0.02 [-0.09,0.13]	-0.00 [-0.11,0.11]	-0.05 [-0.15,0.06]
Hispanic	-0.10* [-0.18,-0.02]	-0.07 [-0.17,0.03]	-0.01 [-0.09,0.07]	0.07+ [-0.01,0.16]	-0.10+ [-0.21,0.01]	-0.07 [-0.17,0.03]	-0.08 [-0.18,0.02]	-0.10* [-0.20,-0.00]
Income	0.01 [-0.02,0.04]	-0.02 [-0.06,0.02]	0.01 [-0.02,0.04]	0.02 [-0.01,0.06]	-0.02 [-0.06,0.02]	0.02 [-0.02,0.06]	-0.00 [-0.04,0.04]	0.01 [-0.02,0.05]

Age: 24–44	−0.04	−0.04	0.01	0.10*	0.04	−0.03	−0.01	−0.06
	[−0.14,0.06]	[−0.15,0.08]	[−0.08,0.10]	[0.01,0.20]	[−0.08,0.16]	[−0.14,0.09]	[−0.13,0.11]	[−0.17,0.05]
Age: 44–64	−0.04	−0.06	0.03	0.10+	0.09	0.02	0.05	−0.10+
	[−0.14,0.06]	[−0.18,0.05]	[−0.06,0.12]	[−0.00,0.20]	[−0.04,0.21]	[−0.10,0.14]	[−0.07,0.16]	[−0.21,0.01]
Age: 65+	0.01	−0.05	0.09+	0.20*	0.13*	0.10	0.08	−0.05
	[−0.09,0.12]	[−0.17,0.08]	[−0.01,0.19]	[0.09,0.30]	[0.00,0.27]	[−0.03,0.23]	[−0.04,0.20]	[−0.17,0.07]
Female	−0.03	0.01	0.01	−0.01	−0.01	0.01	0.03	−0.03
	[−0.07,0.02]	[−0.04,0.06]	[−0.04,0.05]	[−0.06,0.03]	[−0.07,0.04]	[−0.05,0.07]	[−0.03,0.08]	[−0.09,0.02]
β_0	0.94*	0.93*	0.80*	0.51*	0.92*	0.64*	0.73*	1.00*
	[0.82,1.06]	[0.78,1.07]	[0.68,0.91]	[0.38,0.63]	[0.76,1.07]	[0.49,0.79]	[0.58,0.88]	[0.86,1.14]
N	339	341	342	341	342	343	341	341
R^2	0.26	0.24	0.09	0.16	0.43	0.32	0.35	0.32

Note: OLS coefficients presented with 95 percent confidence intervals in brackets. For scale-validation purposes, models exclude individuals who completed the survey in less than half of the anticipated completion time (7 minutes for a 15- to 20-minute survey). Additional information about these models can be found in the main text.

Table A3.4 **Models Used to Build Figure 3.3 (GSS Models)**

	Sci.	Profs.	Drs.	Econ.	Fauci	Yellen	Walensky	Clim. Sci.
Anti-Intel. (Sci.)	-0.18* [-0.22,-0.13]	-0.14* [-0.19,-0.08]	-0.13* [-0.17,-0.08]	-0.08* [-0.13,-0.04]	-0.15* [-0.21,-0.09]	-0.11* [-0.17,-0.05]	-0.15* [-0.21,-0.10]	-0.18* [-0.24,-0.13]
College Educ.	0.06+ [-0.00,0.12]	0.08* [0.02,0.14]	0.04 [-0.01,0.09]	0.02 [-0.04,0.08]	-0.01 [-0.06,0.03]	0.06* [0.01,0.11]	0.06+ [-0.01,0.12]	0.03 [-0.03,0.08]
Ideo. (1 = Conservative)	-0.17* [-0.28,-0.06]	-0.15* [-0.26,-0.04]	-0.10* [-0.19,-0.01]	-0.16* [-0.26,-0.05]	-0.04 [-0.13,0.04]	-0.01 [-0.10,0.08]	-0.24* [-0.36,-0.13]	-0.20* [-0.31,-0.09]
Party ID (1 = GOP)	-0.25* [-0.33,-0.16]	-0.26* [-0.34,-0.17]	-0.09* [-0.16,-0.02]	-0.17* [-0.26,-0.09]	-0.03 [-0.09,0.04]	-0.10* [-0.17,-0.03]	-0.33* [-0.42,-0.24]	-0.14* [-0.23,-0.06]
Rel. Service Attendance	0.08* [0.00,0.16]	0.06 [-0.01,0.14]	-0.04 [-0.10,0.02]	-0.03 [-0.10,0.05]	0.03 [-0.03,0.09]	0.03 [-0.04,0.09]	0.06 [-0.02,0.14]	-0.04 [-0.11,0.03]
Race = Black	0.05 [-0.06,0.16]	0.04 [-0.07,0.14]	-0.03 [-0.12,0.05]	-0.01 [-0.11,0.10]	-0.06 [-0.14,0.03]	0.03 [-0.06,0.12]	0.02 [-0.09,0.14]	0.00 [-0.10,0.10]
Hispanic	-0.07 [-0.17,0.03]	-0.08 [-0.18,0.02]	-0.10* [-0.18,-0.02]	-0.07 [-0.17,0.02]	-0.01 [-0.08,0.07]	0.07+ [-0.01,0.15]	-0.10+ [-0.21,0.01]	-0.10* [-0.20,-0.01]
Income	0.02 [-0.02,0.06]	0.00 [-0.03,0.04]	0.01 [-0.01,0.04]	-0.02 [-0.05,0.02]	0.01 [-0.01,0.04]	0.03 [-0.01,0.06]	-0.02 [-0.06,0.02]	0.02 [-0.02,0.05]

	(1)	(2)	(3)	(4)	(5)	(6)	(7)	(8)
Age: 24–44	-0.01	0.01	-0.00	-0.02	0.03	0.12*	0.06	-0.03
	[-0.13,0.10]	[-0.10,0.13]	[-0.10,0.09]	[-0.13,0.10]	[-0.06,0.12]	[0.02,0.22]	[-0.06,0.18]	[-0.14,0.08]
Age: 44–64	0.02	0.05	-0.02	-0.06	0.03	0.09+	0.10	-0.09
	[-0.10,0.13]	[-0.06,0.16]	[-0.11,0.07]	[-0.17,0.06]	[-0.06,0.12]	[-0.00,0.19]	[-0.03,0.22]	[-0.19,0.02]
Age: 65+	0.10	0.09	0.04	-0.04	0.09*	0.19*	0.15*	-0.03
	[-0.03,0.22]	[-0.03,0.21]	[-0.06,0.14]	[-0.16,0.08]	[0.00,0.19]	[0.09,0.30]	[0.02,0.28]	[-0.14,0.09]
Female	0.01	0.03	-0.01	0.01	0.01	-0.02	0.00	-0.02
	[-0.05,0.06]	[-0.02,0.09]	[-0.05,0.03]	[-0.04,0.07]	[-0.03,0.05]	[-0.06,0.03]	[-0.06,0.06]	[-0.07,0.03]
β_0	0.68*	0.75*	0.91*	0.95*	0.82*	0.55*	0.89*	0.98*
	[0.54,0.83]	[0.61,0.89]	[0.80,1.03]	[0.81,1.08]	[0.72,0.93]	[0.43,0.67]	[0.74,1.05]	[0.84,1.11]
N	343	341	339	341	342	341	342	341
R^2	0.34	0.39	0.32	0.29	0.16	0.19	0.44	0.36

Note: OLS coefficients presented with 95 percent confidence intervals in brackets. For scale-validation purposes, models exclude individuals who completed the survey in less than half of the anticipated completion time. Additional information about these models can be found in the main text.

Table A3.5 **Summary Statistics for Supplemental Lucid Study (2021)**

Variable	Mean	SD	Min	Max	N
Anti-Intel. (ANES)	0.481	0.325	0	1	478
Anti-Intel. (GSS)	0.613	0.488	0	1	478
Ideology (1 = Cons.)	0.47	0.306	0	1	478
PID (1 = GOP)	0.417	0.398	0	1	455
Religiosity	0.379	0.368	0	1	478
Educ. (1 = College)	0.435	0.496	0	1	478
Race = Black	0.092	0.289	0	1	468
Ethnicity = Hispanic	0.121	0.327	0	1	478
Income	0.371	0.319	0	1	455
Age 18–24	0.121	0.327	0	1	478
Age 25–44	0.385	0.487	0	1	478
Age 44–64	0.314	0.465	0	1	478
Age 65+	0.18	0.385	0	1	478
Gender = Female	0.517	0.5	0	1	478

Note: Unweighted sample summary statistics for the supplemental 2021 Lucid survey. N represents the number of non-missing observations on each variable.

Appendix Materials

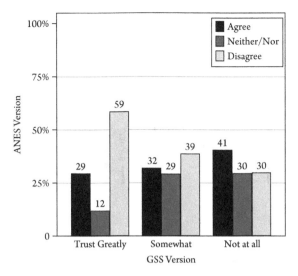

Figure S3.1 Replication of Figure 3.1 with the inclusion of potential satisficers
Note: Analyses include respondents who completed the survey in less than half of the survey's anticipated completion time. Figure S3.1 is otherwise analogous to Figure 3.1 in the main text. Please refer to Figure 3.1 and my discussion of the importance of accounting for satisficing in these validation analyses for additional information.

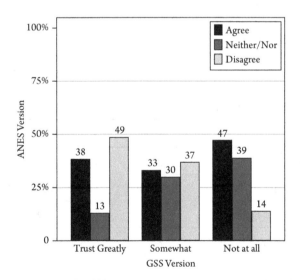

Figure S3.2 Replication of Figure 3.2 with the inclusion of potential satisficers
Note: Analyses include respondents who completed the survey in less than half of the survey's anticipated completion time. Figure S.3.2 is otherwise analogous to Figure 3.2 in the main text. Please refer to Figure 3.2 and my discussion of the importance of accounting for satisficing in these validation analyses for additional information.

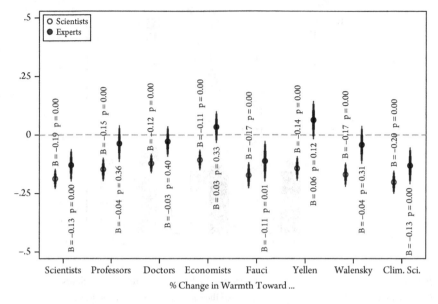

Figure S3.3 Replication of Figure 3.3 with the inclusion of potential satisficers
Note: Analyses include respondents who completed the survey in less than half of the survey's anticipated completion time. Figure S3.3 is otherwise analogous to Figure 3.3 in the main text. Please refer to Figure 3.3 and my discussion of the importance of accounting for satisficing in these validation analyses for additional information.

Supplementary Materials for Chapter 4

Table A4.1 **Sample Summary Statistics for MAID Database**

Variable	Mean	SD	Min	Max	N
Anti-Intel (Quarterly)	32.79	14.19	4	73	137
Mood (Quarterly)	61.04	4.09	53.25	73.27	124
Macro-Partisanship (Quarterly)	56.9	3.64	51.22	64.34	122
Consumer Sentiment (Quarterly)	86.33	12.06	57.67	108.77	134
Climate Sci in Cmte Mtg. Count	4.94	4.15	0	16	137
Economist Testimony Count	41.77	22.92	0	95	122
Envi. Hearing Count: Average	18.51	12.85	0	69	128
Envi. Hearing Count: General	2.04	1.79	0	7	128

Variable	Mean	SD	Min	Max	N
Envi. Hearing Count: Drinking Water	1.57	1.66	0	11	128
Envi. Hearing Count: Waste Disposal	0.48	0.92	0	5	128
Envi. Hearing Count: Hazard. Waste	2.98	2.95	0	18	128
Envi. Hearing Count: Recycling	0.2	0.52	0	3	128
Envi. Hearing Count: Indoor Hazards	0.55	1.02	0	5	128
Envi. Hearing Count: Species & Forest	3.17	3.33	0	16	128
Envi. Hearing Count: Conservation	0.81	1.1	0	6	128
Envi. Hearing Count: R&D	0.58	0.82	0	3	128
Envi. Hearing Count: Other	0.18	0.55	0	4	128

Note: Quarterly summary statistics presented. Anti-Intel is an intervalized measure of anti-intellectualism discussed at length in Chapters 3 and 4 and can theoretically range from 0 to 100. Please refer to those chapters for additional information about the construction of this measure. Policy Mood and Macro-Partisanship are Stimson's measures of policy liberalism and Democratic self-identification, respectively (see Chapter 3 for more information, as well as the citations), and are also theoretically bounded between 0 and 100. *For outcome variables presented in main text figures*: Economist Testimony Count is a count of the total number of times economists testified before Congress between 1949 and 2021, derived from Maher and colleagues' research (see Chapter 3 for additional information about this variable). Climate Sci in Cmte Mtg. is a measure of the total number of references (co-occurrences) between climate or environmental scientists and terms related to congressional testimony (testi*) in all House and Senate committee meeting materials published since 2000–2021, which serves as a proxy for the involvement of climate/environmental scientists in congressional committee proceedings and is used as part of the proxy measure validation exercise in Chapter 8. Envi. Hearing Count variables correspond to the total number of hearings (also a count variable) held on both environmental issues in general and several related subtopics. These data, as well as general and specific topic codes, are derived from the Policy Agendas Project, as discussed in Chapter 4.

Supplementary Materials for Chapter 5

Variable Measurement

GSS Cross-Section

PARTISAN IDENTITY

Q1. Generally speaking, do you usually think of yourself as a Republican, Democrat, Independent, or what?

240   APPENDIX MATERIALS

1. Strong Democrat
2. Not Strong Democrat
3. Lean Democrat
4. Independent
5. Lean Republican
6. Not Strong Republican
7. Strong Republican
8. DK
9. NA

SYMBOLIC IDEOLOGY

Q1. We hear a lot of talk these days about liberals and conservatives. I'm going to show you a seven-point scale on which the political views that people might hold are arranged from extremely liberal (point 1) to extremely conservative (point 7). Where would you place yourself on this scale?

1. Extremely liberal
2. Liberal
3. Slightly liberal
4. Moderate; middle of the road
5. Slightly conservative
6. Conservative
7. Extremely conservative
8. DK
9. NA

LIMITED GOVERNMENT

QUESTION STEMS

Q1. We are faced with many problems in this country, none of which can be solved easily or inexpensively. I'm going to name some of these problems, and for each one I'd like you to name some of these problems, and for each one I'd like you to tell me whether you think we're spending too much money on it, too little money, or about the right amount.

A. Solving problems of big cities
B. Halting rising crime rate
C. Dealing with drug addiction
D. Improving nation's education system
E. Improving conditions of Blacks
F. Foreign aid
G. Welfare

1. Too little
2. About right
3. Too much
8. DK
9. NA

RELIGIOSITY
How often do you attend religious services?

0. Never
1. Less than once a year
2. Once a year
3. Several times a year
4. Once a month
5. 2–3 times a month
6. Nearly every week
7. Every week
8. More than once a week
9. DK/NA

HOUSEHOLD INCOME
In which of these groups did your total family income, from all sources, fall last year before taxes, that is? Just tell me the letter.

1 Less than $1000
2 $1000 to 2999
3 $3000 to 3999
4 $4000 to 4999
5 $5000 to 5999
6 $6000 to 6999
7 $7000 to 7999
8 $8000 to 9999
9 $10,000 – 14,999
10 $15,000 – 19,999
11 $2,0000 – 24,999
12 $25,000 or more
13 Refused
98 Don't know
99 No answer

APPENDIX MATERIALS

2016 CSPP

PARTISAN IDENTITY
Generally speaking, do you usually think of yourself as a Republican, a Democrat, an Independent, or what?

<1>Republican
<2>Democrat
<3>Independent
<4>Other Party

THEN BRANCH IF Q1==1 | Q1==2
Would you call yourself a strong [Democrat/Republican] or a not very strong Democrat/Republican?

<1>Strong Democrat/Republican
<2>Not very strong Democrat/Republican THEN BRANCH IF Q1==3

Do you think of yourself as closer to the Republican Party or the Democratic Party?

<1>Democratic
<2>Republican
<3>Neither

SYMBOLIC IDEOLOGY
Q1. We hear a lot of talk these days about liberals and conservatives. Here is a seven-point scale on which the political views that people might hold are arranged from extremely liberal to extremely conservative. Where would you place yourself on this scale?

<1>Extremely liberal
<2>Liberal
<3>Slightly liberal
<4>Moderate; middle of the road
<5>Slightly conservative
<6>Conservative
<7>Extremely conservative

LIMITED GOVERNMENT
Q1. Some people think the government should provide fewer services even in areas such as health and education in order to reduce spending. Other people feel it is important for the government to provide many more services even if it means

an increase in spending. Many also have opinions that fall in between. What is your opinion? Please note that you must move the slider in order to register a response.

1   - FEWER SERVICES
2
3
4
5
6
7   - MORE SERVICES

RELIGIOSITY
Q1. How often do you attend religious services?

<1>Never
<2>Hardly ever, except holidays
<3>Less than once a month
<4>About once a month
<5>Two to three times a month
<6>Once a week
<7>More than once a week

HOUSEHOLD INCOME
We would like to get an estimate of your total household income in the past 12 months before taxes. Please select one of the items from the list below:

<1> Less than $10,000
<2> $10,000 – $14,999
<3> $15,000 – $24,999
<4> $25,000 – $34,999
<5> $35,000 – $49,999
<6> $50,000 – $74,999
<7> $75,000 – $99,999
<8> $100,000 – $149,999
<9>$150,000 – $199,999
<10>$200,000 or more

2019 ANES

PARTISAN IDENTITY
Generally speaking, do you usually think of yourself as a Democrat, a Republican, an independent, or what?

244 APPENDIX MATERIALS

Q1. Generally speaking, do you usually think of yourself as [a Democrat, a Republican/a Republican, a Democrat], an independent, or what?

1. Democrat
2. Republican
3. Independent
4. Something Else

THEN BRANCH IF Q1==1 | Q1==2

Q2. Would you call yourself a strong [Democrat/Republican] or a not very strong [Democrat/Republican]?

1. Strong
2. Not very strong THEN BRANCH IF Q1==3

Do you think of yourself as closer to the Republican Party or to the Democratic Party?

1. Closer to Republican
2. Closer to Democratic
3. Neither

SYMBOLIC IDEOLOGY

Q1. When it comes to politics, would you describe yourself, and these groups, as liberal, conservative, or neither liberal nor conservative?

Mark one answer in each row.

1. Very liberal
2. Somewhat liberal
3. Closer to liberals
4. Neither liberal nor conservative
5. Closer to conservatives
6. Somewhat conservative
7. Very conservative

LIMITED GOVERNMENT
Not available.

RELIGIOSITY

Q1. Lots of things come up that keep people from attending religious services even if they want to. Thinking about your life these days, do you ever attend religious services, apart from occasional weddings, baptisms or funerals?

Appendix Materials

1. Yes
2. No
-8. Don't know
-9. Refused

THEN BRANCH IF Q1==1

Q2. Do you go to religious services every week, almost every week, once or twice a month, a few times a year, or never?

1. Every week
2. Almost every week
3. Once or twice a month
4. A few times a year
5. Never

HOUSEHOLD INCOME

The next question is about [the total combined income of all members of your family/your total income] during the past 12 months. This includes money from jobs, net income from business, farm or rent, pensions, dividends, interest, Social Security payments, and any other money income received by members of your family who are 15 years of age or older. What was the total income of your family during the past 12 months? TYPE THE NUMBER. YOUR BEST GUESS IS FINE.

RECODE CATEGORIES:

1 Less than $10,000
2 $10,000–$19,999
3 $20,000–$29,999
4 $30,000–$39,999
5 $40,000–$49,999
6 $50,000–$59,999
7 $60,000–$69,999
8 $70,000–$79,999
9 $80,000–$99,999
10 $100,000–$119,999
11 $120,000–$149,999
12 $150,000–$199,999
13 $200,000–$249,999
14 $250,000–$349,999
15 $350,000–$499,999
16 $500,000 or more
97 Prefer not to say

246   APPENDIX MATERIALS

2020 ANES

PARTISAN IDENTITY

Q1. Generally speaking, do you usually think of yourself as [a Democrat, a Republican/a Republican, a Democrat], an independent, or what?

  0. No preference {VOL}
  1. Democrat
  2. Republican
  3. Independent
  5. Other party {SPECIFY}
−4. Technical error
−8. Don't know
−9. Refused

THEN BRANCH OF Q1==1 | Q1==2

Q2. Would you call yourself a strong [Democrat/Republican] or a not very strong [Democrat/Republican]?

  1. Strong
  2. Not very strong
−1. Inapplicable
−9. Refused

THEN BRANCH IF Q1==3

Do you think of yourself as closer to the Republican Party or to the Democratic Party?

  1. Closer to Republican
  2. Neither {VOL in video and phone}
  3. Closer to Democratic

−1. Inapplicable
−8. Don't know
−9. Refused

SYMBOLIC IDEOLOGY

Q1. Where would you place yourself on this scale, or haven't you thought much about this?

  1. Extremely liberal
  2. Liberal

Appendix Materials

3. Slightly liberal
4. Moderate; middle of the road
5. Slightly conservative
6. Conservative
7. Extremely conservative
99. Haven't thought much about this
−8. Don't know
−9. Refused IF Q1 == 99

Q2. If you had to choose, would you consider yourself a liberal or a conservative?

1. Liberal
2. Conservative
3. Moderate {VOL, video/phone only}
−1. Inapplicable
−4. Technical error
−8. Don't know
−9. Refused

LIMITED GOVERNMENT
Q1. QUESTION STEMS

A. What about Social Security? Should federal spending on Social Security be increased, decreased, or kept the same?
B. What about public schools? Should federal spending on public schools be increased, decreased, or kept the same?
C. What about welfare programs? Should federal spending on welfare programs be increased, decreased, or kept the same?
D. What about building and repairing highways? Should federal spending on building and repairing highways be increased, decreased, or kept the same?
E. What about aid to the poor? Should federal spending on aid to the poor be increased, decreased, or kept the same?

1. Increased
2. Decreased
3. Kept the same

THEN BRANCH IF Q1==1 | Q1==2
Q2. Should it be [increased/decreased] a lot or a little?

1. A lot
2. A little

−1. Inapplicable

−9. Refused

RELIGIOSITY

Q1. Lots of things come up that keep people from attending religious services even if they want to. Thinking about your life these days, do you ever attend religious services, apart from occasional weddings, baptisms or funerals?

   1. Yes

   2. No

−8. Don't know

−9. Refused

THEN BRANCH IF Q1 == 1

Q2. Do you go to religious services every week, almost every week, once or twice a month, a few times a year, or never?

   1. Every week

   2. Almost every week

   3. Once or twice a month

   4. A few times a year

   5. Never

−1. Inapplicable

−8. Don't know

−9. Refused

HOUSEHOLD INCOME

The next question is about [the total combined income of all members of your family/your total income] during the past 12 months. This includes money from jobs, net income from business, farm or rent, pensions, dividends, interest, Social Security payments, and any other money income received by members of your family who are 15 years of age or older. What was the total income of your family during the past 12 months? TYPE THE NUMBER. YOUR BEST GUESS IS FINE.

RECODE CATEGORIES:

1   Less than $10,000

2   $10,000–$19,999

3   $20,000–$29,999

4   $30,000–$39,999

5 $40,000–$49,999
 6 $50,000–$59,999
 7 $60,000–$69,999
 8 $70,000–$79,999
 9 $80,000–$99,999
10 $100,000–$119,999
11 $120,000–$149,999
12 $150,000–$199,999
13 $200,000–$249,999
14 $250,000–$349,999
15 $350,000–$499,999
16 $500,000 or more
97 Prefer not to say

2020–2021 SciPol

PARTISAN IDENTITY
Measured in an initial inventory survey from Lucid Theorem.

SYMBOLIC IDEOLOGY
"We hear a lot of talk these days about liberals and conservatives. Here is a seven-point extremely conservative.

Where would you place yourself on this scale?"

1 Extremely Liberal
2 Liberal
3 Slightly Liberal
4 Moderate; Middle of the road
5 Slightly Conservative
6 Conservative
7 Extremely Conservative

LIMITED GOVERNMENT
Not available.

RELIGIOSITY
Not available.

HOUSEHOLD INCOME
Measured in an initial inventory survey from Lucid Theorem. Recode values are as follows:

1 Less than $14,999
2 $15,000 to $19,999
3 $20,000 to $24,999
4 $25,000 to $29,999
5 $30,000 to $34,999
6 $35,000 to $39,999
7 $40,000 to $44,999
8 $45,000 to $49,999
9 $50,000 to $54,999
10 $55,000 to $59,999
11 $60,000 to $64,999
12 $65,000 to $69,999
13 $70,000 to $74,999
14 $75,000 to $79,999
15 $80,000 to $84,999
16 $85,000 to $89,999
17 $90,000 to $94,999
18 $95,000 to $99,999
19 $100,000 to $124,999
20 $125,000 to $149,999
21 $150,000 to $174,999
22 $175,000 to $199,999
23 $200,000 to $249,999
24 $250,000 and above

Table A5.1a **Models Used to Produce Figures 5.1, 5.3, 5.5, and 5.7**

	74	75	76	77	78	80	82	83	84
College Educ.	-0.61*	-0.51*	-0.72*	-0.59*	-0.95*	-0.77*	-0.67*	-0.75*	-0.82*
	[-0.96,-0.27]	[-0.84,-0.19]	[-1.06,-0.37]	[-0.92,-0.25]	[-1.29,-0.61]	[-1.08,-0.45]	[-0.96,-0.37]	[-1.16,-0.34]	[-1.21,-0.43]
Limited Govt. Index	-0.12	-0.26	-0.34	0.13	0.06	0.55	0.35	0.04	-0.50
	[-0.88,0.64]	[-0.97,0.46]	[-1.06,0.37]	[-0.57,0.83]	[-0.72,0.85]	[-0.15,1.26]	[-0.37,1.07]	[-0.98,1.05]	[-1.71,0.72]
Ideo. (1 = Conservative)	-0.09	0.28	-0.08	0.18	0.07	0.62+	0.17	-0.28	0.10
	[-0.71,0.54]	[-0.30,0.86]	[-0.70,0.55]	[-0.40,0.76]	[-0.55,0.70]	[-0.08,1.32]	[-0.38,0.72]	[-1.12,0.57]	[-0.70,0.90]
Party ID (1 = GOP)	-0.21	-0.23	-0.06	-0.18	-0.00	-0.60*	-0.40+	-0.18	-0.16
	[-0.63,0.20]	[-0.64,0.17]	[-0.47,0.34]	[-0.56,0.21]	[-0.42,0.41]	[-1.01,-0.18]	[-0.80,0.00]	[-0.73,0.36]	[-0.69,0.38]
Rel. Service Attendance	-0.03	0.11	0.45*	0.07	0.36+	-0.09	0.16	0.50+	0.13
	[-0.44,0.38]	[-0.27,0.48]	[0.07,0.82]	[-0.30,0.44]	[-0.00,0.72]	[-0.49,0.31]	[-0.21,0.52]	[-0.03,1.02]	[-0.35,0.61]
Race = Black	1.25*	0.55*	0.54*	0.40+	0.91*	0.63*	0.77*	-0.10	0.66*
	[0.76,1.74]	[0.10,1.00]	[0.01,1.07]	[-0.01,0.82]	[0.39,1.43]	[0.10,1.16]	[0.46,1.08]	[-0.69,0.48]	[0.12,1.21]
Race = Other	-13.76*	-0.15	-0.43	-0.58	-0.23	-0.65	0.41	-0.25	0.26
	[-14.94,-12.58]	[-2.01,1.70]	[-1.80,0.93]	[-1.85,0.69]	[-1.42,0.96]	[-2.22,0.92]	[-0.58,1.41]	[-1.60,1.10]	[-0.88,1.40]
Income	-0.48+	-0.04	-0.48+	-0.47+	-0.45	-0.36	-0.36	-0.22	-0.55
	[-1.03,0.07]	[-0.56,0.49]	[-0.99,0.03]	[-1.02,0.07]	[-1.00,0.10]	[-0.90,0.19]	[-0.83,0.11]	[-1.00,0.56]	[-1.29,0.19]

(Continued)

Table A5.1a **Continued**

	74	75	76	77	78	80	82	83	84
Age: 24–44	0.33+	0.46*	0.18	−0.01	−0.11	0.05	0.37+	0.68*	0.19
	[−0.06,0.72]	[0.10,0.82]	[−0.22,0.58]	[−0.40,0.38]	[−0.49,0.26]	[−0.33,0.43]	[−0.00,0.75]	[0.12,1.24]	[−0.49,0.87]
Age: 44–64	0.39+	0.20	0.24	−0.40+	−0.17	0.08	0.40*	0.67*	0.33
	[−0.03,0.80]	[−0.20,0.60]	[−0.18,0.66]	[−0.81,0.01]	[−0.59,0.25]	[−0.34,0.49]	[0.01,0.79]	[0.04,1.30]	[−0.40,1.05]
Age: 65+	0.29	0.71*	0.22	0.31	0.03	0.26	0.15	0.95*	0.43
	[−0.19,0.77]	[0.21,1.21]	[−0.23,0.68]	[−0.22,0.84]	[−0.46,0.51]	[−0.21,0.73]	[−0.32,0.61]	[0.24,1.66]	[−0.28,1.13]
Female	0.12	−0.07	0.05	0.32*	0.29*	0.21+	0.44*	0.37*	0.55*
	[−0.14,0.38]	[−0.31,0.18]	[−0.21,0.30]	[0.08,0.56]	[0.05,0.54]	[−0.04,0.46]	[0.20,0.67]	[0.02,0.72]	[0.24,0.87]
τ_1	−0.05	−0.06	−0.25	−0.46	−0.56+	−0.10	0.09	0.30	−0.23
	[−0.64,0.55]	[−0.66,0.53]	[−0.84,0.34]	[−1.08,0.16]	[−1.19,0.08]	[−0.73,0.53]	[−0.52,0.70]	[−0.64,1.24]	[−1.10,0.64]
τ_2	2.56*	2.91*	2.33*	2.69*	2.48*	2.71*	3.32*	3.36*	2.91*
	[1.91,3.22]	[2.26,3.56]	[1.70,2.96]	[2.02,3.35]	[1.79,3.16]	[2.05,3.36]	[2.66,3.97]	[2.32,4.40]	[1.91,3.91]
N	1146	1203	1156	1248	1249	1191	1454	681	809

Note: Ordered logistic regression coefficients with 95 percent CIs in brackets. Outcome variable is a three-point ordinal measure of anti-intellectual attitude endorsement. Please refer to the main text for additional information about these models.

Table A5.1b **Models Used to Produce Figures 5.1, 5.3, 5.5, and 5.7**

	86	87	88	89	90	91	93	94	96	98
College Educ.	−0.62*	−1.00*	−0.36+	−0.86*	−0.61*	−0.46*	−0.60*	−0.73*	−0.87*	−0.74*
	[−0.93,−0.32]	[−1.30,−0.70]	[−0.73,0.00]	[−1.24,−0.48]	[−1.00,−0.21]	[−0.84,−0.08]	[−0.93,−0.27]	[−0.97,−0.48]	[−1.12,−0.61]	[−1.00,−0.4¿9]
Limited	0.16	0.31	0.55	0.10	1.75*	0.70	0.08	0.16	0.55	1.08¿*
Govt. Index	[−0.76,1.08]	[−0.68,1.31]	[−0.53,1.62]	[−1.05,1.24]	[0.54,2.96]	[−0.42,1.81]	[−1.08,1.24]	[−0.58,0.90]	[−0.26,1.36]	[0.29,1.87]
Ideo. (1 =	−0.23	0.27	0.12	0.90*	0.39	−0.19	0.19	0.56*	0.90*	¿0.04
Conservative)	[−0.86,0.40]	[−0.28,0.82]	[−0.65,0.89]	[0.15,1.65]	[−0.42,1.20]	[−0.99,0.61]	[−0.51,0.89]	[0.01,1.11]	[0.31,1.49]	[−0.52,0.60]
Party ID	0.21	−0.13	0.00	−0.65*	−0.21	−0.47+	0.03	0.06	−0.35+	0.08¿
(1 = GOP)	[−0.20,0.62]	[−0.52,0.25]	[−0.49,0.50]	[−1.12,−0.17]	[−0.71,0.29]	[−0.94,0.01]	[−0.46,0.51]	[−0.31,0.42]	[−0.73,0.03]	[−0.33,0.49]
Rel. Service	0.24	0.08	0.04	0.20	0.33	0.46+	−0.07	0.00	0.38*	¿0.24
Attendance	[−0.14,0.63]	[−0.31,0.46]	[−0.44,0.52]	[−0.27,0.68]	[−0.18,0.84]	[−0.06,0.97]	[−0.55,0.42]	[−0.33,0.34]	[0.02,0.74]	[−0.11,0.59]
Race = Black	1.05*	0.48*	0.10	0.57*	1.47*	0.44+	1.06*	0.87*	0.80*	0.59*
	[0.58,1.52]	[0.18,0.78]	[−0.44,0.64]	[0.03,1.10]	[0.94,2.00]	[−0.07,0.94]	[0.55,1.57]	[0.46,1.29]	[0.38,1.23]	[0.24,0.93]
Race = Other	−0.40	0.12	0.76*	0.14	0.66	0.30	0.20	−0.15	−0.38	0.27
	[−1.32,0.52]	[−0.66,0.91]	[0.13,1.38]	[−0.87,1.14]	[−0.14,1.47]	[−0.30,0.90]	[−0.52,0.91]	[−0.72,0.43]	[−0.90,0.15]	[−0.22,0.76]
Income	−0.27	−0.67*	−0.42	−0.43	−1.52*	−0.24	0.07	−0.28	−0.41	−1.19*
	[−0.82,0.28]	[−1.21,−0.13]	[−1.14,0.30]	[−1.21,0.35]	[−2.24,−0.80]	[−0.92,0.45]	[−0.63,0.78]	[−0.86,0.30]	[−1.07,0.25]	[−1.81,−0.57]

(Continued)

Table A5.1b **Continued**

	86	87	88	89	90	91	93	94	96	98
Age: 24–44	0.15 [−0.28,0.59]	0.31 [−0.06,0.68]	0.45 [−0.15,1.06]	0.16 [−0.33,0.66]	0.00 [−0.59,0.60]	0.16 [−0.40,0.72]	0.35 [−0.22,0.93]	0.52+ [−0.01,1.05]	0.34 [−0.11,0.79]	1.16* [0.69,1.62]
Age: 44–64	0.38 [−0.09,0.86]	0.32 [−0.06,0.71]	0.49 [−0.15,1.12]	0.52+ [−0.01,1.05]	0.18 [−0.46,0.82]	0.75* [0.12,1.38]	0.53+ [−0.07,1.12]	0.83* [0.28,1.38]	0.32 [−0.16,0.79]	1.04* [0.54,1.53]
Age: 65+	0.55* [0.04,1.05]	0.33 [−0.13,0.79]	0.59+ [−0.05,1.23]	0.16 [−0.45,0.76]	−0.07 [−0.73,0.60]	0.29 [−0.33,0.91]	0.93* [0.28,1.59]	0.83* [0.27,1.40]	0.14 [−0.40,0.68]	0.82* [0.29,1.35]
Female	0.43* [0.18,0.67]	0.17 [−0.06,0.39]	0.37* [0.07,0.67]	0.18 [−0.12,0.48]	−0.09 [−0.42,0.23]	0.15 [−0.16,0.47]	0.52* [0.22,0.83]	0.11 [−0.11,0.32]	0.53* [0.30,0.76]	0.38* [0.15,0.61]
τ_1	0.03 [−0.67,0.74]	−0.20 [−0.88,0.47]	0.28 [−0.55,1.10]	−0.11 [−1.07,0.85]	−0.75 [−1.74,0.25]	0.04 [−0.77,0.86]	0.44 [−0.40,1.28]	0.40 [−0.33,1.13]	0.42 [−0.39,1.23]	0.36 [−0.36,1.08]
τ_2	3.10* [2.36,3.84]	2.68* [2.00,3.37]	3.41* [2.51,4.31]	3.07* [2.06,4.08]	2.59* [1.57,3.62]	2.98* [2.14,3.83]	3.57* [2.70,4.43]	3.35* [2.57,4.12]	3.42* [2.56,4.28]	3.20* [2.46,3.95]
N	1225	1449	817	826	701	816	835	1578	1451	1458

Table A5.1c **Models Used to Produce Figures 5.1, 5.3, 5.5, and 5.7**

	00	02	04	06	08	10	12	14	16	18
College Educ.	−0.77* [−1.02,−0.51]	−0.38* [−0.72,−0.04]	−0.98* [−1.38,−0.59]	−0.78* [−1.03,−0.53]	−0.75* [−1.06,−0.45]	−0.91* [−1.21,−0.60]	−0.56* [−0.86,−0.26]	−0.65* [−0.91,−0.40]	−0.76* [−1.02,−0.50]	−1.13* [−1.45,−0.81]
Limited Govt. Index	0.42 [−0.49,1.33]	0.94 [−0.22,2.10]	1.69* [0.36,3.02]	0.03 [−0.85,0.91]	0.45 [−0.56,1.45]	−0.15 [−1.19,0.90]	0.60 [−0.46,1.65]	0.49 [−0.44,1.42]	0.46 [−0.37,1.29]	1.17* [0.14,2.19]
Ideo. (1 = Conservative)	0.57* [0.01,1.13]	0.80* [0.00,1.61]	0.61 [−0.21,1.44]	0.39 [−0.19,0.98]	0.31 [−0.36,0.98]	0.02 [−0.65,0.69]	−0.52 [−1.32,0.27]	0.82* [0.14,1.50]	0.46+ [−0.07,1.00]	0.82* [0.10,1.55]
Party ID (1 = GOP)	0.09 [−0.31,0.49]	−0.13 [−0.68,0.41]	0.12 [−0.45,0.69]	0.06 [−0.36,0.48]	0.32 [−0.15,0.80]	0.51+ [−0.03,1.04]	0.55+ [−0.01,1.11]	0.34 [−0.12,0.80]	0.38+ [−0.05,0.81]	0.59* [0.05,1.13]
Rel. Service Attendance	0.35+ [−0.01,0.70]	0.48* [0.01,0.96]	0.30 [−0.23,0.82]	0.32+ [−0.03,0.67]	0.36 [−0.08,0.79]	0.90* [0.49,1.31]	0.68* [0.26,1.10]	0.43* [0.05,0.81]	0.69* [0.35,1.03]	0.09 [−0.32,0.51]
Race = Black	0.77* [0.41,1.14]	0.94* [0.41,1.47]	1.51* [0.91,2.10]	0.75* [0.35,1.14]	0.76* [0.22,1.30]	0.25 [−0.19,0.70]	0.60* [0.14,1.05]	0.64* [0.26,1.02]	0.71* [0.36,1.06]	1.09* [0.70,1.49]
Race = Other	0.32 [−0.19,0.83]	−0.33 [−1.09,0.43]	0.52* [0.00,1.05]	0.38* [0.01,0.75]	0.27 [−0.22,0.75]	0.48+ [−0.01,0.97]	−0.38 [−0.85,0.09]	0.17 [−0.23,0.57]	−0.12 [−0.55,0.31]	0.56* [0.05,1.07]
Income	−0.82* [−1.42,−0.22]	−0.85+ [−1.74,0.05]	−0.17 [−1.15,0.81]	0.09 [−0.60,0.77]	−0.19 [−1.01,0.62]	−0.58+ [−1.23,0.07]	−1.12* [−1.94,−0.30]	−0.77* [−1.48,−0.06]	0.21 [−0.37,0.79]	−0.05 [−0.71,0.61]

(*Continued*)

Table A5.1c **Continued**

	00	02	04	06	08	10	12	14	16	18
Age: 24–44	0.01	0.14	0.57	0.81*	−0.17	1.06*	0.76*	0.22	0.37	0.64*
	[−0.41,0.43]	[−0.45,0.74]	[−0.14,1.28]	[0.34,1.28]	[−0.80,0.46]	[0.54,1.58]	[0.18,1.34]	[−0.35,0.80]	[−0.07,0.81]	[0.10,1.18]
Age: 44–64	0.23	−0.22	0.70+	1.03*	0.19	1.07*	0.91*	0.33	0.57*	0.59*
	[−0.20,0.66]	[−0.84,0.39]	[−0.02,1.43]	[0.55,1.51]	[−0.46,0.84]	[0.54,1.60]	[0.34,1.48]	[−0.24,0.91]	[0.13,1.00]	[0.06,1.12]
Age: 65+	0.05	0.09	0.68+	1.00*	0.19	0.75*	0.61*	0.25	0.58*	0.35
	[−0.45,0.55]	[−0.62,0.80]	[−0.11,1.47]	[0.47,1.53]	[−0.48,0.86]	[0.14,1.37]	[0.01,1.21]	[−0.38,0.88]	[0.12,1.05]	[−0.20,0.90]
Female	0.08	0.00	0.33+	0.41*	0.28+	0.27+	0.30*	0.10	0.39*	0.55*
	[−0.16,0.32]	[−0.30,0.31]	[−0.01,0.66]	[0.17,0.65]	[−0.01,0.57]	[−0.01,0.55]	[0.01,0.59]	[−0.14,0.34]	[0.16,0.62]	[0.28,0.83]
τ_1	−0.23	−0.31	1.38*	1.20*	0.10	0.64	−0.06	0.10	1.17*	1.47*
	[−0.94,0.48]	[−1.38,0.75]	[0.32,2.45]	[0.38,2.01]	[−0.88,1.09]	[−0.18,1.46]	[−1.10,0.97]	[−0.84,1.04]	[0.46,1.89]	[0.65,2.29]
τ_2	2.55*	2.64*	4.77*	4.39*	3.56*	4.04*	2.97*	3.20*	4.49*	4.62*
	[1.83,3.27]	[1.55,3.72]	[3.63,5.91]	[3.53,5.25]	[2.54,4.58]	[3.13,4.94]	[1.87,4.06]	[2.22,4.17]	[3.72,5.26]	[3.74,5.51]
N	1378	766	723	1590	1099	1114	1062	1392	1502	1176

Table A5.2 **Models Used to Produce Figures 5.2, 5.4, 5.7, and 5.9**

	CSPP 6/16	CSPP 9/16	ANES 12/19	SciPol 4/20	SciPol 6/20	SciPol 8/20	SciPol 10/20	SciPol 12/20	ANES 12/20	SciPol 2/21
College Educ.	−0.29* [−0.43,−0.16]	−0.36* [−0.54,−0.17]	−0.40* [−0.58,−0.21]	−0.09 [−0.44,0.27]	−0.01 [−0.37,0.35]	0.39+ [−0.03,0.81]	0.58* [0.20,0.97]	0.32 [−0.11,0.75]	−0.40* [−0.60,−0.21]	0.06 [−0.25,0.37]
Ideo. (1 = Conservative)	0.77* [0.46,1.07]	1.12* [0.72,1.52]	1.37* [0.89,1.85]	−0.32 [−1.05,0.41]	−0.39 [−1.14,0.37]	0.22 [−0.50,0.94]	0.42 [−0.13,0.97]	0.76* [0.20,1.33]	0.24* [0.16,0.33]	0.74* [0.17,1.30]
Party ID (1 = GOP)	0.35* [0.12,0.58]	0.10 [−0.21,0.41]	1.01* [0.65,1.38]	0.78* [0.24,1.31]	1.17* [0.65,1.68]	1.34* [0.77,1.90]	1.08* [0.64,1.53]	−0.29 [−0.73,0.16]	0.60* [0.22,0.98]	0.06 [−0.35,0.46]
Limited Govt. Index	−0.06 [−0.33,0.21]	0.41* [0.11,0.72]	−	−	−	−	−	−	0.76* [0.07,1.45]	−
Rel. Service Attendance	0.33* [0.14,0.51]	0.34* [0.09,0.59]	0.06 [−0.21,0.32]	−	−	−	−	−	0.21 [−0.08,0.50]	−
Race = Black	0.15 [−0.06,0.35]	0.17 [−0.11,0.44]	0.45* [0.15,0.74]	0.54* [0.06,1.01]	0.05 [−0.40,0.51]	0.17 [−0.42,0.77]	0.43+ [−0.04,0.90]	−0.44 [−0.96,0.09]	0.43* [0.10,0.75]	−0.04 [−0.42,0.34]
Race = Hispanic	−0.07 [−0.25,0.11]	0.03 [−0.23,0.28]	0.16 [−0.11,0.44]	0.44+ [−0.05,0.93]	0.36 [−0.16,0.87]	0.44+ [−0.01,0.89]	0.04 [−0.40,0.47]	−0.37 [−0.86,0.13]	−0.13 [−0.43,0.17]	0.02 [−0.42,0.45]

(Continued)

	CSPP 6/16	CSPP 9/16	ANES 12/19	SciPol 4/20	SciPol 6/20	SciPol 8/20	SciPol 10/20	SciPol 12/20	ANES 12/20	SciPol 2/21
Income	−0.35*	−0.65*	−0.64*	0.22	−0.54+	−0.16	0.14	0.31	−0.52*	−0.23
	[−0.64,−0.05]	[−1.05,−0.26]	[−1.03,−0.25]	[−0.36,0.79]	[−1.14,0.05]	[−0.83,0.50]	[−0.37,0.65]	[−0.37,0.98]	[−0.86,−0.19]	[−0.70,0.24]
Age: 24–44	0.47*	0.08	0.51*	−0.05	−0.02	0.19	−0.21	−0.15	0.22	0.55*
	[0.13,0.80]	[−0.50,0.66]	[0.11,0.92]	[−0.62,0.52]	[−0.70,0.67]	[−0.52,0.91]	[−0.72,0.30]	[−0.61,0.32]	[−0.24,0.68]	[0.15,0.96]
Age: 44–64	0.46*	0.16	0.81*	−0.52+	−0.42	−0.39	−1.10*	−0.32	0.22	−0.23
	[0.14,0.79]	[−0.41,0.74]	[0.41,1.21]	[−1.09,0.05]	[−1.11,0.27]	[−1.14,0.36]	[−1.61,−0.58]	[−0.84,0.20]	[−0.24,0.68]	[−0.66,0.21]
Age: 65+	0.42*	0.11	0.79*	−0.84*	−0.76*	−0.65+	−1.50*	−0.98*	0.41+	−0.57*
	[0.07,0.76]	[−0.48,0.70]	[0.38,1.21]	[−1.50,−0.19]	[−1.49,−0.02]	[−1.42,0.11]	[−2.06,−0.93]	[−1.60,−0.36]	[−0.05,0.88]	[−1.03,−0.11]
Female	−0.07	−0.06	−0.13	−0.36*	−0.10	−0.24	−0.58*	−0.34*	0.15	−0.30*
	[−0.20,0.06]	[−0.23,0.12]	[−0.30,0.03]	[−0.67,−0.06]	[−0.40,0.20]	[−0.56,0.07]	[−0.88,−0.29]	[−0.68,−0.00]	[−0.03,0.34]	[−0.54,−0.05]
τ_1	−2.28*	−2.35*	−0.80*	−1.61*	−1.85*	−0.98*	−1.65*	−1.61*	−0.16	−1.50*
	[−2.67,−1.88]	[−3.01,−1.69]	[−1.23,−0.37]	[−2.38,−0.85]	[−2.61,−1.08]	[−1.77,−0.19]	[−2.27,−1.03]	[−2.15,−1.06]	[−0.69,0.38]	[−1.98,−1.01]
τ_2	−0.62*	−0.72*	0.81*	−0.84*	−0.94*	−0.01	−0.77*	−1.04*	1.04*	−0.60*
	[−0.99,−0.24]	[−1.36,−0.08]	[0.38,1.25]	[−1.57,−0.10]	[−1.72,−0.17]	[−0.78,0.76]	[−1.38,−0.16]	[−1.57,−0.51]	[0.50,1.57]	[−1.07,−0.13]
τ_3	1.03*	0.97*	2.56*	−0.15	−0.25	0.68+	−0.23	−0.56*	3.20*	−0.05
	[0.65,1.41]	[0.33,1.61]	[2.12,3.00]	[−0.87,0.58]	[−1.02,0.52]	[−0.08,1.43]	[−0.85,0.39]	[−1.10,−0.03]	[2.64,3.76]	[−0.52,0.42]

τ_4	2.62*	2.71*	3.71*	0.83*	0.78+	1.63*	0.87*	0.41	4.27*	0.93*
	[2.24,3.01]	[2.06,3.36]	[3.24,4.19]	[0.11,1.55]	[−0.00,1.57]	[0.88,2.39]	[0.26,1.49]	[−0.13,0.94]	[3.70,4.83]	[0.46,1.41]
τ_5	–	–	–	1.53*	1.47*	2.30*	1.48*	1.11*	–	1.61*
				[0.81,2.25]	[0.68,2.26]	[1.52,3.08]	[0.87,2.10]	[0.56,1.66]		[1.14,2.07]
τ_6	–	–	–	2.44*	2.37*	3.37*	2.27*	2.00*	–	2.50*
				[1.69,3.18]	[1.53,3.20]	[2.56,4.18]	[1.64,2.90]	[1.41,2.59]		[2.00,3.01]
N	3271	1844	2351	916	850	829	870	898	3162	1334

Note: Ordered logistic regression coefficients with 95 percent CIs in brackets. Outcome variables are ordinal measures of anti−intellectual attitude endorsement. Please refer to the main text for additional information about these models.

Table A5.3 **Models Used to Produce Table 5.1 (Reverse Causality Test Summary)**

	AI ← X	AI → PID	GSS AI → Ideo.	AI → Lim. Gov.	AI → Relig.	AI ← X	AI → PID	CSPP AI → Ideo.	AI → Lim. Gov.
Anti-Intellectualism	2.60* [2.17,3.04]	0.12 [−0.24,0.47]	0.08 [−0.31,0.47]	0.03* [0.00,0.05]	0.05* [0.00,0.10]	3.59* [3.19,3.99]	0.16 [−0.26,0.58]	0.18 [−0.21,0.56]	0.29 [−0.06,0.64]
Party ID (1 = GOP)	0.55* [0.14,0.97]	7.39* [6.70,8.08]	1.66* [1.27,2.04]	0.04* [0.02,0.06]	0.02 [−0.03,0.06]	0.00 [−0.31,0.32]	15.26* [14.40,16.13]	0.83* [0.48,1.18]	0.43* [0.12,0.74]
Ideo. (1 = Conservative)	−0.18 [−0.74,0.38]	0.85* [0.39,1.32]	4.63* [3.98,5.28]	0.04* [0.01,0.07]	0.07* [0.01,0.13]	0.67* [0.25,1.08]	1.17* [0.68,1.67]	11.86* [11.16,12.56]	1.02* [0.61,1.43]
Limited Govt. Index	−0.31 [−1.10,0.48]	0.76* [0.04,1.49]	1.66* [0.90,2.42]	0.50* [0.45,0.55]	−0.06 [−0.15,0.04]	0.50* [0.12,0.87]	0.38+ [−0.05,0.80]	0.67* [0.28,1.06]	4.04* [3.63,4.45]
Female	0.32* [0.10,0.53]	−0.08 [−0.26,0.10]	0.05 [−0.14,0.24]	−0.01 [−0.02,0.00]	0.02+ [−0.00,0.05]	−0.05 [−0.23,0.13]	0.10 [−0.11,0.31]	−0.11 [−0.30,0.08]	−0.10 [−0.27,0.07]
Race = Black	0.69* [0.31,1.07]	−0.88* [−1.21,−0.56]	0.34+ [−0.04,0.73]	−0.05* [−0.07,−0.03]	0.06* [0.01,0.11]	0.15 [−0.13,0.42]	−0.42* [−0.77,−0.07]	−0.04 [−0.34,0.26]	0.02 [−0.27,0.30]
Race = Hispanic	−	−	−	−	−	0.04 [−0.22,0.30]	−0.18 [−0.48,0.11]	−0.07 [−0.35,0.22]	−0.14 [−0.39,0.11]

Populism	—	—	—	—	0.15* [0.02,0.27]	0.04 [-0.10,0.18]	0.03 [-0.10,0.16]	0.00 [-0.12,0.12]
College Educ.	-0.04 [-0.22,0.14]	-0.30* [-0.48,-0.11]	0.01+ [-0.00,0.03]	0.02 [-0.01,0.05]	-0.27* [-0.46,-0.09]	0.06 [-0.16,0.27]	-0.09 [-0.29,0.11]	-0.15 [-0.32,0.03]
Race = Other	0.04 [-0.37,0.45]	-0.24 [-0.61,0.14]	0.01 [-0.02,0.03]	0.04+ [-0.00,0.09]	0.14 [-0.22,0.49]	—	—	—
Rel. Service Attendance	0.28* [0.02,0.53]	0.96* [0.68,1.24]	0.00 [-0.02,0.02]	0.71* [0.67,0.75]	0.32* [0.07,0.57]	-0.36* [-0.66,-0.06]	0.54* [0.27,0.82]	0.02 [-0.22,0.27]
Income	-0.03 [-0.45,0.39]	0.41 [-0.14,0.96]	-0.02 [-0.06,0.02]	0.00 [-0.07,0.07]	-0.41* [-0.82,-0.01]	0.13 [-0.34,0.59]	-0.21 [-0.64,0.23]	0.23 [-0.16,0.63]
Age 25–44	0.18 [-0.18,0.54]	0.30 [-0.10,0.70]	-0.01 [-0.03,0.02]	-0.02 [-0.07,0.03]	0.09 [-0.52,0.69]	0.31 [-0.47,1.09]	0.82* [0.09,1.55]	0.02 [-0.62,0.65]
Age 45–65	0.15 [-0.21,0.50]	0.39+ [-0.01,0.80]	-0.01 [-0.03,0.02]	-0.00 [-0.05,0.05]	0.14 [-0.46,0.74]	0.31 [-0.45,1.08]	0.85* [0.13,1.57]	-0.14 [-0.77,0.49]
Age 65+	0.04 [-0.35,0.44]	0.32 [-0.14,0.77]	-0.02 [-0.04,0.01]	0.04 [-0.01,0.09]	0.09 [-0.52,0.70]	0.38 [-0.40,1.16]	0.84* [0.10,1.57]	-0.33 [-0.97,0.31]
β_0	—	—	0.18* [0.14,0.22]	0.05 [-0.03,0.14]	—	—	—	—

(Continued)

Table A5.3 **Continued**

	AI ← X	AI → PID	GSS AI → Ideo.	AI → Lim. Gov.	AI → Relig.	AI ← X	AI → PID	CSPP AI → Ideo.	AI → Lim. Gov.
τ_1	0.76*	0.71*	0.33	–	–	−0.32	2.58*	1.66*	−0.61
	[0.04,1.47]	[0.14,1.29]	[−0.35,1.01]			[−1.11,0.47]	[1.61,3.55]	[0.76,2.57]	[−1.42,0.19]
τ_2	4.12*	2.67*	2.38*	–	–	1.48*	5.35*	4.49*	0.75+
	[3.36,4.88]	[2.08,3.27]	[1.73,3.02]			[0.70,2.26]	[4.36,6.34]	[3.57,5.41]	[−0.05,1.55]
τ_3	–	3.94*	3.46*	–	–	3.42*	7.31*	5.73*	2.22*
		[3.31,4.57]	[2.79,4.12]			[2.63,4.21]	[6.29,8.33]	[4.79,6.67]	[1.42,3.02]
τ_4	–	5.35*	5.92*	–	–	5.39*	10.56*	9.31*	3.45*
		[4.66,6.04]	[5.18,6.67]			[4.58,6.21]	[9.45,11.68]	[8.32,10.31]	[2.63,4.26]
τ_5	–	6.63*	7.00*	–	–	–	12.51*	10.54*	4.30*
		[5.86,7.39]	[6.22,7.77]				[11.34,13.69]	[9.52,11.56]	[3.47,5.12]
τ_6	–	8.42*	9.26*	–	–	–	15.51*	13.54*	4.91*
		[7.59,9.25]	[8.36,10.15]				[14.26,16.76]	[12.45,14.63]	[4.08,5.74]
N	2068	2066	2084	2114	2111	1833	1814	1830	1791

Note: Ordered logistic regression coefficients from the GSS and CSPP panel studies, with 95 percent CIs in brackets. Outcome variable in columns one and six are ordinal measures of anti-intellectual attitude endorsement (left-facing arrows). Hypothesized static influences on anti-intellectual attitude endorsement are the outcome variables in all other models (right-facing arrow). In both cases, outcome variable data are derived from the most recent survey wave for which data are available (Wave 3 for GSS, Wave 2 for CSPP), controlling for each quantity measured in the first panel wave. Please refer to the main text for additional information about these models.

Table A5.4 **Models Used to Produce Figure 5.9 (Tea Party, GSS)**

	Lim. Gov	*Ideo.*	*PID*	*Relig.*
College Educ.	−0.72*	−0.71*	−0.71*	−0.72*
	[−0.77,−0.66]	[−0.77,−0.66]	[−0.77,−0.65]	[−0.77,−0.66]
Limited Govt.	0.10	0.20*	0.20*	0.20*
Index	[−0.07,0.27]	[0.04,0.36]	[0.04,0.36]	[0.04,0.36]
Post Obama	−0.14+	−0.18*	−0.18*	−0.06
(08)	[−0.30,0.01]	[−0.33,−0.03]	[−0.29,−0.08]	[−0.16,0.03]
Ideo.	0.36*	0.26*	0.34*	0.36*
(1 = Conservative)	[0.24,0.48]	[0.14,0.39]	[0.22,0.46]	[0.25,0.48]
Party ID	0.01	0.01	−0.08+	0.01
(1 = GOP)	[−0.07,0.09]	[−0.07,0.09]	[−0.17,0.00]	[−0.07,0.09]
Rel. Service	0.26*	0.26*	0.26*	0.19*
Attendance	[0.19,0.34]	[0.19,0.33]	[0.18,0.33]	[0.11,0.27]
Race = Black	0.71*	0.71*	0.72*	0.71*
	[0.63,0.79]	[0.63,0.79]	[0.64,0.80]	[0.63,0.79]
Race = Other	0.16*	0.17*	0.18*	0.16*
	[0.05,0.27]	[0.06,0.28]	[0.06,0.29]	[0.05,0.28]
Income	−0.31*	−0.31*	−0.30*	−0.31*
	[−0.42,−0.21]	[−0.42,−0.20]	[−0.41,−0.20]	[−0.42,−0.20]
Age: 24–44	0.32*	0.32*	0.32*	0.32*
	[0.23,0.41]	[0.23,0.40]	[0.23,0.40]	[0.23,0.41]
Age: 44–64	0.40*	0.39*	0.39*	0.40*
	[0.31,0.49]	[0.30,0.48]	[0.30,0.48]	[0.31,0.49]
Age: 65+	0.40*	0.40*	0.41*	0.40*
	[0.31,0.50]	[0.30,0.50]	[0.31,0.50]	[0.30,0.50]
Female	0.27*	0.27*	0.27*	0.27*
	[0.22,0.32]	[0.22,0.32]	[0.22,0.32]	[0.22,0.32]
Lim.	0.68*	−	−	−
Gov. X Post−08	[0.27,1.09]			
Ideo. X Post−08	−	0.54*	−	−
		[0.27,0.80]		

(*Continued*)

APPENDIX MATERIALS

Table A5.4 **Continued**

	Lim. Gov	*Ideo.*	*PID*	*Relig.*
PID X Post–08	–	–	0.62* [0.44,0.80]	–
Relig. X Post–08	–	–	–	0.38* [0.21,0.55]
τ_1	0.24* [0.10,0.38]	0.23* [0.09,0.36]	0.23* [0.09,0.37]	0.24* [0.11,0.38]
τ_2	3.23* [3.09,3.38]	3.22* [3.07,3.37]	3.23* [3.08,3.37]	3.24* [3.09,3.38]
N	33095	33095	33095	33095

Note: Ordered logistic regression coefficients with 95 percent CIs in brackets. Outcome variable is a three point measure of anti-intellectualism in the GSS time series studies. Please refer to the main text for additional information about these models.

Table A5.5 **Models Used to Produce Figure 5.10 (Tea Party, CSPP)**

DV = Anti-Intellectualism	
Tea Party Support	0.50* [0.31,0.70]
Populism	0.80* [0.66,0.95]
College Educ.	−0.29* [−0.50,−0.08]
Race = Black	0.12 [−0.53,0.77]
Hispanic	−0.30+ [−0.61,0.00]
Income	−0.13 [−0.59,0.32]
Age 25–44	0.03 [−0.59,0.65]
Age 45–65	0.24 [−0.37,0.85]

	0.28
Age 65+	[−0.35,0.91]
Female	−0.08
	[−0.28,0.12]
τ_1	−0.83*
	[−1.66,−0.01]
τ_2	0.99*
	[0.20,1.78]
τ_3	2.69*
	[1.89,3.49]
τ_4	4.41*
	[3.59,5.23]
N	1366

Note: Ordered logistic regression coefficients with 95 percent CIs in brackets. Outcome variable is an ordinal measure of anti-intellectualism in the CSPP panel study (Wave 1). Please refer to the main text for additional information about these models.

Table A5.6 **Summary Statistics for GSS, ANES, CSPP, and SciPol Surveys**

Variable	Mean	SD	Min	Max	N
		GSS			
Anti-Intel.	0.322	0.306	0	1	40784
Ideology (1 = Cons.)	0.517	0.23	0	1	55328
PID (1 = GOP)	0.445	0.331	0	1	63324
Religiosity	0.47	0.341	0	1	64219
Lim. Govt.	0.377	0.165	0	1	61330
Educ. (1 = College)	0.22	0.414	0	1	64641
Race = Black	0.142	0.349	0	1	64814
Race = Other	0.055	0.229	0	1	64814
Income	0.824	0.258	0	1	56488
Age 18–24	0.101	0.301	0	1	64814

(*Continued*)

Table A5.6 **Continued**

Variable	Mean	SD	Min	Max	N
Age 25–44	0.412	0.492	0	1	64814
Age 44–64	0.304	0.46	0	1	64814
Age 65+	0.183	0.387	0	1	64814
Gender = Female	0.559	0.497	0	1	64814
	CSPP 2016				
Anti-Intel.	0.574	0.264	0	1	5507
Ideology (1 = Cons.)	0.52	0.286	0	1	5478
PID (1 = GOP)	0.448	0.379	0	1	5461
Religiosity	0.38	0.358	0	1	7054
Lim. Govt.	0.469	0.295	0	1	5365
Educ. (1 = College)	0.454	0.498	0	1	7104
Race = Blacknh	0.136	0.343	0	1	7104
Race = Hispanic	0.171	0.376	0	1	7104
Income	0.5	0.236	0	1	7026
Age 18–24	0.047	0.213	0	1	7002
Age 25–44	0.297	0.457	0	1	7002
Age 45–64	0.44	0.496	0	1	7002
Age 65+	0.216	0.412	0	1	7002
Gender = Female	0.618	0.486	0	1	7104
	ANES 2019				
Anti-Intel.	0.494	0.287	0	1	2999
Ideology (1 = Cons.)	0.536	0.316	0	1	2739
PID (1 = GOP)	0.477	0.364	0	1	2887
Religiosity	0.263	0.381	0	1	2998
Educ. (1 = College)	0.309	0.462	0	1	3000
Race = Blacknh	0.11	0.313	0	1	3000

Appendix Materials

Variable	Mean	SD	Min	Max	N
Race = Hispanic	0.119	0.323	0	1	3000
Income	0.339	0.231	0	1	2591
Age 18–24	0.066	0.248	0	1	3000
Age 25–44	0.356	0.479	0	1	3000
Age 45–64	0.361	0.48	0	1	3000
Age 65+	0.217	0.413	0	1	3000
Gender = Female	0.533	0.499	0	1	3000
ANES 2020					
Anti-Intel.	0.411	0.282	0	1	7360
Ideology (1 = Cons.)	4.105	1.66	1	7	8160
PID (1 = GOP)	0.481	0.376	0	1	8245
Religiosity	0.635	0.312	0	1	3979
Lim. Govt.	0.321	0.18	0	1	8268
Educ. (1 = College)	0.44	0.496	0	1	8280
Race = Blacknh	0.088	0.283	0	1	8280
Race = Hispanic	0.092	0.289	0	1	8280
Income	0.512	0.322	0	1	7665
Age 18–24	0.051	0.22	0	1	7926
Age 25–44	0.329	0.47	0	1	7926
Age 45–64	0.338	0.473	0	1	7926
Age 65+	0.282	0.45	0	1	7926
Gender = Female	0.537	0.499	0	1	8280
SciPol 2020–2021					
Anti-Intel.	0.279	0.255	0	1	6494
Ideology (1 = Cons.)	0.481	0.303	0	1	6488
PID (1 = GOP)	0.466	0.403	0	1	6068

(*Continued*)

Table A5.6 **Continued**

Variable	Mean	SD	Min	Max	N
Educ. (1 = College)	0.46	0.498	0	1	6499
Race = Black	0.126	0.332	0	1	6315
Race = Hispanic	0.122	0.328	0	1	6499
Income	0.384	0.329	0	1	6184
Age 18–24	0.136	0.343	0	1	6499
Age 25–44	0.375	0.484	0	1	6499
Age 45–64	0.337	0.473	0	1	6499
Age 65+	0.151	0.358	0	1	6499
Gender = Female	0.513	0.5	0	1	6499

Note: Unweighted sample summary statistics for the GSS, ANES, CSPP, and SciPol surveys. In surveys with multiple cross-sections, summary statistics are pooled across survey waves. N represents the number of non-missing observations on each variable.

Supplementary Materials for Chapter 6

Science Knowledge Test (Question Wording and Coding Protocol)

NOTE: CORRECT ANSWERS ARE DESIGNATED WITH AN ASTERISK CORRECT ANSWERS RECEIVE A SCORE OF 1; 0 OTHERWISE.

PREAMBLE: Now, I would like to ask you a few short questions like those you might see on a television game show. For each statement that I read, please tell me if it is true or false. If you don't know or aren't sure, just tell me so, and we will skip to the next question. Remember true, false, or don't know.

1. The center of the earth is very hot.
   True *
   False
   DK
2. All radioactivity is manmade.
   True
   False *
   DK

Appendix Materials

3. It is the father's gene that decides whether the baby is a boy or a girl.
   True *
   False
   DK

4. Electrons are smaller than atoms.
   True *
   False
   DK

5. Antibiotics kill viruses as well as bacteria.
   True
   False *
   DK

6. The universe began with a huge explosion.
   True *
   False
   DK

7. The continents have been moving their locations for millions of years and will continue to move in the future.
   True *
   False
   DK

8. Human beings, as we know them today, developed from earlier species of animals.
   True *
   False
   DK

9. Does the Earth go around the Sun, or the Sun go around the Earth?
   Earth around Sun *
   Sun around Earth
   DK

10. How long does it take for the Earth to go around the Sun: one day, one month, or one year?
    One day
    One month
    One year *
    DK

11. Lasers work by focusing sound waves.
    True
    False *
    DK

APPENDIX MATERIALS

Table A6.1 **Full Model Output Used to Produce Figure 6.1**

DV = Anti-Intellectualism	
Science Knowledge	0.06 [−0.07,0.19]
Science Interest	−0.13* [−0.22,−0.04]
Party ID (1 = Republican)	−0.00 [−0.10,0.10]
Ideology (Conservatism)	0.01 [−0.12,0.13]
Limited Govt. Scale	0.02 [−0.15,0.19]
Rel. Serv. Attend.	−0.06 [−0.15,0.02]
β_0	0.38* [0.25,0.51]
N	3464

Note: Fixed effect panel regression model coefficients presented with 95 percent confidence intervals in brackets. Please refer to the main text in Chapter 6 for additional information.

Table A6.2 **Full Model Output Used to Produce Table 6.1**

DV =	Sci. Interest $AI \rightarrow X$	Sci. Knowledge $AI \rightarrow X$	Anti-Intellectualism $AI \leftarrow X$
Science Interest	0.48* [0.39,0.58]	0.01 [−0.05,0.08]	−0.10* [−0.19,−0.01]
Science Knowledge	0.06 [−0.05,0.17]	0.54* [0.46,0.63]	−0.16* [−0.30,−0.03]
Anti-Intellectualism	−0.01 [−0.09,0.06]	0.02 [−0.04,0.07]	0.34* [0.25,0.42]
Party ID (1 = GOP)	−0.03 [−0.11,0.05]	0.03 [−0.04,0.09]	0.07 [−0.02,0.15]

DV =	Sci. Interest	Sci. Knowledge	Anti-Intellectualism
	$AI \rightarrow X$	$AI \rightarrow X$	$AI \leftarrow X$
Ideo. (1 = Conservative)	−0.09	−0.07	−0.01
	[−0.20,0.02]	[−0.16,0.02]	[−0.13,0.10]
Female	−0.06*	−0.03*	0.02
	[−0.10,−0.01]	[−0.06,−0.00]	[−0.03,0.06]
College Educ.	0.01	0.05*	−0.07*
	[−0.04,0.06]	[0.03,0.08]	[−0.12,−0.02]
Race = Black	−0.02	−0.08*	0.08*
	[−0.09,0.05]	[−0.14,−0.03]	[0.01,0.16]
Race = Other	0.01	0.00	0.08
	[−0.08,0.09]	[−0.05,0.05]	[−0.02,0.19]
β_0	0.34*	0.37*	0.38*
	[0.21,0.46]	[0.28,0.47]	[0.24,0.51]
N	540	541	741
r2	0.29	0.47	0.24

Note: Cross-lagged regression models present OLS coefficients with 95 percent confidence intervals in brackets. Models are calculated in-between the surveys' first and final waves. Please refer to the main text in Chapter 6 for additional information.

Table A6.3 **Full Model Output Used to Produce Table 6.2**

	College Educ.	Not College Educ.	Current College
Science Knowledge	−0.09	0.09	0.25
	[−0.31,0.14]	[−0.02,0.19]	[−0.18,0.67]
Science Interest	−0.16*	−0.15*	−0.41*
	[−0.30,−0.03]	[−0.22,−0.08]	[−0.76,−0.06]
β_0	0.42*	0.39*	0.37+
	[0.20,0.63]	[0.31,0.48]	[−0.00,0.74]
N	1349	2960	219

Note: Fixed effect regression coefficients presented with 95 percent confidence intervals in brackets. Note that *current college* refers to respondents' whose educational attainment changed from not holding a college degree to holding a college degree within the duration of the panel. Please refer to the main text in Chapter 6 for additional information.

Supplementary Materials for Chapter 7

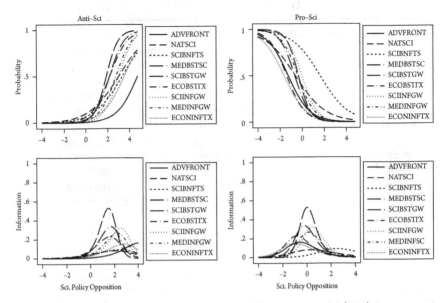

Figure S7.1 Expert policy role orientations: Graded response model (IRT) diagnostics and summary

Note: Category characteristic curves (top row) and item information functions (bottom row) presented; evaluated at the minimum (right-side panels) and maximum (left-side panels) values of each constituent item used to build the expert policy role index. Both sets of quantities are derived from a graded response modeling application of item response theory.

Graded response models work by estimating two sets of parameters, known as *difficulty* and *discrimination* parameters. Difficulty parameters are calculated for each *level* (i.e., response option) for every constituent item in the resulting scale, whereas discrimination parameters are calculated at the question level. The parameters can be interpreted as follows. Response options that are very *difficult* (i.e., a larger absolute value for the difficulty parameter) are endorsed by relatively few people but imply that most respondents who select those options earn very high (if positive) or low (if negative) scores on the latent scale. Questions with difficult response options, however, may not be very *discriminating*—or informative with respect to whether people earn above or below a particular scale point—given their rarity in the population. Comparatively *easier* responses (or those endorsed by a greater proportion of the sample) may be highly discriminating if respondents fail to select that option consistently earn low scores on the latent scale across all other items, while those who select it earn comparatively higher scores.

Item characteristic curves can be thought about as a more reader-friendly way to summarize information about question difficulty. These curves denote the probability (y-axis) that respondents earn a particular score on latent scale (x-axis) if they select either the most (left side) or least (right side) anti-expert response to each question summarized in the main text (Table 7.1). The S-shaped curves in the figure's first panel suggest that respondents are very unlikely to earn a low score when they select the most anti-expert option and very likely to do so when they do. The opposite is true of the figure's second panel (i.e., when respondents indicate positivity toward the role that experts play in the policymaking process). As virtually every line expresses the anticipated pattern of effects across top-row panels, we can say that the resulting scale not only seems to substantively measure what it purports to measure but also that no variables stand out as being particularly poor indicators of the underlying latent concept. The one exception to this general pattern of results may be the category characteristic curve associated with the *general science funding* item ADVFRONT (see Table 7.1), which exhibits more of a J-shaped curve in the top row's leftmost panel. This pattern indicates that higher scores on this variable are associated only with *very* strong levels of opposition to the role that experts play in the policymaking process. However, given that I do not observe this pattern in the rightmost portion of the figure, and considering that the variable's effect moves in the correct direction, I consider scores on this measure to pose a particularly difficult test of whether respondents resent the role that experts play in the policymaking process.

Conversely, the information curves presented at the bottom of the figure can be thought about as an extension of each question's discrimination parameter. More kurtotic (higher-peaked) curves indicate higher levels of discrimination (more information) at a corresponding point on the x-axis. The results suggest that the science funding item natsci is particularly informative at determining who earns low versus high scores on the latent scale when respondents endorse the most pro-expert option (right-side figure), and between low versus high levels of opposition for those selecting the most anti-expert option (left side). Most items exhibit similar (albeit less informative) patterns, again with the exception of the ADVFRONT item for those who express the most anti-expert opinions (left side) and the benefits of scientific research item (right side) for those expressing the most pro-expert option. In both cases, these items are comparatively better at discerning who earns very high (from less high) scores on the latent scale.

Table S7.1 **Full Model Output Used to Produce Figure 7.2**

	AI → EPR	AI ← EPR
AI	0.05* [0.04,0.06]	–
EPR	–	0.21* [0.15,0.26]
Party ID (1 = Republican)	0.00 [−0.02,0.02]	−0.01 [−0.06,0.04]
Ideology (Conservatism)	0.01 [−0.01,0.03]	0.00 [−0.04,0.04]
Limited Govt. Scale	0.09* [0.06,0.13]	−0.01 [−0.08,0.06]
Rel. Serv. Attend.	0.00 [−0.02,0.02]	−0.02 [−0.06,0.02]
College	0.02+ [−0.00,0.04]	−0.05* [−0.09,−0.00]
β_0	0.33* [0.30,0.35]	0.28* [0.23,0.33]
N	7977	7977

Note: Fixed effect panel regression model coefficients presented with 95 percent confidence intervals in parentheses. Please see the note accompanying Figure 7.2 in the main text for additional information about these models.

Supplementary Materials for Chapter 8

Table S8.1 **Full Model Output Used to Produce Figure 8.1**

	Warming ANES 19	Anthro SciPol	Concern ANES '20	Concern SciPol
	Logistic	Logistic	OLS	OLS
Anti−Intel.	−0.90* [−1.33,−0.48]	−1.27* [−1.47,−1.07]	−0.17* [−0.22,−0.12]	0.04* [0.02,0.07]
Party ID (1 = GOP)	−1.48* [−1.96,−1.00]	−1.07* [−1.24,−0.90]	−0.22* [−0.28,−0.17]	−0.18* [−0.21,−0.16]

Appendix Materials

	Warming ANES 19	Anthro SciPol	Concern ANES '20	Concern SciPol
	Logistic	Logistic	OLS	OLS
Ideo. (1 = Conservative)	−1.84* [−2.46,−1.22]	−1.38* [−1.60,−1.16]	−0.05* [−0.06,−0.04]	−0.25* [−0.28,−0.22]
Limited Govt. Index	−	−	−0.37* [−0.44,−0.29]	−
College Educ.	0.37* [0.10,0.64]	0.14* [0.00,0.28]	0.01 [−0.02,0.03]	0.04* [0.03,0.06]
Rel. Service Attendance	−0.33* [−0.65,−0.01]	−	−0.02 [−0.06,0.02]	−
Race = Black	0.04 [−0.44,0.51]	−0.67* [−0.88,−0.47]	−0.07* [−0.11,−0.02]	−0.04* [−0.07,−0.02]
Eth. = Hispanic	−0.11 [−0.51,0.30]	−0.17+ [−0.37,0.03]	0.04+ [−0.00,0.08]	−0.00 [−0.03,0.02]
Income	0.13 [−0.45,0.71]	0.42* [0.20,0.64]	0.00 [−0.04,0.04]	0.11* [0.09,0.14]
Age: 24–44	−0.72* [−1.36,−0.09]	0.13 [−0.08,0.34]	−0.02 [−0.08,0.04]	0.04* [0.02,0.07]
Age: 44–64	−0.62+ [−1.24,0.00]	−0.12 [−0.34,0.09]	0.00 [−0.05,0.06]	0.02+ [−0.00,0.05]
Age: 65+	−0.34 [−0.99,0.31]	−0.01 [−0.26,0.24]	0.01 [−0.05,0.07]	0.02 [−0.01,0.05]
Female	0.05 [−0.19,0.28]	−0.16* [−0.29,−0.04]	0.01 [−0.02,0.03]	0.01 [−0.01,0.02]
April 2020	−	0.00 [0.00,0.00]	−	0.00 [0.00,0.00]
June 2020	−	−0.12 [−0.33,0.08]	−	−0.04* [−0.07,−0.02]
Aug. 2020	−	0.04 [−0.16,0.24]	−	−0.01 [−0.03,0.02]
Oct. 2020	−	0.03 [−0.17,0.23]	−	0.03* [0.00,0.05]

(Continued)

Table S8.1 **Continued**

	Warming ANES 19	*Anthro* SciPol	*Concern* ANES '20	*Concern* SciPol
	Logistic	*Logistic*	OLS	OLS
Dec. 2020	–	−0.08 [−0.28,0.13]	–	0.00 [−0.02,0.03]
Feb. 2021	–	−0.01 [−0.23,0.21]	–	−0.01 [−0.04,0.01]
β_0	4.09* [3.34,4.84]	1.86* [1.57,2.15]	1.13* [1.07,1.20]	0.77* [0.74,0.81]
N	2350	5095	3157	5096

* p < 0.05; + p < 0.10

Note: Logistic and OLS parameters presented with 95 percent confidence intervals in brackets. Please refer to Chapter 8 for a description of each outcome variable and additional information about these models.

Table S8.2 **Full Model Output Used to Produce Figure 8.2**

	Spending ANES 20	*Reg. Biz.* ANES 20	*Reg. Polluters* ANES '19	*Fuel Eff.* ANES '19
	O. Logistic	O. Logistic	O. Logistic	O. Logistic
Anti−Intel.	1.12* [0.71,1.52]	0.98* [0.60,1.36]	1.63* [1.23,2.03]	1.41* [1.04,1.78]
Party ID (1 = GOP)	0.74* [0.31,1.17]	1.30* [0.87,1.74]	1.57* [1.18,1.96]	1.00* [0.68,1.33]
Ideo. (1 = Conservative)	0.36* [0.26,0.46]	0.39* [0.28,0.49]	2.74* [2.20,3.28]	2.38* [1.99,2.77]
Limited Govt. Index	5.53* [4.78,6.28]	2.83* [2.15,3.52]	–	–
College Educ.	−0.02 [−0.24,0.19]	−0.06 [−0.26,0.14]	−0.16 [−0.38,0.05]	−0.36* [−0.55,−0.17]
Rel. Service Attendance	0.48* [0.15,0.82]	0.12 [−0.21,0.45]	0.22 [−0.04,0.49]	0.00 [−0.23,0.24]

Appendix Materials

	Spending ANES 20	Reg. Biz. ANES 20	Reg. Polluters ANES '19	Fuel Eff. ANES '19
	O. Logistic	O. Logistic	O. Logistic	O. Logistic
Race = Black	0.49*	−0.01	0.26+	0.26+
	[0.14,0.83]	[−0.41,0.38]	[−0.05,0.57]	[−0.05,0.56]
Eth. = Hispanic	−0.58*	−0.53*	0.32*	0.34*
	[−0.96,−0.20]	[−0.91,−0.15]	[0.04,0.60]	[0.00,0.68]
Income	0.04	−0.25	0.39+	−0.25
	[−0.31,0.39]	[−0.62,0.11]	[−0.06,0.84]	[−0.67,0.17]
Age: 24–44	0.03	0.21	0.23	0.13
	[−0.50,0.57]	[−0.30,0.71]	[−0.18,0.65]	[−0.27,0.53]
Age: 44–64	−0.00	0.13	0.35+	0.11
	[−0.53,0.53]	[−0.36,0.63]	[−0.06,0.76]	[−0.29,0.52]
Age: 65+	0.11	0.37	0.13	−0.13
	[−0.42,0.64]	[−0.13,0.87]	[−0.30,0.55]	[−0.56,0.30]
Female	−0.07	−0.18+	−0.23*	−0.01
	[−0.28,0.13]	[−0.37,0.02]	[−0.41,−0.05]	[−0.18,0.16]
τ_1	3.86*	2.24*	−6.33*	−5.83*
	[3.27,4.44]	[1.61,2.86]	[−8.32,−4.34]	[−7.36,−4.31]
τ_2	4.92*	3.08*	2.70*	1.81*
	[4.32,5.51]	[2.44,3.71]	[2.24,3.17]	[1.36,2.26]
τ_3	7.73*	3.80*	3.81*	3.01*
	[7.07,8.39]	[3.16,4.44]	[3.33,4.28]	[2.55,3.47]
τ_4	8.77*	5.03*	5.07*	4.32*
	[8.09,9.44]	[4.35,5.70]	[4.58,5.56]	[3.85,4.79]
τ_5	–	5.87*	5.76*	5.03*
		[5.18,6.56]	[5.25,6.26]	[4.55,5.50]
τ_6	–	6.63*	–	–
		[5.92,7.34]		
N	3157	2731	2351	2351

* p < 0.05; + p < 0.10

Note: Ordered logistic regression parameters presented with 95 percent confidence intervals in brackets. Please refer to Chapter 8 for a description of each outcome variable and additional information about these models.

Table S8.3 **Full Model Output Used to Produce Figure 8.3**

	Pow. Plants SciPol	Paris SciPol	Carbon Tax SciPol	Fuel Eff. SciPol	Green Jobs SciPol	Disaster Ins. SciPol
	O. Logistic	O. Logistic	O. Logistic	O. Logistic	O. Logistic	O. Logistic
Anti–Intel.	0.87*	0.72*	0.24	0.79*	0.73*	0.28
	[0.26,1.47]	[0.12,1.33]	[−0.35,0.83]	[0.20,1.38]	[0.18,1.28]	[−0.26,0.83]
Party ID (1 = GOP)	0.31	0.98*	0.25	0.65*	0.34	0.53+
	[−0.17,0.79]	[0.51,1.46]	[−0.19,0.70]	[0.20,1.11]	[−0.15,0.83]	[−0.00,1.06]
Ideo. (1 = Conservative)	2.20*	1.45*	1.55*	2.02*	1.29*	1.25*
	[1.48,2.91]	[0.77,2.14]	[0.89,2.22]	[1.28,2.75]	[0.56,2.01]	[0.44,2.05]
College Educ.	−0.37*	−0.29	−0.27	−0.39*	−0.33+	−0.23
	[−0.72,−0.02]	[−0.64,0.07]	[−0.63,0.10]	[−0.73,−0.04]	[−0.70,0.03]	[−0.58,0.12]
Race = Black	0.55*	0.62*	0.61*	0.50+	0.11	0.14
	[0.10,1.00]	[0.16,1.08]	[0.16,1.06]	[−0.01,1.00]	[−0.45,0.67]	[−0.39,0.68]
Eth. = Hispanic	0.19	0.19	0.05	0.24	0.10	0.27
	[−0.39,0.77]	[−0.36,0.74]	[−0.42,0.52]	[−0.31,0.80]	[−0.40,0.59]	[−0.24,0.77]
Income	0.11	−0.01	−0.02	0.07	0.23+	−0.03
	[−0.13,0.35]	[−0.25,0.22]	[−0.26,0.22]	[−0.16,0.30]	[−0.03,0.50]	[−0.27,0.22]
Age: 24–44	−0.55*	−0.16	−0.42	−0.24	−0.49+	−0.69*
	[−1.09,−0.00]	[−0.70,0.37]	[−1.01,0.16]	[−0.78,0.31]	[−1.03,0.05]	[−1.24,−0.14]

Age: 44–64	−0.94* [−1.49,−0.38]	−0.54+ [−1.08,0.00]	−0.63* [−1.22,−0.04]	−0.75* [−1.28,−0.22]	−0.94* [−1.48,−0.39]	−1.06* [−1.61,−0.51]
Age: 65+	−0.46 [−1.07,0.14]	−0.28 [−0.88,0.32]	−0.35 [−1.01,0.32]	−0.45 [−1.04,0.14]	−0.95* [−1.55,−0.35]	−0.85* [−1.46,−0.24]
Female	−0.57* [−0.88,−0.27]	−0.66* [−0.96,−0.35]	−0.45* [−0.75,−0.15]	−0.29+ [−0.59,0.01]	−0.27+ [−0.58,0.04]	−0.52* [−0.83,−0.20]
June 2020	0.00 [0.00,0.00]	0.00 [0.00,0.00]	0.00 [0.00,0.00]	0.00 [0.00,0.00]	0.00 [0.00,0.00]	0.00 [0.00,0.00]
τ_1	−0.33 [−1.12,0.47]	−0.06 [−0.79,0.68]	−0.80+ [−1.70,0.09]	0.08 [−0.79,0.94]	0.15 [−0.70,1.00]	−1.03* [−1.83,−0.23]
τ_2	1.21* [0.41,2.00]	1.26* [0.53,2.00]	0.63 [−0.27,1.53]	1.51* [0.64,2.37]	1.52* [0.65,2.38]	0.50 [−0.31,1.31]
τ_3	2.79* [1.96,3.63]	2.71* [1.96,3.45]	2.05* [1.13,2.96]	2.94* [2.06,3.82]	2.91* [2.01,3.80]	1.86* [1.02,2.70]
τ_4	3.77* [2.93,4.61]	3.47* [2.71,4.22]	2.96* [2.00,3.92]	4.00* [3.13,4.88]	3.78* [2.78,4.77]	2.92* [2.01,3.84]
N	889	888	889	890	890	888

* p < 0.05; + p < 0.10

Note: Ordered logistic regression parameters presented with 95 percent confidence intervals in brackets. Please refer to Chapter 8 for a description of each outcome variable and additional information about these models.

Table S8.4 **Full Model Output Used to Produce Figure 8.4**

	Flu Sick SciPol	COVID Lab SciPol	MMR Autism SciPol	5G Sick SciPol	COVID Lab ANES '20	Hydrox. ANES '20
	Logit	Logit	O. Logit	Logit	Logit	Logit
Anti-Intel.	−0.76*	−0.78*	−2.78*	−0.86*	−1.10*	−0.77*
	[−0.98,−0.54]	[−0.97,−0.59]	[−2.95,−2.60]	[−1.20,−0.51]	[−1.53,−0.67]	[−1.22,−0.32]
Party ID (1 = GOP)	−0.23*	−0.83*	−0.22*	−0.50*	−1.19*	−1.71*
	[−0.42,−0.04]	[−1.00,−0.66]	[−0.36,−0.08]	[−0.81,−0.18]	[−1.61,−0.77]	[−2.22,−1.21]
Ideo. (1 = Conservative)	−0.53*	−0.96*	−0.04	−0.20	−0.19*	−0.27*
	[−0.77,−0.29]	[−1.18,−0.74]	[−0.22,0.15]	[−0.61,0.21]	[−0.29,−0.10]	[−0.39,−0.15]
College Educ.	0.08	0.50*	0.05	0.11	0.57*	0.14
	[−0.08,0.24]	[0.37,0.64]	[−0.06,0.16]	[−0.12,0.35]	[0.34,0.81]	[−0.11,0.39]
Race = Black	−0.60*	−0.82*	−0.63*	−0.38*	−0.77*	−0.21
	[−0.83,−0.37]	[−1.04,−0.59]	[−0.80,−0.47]	[−0.74,−0.01]	[−1.15,−0.39]	[−0.69,0.27]
Eth. = Hispanic	−0.15	−0.29*	−0.23*	−0.16	−0.78*	−0.10
	[−0.37,0.07]	[−0.49,−0.09]	[−0.39,−0.07]	[−0.52,0.19]	[−1.17,−0.39]	[−0.57,0.36]
Income	0.58*	0.37*	−0.37*	0.45*	0.57*	0.32
	[0.34,0.82]	[0.16,0.58]	[−0.55,−0.20]	[0.08,0.83]	[0.18,0.95]	[−0.12,0.75]
Age: 24–44	−0.20+	−0.25*	−0.35*	0.12	−0.55*	0.31
	[−0.43,0.03]	[−0.46,−0.04]	[−0.52,−0.18]	[−0.26,0.50]	[−1.06,−0.04]	[−0.23,0.85]

Age: 44–64	−0.01 [−0.25,0.22]	−0.18+ [−0.40,0.03]	−0.04 [−0.22,0.13]	−0.09 [−0.48,0.29]	−0.61* [−1.11,−0.11]	0.34 [−0.19,0.87]
Age: 65+	0.76* [0.47,1.05]	−0.07 [−0.31,0.17]	0.47* [0.27,0.67]	0.20 [−0.23,0.63]	−0.26 [−0.76,0.25]	0.57* [0.03,1.12]
Female	0.02 [−0.12,0.16]	−0.19* [−0.31,−0.06]	0.19* [0.09,0.29]	−0.50* [−0.71,−0.28]	−0.17 [−0.39,0.05]	−0.32* [−0.56,−0.08]
Rel. Service Attendance	−	−	−	−	0.29 [−0.07,0.65]	−0.13 [−0.52,0.26]
Aug. 2020	0.00 [0.00,0.00]	−0.05 [−0.26,0.16]	−0.06 [−0.23,0.11]	−	−	−
Oct. 2020	0.01 [−0.20,0.21]	−0.15 [−0.35,0.06]	−0.29* [−0.46,−0.12]	−	−	−
Dec. 2020	−0.13 [−0.33,0.08]	−0.30* [−0.51,−0.09]	−0.29* [−0.46,−0.12]	−	−	−
Feb. 2021	−0.14 [−0.32,0.05]	−0.23* [−0.42,−0.04]	0.03 [−0.12,0.19]	−	−	−
April 2020	−	0.00 [0.00,0.00]	0.00 [0.00,0.00]	0.00 [0.00,0.00]	−	−

(Continued)

Table S8.4 **Continued**

	Flu Sick SciPol	COVID Lab SciPol	MMR Autism SciPol	5G Sick SciPol	COVID Lab ANES '20	Hydrox. ANES '20
June 2020	–	−0.04	0.18*	0.15	–	–
	[−0.24,0.17]	[0.01,0.35]	[−0.06,0.35]			
β_0	1.20*	0.45*	–	−0.13	1.82*	3.25*
	[0.90,1.51]	[0.17,0.72]		[−0.58,0.32]	[1.18,2.45]	[2.56,3.95]
τ_1	–	–	−3.75*	–	–	–
			[−4.00,−3.50]			
τ_2	–	–	−2.00*	–	–	–
			[−2.24,−1.77]			
τ_3	–	–	−0.39*	–	–	–
			[−0.62,−0.16]			
N	3988	5795	5793	1786	3120	3116

* $p < 0.05$; + $p < 0.10$

Note: Logistic and ordered logistic regression parameters presented with 95 percent confidence intervals in brackets. Please refer to Chapter 8 for a description of each outcome variable and additional information about these models.

Table S8.5 **Full Model Output Used to Produce Figure 8.5**

	Flu Uptake SciPol	COVID Uptake SciPol	Mand. Vax SciPol	Mand Vax ANES '20	Sci. COVID Policy ANES '20	COVID Restrict. ANES '20
	O. Logit	O. Logit	Logit	O. Logit	O. Logit	Logit
Anti-Intel.	−0.03	0.38*	−0.37*	0.48*	−1.84*	−1.04*
	[−0.32,0.26]	[0.07,0.68]	[−0.55,−0.19]	[0.09,0.87]	[−2.24,−1.44]	[−1.50,−0.57]
Party ID (1 = GOP)	0.44*	0.47*	−0.37*	0.40+	−1.39*	−1.64*
	[0.18,0.69]	[0.20,0.74]	[−0.52,−0.21]	[−0.00,0.80]	[−1.79,−0.98]	[−2.19,−1.09]
Ideo. (1 = Conservative)	0.13	0.55*	−0.50*	0.18*	−0.26*	−0.34*
	[−0.21,0.47]	[0.20,0.90]	[−0.70,−0.30]	[0.09,0.28]	[−0.35,−0.16]	[−0.49,−0.20]
College Educ.	−0.36*	−0.40*	0.06	0.02	0.07	0.11
	[−0.57,−0.16]	[−0.60,−0.19]	[−0.07,0.19]	[−0.18,0.22]	[−0.12,0.27]	[−0.16,0.38]
Race = Black	0.46*	0.69*	−0.79*	0.58*	0.34+	0.67*
	[0.18,0.75]	[0.39,0.99]	[−0.98,−0.60]	[0.22,0.93]	[−0.03,0.72]	[0.05,1.29]
Eth. = Hispanic	0.22	0.31*	−0.29*	−0.01	0.41*	0.71*
	[−0.06,0.50]	[0.02,0.60]	[−0.47,−0.11]	[−0.35,0.32]	[0.04,0.79]	[0.22,1.20]
Income	−0.63*	−0.80*	0.26*	−0.70*	0.34+	−0.10
	[−0.95,−0.30]	[−1.13,−0.46]	[0.06,0.45]	[−1.02,−0.39]	[−0.00,0.69]	[−0.54,0.34]

(*Continued*)

Table S8.5 **Continued**

	Flu Uptake SciPol	COVID Uptake SciPol	Mand. Vax SciPol	Mand Vax ANES '20	Sci. COVID Policy ANES '20	COVID Restrict. ANES '20
Age: 24–44	0.02 [−0.27,0.31]	−0.20 [−0.50,0.10]	0.09 [−0.10,0.28]	0.13 [−0.28,0.54]	−0.20 [−0.65,0.26]	−0.13 [−0.69,0.43]
Age: 44–64	−0.23 [−0.52,0.07]	−0.42* [−0.73,−0.12]	0.35* [0.16,0.55]	−0.58* [−0.99,−0.17]	0.24 [−0.21,0.68]	0.03 [−0.53,0.58]
Age: 65+	−1.29* [−1.66,−0.92]	−1.13* [−1.50,−0.76]	0.63* [0.40,0.86]	−1.32* [−1.74,−0.89]	0.35 [−0.11,0.81]	0.41 [−0.18,1.00]
Female	0.05 [−0.12,0.23]	0.20* [0.01,0.38]	0.11+ [−0.01,0.22]	−0.11 [−0.30,0.09]	0.10 [−0.09,0.29]	0.41* [0.17,0.66]
April 2020	0.00 [0.00,0.00]	0.00 [0.00,0.00]	0.00 [0.00,0.00]	–	–	–
June 2020	−0.01 [−0.18,0.16]	0.22* [0.04,0.39]	0.05 [−0.15,0.25]	–	–	–
Aug. 2020	–	–	−0.28* [−0.48,−0.07]	–	–	–
Oct. 2020	–	–	−0.36* [−0.56,−0.16]	–	–	–

Dec. 2020	–	–	−0.43* [−0.62,−0.23]	–	–	–
Feb. 2021	–	–	−0.42* [−0.60,−0.24]	–	–	–
Rel. Service Attendance	–	–	–	−0.25 [−0.57,0.07]	0.04 [−0.29,0.37]	0.08 [−0.33,0.50]
β_0	–	–	1.04* [0.78,1.30]	–	–	3.92* [3.14,4.69]
τ_1	−0.58* [−0.95,−0.21]	−0.04 [−0.42,0.34]	–	0.36 [−0.14,0.86]	−6.77* [−7.47,−6.08]	–
τ_2	0.16 [−0.21,0.52]	1.33* [0.94,1.72]	–	1.07* [0.56,1.57]	−5.36* [−5.98,−4.74]	–
τ_3	0.89* [0.52,1.26]	2.37* [1.97,2.77]	–	1.20* [0.70,1.69]	−3.60* [−4.18,−3.02]	–
τ_4	1.59* [1.21,1.97]	–	–	2.35* [1.85,2.86]	−1.99* [−2.55,−1.42]	–

(Continued)

	Flu Uptake SciPol	COVID Uptake SciPol	Mand. Vax SciPol	Mand Vax ANES '20	Sci. COVID Policy ANES '20	COVID Restrict. ANES '20
τ_5	–	–	–	2.52* [2.02,3.03]	–	–
τ_6	–	–	–	3.15* [2.64,3.66]	–	–
N	1789	1793	5788	3156	3162	3161

* $p < 0.05$; + $p < 0.10$

Note: Logistic and ordered logistic regression parameters presented with 95 percent confidence intervals in brackets. Please refer to Chapter 8 for a description of each outcome variable and additional information about these models.

Table S8.6 **Full Model Output Used to Produce Figure 8.5**

	Mask	No Dine-in	No Travel	Soc. Distance	Close Schools	Close Restaurants	No Gather	Shelter
	SciPol	SciPol	SciPol	ANES '20	ANES '20	ANES '20		
	Logit	Logit	Logit	Logit	O. Logit	O. Logit	O. Logit	O. Logit
Anti-Intel.	-1.70* [-1.91,-1.49]	-1.41* [-1.60,-1.23]	-0.71* [-0.89,-0.53]	-1.79* [-2.00,-1.59]	0.50* [0.34,0.66]	0.24* [0.08,0.40]	0.62* [0.45,0.78]	0.24* [0.08,0.40]
Party ID (1 = GOP)	-0.40* [-0.58,-0.22]	-0.57* [-0.73,-0.41]	-0.18* [-0.34,-0.02]	-0.31* [-0.48,-0.14]	0.87* [0.73,1.01]	0.66* [0.52,0.80]	0.93* [0.79,1.08]	0.99* [0.85,1.13]
Ideo. (1 = Conservative)	0.22+ [-0.00,0.44]	-0.17 [-0.38,0.04]	-0.03 [-0.23,0.18]	0.02 [-0.20,0.23]	0.80* [0.62,0.99]	0.96* [0.78,1.14]	0.77* [0.59,0.96]	0.84* [0.66,1.02]
College Educ.	-0.04 [-0.20,0.11]	0.04 [-0.09,0.17]	0.34* [0.21,0.47]	-0.05 [-0.20,0.09]	0.06 [-0.06,0.17]	-0.12* [-0.24,-0.01]	-0.08 [-0.20,0.03]	-0.14* [-0.25,-0.02]
Race = Black	-0.40* [-0.61,-0.19]	-0.13 [-0.32,0.07]	-0.06 [-0.26,0.13]	-0.11 [-0.32,0.10]	0.23* [0.06,0.40]	0.22* [0.05,0.39]	0.20* [0.02,0.38]	0.11 [-0.06,0.28]
Eth. = Hispanic	-0.39* [-0.59,-0.19]	-0.07 [-0.26,0.12]	0.21* [0.03,0.40]	-0.23* [-0.42,-0.03]	0.27* [0.10,0.43]	0.15+ [-0.01,0.31]	0.13 [-0.03,0.29]	0.06 [-0.10,0.23]
Income	0.22+ [-0.01,0.45]	0.20+ [-0.00,0.40]	0.90* [0.71,1.10]	0.05 [-0.17,0.27]	-0.42* [-0.59,-0.24]	-0.40* [-0.58,-0.23]	-0.42* [-0.60,-0.24]	-0.39* [-0.56,-0.21]

(Continued)

Table S8.6 **Continued**

	Mask SciPol	No Dine-in SciPol	No Travel SciPol	Soc. Distance ANES '20	Close Schools ANES '20	Close Restaurants ANES '20	No Gather	Shelter
Age: 24–44	0.46* [0.25,0.66]	0.44* [0.24,0.63]	0.03 [−0.17,0.23]	0.44* [0.25,0.64]	−0.27* [−0.44,−0.10]	−0.16+ [−0.32,0.01]	−0.39* [−0.56,−0.23]	−0.32* [−0.49,−0.15]
Age: 44–64	0.92* [0.71,1.13]	0.77* [0.58,0.97]	0.03 [−0.17,0.23]	1.08* [0.87,1.29]	−0.38* [−0.56,−0.21]	−0.29* [−0.46,−0.13]	−0.67* [−0.84,−0.50]	−0.50* [−0.67,−0.32]
Age: 65+	1.69* [1.40,1.98]	1.28* [1.05,1.52]	0.14 [−0.09,0.37]	1.80* [1.52,2.09]	−0.40* [−0.60,−0.20]	−0.58* [−0.78,−0.38]	−1.06* [−1.26,−0.85]	−0.85* [−1.05,−0.65]
Female	0.54* [0.41,0.67]	0.25* [0.13,0.37]	0.11+ [−0.00,0.23]	0.50* [0.37,0.63]	−0.19* [−0.29,−0.08]	−0.15* [−0.25,−0.05]	−0.23* [−0.33,−0.12]	−0.21* [−0.31,−0.11]
April 2020	0.00 [0.00,0.00]	0.00 [0.00,0.00]	0.00 [0.00,0.00]	0.00 [0.00,0.00]	0.00 [0.00,0.00]	0.00 [0.00,0.00]	0.00 [0.00,0.00]	0.00 [0.00,0.00]
June 2020	0.37* [0.15,0.58]	−0.69* [−0.91,−0.48]	−0.43* [−0.63,−0.24]	−0.28* [−0.51,−0.05]	0.52* [0.33,0.70]	0.31* [0.14,0.49]	0.37* [0.19,0.56]	0.36* [0.18,0.54]
Aug. 2020	0.60* [0.38,0.82]	−1.00* [−1.22,−0.79]	−0.53* [−0.73,−0.34]	−0.33* [−0.56,−0.11]	0.62* [0.44,0.80]	0.53* [0.35,0.70]	0.51* [0.32,0.69]	0.60* [0.42,0.77]

Oct. 2020	0.54* [0.32,0.75]	−1.31* [−1.52,−1.10]	−0.61* [−0.80,−0.41]	−0.56* [−0.78,−0.34]	0.69* [0.51,0.88]	0.54* [0.36,0.71]	0.45* [0.27,0.64]	0.68* [0.50,0.86]
Dec. 2020	0.88* [0.65,1.10]	−1.06* [−1.28,−0.85]	−0.49* [−0.68,−0.30]	−0.37* [−0.60,−0.15]	0.97* [0.78,1.15]	0.67* [0.50,0.85]	0.56* [0.38,0.74]	0.87* [0.69,1.04]
Feb. 2021	1.07* [0.86,1.28]	−0.90* [−1.10,−0.70]	−0.61* [−0.78,−0.43]	−0.05 [−0.26,0.16]	1.11* [0.94,1.27]	0.73* [0.57,0.89]	0.57* [0.40,0.73]	0.85* [0.69,1.01]
β_0	0.46* [0.17,0.74]	1.39* [1.11,1.66]	−0.31* [−0.57,−0.05]	1.19* [0.90,1.48]	—	—	—	—
τ_1	—	—	—	—	1.04* [0.79,1.28]	0.38* [0.15,0.61]	0.69* [0.45,0.93]	0.43* [0.19,0.66]
τ_2	—	—	—	—	2.50* [2.25,2.75]	1.77* [1.53,2.01]	2.16* [1.91,2.40]	1.93* [1.69,2.17]
τ_3	—	—	—	—	3.72* [3.45,3.98]	3.09* [2.84,3.34]	3.41* [3.15,3.66]	3.23* [2.98,3.48]
N	5795	5795	5795	5795	5789	5788	5790	5791

* $p < 0.05$; + $p < 0.10$

Note: Logistic and ordered logistic regression parameters presented with 95 percent confidence intervals in brackets. Please refer to Chapter 8 for a description of each outcome variable and additional information about these models.

Table S8.7 **Full Model Output Used to Produce Figure 8.7**

	Immigration = Good ANES '20	Economy = Worse in 2020 ANES '20
	Logit	Logit
Anti-Intel.	−0.61* [−1.02,−0.20]	−0.66* [−1.07,−0.25]
Party ID (1 = GOP)	−0.87* [−1.29,−0.44]	−1.55* [−1.98,−1.12]
Ideo. (1 = Conservative)	−0.13* [−0.23,−0.03]	−0.12* [−0.22,−0.02]
College Educ.	0.54* [0.31,0.76]	0.14 [−0.09,0.37]
Rel. Service Attendance	0.63* [0.28,0.98]	−0.01 [−0.37,0.34]
Race = Black	−0.42* [−0.78,−0.07]	0.26 [−0.15,0.67]
Eth. = Hispanic	0.56* [0.17,0.96]	−0.15 [−0.52,0.22]
Income	0.94* [0.57,1.31]	0.05 [−0.34,0.44]
Age: 24–44	−0.01 [−0.47,0.44]	0.42+ [−0.08,0.92]
Age: 44–64	−0.02 [−0.47,0.43]	0.67* [0.18,1.17]
Age: 65+	0.35 [−0.11,0.82]	0.75* [0.24,1.25]
Female	−0.27* [−0.49,−0.06]	0.21+ [−0.01,0.43]
β_0	0.71* [0.14,1.27]	1.28* [0.64,1.92]
N	3152	3143

* $p < 0.05$; + $p < 0.10$

Note: Logistic regression parameters presented with 95 percent confidence intervals in brackets. Please refer to Chapter 8 for a description of each outcome variable and additional information about these models.

Table S8.8a **Full Model Output Used to Produce Figure 8.8 (Fixed Effects)**

	Avg.	Gen.	Waste	Hazard	Recycle	Indoor	Species	Conservation	R&D
Mood (t−1)	0.00	−0.02	−0.05	0.08	−0.03	0.05	0.01	−0.05	0.04
	(0.03)	(0.04)	(0.04)	(0.08)	(0.04)	(0.07)	(0.04)	(0.07)	(0.06)
M.P. (t−1)	0.07	−0.07	0.04	0.08	0.05	−0.04	0.23*	−0.03	0.20
	(0.05)	(0.09)	(0.18)	(0.15)	(0.07)	(0.14)	(0.08)	(0.12)	(0.16)
Sent. (t−1)	−0.00	−0.03+	−0.03+	−0.04+	−0.00	0.01	−0.00	−0.00	−0.00
	(0.01)	(0.01)	(0.02)	(0.02)	(0.01)	(0.02)	(0.01)	(0.02)	(0.02)
AI (t−1)	−0.01+	−0.01	−0.00	0.00	−0.01+	−0.01	−0.01	−0.01	−0.02+
	(0.00)	(0.01)	(0.01)	(0.01)	(0.01)	(0.01)	(0.01)	(0.01)	(0.01)
β_0	−2.20	9.61	5.46	7.85	1.29	15.54	−12.01*	6.38	2.89
	(3.41)	(6.83)	(10.00)	(1132.25)	(5.46)	(2528.41)	(5.86)	(8.89)	(1012.52)
N	118	118	118	95	118	71	118	118	103

* $p < 0.05$; + $p < 0.10$

Note: Fixed effect negative binomial regression parameters presented with 95 percent confidence intervals in brackets. Please refer to Chapter 8 for additional information about these models. A master list of outcome variable codings can be found at the Policy Agendas Project at https://www.comparativeagendas.net/.

Table S8.8b **Full Model Output Used to Produce Figure 8.8 (Random Effects)**

	Avg.	Gen.	Waste	Hazard	Recycle	Indoor	Species	Conservation	R&D
Mood (t−1)	0.01	−0.01	0.01	0.07	−0.02	0.03	−0.01	−0.01	0.00
	(0.02)	(0.02)	(0.03)	(0.05)	(0.03)	(0.06)	(0.02)	(0.03)	(0.04)
M.P. (t−1)	−0.02	−0.04	0.03	−0.07	−0.06+	−0.05	−0.06+	0.01	−0.04
	(0.02)	(0.03)	(0.03)	(0.06)	(0.03)	(0.08)	(0.03)	(0.04)	(0.05)
Sent. (t−1)	−0.01*	−0.01	−0.01	−0.04*	−0.02*	−0.01	−0.01	−0.00	−0.01
	(0.01)	(0.01)	(0.01)	(0.02)	(0.01)	(0.02)	(0.01)	(0.01)	(0.01)
AI (t−1)	−0.00	0.00	0.01	−0.00	−0.01	−0.01	−0.00	−0.01	−0.02*
	(0.00)	(0.01)	(0.01)	(0.01)	(0.01)	(0.01)	(0.01)	(0.01)	(0.01)
β_0	2.73	4.54+	−0.58	3.81	7.29*	17.09	4.98+	2.03	18.68
	(1.94)	(2.74)	(3.19)	(6.14)	(3.21)	(828.37)	(2.77)	(3.79)	(830.50)
ln(r)	2.84*	4.91+	3.83*	2.51*	2.21*	14.81	2.81*	4.07*	16.85
	(0.66)	(2.74)	(1.07)	(0.85)	(0.50)	(828.33)	(0.70)	(1.66)	(830.48)
ln(s)	4.68*	4.29	2.92*	0.91	2.04*	−0.68	3.15*	2.94	1.30+
	(0.76)	(3.04)	(1.23)	(0.76)	(0.66)	(0.42)	(0.81)	(1.90)	(0.68)
N	120	120	120	120	120	120	120	120	120

*p < 0.05; +p < 0.10

Note: Random effect negative binomial regression parameters presented with 95 percent confidence intervals in brackets. Please refer to Chapter 8 for additional information about these models. A master list of outcome variable codings can be found at the Policy Agendas Project at https://www.comparativeagendas.net/.

Table S8.9a **Full Model Output Used to Produce Figure 8.9 (Fixed FX)**

	Avg.	Gen.	HC	Insur.	Drug Ind.	I.	Liab.	Work.	Dis.	Child.	Mental	Long	Drug C.	Tobac.	Drug Ab..	R&D
Mood (t−1)	0.00	−0.06	−0.01	0.01	0.03	−0.01	−0.06	0.01	0.00	0.07	0.01	0.06	−0.07	0.00	−0.03	−0.10
	(0.02)	(0.05)	(0.04)	(0.04)	(0.04)	(0.08)	(0.06)	(0.06)	(0.04)	(0.06)	(0.04)	(0.06)	(0.12)	(0.04)	(0.05)	(0.10)
M.P. (t−1)	0.08+	−0.05	−0.02	0.22*	−0.07	−0.25+	−0.18*	0.14	0.01	−0.00	0.07	0.11	0.05	0.01	−0.00	−0.36
	(0.04)	(0.08)	(0.08)	(0.08)	(0.07)	(0.13)	(0.09)	(0.14)	(0.08)	(0.12)	(0.07)	(0.14)	(0.29)	(0.08)	(0.10)	(0.26)
Sent. (t−1)	−0.01	−0.03+	−0.04*	0.00	−0.01	0.02	−0.01	−0.04+	0.01	0.02	−0.01	0.03	0.03	−0.01	0.01	−0.09+
	(0.01)	(0.02)	(0.02)	(0.01)	(0.01)	(0.03)	(0.02)	(0.02)	(0.01)	(0.02)	(0.01)	(0.02)	(0.04)	(0.02)	(0.02)	(0.05)
AI (t−1)	−0.01	−0.01	0.01	−0.00	−0.01	−0.01	−0.01	−0.01	−0.01	−0.01	−0.00	−0.01	−0.00	−0.01	−0.01	−0.01
	(0.00)	(0.01)	(0.01)	(0.01)	(0.01)	(0.01)	(0.01)	(0.01)	(0.01)	(0.01)	(0.01)	(0.01)	(0.02)	(0.01)	(0.01)	(0.02)
β_0	−2.30	9.49	5.65	−11.93*	4.07	13.50	15.51*	−3.11	−0.24	−1.44	−2.35	−9.45	0.59	1.36	2.25	36.38+
	(3.20)	(6.99)	(5.77)	(5.84)	(5.19)	(10.68)	(7.26)	(8.56)	(6.38)	(13.01)	(5.99)	(10.39)	(18.58)	(6.32)	(7.50)	(19.95)
N	118	118	115	118	118	92	102	107	118	115	115	92	48	118	114	76

* $p < 0.05$; + $p < 0.10$

Note: Fixed effect negative binomial regression parameters presented with 95 percent confidence intervals in brackets. Please refer to Chapter 8 for additional information about these models. A master list of outcome variable codings can be found at the Policy Agendas Project at https://www.comparativeagendas.net/.

Table S8.9b **Full Model Output Used to Produce Figure 8.9 (Random FX)**

	Avg.	Gen.	HC	Insur.	Drug Ind.	I.	Liab.	Work.	Dis.	Child.	Mental	Long	Drug C.	Tobac.	Drug Ab..	R&D
Mood (t−1)	0.01	0.00	0.00	−0.01	0.03	−0.01	−0.04	0.03	0.02	0.01	0.03	0.04	−0.03	0.02	−0.03	−0.07
	(0.01)	(0.02)	(0.03)	(0.02)	(0.02)	(0.05)	(0.03)	(0.04)	(0.02)	(0.03)	(0.03)	(0.04)	(0.09)	(0.03)	(0.03)	(0.07)
M.P. (t−1)	−0.05*	−0.03	−0.10*	−0.05+	−0.06*	−0.14*	−0.16*	0.06	−0.07*	−0.05	0.01	−0.24*	−0.16	0.01	−0.07*	−0.13
	(0.02)	(0.03)	(0.04)	(0.03)	(0.02)	(0.06)	(0.04)	(0.04)	(0.03)	(0.03)	(0.03)	(0.05)	(0.12)	(0.04)	(0.04)	(0.09)
Sent. (t−1)	−0.01*	−0.02*	−0.04*	−0.01	−0.02*	−0.01	−0.02	−0.00	−0.00	−0.02+	−0.01	0.00	0.03	0.00	0.02	0.01
	(0.00)	(0.01)	(0.01)	(0.01)	(0.01)	(0.02)	(0.01)	(0.01)	(0.01)	(0.01)	(0.01)	(0.01)	(0.03)	(0.01)	(0.01)	(0.02)
AI (t−1)	−0.00	−0.00	0.01*	−0.00	−0.01	−0.02+	−0.00	−0.01	−0.00	−0.01	−0.01	−0.01	−0.01	−0.01	−0.01	−0.01
	(0.00)	(0.01)	(0.01)	(0.01)	(0.01)	(0.01)	(0.01)	(0.01)	(0.01)	(0.01)	(0.01)	(0.01)	(0.02)	(0.01)	(0.01)	(0.01)
β_0	4.15*	4.12	9.19*	5.77*	3.94+	10.22+	12.71*	−3.28	4.21	6.14+	−0.40	11.97*	10.16	−0.33	5.85+	14.02
	(1.67)	(2.78)	(3.73)	(2.71)	(2.36)	(5.58)	(3.99)	(4.34)	(2.61)	(3.56)	(3.36)	(4.83)	(11.32)	(3.48)	(3.52)	(11.10)
ln(r)	4.02*	19.06	1.79*	2.63*	16.37	2.52*	4.81	3.02*	4.30	6.19	2.25*	3.82*	2.21	2.56*	2.91*	4.17
	(1.58)	(785.28)	(0.42)	(0.72)	(655.88)	(0.92)	(9.86)	(0.83)	(2.69)	(4.95)	(0.60)	(1.18)	(1.93)	(0.55)	(0.71)	(7.05)
ln(s)	6.14*	19.27	1.52*	3.09*	16.27	1.67	4.69	1.53+	4.43	4.19	2.05*	2.31	−0.80	1.81*	2.41*	0.09
	(1.69)	(785.28)	(0.50)	(0.87)	(655.88)	(1.16)	(10.21)	(0.89)	(2.94)	(5.60)	(0.77)	(1.43)	(0.57)	(0.62)	(0.86)	(0.65)
N	120	120	120	120	120	120	120	120	120	120	120	120	120	120	120	120

*p < 0.05; +p < 0.10

Note: Random effect negative binomial regression parameters presented with 95 percent confidence intervals in brackets. Please refer to Chapter 8 for additional information about these models. A master list of outcome variable codings can be found at the Policy Agendas Project at https://www.comparativeagendas.net/.

Table S8.10a **Full Model Output Used to Replicate Figure 8.8, for Health-Related Hearings (Fixed FX)**

	Avg.	Gen.	Interest Rate	Unempl.	Mon. Policy	Ntl Budget	Tax Code	Industry
Mood (t−1)	−0.01	−0.01	−0.28*	−0.04	−0.03	−0.04	−0.05	0.02
	(0.03)	(0.04)	(0.10)	(0.06)	(0.04)	(0.04)	(0.07)	(0.03)
M.P. (t−1)	0.07	0.05	0.02	0.03	0.02	−0.07	−0.07	0.10*
	(0.05)	(0.08)	(0.12)	(0.11)	(0.08)	(0.05)	(0.13)	(0.04)
Sent. (t−1)	−0.01	−0.02	−0.03	−0.04*	0.00	0.00	0.02	−0.01
	(0.01)	(0.01)	(0.03)	(0.02)	(0.01)	(0.01)	(0.02)	(0.01)
AI (t−1)	−0.00	−0.00	0.00	−0.00	−0.00	−0.00	−0.00	−0.01*
	(0.00)	(0.01)	(0.01)	(0.01)	(0.01)	(0.01)	(0.01)	(0.00)
β_0	−1.86	0.61	34.24	6.28	2.67	7.02	5.27	−4.50
	(4.24)	(5.97)	(1054.42)	(8.89)	(6.58)	(4.94)	(10.54)	(3.48)
N	118	118	53	109	118	118	106	115

* $p < 0.05$; + $p < 0.10$

Note: Fixed effect negative binomial regression parameters presented with 95 percent confidence intervals in brackets. Please refer to Chapter 8 for additional information about these models. A master list of outcome variable codings can be found at the Policy Agendas Project at https://www.comparativeagendas.net/.

Table S8.10b **Full Model Output Used to Replicate Figure 8.8, for Health-Related Hearings (Random FX)**

	Avg.	Gen.	Interest Rate	Unempl.	Mon. Policy	Ntl Budget	Tax Code	Industry
Mood (t−1)	−0.01	0.03	−0.16*	−0.02	−0.03	−0.01	−0.08*	−0.00
	(0.02)	(0.02)	(0.07)	(0.03)	(0.02)	(0.03)	(0.04)	(0.02)
M.P. (t−1)	0.02	0.06*	0.05	−0.04	−0.01	0.00	0.06	0.01
	(0.02)	(0.02)	(0.09)	(0.04)	(0.03)	(0.03)	(0.04)	(0.02)
Sent. (t−1)	−0.02*	−0.02*	−0.02	−0.03*	−0.02*	−0.01	−0.02	−0.01*
	(0.01)	(0.01)	(0.02)	(0.01)	(0.01)	(0.01)	(0.01)	(0.00)
AI (t−1)	−0.01	0.00	0.00	−0.01	0.00	−0.01	−0.00	−0.01+
	(0.00)	(0.01)	(0.01)	(0.01)	(0.01)	(0.01)	(0.01)	(0.00)
β_0	1.93	−1.78	23.14	8.34*	5.94*	1.99	2.27	1.71
	(1.98)	(2.40)	(941.57)	(3.95)	(2.80)	(3.00)	(4.11)	(1.61)
ln(r)	3.41*	5.07*	14.10	4.37*	4.69*	2.32*	17.28	5.06
	(1.00)	(2.47)	(941.52)	(1.28)	(1.04)	(0.68)	(1241.95)	(4.07)
ln(s)	5.01*	4.71+	−1.16*	2.11*	3.10*	3.07*	17.09	8.09+
	(1.10)	(2.61)	(0.43)	(0.96)	(1.11)	(0.81)	(1241.95)	(4.16)
N	120	120	120	120	120	120	120	117

* $p < 0.05$; + $p < 0.10$

Note: Random effect negative binomial regression parameters presented with 95 percent confidence intervals in brackets. Please refer to Chapter 8 for additional information about these models. A master list of outcome variable codings can be found at the Policy Agendas Project at https://www.comparativeagendas.net/.

Table S8.11 **Reverse Causality Checks for Figures 8.8 and 8.9**

	Envi (FE)	Envi (RE)	Econ (FE)	Econ (RE)
Mood (t−1)	−0.05*	−0.03*	−0.05*	−0.03*
	(0.02)	(0.01)	(0.02)	(0.01)
M.P. (t−1)	−0.03	−0.01	−0.04	−0.02
	(0.03)	(0.01)	(0.03)	(0.01)
Sent. (t−1)	−0.01	−0.00	−0.01	−0.00
	(0.01)	(0.00)	(0.01)	(0.00)
Hearings (t−1)	0.01	0.00	−	−
	(0.00)	(0.00)		
Testimony (t−1)	−	−	0.00	−0.00
			(0.00)	(0.00)
β_0	7.54*	4.25*	7.48*	4.47*
	(2.32)	(1.28)	(2.38)	(1.29)
ln(r)	−	4.47*	−	4.59*
		(1.46)		(1.83)
ln(s)	−	6.13*	−	6.31*
		(1.57)		(1.95)
N	118	120	115	118

* $p < 0.05$; + $p < 0.10$

Note: Fixed effect negative binomial regression parameters presented with 95 percent confidence intervals in brackets. Please refer to Chapter 8 for additional information about these models. Note that reverse causality tests are limited to just those models that document significant effects of anti-intellectualism on policy responsiveness. For the sake of brevity, I further limit analysis to just the pooled count model in the hearing count case (environmental policies), as this model exhibited a similarly sized and more precise estimate of the effects of anti-intellectualism as all others.

REFERENCES

Abbott, A. (2019). Fresh push for "failed" Alzheimer's drug. *Nature.* doi.org/10.1038/d41586-019-03261-5

Abramowitz, A. A. (2001). "Mr. Mayhew, meet Mr. DeLay," or the electoral connection in the post-reform Congress. *PS: Political Science & Politics, 34*(2), 257.

Abramowitz, A. I. (2012). Grand old Tea Party: Partisan polarization and the rise of the Tea Party movement. In *Steep* (pp. 195–211). University of California Press.

Abrams, D., & Hogg, M. A. (1988). Comments on the motivational status of self-esteem in social identity and intergroup discrimination. *European Journal of Social Psychology, 18*(4), 317–334.

Achen, C. H., & Bartels, L. M. (2017). *Democracy for realists: Why elections do not produce responsive government.* Princeton University Press.

Alaa, E., Ed, L., & Ashley, K. (2021). Deflated health care workers and desperate patients clash over alternative Covid treatments. *CNN.* https://www.cnn.com/2021/12/24/us/doctors-patients-threats-coronavirus-treatments/index.html

Alford, J. R., Funk, C. L., & Hibbing, J. R. (2005). Are political orientations genetically transmitted? *American Political Science Review, 99*(2), 153–167.

Allison, P. D., & Waterman, R. P. (2002). Fixed effects negative binomial regression models. *Sociological Methodology, 32*(1), 247–265.

Allum, N., Sturgis, P., Tabourazi, D., & Brunton-Smith, I. (2008). Science knowledge and attitudes across cultures: A meta-analysis. Public Understanding of Science, *17*(1), 35–54.

American Institute of Physics, AIP. (2021). Biden orders review of federal scientific integrity policies. Science Policy News from AIP. https://www.aip.org/fyi/2021/biden-orders-review-federal-scientific-integrity-policies

Amin, A. B., Bednarczyk, R. A., Ray, C. E., Melchiori, K. J., Graham, J., Huntsinger, J. R., & Omer, S. B. (2017). Association of moral values with vaccine hesitancy. *Nature Human Behaviour, 1*(12), 873–880.

Andersen, K. G., Rambaut, A., Lipkin, W. I., Holmes, E. C., & Garry, R. F. (2020). The proximal origin of SARS-CoV-2. *Nature Medicine, 26*(4), 450–452.

Ansolabehere, S., Rodden, J., & Snyder Jr., J. M. (2008). The strength of issues: Using multiple measures to gauge preference stability, ideological constraint, and issue voting. *American Political Science Review, 102*(2), 215–232.

Anson, I. G. (2018). Partisanship, political knowledge, and the Dunning Kruger effect. *Political Psychology, 39*(5), 1173–1192.

Arceneaux, K., & Vander Wielen, R. J. (2017). *Taming intuition: How reflection minimizes partisan reasoning and promotes democratic accountability.* Cambridge University Press.

Argue, A., Johnson, D. R., & White, L. K. (1999). Age and religiosity: Evidence from a three-wave panel analysis. *Journal for the Scientific Study of Religion, 38*(3), 423–435.

REFERENCES

Arnone, M. P., & Small, R. V. (1995). Arousing and sustaining curiosity: Lessons from the ARCS model. In *Proceedings of the Annual National Conference of the Association of Educational Communications and Technology (AECT)*, Anaheim, CA.

Ashraf, H. (2001). US expert group rejects link between MMR and autism. *The Lancet, 357*(9265), 1341.

Associated Press, AP. (2019). Trump threatens to cut funding for colleges "hostile to free speech." *Associated Press: Reprinted in the Guardian*. https://www.theguardian.com/us-news/2019/mar/21/college-university-free-speech-funding

Atkeson, L. R., & Rapoport, R. B. (2003). The more things change the more they stay the same: Examining gender differences in political attitude expression, 1952–2000. *Public Opinion Quarterly, 67*(4), 495–521.

Bafumi, J., & Shapiro, R. Y. (2009). A new partisan voter. *The Journal of Politics, 71*(1), 1–24.

Baetschmann, G., Staub, K. E., & Winkelmann, R. (2015). Consistent estimation of the fixed effects ordered logit model. *Journal of the Royal Statistical Society*. Series A (Statistics in Society), *178*(3), 685–703.

Barker, D. C., Detamble, R., & Marietta, M. (2022). Intellectualism, anti-intellectualism, and epistemic hubris in red and blue America. American Political Science Review, *116*(1), 38–53.

Bartlett, B. (2020). The GOP's murderous anti-intellectualism. *The New Republic*. https://newrepublic.c murderous-anti-intellectualism

Bauer, L., Broady, K., Edelberg, W., & O'Donnell, J. (2020). Ten facts about COVID-19 and the U.S. economy. *Brookings*. https://www.brookings.edu/research/ten-facts-about-covid-19-and-the-u-s-economy/

Beattie, P., & Snider, D. (2019). Knowledge in international relations: Susceptibilities to motivated reasoning among experts and non-experts. *Journal of Social and Political Psychology, 7*(1), 172–191.

Beck, P. A., & Jennings, M. K. (1975). Parents as "middlepersons" in political socialization. *The Journal of Politics, 37*(1), 83–107.

Benegal, S. D., & Scruggs, L. A. (2018). Correcting misinformation about climate change: The impact of partisanship in an experimental setting. *Climatic Change, 148*(1), 61–80.

Berinsky, A. J. (2002). Silent voices: Social welfare policy opinions and political equality in America. *American Journal of Political Science, 46*(2), 276–287.

Berinsky, A. J. (2013). *Silent voices*. Princeton University Press.

Berinsky, A. J. (2017). Rumors and health care reform: Experiments in political misinformation. *British Journal of Political Science, 47*(2), 241–262.

Besley, J. C., & Tanner, A. H. (2011). What science communication scholars think about training scientists to communicate. *Science Communication, 33*(2), 239–263.

Besley, J. C., Dudo, A. D., Yuan, S., & Abi Ghannam, N. (2016). Qualitative interviews with science communication trainers about communication objectives and goals. *Science Communication, 38*(3), 356–381.

Besley, J. (2018). Science & technology: Public attitudes and understanding. In Science & Engineering Indicators 2018. National Science Board—National Science Foundation. https://www.nsf.gov/statistics/2018/nsb20181/assets/nsb20181.pdf

Bevan, S., Jennings, W., & Pickup, M. (2019). Problem detection in legislative oversight: An analysis of legislative committee agendas in the UK and US. *Journal of European Public Policy, 26*(10), 1560–1578.

Biden, J. R. (2021). Memorandum on restoring trust in government through scientific integrity and evidence-based policymaking. *The White House Briefing Room*. https://www.whitehouse.room/presidential-actions/2021/01/27/memorandum-on-restoring-trust-in-government-through-scientific-integrity-and-evidence-based-policymaking/

Biesecker, M. & Kealoha Causey, A. (2017). Emails reiterate EPA chief's ties to fossil fuel interests. *The Associated Press*. https://apnews.com/united-states-government-f8797e5c55764ff39429b21372d2acee

Blake, A. (2021). The GOP: The new know-nothing party. *The Washington Post*. https://www.washingtonpost.com/politics/2021/02/04/kevin-mccarthy-know-nothing-gop/

References

Blank, J. M., & Shaw, D. (2015). Does partisanship shape attitudes toward science and public policy? The case for ideology and religion. *The ANNALS of the American Academy of Political and Social Science*, *658*(1), 18–35.

Besley, J. C. (2015). Predictors of perceptions of scientists: Comparing 2001 and 2012. *Bulletin of Science, Technology & Society*, *35*(1–2), 3–15.

Bevan, S. (2019). Gone fishing: The creation of the comparative agendas project master codebook. In *Comparative Policy Agendas* (pp. 17–34). Oxford University Press.

Bloom, J. D., Chan, Y. A., Baric, R. S., Bjorkman, P. J., Cobey, S., Deverman, B. E., ... & Relman, D. A. (2021). Investigate the origins of COVID-19. *Science*, *372*(6543), 694–694.

Bode, L., & Vraga, E. K. (2015). In related news, that was wrong: The correction of misinformation through related stories functionality in social media. *Journal of Communication*, *65*(4), 619–638.

Bode, L., & Vraga, E. (2021). The Swiss cheese model for mitigating online misinformation. *Bulletin of the Atomic Scientists*, *77*(3), 129–133.

Boffey, P. M., Carter, L. J., & Hamilton, A. (1970). Nixon budget: Science funding remains tight. *Science*. *167*(3919), 845–848.

Bogel-Burroughs, N., Dewan, S., & Gray, K. (2020). F.B.I. says Michigan anti-government group plotted to kidnap Gov. Gretchen Whitmer. *The New York Times*. https://www.nytimes.com/2whitmer-michigan-militia.html

Bolsen, T., Druckman, J. N., & Cook, F. L. (2014). The influence of partisan motivated reasoning on public opinion. *Political Behavior*, *36*(2), 235–262.

Borjas, G. J. (2018). Lessons from immigration economics. *The Independent Review*, *22*(3), 329–340.

Brossard, D., Scheufele, D. A., Kim, E., & Lewenstein, B. V. (2009). Religiosity as a perceptual filter: Examining processes of opinion formation about nanotechnology. *Public Understanding of Science*, *18*(5), 546–558.

Bruggers, J. & Green, A. (2021) Two years ago, Florida Gov. Ron DeSantis was praised for appointing science and resilience officers. Now, both posts are vacant. *Inside Climate News*. https://insideclimatenews.org/news/17032021/florida-gov-ron-desantis-was-praised-for-appointing-science-and-resilience-officers-now-both-posts-are-vacant/

Brulle, R. J., Carmichael, J., & Jenkins, J. C. (2012). Shifting public opinion on climate change: An empirical assessment of factors influencing concern over climate change in the US, 2002–2010. *Climatic Change*, *114*(2), 169–188.

Brulle, R. J. (2018, March). Critical reflections on the march for science. *Sociological Forum*, *33*(1), 255–258.

Bruns, A., Harrington, S., & Hurcombe, E. (2020). Covid19? Corona? 5G? or both?: The dynamics of COVID-19/5G conspiracy theories on Facebook. *Media International Australia*, *177*(1), 12–29.

Bullock, J. G., & Lenz, G. (2019). Partisan bias in surveys. *Annual Review of Political Science*, *22*, 325–342.

Claassen, R. L., & Povtak, A. (2010). The Christian right thesis: Explaining longitudinal change in participation among evangelical Christians. *The Journal of Politics*, *72*(1), 2–15.

Cacioppo, J. T., & Petty, R. E. (1982). The need for cognition. *Journal of Personality and Social Psychology*, *42*(1), 116.

Callaghan, T., Motta, M., Sylvester, S., Trujillo, K. L., & Blackburn, C. C. (2019). Parent psychology and the decision to delay childhood vaccination. *Social Science & Medicine*, *238*, 112407.

Callaghan, T., Moghtaderi, A., Lueck, J. A., Hotez, P., Strych, U., Dor, A., ... & Motta, M. (2021). Correlates and disparities of intention to vaccinate against COVID-19. *Social Science & Medicine*, *272*, 113638.

Callaghan, T., David W., Kirby G., Tasmiah N., Abigail S., Julia S., Ali M., & Matthew M. (2022). Imperfect messengers? An analysis of vaccine confidence among primary care physicians. *Vaccine* *40*(18), 2588–2603.

Campbell, A., Converse, P. E., Miller, W. E., & Stokes, D. E. (1960). *The American Voter*. University of Chicago Press.

REFERENCES

Carlton, J. S., Perry-Hill, R., Huber, M., & Prokopy, L. S. (2015). The climate change consensus extends beyond climate scientists. *Environmental Research Letters, 10*(9), 094025.

Carter, J. (2020). The American public still trusts scientists, says a new pew survey. *Scientific American.* https://www.scientificamerican.com/article/the-american-public-still-trusts-scientists-says-a-new-pew-survey/

Carter, J., Berman, E., Desikan, A., Johnson, C., & Goldman, G. (2019). The state of science in the Trump era: Damage done, lessons learned, and a path to progress. *Center for Science & Democracy at the Union of Concerned Scientists.* https://www.ucsusa.org/sites/default/files/attrump-2yrs-report.pdf?utm medium=email&utm source=FYI&dmi=1ZJN,63X1U,R7OZG8,NZXQK

Carter, J., Berman, E., Desikan, A., Johnson, C., & Goldman, G. (2020). The state of science in the Trump era. Union of Concerned Scientists. https://www.ucsusa.org/resources/state-science-trump-era

Centers for Disease Control, CDC (2020). What is social distancing? https://www.cdc.gov/coronavirus/2019-ncov/prevent-getting-sick/social-distancing.html

Centers for Disease Control, CDC (2021). Misconceptions about flu vaccines. https://www.cdc.gov/flu/prevent/misconceptions.htm

Ceballos, A. (2021). DeSantis attacks 'critical race theory' as state looks to change teaching guidelines. *The Miami Herald.* https://www.miamiherald.com/news/politics-government/state-politics/article251909718.html

Chaiken, S. (1987). The heuristic model of persuasion. In Social influence: The Ontario symposium (Vol. 5, pp. 3–39).

Chan, M. P. S., Jones, C. R., Hall Jamieson, K., & Albarracin, D. (2017). Debunking: A meta-analysis of the psychological efficacy of messages countering misinformation. *Psychological Science, 28*(11), 1531–1546.

Chappell, B. (2022). A Texas lawmaker is targeting 850 books that he says could make students feel uneasy. National Public Radio (NPR). https://www.npr.org/2021/10/28/1050013664/texas-lawmaker-matt-krause-launches-inquiry-into-850-books

Chen, M., & Kianifard, F. (1999). Application of Goodman-Kruskal's gamma for ordinal data, in comparing several ordered treatments: A Different approach. *Biometrical Journal: Journal of Mathematical Methods in Biosciences, 41*(4), 491–498.

Chiacu, D., & Volcovici, V. (2017). EPA Chief Pruitt refuses to link CO2 and global warming. *Scientific American.* https://www.scientificamerican.com/article/epa-chief-pruitt-refuses-to-link-co2-and-global-warming/

Chinn, S., Lane, D. S., & Hart, P. S. (2018). In consensus we trust? Persuasive effects of scientific consensus communication. *Public Understanding of Science, 27*(7), 807–823.

Cineas, F. (2020). Critical race theory, and Trump's war on it, explained. *Vox.* https://www.vox.com/2020race-theory-diversity-training-trump

Clark, C. J., Liu, B. S., Winegard, B. M., & Ditto, P. H. (2019). Tribalism is human nature. *Current Directions in Psychological Science, 28*(6), 587–592.

Clayton, K., Blair, S., Busam, J. A., Forstner, S., Glance, J., Green, G.,... & Nyhan, B. (2020). Real solutions for fake news? Measuring the effectiveness of general warnings and fact-check tags in reducing belief in false stories on social media. *Political behavior, 42,* 1073–1095.

Cole, J. (2021). Anti-science republicans like Jim Jordan have blood on their hands. *Common Dreams.* https://www.commondreams.org/views/2021/04/16/anti-science-republicans-jim-jordan-have-blood-their-hands

Coll, S. (2020). Woodrow Wilson's case of the flu, and how pandemics change history. *The New Yorker.* https://www.newyorker.com/news/daily-comment/woodrow-wilsons-case-of-the-flu-and-how-pandemics-change-history

Collingwood, L., Lajevardi, N., & Oskooii, K. A. (2018). A change of heart? Why individual-level public opinion shifted against Trump's "Muslim Ban." *Political Behavior, 40*(4), 1035–1072.

Compton, J. (2013). Inoculation theory. In *The Sage Handbook of Persuasion: Developments in Theory and Practice* (2, pp. 220–237).

References

Converse, P. E. (1964). The nature of belief systems in mass publics. *Critical Review, 18*(1–3), 1–74.

Cook, J., Oreskes, N., Doran, P. T., Anderegg, W. R., Verheggen, B., Maibach, E. W., . . . & Rice, K. (2016). Consensus on consensus: A synthesis of consensus estimates on human-caused global warming. *Environmental Research Letters, 11*(4), 048002.

Couric, K. & Goldsmith, B. (2018). What Sarah Palin saw clearly. *The Atlantic.* https://www.theatlantic.com/ide sarah-palin-understood-about-politics/572389/

Cundiff, J. L., Danube, C. L., Zawadzki, M. J., & Shields, S. A. (2018). Testing an intervention for recognizing and reporting subtle gender bias in promotion and tenure decisions. *The Journal of Higher Education, 89*(5), 611–636.

Darmofal, D. (2005). Elite cues and citizen disagreement with expert opinion. *Political Research Quarterly, 58*(3), 381–395.

DeJarnette, N. (2012). America's children: Providing early exposure to STEM (science, technology, engineering and math) initiatives. *Education, 133*(1), 77–84.

Dejarnette, N. K. (2016). America's children: Providing early exposure to STEM (science, technology, engineering and math) initiatives. *Reading Improvement, 53*(4), 181–187.

Deshais, N. (2019). The doctor and the pandemic: Spokane's 1918 fight against the Spanish influenza. *The Spokesman-Review.* https://www.spokesman.com/stories/2019/jan/20/the-doctor-and-the-pandemic-spokanes-1918-fight-ag/

Diamond, D. (2021). Feuds, fibs and finger-pointing: Trump officials say coronavirus response was worse than known. *The Washington Post.* https://www.washingtonpost.com/health/2021/03/29/trump-officials-tell-all-coronavirus-response/

Diermeier, D., & Feddersen, T. J. (2000). Information and congressional hearings. *American Journal of Political Science, 44*(1), 51–65.

Dolan, K., & Hansen, M. A. (2020). The variable nature of the gender gap in political knowledge. *Journal of Women, Politics & Policy, 41*(2), 127–143.

Douglas, K. M. (2021). COVID-19 conspiracy theories. *Group Processes & Intergroup Relations, 24*(2), 270–275.

Druckman, J. N., Leeper, T. J., & Slothuus, R. (2018). Motivated responses to political communications: Framing, party cues, and science information. In *The feeling, thinking citizen* (pp. 125–150). Routledge.

Dunning, D. (2011). The Dunning Kruger effect: On being ignorant of one's own ignorance. In *Advances in experimental social psychology* (Vol. 44, pp. 247–296). Academic Press.

Dyer, O. (2020). Covid-19: Trump stokes protests against social distancing measures. *BMJ; 369,* m1596.

Dyer, O. (2020). Trump claims public health warnings on COVID-19 are a conspiracy against him. *BMJ, 368,* m941.

Dyer, O. (2020). Covid-19: Trump declares intention to "re-open economy" within weeks against experts' advice. *BMJ, 2020*(368), m1217.

Egan, P. J. (2020). Identity as dependent variable: How Americans shift their identities to align with their politics. *American Journal of Political Science, 64*(3), 699–716.

Ellis, C., & Stimson, J. A. (2012). *Ideology in America.* Cambridge University Press.

Elliott, D. (2016). Is Donald Trump a modern-day George Wallace? National Public Radio (NPR). https://www.npr.org/2016/04/22/475172438/donald-trump-and-george-wallace-riding-the-rage

Ehret, P. J., Van Boven, L., & Sherman, D. K. (2018). Partisan barriers to bipartisanship: Understanding climate policy polarization. *Social Psychological and Personality Science, 9*(3), 308–318.

Enders, A. M., Uscinski, J. E., Klofstad, C., & Stoler, J. (2020). The different forms of COVID-19 misinformation and their consequences. *The Harvard Kennedy School Misinformation Review, 1*(8).

Englund, M. M., Luckner, A. E., Whaley, G. J., & Egeland, B. (2004). Children's achievement in early elementary school: Longitudinal effects of parental involvement, expectations, and quality of assistance. *Journal of Educational Psychology, 96*(4), 723.

Enright, M. (2016). Donald Trump is not the first to terrify U.S. political elites in a presidential election - Michael's essay. *CBC*. https://www.cbc.ca/radio/sunday/the-angry-populism-of-68-sadik-khan-on-urban-revolution-margot-bentley-justice-abella-goes-to-yale-1.3600952/donald-trump-is-not-the-first-to-terrify-u-s-political-elites-in-a-presidential-election-michael-s-essay-1.3600972

Enserink, M., & Cohen, J. (2020). Fact-checking Judy Mikovits, the controversial virologist attacking Anthony Fauci in a viral conspiracy video. *Science, 8*.

Falk, J. H., Storksdieck, M., & Dierking, L. D. (2007). Investigating public science interest and understanding: Evidence for the importance of free-choice learning. *Public Understanding of Science, 16*(4), 455–469.

Fasce, A., Adrián-Ventura, J., Lewandowsky, S., & van der Linden, S. (2023). Science through a tribal lens: A group-based account of polarization over scientific facts. *Group Processes & Intergroup Relations, 26*(1), 3–23.

FDA (2021). FDA grants accelerated approval for Alzheimer's drug. *Food & Drug Administration, News Release*. https://www.fda.gov/news-events/press-announcements/fda-grants-accelerated-approval-alzheimers-drug

Fearnow, B. (2020). Sarah Palin blasts Obama book tying her to "anti-intellectuals," says GOP dislikes Trump, "never liked me." *Newsweek*. https://www.newsweek.com/sarah-palin-blasts-obama-book-tying-her-anti-intellectuals-says-gop-dislikes-trump-never-1547499

Featherstone, J. D., Bell, R. A., & Ruiz, J. B. (2019). Relationship of people's sources of health information and political ideology with acceptance of conspiratorial beliefs about vaccines. *Vaccine, 37*(23), 2993–2997.

Feldman, L., Maibach, E. W., Roser-Renouf, C., & Leiserowitz, A. (2012). Climate on cable: The nature and impact of global warming coverage on Fox News, CNN, and MSNBC. *The International Journal of Press/Politics, 17*(1), 3–31.

Fenno, R. F. (1977). US House members in their constituencies: An exploration. *American Political Science Review, 71*(3), 883–917.

Fernbach, P. M., Light, N., Scott, S. E., Inbar, Y., & Rozin, P. (2019). Extreme opponents of genetically modified foods know the least but think they know the most. *Nature Human Behaviour, 3*(3), 251–256.

Feuerstein, A., Herper, M., & Garde, D. (2021). Inside "Project Onyx": How Biogen used an FDA back channel to win approval of its polarizing Alzheimer's drug. *STAT News*. https://www.statnews.com/2021/06/29/biogen-fda-alzheimers-drug-approval-aduhelm-project-onyx/

Fisher, D. R., Waggle, J., & Leifeld, P. (2013). Where does political polarization come from? Locating polarization within the US climate change debate. *American Behavioral Scientist, 57*(1), 70–92.

Fisher, D. R. (2018, March). Scientists in the resistance. *Sociological Forum, 33*(1), 247–250.

Fiske, S. T., & Dupree, C. (2014). Gaining trust as well as respect in communicating to motivated audiences about science topics. *Proceedings of the National Academy of Sciences, 111*(Supplement 4), 13593–13597.

Fiske, S. T. (2000). Stereotyping, prejudice, and discrimination at the seam between the centuries: Evolution, culture, mind, and brain. *European Journal of Social Psychology, 30*(3), 299–322.

Fiske, S. T. (2018). *Social beings: Core motives in social psychology*. John Wiley & Sons.

Fleshler, D. (2021). Handpicked experts assure Gov. DeSantis his COVID critics are wrong. *South Florida Sun Sentinel*. https://www.sun-sentinel.com/coronavirus/fl-ne-desantis-covid-scientists-20210318-5wpcx3kjyvauvnanntmhxqkcmq-story.html

Forman, C. (2021). Hundreds of Oklahomans gather at Capitol to oppose COVID-19 vaccine, mask mandates. *The Oklahoman*. https://www.oklahoman.com/story/news/2021/11/16/oklahoma-covid-biden-vaccine-mask-mandate-oklahomans-protest-rally-against/6384231001/

Friedman, L. (2019). White House tried to stop climate science testimony, documents show. *The New York Times*. https://www.nytimes.com/2019/06/08/climate/rod-schoonover-testimony.html

References

Funke, D. (2020). Conspiracy theorist spreads false claim about Fauci, patents and COVID-19. PolitiFact. https://www.politifact.com/factchecks/2020/may/12/jerome-corsi/conspiracy-theorist-spreads-false-claim-about-fauc/

Funk, C., Kennedy, B., & Johnson, C. (2020). Trust in medical scientists has grown in U.S., but mainly among Democrats. Pew Research Center. https://www.pewresearch.org/science/2020/05/in-medical-scientists-has-grown-in-u-s-but-mainly-among-democrats/

Funk, C., & Hefferson, M. (2019). Most Americans have positive image of research scientists, but fewer see them as good communicators. Pew Research Center. https://www.pewresearch.org/fact-tank/2019/08/19/most-americans-have-positive-image-of-research-scientists-but-fewer-see-them-as-good-communicators/

Funk, C., Hefferon, M., Kennedy, B., & Johnson, C. (2019). Trust and mistrust in Americans' views of scientific experts. Pew Research Center. https://www.pewresearch.org/science/2019/08/02/tand-mistrust-in-americans-views-of-scientific-experts/

Funk, C., Rainie, L., & Page, D. (2015). Public and scientists' views on science and society. Pew Research Center, 29. https://www.pewresearch.org/science/2015/01/29/public-and-scientists-views-on-science-and-society/

Gadarian, S. K., Goodman, S. W., & Pepinsky, T. B. (2021). Partisanship, health behavior, and policy attitudes in the early stages of the COVID-19 pandemic. *PLOS ONE, 16*(4), e0249596.

Gallup (2019). Wellcome global monitor—First wave findings. https://wellcome.org/reports/wellcome-global-monitor/2018

Gancarski, A. G. (2021). Ironic? Ron DeSantis slams Anthony Fauci for too many interviews during pandemic. *Florida Politics*. https://floridapolitics.com/archives/433736-fauci-ouchie/

Gauchat, G., & Andrews, K. T. (2018). The cultural-cognitive mapping of scientific professions. *American Sociological Review, 83*(3), 567–595.

Geleris, J., Sun, Y., Platt, J., Zucker, J., Baldwin, M., Hripcsak, G.,...& Schluger, N. W. (2020). Observational study of hydroxychloroquine in hospitalized patients with COVID-19. *New England Journal of Medicine, 382*(25), 2411–2418.

Gervais, B. T., & Morris, I. L. (2018). *Reactionary Republicanism: How the Tea Party in the House paved the way for Trump's victory*. Oxford University Press.

Gillman, T. J. (2014). In DC, Gov. Rick Perry talks 2016, Ted Cruz, climate change, border security. *The Dallas Morning News*. https://www.dallasnews.com/news/politics/2014/06/19/in-dc-gov-rick-perry-talks-2016-ted-cruz-climate-change-border-security/

Gancarski, A. G. (2021).Teaching kids to "attack cops": Ron DeSantis adds fuel to critical race theory fire. Florida Politics. https://floridapolitics.com/archives/436040-ron-desantis-crt-attack-cops/

Garde, D., & Florko, N. (2021). Calls grow for an investigation into FDA approval of Biogen's Alzheimer's drug. *STAT News*. https://www.statnews.com/2021/06/30/calls-investigation-fda-approval-biogen-alzheimers-drug/

Gardner, A. (2010).Gauging the scope of the tea party movement in America. *The Washington Post*. https://www.washingtonpost.com/wp-srv/special/politics/tea-party-canvass/

Gauchat, G. W. (2008). A test of three theories of anti-science attitudes. *Sociological Focus, 41*(4), 337–357.

Gauchat, G. (2011). The cultural authority of science: Public trust and acceptance of organized science. *Public Understanding of Science, 20*(6), 751–770.

Gauchat, G. (2012). Politicization of science in the public sphere: A study of public trust in the United States, 1974 to 2010. *American Sociological Review, 77*(2), 167–187.

Gauchat, G. (2015). The political context of science in the United States: Public acceptance of evidence-based policy and science funding. *Social Forces, 94*(2), 723–746.

Gauchat, G., O'Brien, T., & Mirosa, O. (2017). The legitimacy of environmental scientists in the public sphere. *Climatic Change, 143*(3), 297–306.

Gibson, C. (2017). The march for science was a moment made for Bill Nye. *The Washington Post*. https://www.washingtonpost.com/lifestyle/style/the-march-for-science-was-a-moment-made-for-bill-nye/2017/04/23/bc9429ae-282f-11e7-a616-d7c8a68c1a66story.html

REFERENCES

Gilens, M. (1996). "Race coding" and white opposition to welfare. *American Political Science Review, 90*(3), 593–604.

Gilens, M. (2009). *Why Americans hate welfare: Race, media, and the politics of antipoverty policy.* University of Chicago Press.

Glazer, S. (2021). Expertise under assault. CQ Researcher. http://library.cqpress.com/cqresearcher/docu

Gollust, S. E., Nagler, R. H., & Fowler, E. F. (2020). The emergence of COVID-19 in the US: A public health and political communication crisis. *Journal of Health Politics, Policy and Law, 45*(6), 967–981.

Golman, R., & Loewenstein, G. (2018). Information gaps: A theory of preferences regarding the presence and absence of information. *Decision, 5*(3), 143.

Goldberg, M. (2023). Robert F. Kennedy Jr. and the coalition of the distrustful. *The New York Times.* https://www.nytimes.com/2023/06/30/opinion/robert-f-kennedy-jr-coalition -supporters.html

Good, C. (2013). Tea Party class of 2010: Where are they now? ABC News. https://abcnews. go.com/blo party-class-of-2010-where-are-they-now

Goren, P. (2005). Party identification and core political values. *American Journal of Political Science, 49*(4), 881–896.

Goren, P. (2013). *On voter competence.* Oxford University Press.

Graham, M. H. (2021). "We don't know" means "they're not sure". *Public Opinion Quarterly, 85*(2), 571–593.

Graham, J., Haidt, J., & Nosek, B. A. (2009). Liberals and conservatives rely on different sets of moral foundations. *Journal of Personality and Social Psychology, 96*(5), 1029.

Green, D. P., & Palmquist, B. (1990). Of artifacts and partisan instability. *American Journal of Political Science, 34*(3), 872–902.

Green, D. P., & Palmquist, B. (1994). How stable is party identification? *Political Behavior, 16*(4), 437–466.

Green, D., Palmquist, B., & Schickler, E. (2004). *Partisan hearts and minds.* Yale University Press.

Gross, S.J. (2019). Does Gov. DeSantis believe in climate change? *The Tampa Bay Times.* https:// www.tampabay.com/florida-politics/buzz/2019/01/11/does-gov-desantis-believe-in -climate-change/

Green, D. P., & Palmquist, B. (1990). Of artifacts and partisan instability. *American Journal of Political Science,* 872–902.

Green, D. P., & Palmquist, B. (1994). How stable is party identification?. *Political Behavior, 16*(4), 437–466.

Greenberg, D. S. (1973). Science and Richard Nixon. *New York Times Magazine.*

Grier, P. (2016). The roots of Donald Trump's anti-intellectualism. *The Christian Science Monitor.* https://www.csmonitor.com/USA/Politics/Decoder/2016/0927/The-roots-of-Donald-Trump-s-anti-intellectualism

Grossmann, M., & Hopkins, D. A. (2016). *Asymmetric politics: Ideological Republicans and group interest Democrats.* Oxford University Press.

Grossman, G., Kim, S., Rexer, J. M., & Thirumurthy, H. (2020). Political partisanship influences behavioral responses to governors' recommendations for COVID-19 prevention in the United States. *Proceedings of the National Academy of Sciences, 117*(39), 24144–24153.

Golman, R., & Loewenstein, G. (2015). Curiosity, information gaps, and the utility of knowledge. *Information Gaps, and the Utility of Knowledge* (April 16, 2015), 96–135.

Gonyea, D. (2017). From the start, Obama struggled with fallout from a kind of fake news. National Public Radio (NPR). https://www.npr.org/2017/01/10/509164679/from-the-start-obama-struggled-with-fallout-from-a-kind-of-fake-news

Gray, D.D. (2021). Critical race theory: What it is and what it isn't. The Conversation, US. https:// theconversation.com/critical-race-theory-what-it-is-and-what-it-isnt-162752

Grieve, P. G., and M. A. Hogg. 1999. Subjective uncertainty and intergroup discrimination in the minimal group situation. *Personality and Social Psychology Bulletin, 25*(8), 926–940.

References

Gross, N., & Simmons, S. (2007). The social and political views of American professors. Working Paper presented at a Harvard University Symposium on Professors and Their Politics.

Grossman, G., Kim, S., Rexer, J. M., & Thirumurthy, H. (2020). Political partisanship influences behavioral responses to governors' recommendations for COVID-19 prevention in the United States. *Proceedings of the National Academy of Sciences, 117*(39), 24144–24153.

Gummer, T., & Robmann, J. (2015). Explaining interview duration in web surveys: A multi-level approach. *Social Science Computer Review, 33*(2), 217–234.

Guynn, J. (2021). President Joe Biden rescinds Donald Trump ban on diversity training about systemic racism. *USA Today.* https://www.usatoday.com/story/money/2021/01/20/biden-executive-order-overturns-trump-diversity-training-ban/4236891001/

Hall, R. L., & Deardorff, A. V. (2006). Lobbying as legislative subsidy. *American Political Science Review, 100*(1), 69–84.

Hall, R. L., & Miler, K. C. (2008). What happens after the alarm? Interest group subsidies to legislative overseers. *The Journal of Politics, 70*(4), 990–1005.

Hamel, L., Kearney, A., Kirzinger, A. Lopes, L., & Munana, C. (2020). KFF health tracking poll—September 2020: Top issues in 2020 election, The role of misinformation, and views on a potential coronavirus vaccine. Kaiser Family Foundation Health Tracking Poll. https://www.kff.org/coronavirus-covid-19/report/kff-health-tracking-poll-september-2020/

Hamilton, L. C., Hartter, J., & Saito, K. (2015). Trust in scientists on climate change and vaccines. *Sage Open, 5*(3), 2158244015602752.

Haltinner, K., & Sarathchandra, D. (2017). Tea Party health narratives and belief polarization: The journey to killing grandma. *AIMS Public Health, 4*(6), 557.

Harris, A. (2021). The GOP's "critical race theory" obsession. *The Atlantic.* https://www.theatlantic.com critical-race-theory-fixation-explained/618828/

Hatemi, P. K., Alford, J. R., Hibbing, J. R., Martin, N. G., & Eaves, L. J. (2009). Is there a "party" in your genes? *Political Research Quarterly, 62*(3), 584–600.

Heaney, M. T. (2006). Brokering health policy: Coalitions, parties, and interest group influence. *Journal of Health Politics, Policy and Law, 31*(5), 887–944.

Hersh, E. D., & Schaffner, B. F. (2013). Targeted campaign appeals and the value of ambiguity. *The Journal of Politics, 75*(2), 520–534.

Hensley, S., Hamilton, J. & Wamsley, L. (2021). The FDA has approved a New Alzheimer's drug—Here's why that's controversial. National Public Radio (NPR). https://www.npr.org/2021/06/07/1003964235/fda-approves-controversial-alzheimers-drug-aducanumab

Heyward, G. (2021). Georgia's university system takes on tenure. *The New York Times.* https://www.nytimes.com/2021/10/13/us/georgia-university-system-tenure.html

Hmielowski, J. D., Feldman, L., Myers, T. A., Leiserowitz, A., & Maibach, E. (2014). An attack on science? Media use, trust in scientists, and perceptions of global warming. *Public Understanding of Science, 23*(7), 866–883.

Howard, J., Huang, A., Li, Z., Tufekci, Z., Zdimal, V., Van Der Westhuizen, H. M., ... & Rimoin, A. W. (2021). An evidence review of face masks against COVID-19. Proceedings of the National Academy of Sciences, 118(4), e2014564118.

Hviid, A., Hansen, J. V., Frisch, M., & Melbye, M. (2019). Measles, mumps, rubella vaccination and autism: A nationwide cohort study. *Annals of Internal Medicine, 170*(8), 513–520.

Hofstadter, R. (1963). *Anti-intellectualism in American life* (3rd ed., Vol. 713). Vintage.

Holan, A. D. (2009). PolitiFact's lie of the year: "Death panels." PolitiFact. https://www.politifact.com/ar lie-year-death-panels/

Hooghe, M., & Dassonneville, R. (2018). Explaining the Trump vote: The effect of racist resentment and anti-immigrant sentiments. *PS: Political Science & Politics, 51*(3), 528–534.

Hopkins, D. J., & Ladd, J. M. (2014). The consequences of broader media choice: Evidence from the expansion of Fox News. *Quarterly Journal of Political Science, 9*(1), 115–135.

Hovland, C. I., & Weiss, W. (1951). The influence of source credibility on communication effectiveness. *Public Opinion Quarterly, 15*(4), 635–650.

Huber, R. A., Fesenfeld, L., & Bernauer, T. (2020). Political populism, responsiveness, and public support for climate mitigation. *Climate Policy, 20*(3), 373–386.

Hughes, L., & Lipscy, P. Y. (2013). The politics of energy. *Annual Review of Political Science, 16,* 449–469.

Huddy, L. (2001). From social to political identity: A critical examination of social identity theory. *Political Psychology, 22*(1), 127–156.

Huddy, L. 2003. Group identity and intergroup cohesion. In L. Huddy, D. O. Sears, and J. Levy (Eds.), *Oxford handbook of political psychology* (pp. 511–558). Oxford University Press.

Huddy, L., Mason, L., & Aarøe, L. (2015). Expressive partisanship: Campaign involvement, political emotion, and partisan identity. *American Political Science Review, 109*(1), 1–17.

Huddy, L., Mason, L., & Horwitz, S. N. (2016). Political identity convergence: On being Latino, becoming a Democrat, and getting active. *RSF: The Russell Sage Foundation Journal of the Social Sciences, 2*(3), 205–228.

Huddy, L., & Bankert, A. (2017). Political partisanship as a social identity. In *Oxford research encyclopedia of politics.* Oxford University Press.

Inglehart, R., & Norris, P. (2017). Trump and the populist authoritarian parties: The silent revolution in reverse. *Perspectives on Politics, 15*(2), 443–454.

Irfan, U. (2018). Why Scott Pruitt lasted so long at the EPA, and what finally did him in. *Vox.* https://www.vox.com/2018/7/7/17540488/scott-pruitt-resigns-epa-trump-jeff-sessions

Intergovernmental Panel on Climate Change. (2018). *Summary for policymakers of IPCC special report on global warming of 1.5°C approved by governments.* https://www.ipcc.ch/2018/10/08/sum for -policymakers-of-ipcc-special-report-on-global-warming-of-1-5c-approved-by-governments/

Iyengar, S., Sood, G., & Lelkes, Y. (2012). Affect, not ideology: Social identity perspective on polarization. *Public Opinion Quarterly, 76*(3), 405–431.

Jamieson, K. H. (2018). Crisis or self-correction: Rethinking media narratives about the well-being of science. *Proceedings of the National Academy of Sciences, 115*(11), 2620–2627.

Jamieson, K. H., McNutt, M., Kiermer, V., & Sever, R. (2019). Signaling the trustworthiness of science. *Proceedings of the National Academy of Sciences, 116*(39), 19231–19236.

Jasanoff, S. (1998). *The fifth branch: Science advisers as policymakers.* Harvard University Press.

Jennings, M. K., & Markus, G. B. (1984). Partisan orientations over the long haul: Results from the three-wave political socialization panel study. *American Political Science Review, 78*(4), 1000–1018.

Jennings, M. K., Stoker, L., & Bowers, J. (2009). Politics across generations: Family transmission reexamined. *The Journal of Politics, 71*(3), 782–799.

Jenkins, W., Berry, E., & Kreider, L. B. (2018). Religion and climate change. *Annual Review of Environment and Resources, 43,* 85–108.

John, P. (2006). The Policy Agendas Project: A review. *Journal of European Public Policy, 13*(7), 975–986.

Jones, B. D., & Baumgartner, F. R. (2004). Representation and agenda setting. *Policy Studies Journal, 32*(1), 1–24.

Joshua A. C. (2018). A New Reality? The Far Right's Use of Cyberharassment against Academics. https://www.aaup.org/article/new-reality-far-rights-use-cyberharassment-against-academics

Joslyn, M. R., & Sylvester, S. M. (2019). The determinants and consequences of accurate beliefs about childhood vaccinations. *American Politics Research, 47*(3), 628–649.

Kahan, D. M., Braman, D., Slovic, P., Gastil, J., & Cohen, G. L. (2008). The future of nanotechnology risk perceptions: an experimental investigation of two hypotheses. Harvard Law School Program on Risk Regulation Research Paper (pp. 8–24).

Kahan, D. M., Braman, D., Slovic, P., Gastil, J., & Cohen, G. (2009). Cultural cognition of the risks and benefits of nanotechnology. *Nature Nanotechnology, 4*(2), 87–90.

Kahan, D. M., Braman, D., Cohen, G. L., Gastil, J., & Slovic, P. (2010). Who fears the HPV vaccine, who doesn't, and why? An experimental study of the mechanisms of cultural cognition. *Law and Human Behavior, 34*(6), 501–516.

Kahan, D. (2010). Fixing the communications failure. *Nature, 463*(7279), 296–297.

Kahan, D. M., Peters, E., Wittlin, M., Slovic, P., Ouellette, L. L., Braman, D., & Mandel, G. (2012). The polarizing impact of science literacy and numeracy on perceived climate change risks. *Nature Climate Change, 2*(10), 732–735.

Kahan, D. M. (2014). Making climate-science communication evidence-based: all the way down. In Culture, politics and climate change (pp. 203–220). Routledge.

Kahan, D. M. (2015). The politically motivated reasoning paradigm, Part 2: Unanswered questions. Emerging trends in the social and behavioral sciences: An interdisciplinary, searchable, and linkable resource, 1–15. doi.org/10.1002/9781118900772.etrds0418

Kahan, D. M., Landrum, A., Carpenter, K., Helft, L., & Hall Jamieson, K. (2017). Science curiosity and political information processing. Political Psychology, 38, 179–199.

Kahan, D. M. (2017a). "Ordinary science intelligence": A science-comprehension measure for study of risk and science communication, with notes on evolution and climate change. Journal of Risk Research, 20(8), 995–1016.

Kahan, D. M. (2017b). On the sources of ordinary science knowledge and extraordinary science ignorance. The Oxford handbook of the science of science communication, 35, 35–50.

Kahan, D. M. (2017c). Misconceptions, misinformation, and the logic of identity-protective cognition. Yale Law & Economics Research Paper, 164.

Kamola, I. (2021). Guest blog: Where does the bizarre hysteria about "critical race theory" come from? Follow the money! Inside HigherEd. https://www.insidehighered.com/blogs/just-visiting/guest-blog-where-does-bizarre-hysteria-about-%E2%80%98critical-race-theory%E2%80%99-come-follow

Kahneman, D., & Klein, G. (2009). Conditions for intuitive expertise: a failure to disagree. American Psychologist, 64(6), 515.

Kahneman, D. (2011). Thinking, fast and slow. Macmillan.

Katov, M. (2021). Suspect pleads guilty in plot to kidnap Michigan governor, turns government witness. National Public Radio (NPR). https://www.npr.org/2021/01/27/961215604/suspect-pleads-guilty-in-plot-to-kidnap-michigan-governor-turns-government-witne

Kellstedt, P. M., Zahran, S., & Vedlitz, A. (2008). Personal efficacy, the information environment, and attitudes toward global warming and climate change in the United States. Risk Analysis: An International Journal, 28(1), 113–126.

Kearney, M. W. (2017). Cross Lagged Panel Analysis. In M. R. Allen (Ed.), The SAGE encyclopedia of communication research methods. Sage.

Kim, N.Y. (2021). Fact-check: Did Dr. Fauci fund research that created COVID-19? Politifact. https://www.politifact.com/factchecks/2021/feb/08/worldnetdaily/no-dr-anthony-fauci-did-not-fund-research-tied-cov/

Kinder, D. R., & Kalmoe, N. P. (2017). Neither liberal nor conservative: Ideological innocence in the American public. University of Chicago Press.

Kilwans, J. (2021). OK bill would pay parents $10K each day their nominated banned books remain in libraries. Newsweek. https://www.newsweek.com/ok-bill-would-pay-parents-10k-each-day-their-nominated-banned-books-remain-libraries-1663511

Kraft, P. W., Lodge, M., & Taber, C. S. (2015). Why people "don't trust the evidence" motivated reasoning and scientific beliefs. The ANNALS of the American Academy of Political and Social Science, 658(1), 121–133.

Krosnick, J. A. (1991). Response strategies for coping with the cognitive demands of attitude measures in surveys. Applied Cognitive Psychology, 5(3), 213–236.

Krosnick, J. A., & MacInnis, B. (2010). Frequent viewers of Fox News are less likely to accept scientists' views of global warming. Report for The Woods Institute for the Environment. http://woods.stanford.edu/docs/surveys/Global-Warming-Fox-News.pdf

Krosnick, J. A., & Berent, M. K. (1993). Comparisons of party identification and policy preferences: The impact of survey question format. American Journal of Political Science, 37(3), 941–964.

Kunda, Z. (1990). The case for motivated reasoning. Psychological Bulletin, 108(3), 480.

Lajevardi, N., & Abrajano, M. (2019). How negative sentiment toward Muslim Americans predicts support for Trump in the 2016 presidential election. The Journal of Politics, 81(1), 296–302.

Landry, C. (2020).Things to come: What must I do to be blessed? Curt Landry Ministries, April 3 Live Stream. https://www.youtube.com/watch?v=KFREvBq24RQ

Lapinski, J. S., Peltola, P., Shaw, G., & Yang, A. (1997). Trends: Immigrants and immigration. The Public Opinion Quarterly, 61(2), 356–383.

Lawson, K. (2021). Woman on professor watchlist goes into hiding after receiving death threats. *Vice*. https://www.vice.com/en/article/3k8qzn/woman-on-professor-watchlist-goes-into-hiding-after-receiving-death-threats

Lazarsfeld, P. F., & Thielens, W. (1957). Social scientists and recent threats to academic freedom. *Social Problems, 5*(3), 244–266.

Leeper, T. J., & Slothuus, R. (2014). Political parties, motivated reasoning, and public opinion formation. *Political Psychology, 35*, 129–156.

Lenzer, J. (2007). Bush says he will veto stem cell funding, despite vote in favour in Congress. *British Medical Journal, 334*, 1243. doi.org/10.1136/bmj.39245.359306.DB

Lenz, G. S. (2013). Follow the leader?: How voters respond to politicians' policies and performance. *University of Chicago Press*.

Levin, L. (2021). Jim Jordan trips over his own asshole trying to debate Anthony Fauci. *Vanity Fair*. https://www.vanityfair.com/news/2021/04/jim-jordan-anthony-fauci-hearing

Levitan, D. (2016). When a President banishes science from the White House. *The Atlantic*. https://www.theatlantic.com/science/archive/2016/10/when-a-president-banishes-science-from-the-white-house/505937/

Lewandowsky, S., Oberauer, K., & Gignac, G. E. (2013). NASA faked the moon landing—therefore, (climate) science is a hoax: An anatomy of the motivated rejection of science. *Psychological Science, 24*(5), 622–633.

Lim, E. T. (2008). The anti-intellectual presidency: The decline of presidential rhetoric from George Washington to George W. Bush. Oxford University Press.

Lindholt, M. F., Jørgensen, F., Bor, A., & Petersen, M. B. (2021). Public acceptance of COVID-19 vaccines: Cross-national evidence on levels and individual-level predictors using observational data. *BMJ Open, 11*(6), e048172.

Little, B. (2020). As the 1918 flu emerged, cover-up and denial helped it spread. History—Stories. https://www.history.com/news/1918-pandemic-spanish-flu-censorship

Liu, X., Vedlitz, A., Stoutenborough, J. W., & Robinson, S. (2015). Scientists' views and positions on global warming and climate change: A content analysis of congressional testimonies. *Climatic Change, 131*(4), 487–503.

Lodge, M., & Taber, C. S. (2013). *The rationalizing voter*. Cambridge University Press.

Loewenstein, G. (1994). The psychology of curiosity: A review and reinterpretation. *Psychological Bulletin, 116*(1), 75.

Lowndes, J. (2018). Populism and race in the United States from George Wallace to Donald Trump. In Routledge Handbook of Global Populism (pp. 190–200). Routledge.

Lunz Trujillo, K. 2022. Rural identity as a contributing factor to anti-intellectualism in the US. *Political Behavior, 44*(3), 1509–1532.

Lupia, A. (2016). Uninformed: Why people know so little about politics and what we can do about it. Oxford University Press.

Lunz Trujillo, K., & Motta, M. (2021). How internet access drives global vaccine skepticism. *International Journal of Public Opinion Research, 33*(3), 551–570.

Lunz Trujillo, K., Motta, M., Callaghan, T., & Sylvester, S. (2021). Correcting misperceptions about the MMR vaccine: Using psychological risk factors to inform targeted communication strategies. *Political Research Quarterly, 74*(2), 464–478.

Lyons, B. A., Montgomery, J. M., Guess, A. M., Nyhan, B., & Reifler, J. (2021). Overconfidence in news judgments is associated with false news susceptibility. *Proceedings of the National Academy of Sciences, 118*(23), 1–10.

Maaravi, Y., Levy, A., Gur, T., Confino, D., & Segal, S. (2021). "The tragedy of the commons": How individualism and collectivism affected the spread of the COVID-19 pandemic. *Frontiers in Public Health 9*(37).

MacKuen, M. B., Erikson, R. S., & Stimson, J. A. (1989). Macropartisanship. *American Political Science Review, 83*(4), 1125–1142.

MaGill, B. (2016). Rick Perry tapped to run the energy agency he once vowed to kill. *Scientific American*. https://www.scientificamerican.com/article/rick-perry-tapped-to-run-the-energy-agency-he-once-vowed-to-kill/

Mahase, E. (2020). Hydroxychloroquine for COVID-19: The end of the line?. *BMJ, 369.* doi.org/10.1136/bmj.m2378

Maher, T. V., Seguin, C., Zhang, Y., & Davis, A. P. (2020). Social scientists' testimony before Congress in the United States between 1946–2016, trends from a new dataset. *PLOS ONE, 15*(3), e0230104.

Malakoff, D. (2021). Biden orders sweeping review of government science integrity policies. *Science.* doi:10.1126/science.abg7913

Mann, T. E., & Ornstein, N. J. (2012). *It's even worse than it looks: How the American constitutional system collided with the new politics of extremism.* Basic Books.

Mann, M., & Schleifer, C. (2020). Love the science, hate the scientists: Conservative identity protects belief in science and undermines trust in scientists. *Social Forces, 99*(1), 305–332.

Margolis, M. F. (2018). *From politics to the pews: How partisanship and the political environment shape religious identity.* University of Chicago Press.

Marquart-Pyatt, S. T., Shwom, R. L., Dietz, T., Dunlap, R. E., Kaplowitz, S. A., McCright, A. M., & Zahran, S. (2011). Understanding public opinion on climate change: A call for research. *Environment: Science and Policy for Sustainable Development, 53*(4), 38–42.

Masci, D. (2009). Scientists and belief. Pew Research Center. https://www.pewforum.org/2009/11/05/scientists-and-belief/

Masciotra, D. (2020). Anti-intellectualism is back—because it never went away. And it's killing Americans. *Salon.* https://www.salon.com/2020/05/30/anti-intellectualism-is-back–because-it-never-went-away-and-its-killing-americans/

Mason, L. (2018). Ideologues without issues: The polarizing consequences of ideological identities. *Public Opinion Quarterly, 82*(S1), 866–887.

Mason, L., & Wronski, J. (2018). One tribe to bind them all: How our social group attachments strengthen partisanship. *Political Psychology, 39,* 257–277.

Maxmen, A., & Mallapaty, S. (2021). The COVID lab-leak hypothesis: What scientists do and don't know. *Nature, 594*(7863), 313–315. https://www.nature.com/articles/d41586-021-01529-3

Maxmen, A., Subbaraman, N., Tollefson, J., Viglione, G., & Witze, A. (2020). What a Joe Biden presidency would mean for five key science issues. *Nature, 586*(7828), 177–180.

Mayhew, D. R. (1974). *Congress: The electoral connection.* Yale University Press.

Mazure, C. Rick Perry: Man of science? (2011). PBS. https://www.pbs.org/wnet/need-to-know/opinion/rick-perry-man-of-scienc/11911/

McCright, A. M., & Dunlap, R. E. (2000). Challenging global warming as a social problem: An analysis of the conservative movement's counter-claims. *Social Problems, 47*(4), 499–522.

McCright, A. M., & Dunlap, R. E. (2010). Anti-reflexivity. *Theory, Culture & Society, 27*(2–3), 100–133.

McCright, A. M., & Dunlap, R. E. (2011). The politicization of climate change and polarization in the American public's views of global warming, 2001–2010. *The Sociological Quarterly, 52*(2), 155–194.

Mede, N. G., & Schäfer, M. S. (2020). Science-related populism: Conceptualizing populist demands toward science. Public Understanding of science, *29*(5), 473–491.

Mejia Davis, E. (2016). Trump is the nominee of George Wallace's American Independent Party in California. CNN. https://edition.cnn.com/2016/11/02/politics/trump-american-independent-party-california/index.html

Mele, C. (2016). Professor watchlist is seen as threat to academic freedom. *The New York Times.* https://www.nytimes.com/2016/11/28/us/professor-watchlist-is-seen-as-threat-to-academic-freedom.html

Miller, J. D. (1998). The measurement of civic scientific literacy. *Public Understanding of Science, 7,* 203–223.

Miller, W. E. (1991). Party identification, realignment, and party voting: Back to the basics. *American Political Science Review, 85*(2), 557–568.

Miller, J. M. (2020). Psychological, political, and situational factors combine to boost COVID-19 conspiracy theory beliefs. *Canadian Journal of Political Science/Revue Canadienne de Science Politique, 53*(2), 327–334.

Mitchell, A., Jurkowitz, M. Oliphant, J. B., Shearer, E. (2020). Americans rate CDC highly, Trump and his administration poorly on getting the facts right about COVID-19. Pew Research Center. https://www.journalism.org/2020/06/29/americans-rate-cdc-highly-trump-and-his-administration-poorly-on-getting-the-facts-right-about-covid-19/

Merkley, E. (2020). Anti-intellectualism, populism, and motivated resistance to expert consensus. *Public Opinion Quarterly, 84*(1), 24–48.

Merkley, E., & Loewen, P. J. (2021). Anti-intellectualism and the mass public's response to the COVID-19 pandemic. *Nature Human Behavior, 5*(6), 706–715.

Merkley, E., & Stecula, D. A. (2018). Party elites or manufactured doubt? The informational context of climate change polarization. *Science Communication, 40*(2), 258–274.

Merkley, E., & Stecula, D. A. (2021). Party cues in the news: Democratic elites, Republican backlash, and the dynamics of climate skepticism. *British Journal of Political Science, 51*(4), 1439–1456.

Mervis, J. (2014). US political scientists relieved that Coburn language is gone. *Science.* https://www.science.org/content/article/us-political-scientists-relieved-coburn-language-gone

Mervis, J. (2020). "Very disappointed." Trump's science adviser has left U.S. researchers wanting more. *Science.* https://www.sciencemag.org/news/2020/10/very-disappointed-trump-s-science-adviser-has-left-us-researchers-wanting-more

Miller, J. D. (1988). The origins of interest in science and mathematics. *ERIC.*

Miri, J. (2021). The fall of Vannevar bush: The forgotten war for control of science policy in Postwar America. *Historical Studies in the Natural Sciences, 51*(4), 507-541.

Mooney, C. (2005). Requiem for an office. *Bulletin of the Atomic Scientists, 61*(5), 40–49.

Mooney, C. (2006). *Looking for a Fight: Is There a Republican War on Science?* Parlor Press.

Motta, M. (2018a). The dynamics and political implications of anti-intellectualism in the United States. *American Politics Research, 46*(3), 465–498.

Motta, M. (2018b). The enduring effect of scientific interest on trust in climate scientists in the United States. *Nature Climate Change, 8*(6), 485–488.

Motta, M. (2018c). The polarizing effect of the March for Science on attitudes toward scientists. *PS: Political Science & Politics, 51*(4), 782–788.

Motta, M., Callaghan, T., & Sylvester, S. (2018). Knowing less but presuming more: Dunning-Kruger effects and the endorsement of anti-vaccine policy attitudes. *Social Science & Medicine, 211*, 274–281.

Motta, M. (2019). Explaining science funding attitudes in the United States: The case for science interest. *Public Understanding of Science, 28*(2), 161–176.

Motta, M., Chapman, D., Haglin, K., & Kahan, D. (2019). Reducing the administrative demands of the science curiosity scale: A validation study. *International Journal of Public Opinion Research, 33*(2), 215–233.

Motta, M., & Callaghan, T. (2020). The pervasiveness and policy consequences of medical folk wisdom in the US. *Scientific Reports, 10*(1), 1–10.

Motta, M. (2020). ANES 2019 pilot study methodology report: Climate change mitigation policy opinion (GW1 & GW2). Available at SSRN 3550819.

Motta, M., Stecula, D., & Farhart, C. (2020). How right-leaning media coverage of COVID-19 facilitated the spread of misinformation in the early stages of the pandemic in the US. *Canadian Journal of Political Science/Revue Canadienne de Science Politique, 53*(2), 335–342.

Motta, M. (2021a). Republicans, not democrats, are more likely to endorse anti-vaccine misinformation. *American Politics Research, 49*(5), 428–438. 1532673X211022639.

Motta, M. (2021b). Political scientists: A profile of congressional candidates with STEM backgrounds. *PS: Political Science & Politics, 54*(2), 202–207.

Motta, M., Callaghan, T., Sylvester, S., & Lunz-Trujillo, K. (2021). Identifying the prevalence, correlates, and policy consequences of anti-vaccine social identity. *Politics, Groups, and Identities, 11*(1), 108–122.

Mudde, C., & Kaltwasser, C. R. (2017). Populism: A very short introduction. Oxford University Press.

References

Mullard, A. (2021). Landmark Alzheimer's drug approval confounds research community. *Nature*. https://pubmed.ncbi.nlm.nih.gov/34103732/

Mullin, M. (2017). Will the March for science backfire by politicizing science? It depends on this. *The Washington Post*. https://www.washingtonpost.com/news/monkey-cage/wp/2017/04/21/themarch-for-science-could-backfire-by-politicizing-science-this-might-help/

Murugan, V. (2009). Stem cell issue: embryonic stem cell research: A decade of debate from Bush to Obama. *The Yale Journal of Biology and Medicine, 82*(3), 101.

National Science Board (2018). Science and engineering indicators 2018. NSB-2018-1. National Science Foundation. https://www.nsf.gov/statistics/indicators/

Nature Editorial Board. (2010). Science scorned. *Nature, 467*, 133. https://www.nature.com/articles/467

Navarro, J. A. (2020). Mask resistance during a pandemic isn't new—in 1918 many Americans were "slackers." *The Conversation, US*. https://theconversation.com/mask-resistance-during-a-pandemic-isnt-new-in-1918-many-americans-were-slackers-141687

Newman, B. J., Shah, S., & Collingwood, L. (2018). Race, place, and building a base: Latino population growth and the nascent Trump campaign for president. *Public Opinion Quarterly, 82*(1), 122–134.

Nichols, T. (2017). *The death of expertise: The campaign against established knowledge and why it matters*. Oxford University Press.

Nicholson, S. P. (2012). Polarizing cues. *American Journal of Political Science, 56*(1), 52–66.

Nisbet, M. C., Scheufele, D. A., Shanahan, J., Moy, P., Brossard, D., & Lewenstein, B. V. (2002). Knowledge, reservations, or promise? A media effects model for public perceptions of science and technology. *Communication Research, 29*(5), 584–608.

Nuccitelli, D. (2015). Congress manufactures doubt and denial in climate change hearing. *The Guardian*. https://www.theguardian.com/environment/climate-consensus-97-per-cent/2015/may/21/cmanufactures-doubt-and-denial-in-climate-change-hearing

Nowlin, M. C. (2021). Political beliefs, views about technocracy, and energy and climate policy preferences. *Public Understanding of Science, 30*(3), 331–348.

Nyhan, B., Reifler, J., Richey, S., & Freed, G. L. (2014). Effective messages in vaccine promotion: A randomized trial. *Pediatrics, 133*(4), e835–e842.

Nyhan, B., & Reifler, J. (2015). Does correcting myths about the flu vaccine work? An experimental evaluation of the effects of corrective information. *Vaccine, 33*(3), 459–464.

Nyhan, B., Porter, E., Reifler, J., & Wood, T. J. (2020). Taking fact-checks literally but not seriously? The effects of journalistic fact-checking on factual beliefs and candidate favorability. *Political Behavior, 42*(3), 939–960.

Nyhan, B. (2017). How marching for science risks politicizing it. *The New York Times*. https://www.nytimes.com/2017/05/02/upshot/how-marching-for-science-risks-politicizing-it.html

Obama, B. (2020). *A promised land*. Crown.

O'Brien, T. L. (2013). Scientific authority in policy contexts: Public attitudes about environmental scientists, medical researchers, and economists. *Public Understanding of Science, 22*(7), 799–816.

O'Brien, T. L., & Noy, S. (2020). Political identity and confidence in science and religion in the United States. *Sociology of Religion, 81*(4), 439–461.

Oliver, J. E., & Wood, T. J. (2018). *Enchanted America: How intuition and reason divide our politics*. University of Chicago Press.

Oliver, J. E., & Rahn, W. M. (2016). Rise of the Trumpenvolk: Populism in the 2016 election. *The ANNALS of the American Academy of Political and Social Science, 667*(1), 189–206.

Olmos, S. (2021). Mask burning rally in Idaho fans COVID-19 worries in Oregon. *Oregon Public Broadcasting*. https://www.opb.org/article/2021/03/08/mask-burning-idaho-oregon-peoples-rights-far-right/

Osmundsen, M., Bor, A., Vahlstrup, P. B., Bechmann, A., & Petersen, M. (2021). Partisan polarization is the primary psychological motivation behind political fake news sharing on Twitter. *American Political Science Review, 115*(3), 999–1015.

Parker, C. S., & Barreto, M. A. (2014). Change they can't believe. In: *The Tea Party and reactionary politics in America-Updated Edition*. Princeton University Press.

Pasek, J. (2016). When will nonprobability surveys mirror probability surveys? Considering types of inference and weighting strategies as criteria for correspondence. *International Journal of Public Opinion Research, 28*(2), 269–291.

Pearce, K. (2020). What is social distancing and how can it slow the spread of COVID-19. March 13, 2020. Johns Hopkins University HUB. https://hub.jhu.edu/2020/03/13/what-is-social-distancing/

Pearson, R. (1998). Former Alabama Governor George C. Wallace dies. *The Washington Post.* https://www.washingtonpost.com/wp-srv/politics/daily/sept98/wallace.htm

Pellegrino, J. W. (2013). Proficiency in science: Assessment challenges and opportunities. *Science, 340*(6130), 320–323.

Pennycook, G., Ross, R. M., Koehler, D. J., & Fugelsang, J. A. (2017). Dunning Kruger effects in reasoning: Theoretical implications of the failure to recognize incompetence. *Psychonomic Bulletin & Review, 24*(6), 1774–1784.

Pennycook, G., & Rand, D. G. (2019). Lazy, not biased: Susceptibility to partisan fake news is better explained by lack of reasoning than by motivated reasoning. *Cognition, 188*, 39–50.

Pennycook, G., Epstein, Z., Mosleh, M., Arechar, A. A., Eckles, D., & Rand, D. G. (2021). Shifting attention to accuracy can reduce misinformation online. *Nature, 592*(7855), 590–595.

Pennycook, G., & Rand, D. G. (2019). Fighting misinformation on social media using crowd-sourced judgments of news source quality. *Proceedings of the National Academy of Sciences, 116*(7), 2521–2526.

Perlstein, R. (2008). Nixonland: The rise of a president and the fracturing of America. Simon and Schuster.

Peters, M. A. (2019). Anti-intellectualism is a virus. *Educational Philosophy and Theory, 51*(4), 357–363.

Perna, L. W., Orosz, K., & Kent, D. C. (2019). The role and contribution of academic researchers in congressional hearings: A critical discourse analysis. *American Educational Research Journal, 56*(1), 111–145.

Peters, J.W. (2018). In name of free speech, states crack down on campus protests. *The New York Times.* https://www.nytimes.com/2018/06/14/us/politics/campus-speech-protests.html

Pickup, M., Stecula, D., & Van Der Linden, C. (2020). Novel coronavirus, old partisanship: COVID-19 attitudes and behaviours in the United States and Canada. *Canadian Journal of Political Science/Revue Canadienne de Science politique, 53*(2), 357–364.

Piketty, T., & Saez, E. (2014). Inequality in the long run. *Science, 344*(6186), 838–843.

Piller, C. (2018). FDA's revolving door: Companies often hire agency staffers who manage their successful drug reviews. *Science Magazine, 5.* http://www.sciencemag.org/news/2018/07/fda-s-revolving-door-companies-often-hire-agency-staffers-who-managed-their-successful

Pornpitakpan, C. (2004). The persuasiveness of source credibility: A critical review of five decades' evidence. *Journal of Applied Social Psychology, 34*(2), 243–281.

Potvin, P., & Hasni, A. (2014). Interest, motivation and attitude towards science and technology at K–12 levels: A systematic review of 12 years of educational research. *Studies in Science Education, 50*(1), 85–129.

Qian, M., & Jiang, J. (2022). COVID-19 and social distancing. *Journal of Public Health, 30*(1): 259–261.

Revkin, A.C. (2006). Climate expert says NASA tried to silence him. *The New York Times.* https://www.nytimes.com/2006/01/29/science/earth/climate-expert-says-nasa-tried-to-silence-him.html

Rigney, D. (1991). Three kinds of anti-intellectualism: Rethinking Hofstadter. *Sociological Inquiry, 61*(4), 434–451.

Riotta, C. (2021). Fauci feared Americans may "start doing dangerous and foolish things" after Trump suggested "injecting" bleach. *The Independent.* https://www.independent.co.uk/news/world/ampolitics/fauci-trump-coronavirus-injecting-bleach-b1793023.html

References 315

Roberts, C., Gilbert, E., Allum, N., & Eisner, L. (2019). Research synthesis: Satisficing in surveys: A systematic review of the literature. *Public Opinion Quarterly, 83*(3), 598–626.

Rohlinger, D. A., & Bunnage, L. (2017). Did the Tea Party movement fuel the Trump-train? The role of social media in activist persistence and political change in the 21st century. *Social Media & Society, 3*(2), 2056305117706786.

Romo, V. (2020). Dr. Scott Atlas, special coronavirus adviser to Trump, resigns. National Public Radio (NPR). https://www.npr.org/2020/11/30/940376041/dr-scott-atlas-special-coronavirus-adviser-to-trump-resigns

Rosa, E. A., & Dietz, T. (2012). Human drivers of national greenhouse-gas emissions. *Nature Climate Change, 2*(8), 581–586.

Rothman, A. J., Desmarais, K. J., & Lenne, R. L. (2020). Moving from research on message framing to principles of message matching: The use of gain-and loss-framed messages to promote healthy behavior. In *Advances in Motivation Science* (Vol. 7, pp. 43–73). Elsevier.

Rummler, O. (2020). Infectious-disease expert: Scott Atlas' herd immunity claims are "pseudoscience." *Axios.* https://www.axios.com/scott-atlas-herd-immunity-coronavirus-c8511115-0f39-4d0a-a1a8-44dd7560c7f1.html

Rutjens, B. T., & Heine, S. J. (2016). The immoral landscape? Scientists are associated with violations of morality. *PLOS ONE, 11*(4), e0152798.

Rutjens, B. T., Sutton, R. M., & van der Lee, R. (2018). Not all skepticism is equal: Exploring the ideological antecedents of science acceptance and rejection. *Personality and Social Psychology Bulletin, 44*(3), 384–405.

Rutledge, P. E. (2020). Trump, COVID-19, and the war on expertise. *The American Review of Public Administration, 50*(6–7), 505–511.

Sachdeva, S. (2016). Religious identity, beliefs, and views about climate change. In *Oxford research encyclopedia of climate science.* Oxford University Press. doi.org/10.1093/acrefore/9780190228620.013.335

Safarpour, A., Trujillo, K. L., Green, J., Pippert, C. H., Lin, J., & Druckman, J. N. (2024). Divisive or Descriptive?: How Americans Understand Critical Race Theory. *Journal of Race, Ethnicity, and Politics,* 1–25.

Sanger-Katz, M. (2020). On coronavirus, Americans still trust the experts. *The New York Times.* https://www.nytimes.com/2020/06/27/upshot/coronavirus-americans-trust-experts.html

Schaffner, B. F., & Roche, C. (2016). Misinformation and motivated reasoning: Responses to economic news in a politicized environment. *Public Opinion Quarterly, 81*(1), 86–110.

Scharmer, A., & Snyder, M. (2021). Political message matching and green behaviors: Strengths and boundary conditions for promoting high-impact behavioral change. *Journal of Environmental Psychology,* 101643. doi.org/10.1016/j.jenvp.2021.101643

Scheitle, C. P., Johnson, D. R., & Ecklund, E. H. (2018). Scientists and religious leaders compete for cultural authority of science. *Public Understanding of Science, 27*(1), 59–75.

Schnakenberg, K. E. (2017). Informational lobbying and legislative voting. *American Journal of Political Science, 61*(1), 129–145.

Schneider, H. (2020). Analysis-Federal Reserve "boneheads" emerge from Trump era unscathed. Reuters. https://www.reuters.com/article/usa-fed-trump/analysis-federal-reserve-boneheads-emerge-from-trump-era-unscathed-idUSKBN28Q1CZ

Schulman, J. (2016). Every insane thing Donald Trump has said about global warming. *Mother Jones.* https://www.motherjones.com/environment/2016/12/trump-climate-timeline/

Schwarz, H. (2015). The many ways in which Donald Trump was once a liberal's liberal. *The Washington Post.* https://www.washingtonpost.com/news/the-fix/wp/2015/07/09/ths-many-ways-in-which-donald-trump-was-once-a-liberals-liberal/

Segovia, F., & Defever, R. (2010). The polls–trends: American public opinion on immigrants and immigration policy. *Public Opinion Quarterly, 74*(2), 375–394.

Self, W. H., Semler, M. W., Leither, L. M., Casey, J. D., Angus, D. C., Brower, R. G., . . . & Brown, S. M. (2020). Effect of hydroxychloroquine on clinical status at 14 days in hospitalized patients with COVID-19: a randomized clinical trial. *JAMA, 324*(21), 2165- 2176.

Simon, H. A. (1956). Rational choice and the structure of the environment. *Psychological Review, 63*(2), 129.

Shafran, J., Jones, B. D., & Dye, C. (2020). Bounded rationality in public administration. In *Oxford research encyclopedia of politics*. Oxford University Press.

Shapiro, W. (2020). How America's newspapers covered up a pandemic. *The New Republic.* https://newrepublic.com/article/157094/americas-newspapers-covered-pandemic

Shane, L. (2019). Trump blasts Mattis as "the world's most overrated general." *Military Times.* https://www.militarytimes.com/news/pentagon-congress/2019/10/17/trump-blasts -mattis-as-the-worlds-most-overrated-general/

Shumow, L., & Miller, J. D. (2001). Parents' at-home and at-school academic involvement with young adolescents. *The Journal of Early Adolescence, 21*(1), 68–91.

Skipper, C. P., Pastick, K. A., Engen, N. W., Bangdiwala, A. S., Abassi, M., Lofgren, S. M., ... & Boulware, D. R. (2020). Hydroxychloroquine in nonhospitalized adults with early COVID-19: A randomized trial. *Annals of Internal Medicine, 173*(8), 623–631.

Skocpol, T., & Williamson, V. (2016). *The Tea Party and the remaking of Republican conservatism.* Oxford University Press.

Sides, J., Tesler, M., & Vavreck, L. (2016). The electoral landscape of 2016. *The ANNALS of the American Academy of Political and Social Science, 667*(1), 50–71.

Sides, J., Tesler, M., & Vavreck, L. (2019). *Identity crisis: The 2016 presidential campaign and the battle for the meaning of America.* Princeton University Press.

Simonov, A., Sacher, S. K., Dube, J. P. H., & Biswas, S. (2020). The persuasive effect of fox news: non-compliance with social distancing during the COVID-19 pandemic (No. w27237). National Bureau of Economic Research.

Smith, R. A. (1995). Interest group influence in the US Congress. *Legislative Studies Quarterly, 20*(1), 89–139.

Smith, K. B., Oxley, D. R., Hibbing, M. V., Alford, J. R., & Hibbing, J. R. (2011). Linking genetics and political attitudes: Reconceptualizing political ideology. *Political Psychology, 32*(3), 369–397.

Smith, V., et al. (2017). An open letter from 1,470 economists on immigration. New American Economy (NAE). https://www.newamericaneconomy.org/feature/an-open-letter-from-1470-economists-on-immigration/

Snyder, M., & DeBono, K. G. (1985). Appeals to image and claims about quality: Understanding the psychology of advertising. *Journal of Personality and Social Psychology, 49*(3), 586.

Sun Sentinel Editorial Board. (2019). Gov. DeSantis goes bold on climate change. Even Rick Scott says it's real. Now what? *South Florida Sun Sentinel.* https://www.sun-sentinel.com/opinion/ editorials/os-op-desantis-climate-change-20190528-zxfc3aq4qbc5xnre27i4bbhp6u -story.html

Stableford, D. (2021). Trump on Fauci: "I listened to him, but I didn't do what he said." *Yahoo News.* https://news.yahoo.com/trump-fauci-i-listened-to-him-but-i-didnt-do-what-he-said -161745694.html

Stecula, D. A., Kuru, O., Albarracin, D., & Jamieson, K. H. (2020). Policy views and negative beliefs about vaccines in the United States, 2019. *American Journal of Public Health, 110*(10), 1561–1563.

Stephan, W. G., & Stephan, C. W. (2013). An integrated threat theory of prejudice. In *Reducing prejudice and discrimination* (pp. 23–45). Psychology Press.

Stimson, J. (2018). *Public opinion in America: Moods, cycles, and swings.* Routledge.

Stone, T. (2021). DeSantis: Florida chooses freedom over Faucism. Real Clear Politics. https:// www.realclearpolitics.com/video/2021/06/04/desantis florida choose freedom over faucism.ht

Stroud, N. J. (2010). Polarization and partisan selective exposure. *Journal of Communication, 60*(3), 556–576.

Stroud, N. J. (2011). *Niche news: The politics of news choice.* Oxford University Press.

Sturgis, P., & Allum, N. (2004). Science in society: re-evaluating the deficit model of public attitudes. *Public Understanding of Science, 13*(1), 55–74.

Sturgis, P., Brunton-Smith, I., & Jackson, J. (2021). Trust in science, social consensus and vaccine confidence. *Nature Human Behaviour, 5*(11), 1528–1534.

Subbaraman, N. Tollefson, J., Viglione, G., & Witze, A. (2021). The latest on Biden's science team: Former senator to lead NASA. *Nature*. https://www.nature.com/articles/d41586-020-03485-w

Suldovsky, B., & Akin, H. (2023). The role of trust in communicating scientific consensus and the environmental benefits of genetically engineered crops: Experimental evidence of a backfire effect. *Environmental Communication, 17*(1), 101–118.

Suldovsky, B., Landrum, A., & Stroud, N. J. (2019). Public perceptions of who counts as a scientist for controversial science. *Public Understanding of Science, 28*(7), 797–811.

Sullivan, S. (2013). The decline of the tea party—in 5 charts. *The Washington Post*. https://www.washingtonpost.com/news/the-fix/wp/2013/12/12/the-decline-of-the-tea-party-in-5-charts/

Sutton, R. M., Petterson, A., & Rutjens, B. T. (2019). Post-truth, anti-truth, and can't handle the-truth: How responses to science are shaped by concerns about its impact. In *Belief systems and the perception of reality*. Routledge.

Swan, J. (2020). Trump eyes new unproven coronavirus "cure." *Axios*. https://www.axios.com/trump-covid-oleandrin-9896f570-6cd8-4919-af3a-65ebad113d41.html

Swire-Thompson, B., & Lazer, D. (2020). Public health and online misinformation: Challenges and recommendations. *Annual Review of Public Health, 41*(1), 433–451.

Taber, C. S., & Lodge, M. (2006). Motivated skepticism in the evaluation of political beliefs. *American Journal of Political Science, 50*(3), 755–769.

Tajfel, H. 1974. Social identity and intergroup behaviour. *Social Science Information 13*(2), 65–93.

Tollefson, J. (2020). Scientists relieved as Joe Biden wins tight US presidential election. *Nature, 587*(7833), 183–185.

Tooby, J., & Cosmides, L. (2010). Groups in mind: The coalitional roots of war and morality. *Human Morality and Sociality: Evolutionary and Comparative Perspectives, 91*, 234.

Tourangeau, R., Rips, L. J., & Rasinski, K. (2000). The psychology of survey response. Cambridge University Press.

Treier, S., & Jackman, S. (2008). Democracy as a latent variable. *American Journal of Political Science, 52*(1), 201–217.

Treier, S., & Hillygus, D. S. (2009). The nature of political ideology in the contemporary elector-ate. *Public Opinion Quarterly, 73*(4), 679–703.

Turner, J. C., Hogg, M. A., Oakes, P. J., Reicher, S. D., & Wetherell, M. S. (1987). *Rediscovering the social group: A self-categorization theory*. Basil Blackwell.

Turner, C. S. V., Gonzalez, J. C., & Wong, K. (2011). Faculty women of color: The critical nexus of race and gender. *Journal of Diversity in Higher Education, 4*, 199–211. doi:10.1037/a0024630

UCUSA (2019). The White House suppressed science from congressional testimony. Union of Concerned Scientists—USA. https://www.ucsusa.org/resources/attacks-on-science/white-house-suppressed-science-congressional-testimony

Ungar, L., Mellers, B., Satop, V., Tetlock, P., & Baron, J. (2012, October) The good judgment proj-ect: A large scale test of different methods of combining expert predictions. In 2012 AAAI Fall Symposium Series.

Uscinski, J. E., Enders, A. M., Klofstad, C., Seelig, M., Funchion, J., Everett, C., . . . & Murthi, M. (2020). Why do people believe COVID-19 conspiracy theories?. *Harvard Kennedy School Misinformation Review, 1*(3) 1–12.

Vakhshouri, S. (2017). The America First energy plan: Renewing the confidence of American energy producers. Atlantic Council Issue Brief. https://svbweb.s3.amazonaws.com/media/new releas The America First Energy Plan web 0817.pdf

van der Linden, S. L., Clarke, C. E., & Maibach, E. W. (2015). Highlighting consensus among medical scientists increases public support for vaccines: evidence from a randomized ex-periment. *BMC Public Health, 15*(1), 1–5.

Van der Linden, S., Leiserowitz, A., Rosenthal, S., & Maibach, E. (2017). Inoculating the public against misinformation about climate change. *Global Challenges, 1*(2), 1600008.

van Der Linden, S., Roozenbeek, J., & Compton, J. (2020). Inoculating against fake news about COVID-19. *Frontiers in Psychology, 11*, 2928.

Van Stekelenburg, A., Schaap, G., Veling, H., & Buijzen, M. (2021). Boosting understanding and identification of scientific consensus can help to correct false beliefs. *Psychological Science, 32*(10), 1549–1565.

Velan, B., Boyko, V., Lerner-Geva, L., Ziv, A., Yagar, Y., & Kaplan, G. (2012). Individualism, acceptance and differentiation as attitude traits in the public's response to vaccination. *Human Vaccines & Immunotherapeutics, 8*(9), 1272–1282.

Viebeck, E. (2012). Poll: Four in 10 believe in Obama healthcare law "death panels." *The Hill*. https://thehill.com/policy/healthcare/258753-poll-four-in-10-believe-in-health-law -death-panels

Villareal, D. (2022). TikTokers launch spam site to curb Glenn Youngkin's "racist snitch" school tip line. *Newsweek*. https://www.newsweek.com/tiktokers-launch-spam-site-curb-glenn-young kins-racist-snitch-school-tip-line-1673779

Walter, N., Cohen, J., Holbert, R. L., & Morag, Y. (2020). Fact-checking: A meta-analysis of what works and for whom. *Political Communication, 37*(3), 350–375.

Walsh, J. (2021). Rush Limbaugh leaves behind a conservative movement no longer interested in truth. That alarms me as a conservative. *Time Magazine*. https://time.com/5915574/ rush-limbaugh-dies-legacy/

Webster, D. M., & Kruglanski, A. W. (1994). Individual differences in need for cognitive closure. *Journal of Personality and Social Psychology, 67*(6), 1049.

Weisberg, D. S., Landrum, A. R., Metz, S. E., & Weisberg, M. (2018). No missing link: Knowledge predicts acceptance of evolution in the United States. *BioScience, 68*(3), 212–222.

Weixel, N. (2021). Fauci, Jim Jordan spar over pandemic restrictions. *The Hill*. https://thehill. com/policy/healthcare/548481-fauci-jim-jordan-spar-over-pandemic-restrictions/

Williamson, V., Skocpol, T., & Coggin, J. (2011). The Tea Party and the remaking of Republican conservatism. *Perspectives on Politics, 9*(1), 25–43.

Wertz, D. C. (2002). Embryo and stem cell research in the United States: History and politics. *Gene Therapy, 9*(11), 674–678.

Whitehead Jr., J. L. (1968). Factors of source credibility. *Quarterly Journal of Speech, 54*(1), 59–63.

Wilson, R. (2017). Census: More Americans have college degrees than ever before. *The Hill*. https://thehill.com/homenews/state-watch/326995-census-more-americans-have-college-degrees-than-ever-before

Winter, N. J. (2008). *Dangerous frames: How ideas about race and gender shape public opinion*. University of Chicago Press.

Yamey, G., & Gonsalves, G. (2020). Donald Trump: a political determinant of covid-19. *BMJ*, 369.

Yardley, W. (2016). Jesse L. Steinfeld, Surgeon General and Tobacco Foe, Dies at 87. *The New York Times*. https://www.nytimes.com/2014/08/07/us/jesse-l-steinfeld-surgeon-general-and -tobacco-foe-dies-at-87.html

Yong, E. (2017).What exactly are people marching for when they march for science? *The Atlantic*. https://www.theatlantic.com/science/archive/2017/03/what-exactly-are-people-marching-for-when-they-march-for-science/518763/

Zaller, J. R. (1992). *The nature and origins of mass opinion*. Cambridge University Press.

Zernike, K. (2015). Rand Paul rode Tea Party fervor to Washington, then yielded. *The New York Times*. https://www.nytimes paul-first-campaign.html

INDEX

For the benefit of digital users, table entries that span two pages (e.g., 52–53) may, on occasion, appear on only one of those pages.

Aducanumab, 26–27
Aduhelm, 26–27
affective and group-centric theory of
 anti-intellectualism generally, 2, 19,
 28–29, 200
 affective phenomenon, anti-intellectualism as, 4–6
 bidirectionality and, 34–35
 correlational research, 34
 dynamic differences, 34
 dynamic inputs (*see* dynamic inputs)
 expert dislike and distrust, group-based
  origins of, 30–32
 group-based phenomenon,
  anti-intellectualism as, 4–6
 group membership and, 29–30
 Integrated Threat Theory (ITT) and, 32–33
 measurement of anti-intellectualism
  (*see* measurement of anti-intellectualism)
 policy-relevant outputs, 33–35
 political psychological inputs, 33–35
 reverse causality and, 34
 schematic design, 35
 Self-Categorization Theory (SCT) and, 32–33
 Social Identity Theory (SIT) and, 32–33
 sstatic inputs (*see* sstatic inputs)
 static differences, 34
 testing of (*see* measurement of
  anti-intellectualism)
 within-person changes in anti-intellectualism
  and, 34–35
affect transfer, 59–60
Affordable Care Act, 47, 49–51
Alzheimer's disease, 26–27
America First Energy Plan, 187–188
"American exceptionalism," lack of evidence
 of, 211–214
American Independent Party, 40, 47, 108–110

American National Election Study (ANES)
 generally, 73
 ANES Time Series Pilot Study, 75–76
 GSS surveys, correspondence with, 85–89
 predictive validation and, 88
Anderson, John, 1
anti-elitism
 anti-intellectualism, as, 9–10, 15
 populism and, 15
anti-intellectualism
 affective theory of (*see* affective and
  group-centric theory of anti-intellectualism)
 "American exceptionalism," lack of evidence
  of, 211–214
 anti-elitism as, 9–10, 15
 anti-rationalism (*see* anti-rationalism)
 anti-science attitudes and, 14–15
 anti-vaccine social identity (AVISD) and, 32
 between-person differences in
  (*see* between-person differences in
  anti-intellectualism)
 bidirectionality thesis and (*see* bidirectionality
  thesis)
 comparative analysis of, 211–214
 conceptualization of, 3, 6
 Congressional response to (*see* Congressional
  response to anti-intellectualism)
 defined, 3
 Dunning–Kruger effect, 8–9
 elite response to, 186–188, (*see also*
  Congressional response to
  anti-intellectualism)
 elites, role of, 16–17
 emerging strains of, 202–205
 expert dislike and distrust, as (*see* expert
  dislike and distrust)
 future research, 24, 215–216

319

anti-intellectualism (*continued*)
  group-centric theory of (*see* affective and
    group-centric theory of anti-intellectualism)
  indicators of, 68, 77–78
  international sphere, in, 211–214
  limited government orientation and, 43–44
  macro anti-intellectualism database (MAID) (*see*
    macro anti-intellectualism database (MAID))
  measurement of (*see* measurement of
    anti-intellectualism)
  meta-ignorance, 8–9
  origin story, 114
  partisan polarization and, 2, 19, 114
  policy consequences of (*see* policy
    consequences of anti-intellectualism)
  populism, relation to, 3, 15–18, 116–117
  prevalence of (*see* prevalence of
    anti-intellectualism)
  religiosity and, 19
  Republican Party and, 19, 91, 102–103, 105
  scholarly focus on, 1–2
  science interest, relation to, 145–147, 201
  science knowledge, relation to, 145–147
  science-related populism contrasted, 15–17
  Tea Party and, 21–22, 51, 136–139
  theoretical framework of (*see* affective and group-
    centric theory of anti-intellectualism)
  unreflective instrumentalism, 8
  within-person changes in (*see* within-person
    changes in anti-intellectualism)
anti-rationalism
  generally, 6
  conceptual problems with, 6–7
  critical thought, relation to, 7
anti-science attitudes
  anti-intellectualism and, 14–15
  dislike and distrust of scientists, 12
  expert dislike and distrust, relation to, 13–14
  experts, scientists as, 12–15
  predictiveness of attitudes, 14
  symbolic ideology and, 42
  Tea Party and, 40
anti-vaccine social identity (AVISD), 32
asymmetric polarization, 47–49
Atlas, Scott, 154

Bachmann., Michele, 49
Barker, D.C., 29
Beck, Glenn, 40, 49
between-person differences in anti-intellectualism
  generally, 21–22, 112–114, 139–140
  analytical strategy in detecting, 114–117
  data, 114–120
  demographic factors, 120
  dynamic reliability of inputs, 115
  empirical results, 123–124

  limited government orientation and, 44,
    118–120, 122, 129–131
  measurement of, 114–120
  model input stability assessment, 121–123
  partisan identity and, 117–118, 122, 124–127
  partisan polarization and, 21–22
  regression models and, 114–117
  religiosity and, 120, 122, 131–133
  reverse causality and, 116, 133–136
  symbolic ideology and, 118, 122, 127–129
  Tea Party and, 136–139
  within-person changes in anti-intellectualism
    and, 115, 117
Biden, Joe
  generally, 204–205
  COVID-19 pandemic and, 13, 22, 60–61
  COVID Response Task Force, 60–61
  Democratic presidential primaries, in, 40
  evidence-based policies and, 199–200
  RFK Jr. and, 211
bidirectionality thesis
  generally, 22–23, 57–58, 152–154, 164–165,
    167, 200
  affective and group-centric theory of
    anti-intellectualism and, 34–35
  affect transfer and, 59–60
  co-constitutive effects, 22–23, 160–161, 163, 201
  COVID-19 pandemic and, 58–59, 61
  data, 156
  empirical results, 160–162
  expert policy role (EPR) orientations and
    (*see* expert policy role (EPR) orientations)
  graded response modeling (GRM) and,
    158–159
  limitations of, 164–165
  populism and, 61–62
  regression models and, 155, 162
  testing, 155
BioGen, 26–27
birth-control education, 45–46
Blank, J.M., 42, 45–46
blanket skepticism, 26–27
book banning, 216
British Tea Act, 49
Bush, George H.W., 125–126
Bush, George W.
  anti-science attitudes of, 21, 48
  partisan polarization and, 125, 139
  stem-cell research and, 39
Bush, Vannevar, 38

Callaghan, Tim, 32
Canada, anti-intellectualism in, 212
censorship, 217–218
Center for the Study of Political Psychology
  (CSPP) Panel Study, 72–75

Index

Centers for Disease Control (CDC)
  COVID-19 pandemic and, 154
  protests against, 1
  public attitudes toward, 103
climate change
  Congressional hearings on, 192
  Congressional response to anti-intellectualism
    and, 192–194
  Democratic Party on, 42
  limited government orientation and, 43
  policy consequences of anti-intellectualism
    for, 23, 176–179
  religiosity and, 46
  Republican Party on, 39, 42, 206–207
  science knowledge and, 55
  survey questions, 168
Coburn, Tom, 39
cognitive closure, 209–210
comparative analysis of anti-intellectualism,
  211–214
Congressional Hearings Database, 189
Congressional Record, 190–191
Congressional response to anti-intellectualism
  climate change and, 192–194
  economic policy and, 195–196
  expert testimony at hearings as indicator, 189
  hearings as indicator, 192
  measuring expert influence in policymaking,
    188–191
  number of hearings as indicator, 190–191
  public health and, 196–197
  robustness checks, 197
conspiracy theories, 49–50, 180
content validation, 20, 66, 78
convergent validation, 20, 66, 78, 85–89
Couric, Katie, 50–51
COVID-19 pandemic
  bidirectionality thesis and, 22, 58–59, 61
  blanket skepticism and, 26–27
  conspiracy theories regarding, 180
  COVID Response Task Force, 60–61
  expert dislike and distrust and, 58–59
  herd-immunity and, 154
  lab leak theory, 153, 180
  mask wearing and, 183–184
  measurement of anti-intellectualism
    and, 75–77
  policy consequences of anti-intellectualism
    for, 23, 179–184
  protests during, 1
  public attitudes toward scientists
    during, 13
  social distancing and, 183–184
  survey questions, 168
critical race theory (CRT), 203–205, 216
cross-sectional survey data, 63
Cuevas, Joshua, 17

David, Edward E., 39
"death panels," 47, 50–51
Democratic Party
  climate change, on, 42
  historical attitudes toward experts, 21–22, 33,
    46–47, 114
  skepticism toward experts, 40
Department of Energy, 188
DeSantis, Ron, 22, 153–154, 204
determination of expert status
  generally, 3, 10–11
  "eye of the beholder" approach, 11–12, 89
  imperfect exercise, as, 11
  scientists as, 12–15
directionally motivated reasoning, 7
DuBridge, Lee Alvin, 38–39
Dunning–Kruger effect, 8–9, 54
dynamic inputs
  generally, 52–53
  epistemic factors, as, 52–53
  science interest as, 56–57
  science knowledge as, 54–56
Dynata, 73–74, 76–77

economic inequality and, 210–211
economic policy
  Congressional hearings on, 195
  Congressional response to anti-intellectualism
    and, 195–196
  policy consequences of anti-intellectualism
    for, 184–186
  survey questions, 168
Eisenhower, Dwight, 9, 37–38
elite response to anti-intellectualism, 186–188.
  See also Congressional response to
    anti-intellectualism
environmental policy
  climate change (*see* climate change)
  policy consequences of anti-intellectualism
    for, 176–179
  survey questions, 168
evolution, 6, 42, 45–46, 132–133
expert dislike and distrust
  anti-expert partisan rhetoric, 41–42
  anti-intellectualism, as, 3, 6–10, 14,
    19–20
  anti-science attitudes, relation to, 13–14
  COVID-19 pandemic and, 58–59
  group-based origins of, 30–32
  indicators of, 66
  partisan polarization and, 33
  populism and, 15–16
  predictiveness of attitudes, 14
  Republican Party and, 33, 37–41
  Tea Party and, 51, 139
  timebound nature of, 47–48

322

INDEX

expert policy role (EPR) orientations. *See also* bidirectionality thesis
   co-constitutive effects with anti-intellectualism, 22–23, 160–161, 163, 201
   distributional summary, 159–160
   empirical results, 160–162
   graded response modeling (GRM) and, 158–159
   measuring, 156–160
   missing data assessment, 159–160
   regression models and, 162
   survey questions, 156
experts
   determination of status as (*see* determination of expert status)
   dislike and distrust of (*see* expert dislike and distrust)
   fallibility of, 24–25
   healthy skepticism toward, 25–27
   inclusiveness of, 11
   measurement of trust in, 67, 71, 73, 75–76
   people, as, 4
   public definitions of, 80–82
   restoring trust in (*see* restoring trust in experts)
   scientists as, 12–15
   trust in, measurement of (*see* trust in experts, measurement of)
   variation among, 25

Facebook, 138
fact checks, 207
Fauci, Anthony
   COVID-19 pandemic and, 22, 112, 153
   criticism of, 102, 153–154
   group membership and, 30
   public attitudes toward, 13–14, 88, 103
First Amendment, 203–204
"folk theories," 55
Food and Drug Administration (FDA), 26–27
future research, 215–216

Gauchat, G., 48–49, 51, 58, 126
General Social Survey (GSS)
   ANES surveys, correspondence with, 85–89
   ballots, 158–159
   GSS Panel Studies, 70–72
   GSS Time Series Studies, 70
   predictive validation and, 88
Goldberg, Michelle, 211
Goldsmith, Brian, 50–51
Goodman, L., 115, 121
graded response modeling (GRM), 158–159
Grassley, Chuck, 47–48

group-centric theory of anti-intellectualism. *See* affective and group-centric theory of anti-intellectualism

healthy skepticism, 25–27
higher education
   perceptions of political bias in, 217
   science interest, enhancing effects of, 143, 148–150, 209
   science knowledge, enhancing effects of, 143, 148–150
Hofstadter, Richard
   generally, 188
   anti-elitism and, 9–10
   anti-intellectualism generally, 1–2, 28–29, 83, 108
   anti-rationalism and, 6–7
   bidirectionality thesis and (*see* bidirectionality thesis)
   conceptualization of anti-intellectualism, 3
   critique of, 5–6
   expert dislike and distrust, on, 19–20
   McCarthyism, on, 37
   populism, on, 15–16
   prevalence of anti-intellectualism, on, 91–92
   scientists, on, 12–13
   unreflective instrumentalism and, 8
Hopper, Grace, 30

ideology. *See* symbolic ideology
immigration, policy consequences of anti-intellectualism for, 185
Inglehart, R., 210
Integrated Threat Theory (ITT)
   generally, 30–32
   affective and group-centric theory of anti-intellectualism and, 32–33
   anti-vaccine social identity (AVISD) and, 32
international sphere, anti-intellectualism in, 211–214
iPoll, 93–95

Johnson, Lyndon, 40
Jordan, Jim, 102–103

Kahan, Dan, 43, 55
Kennedy, Robert F. Jr., 40, 210–211
Killian, James, 38
knowledge deficit model, 7, 54–56
Know-Nothing Party, 91, 102–103
Kruse, Matt, 216
Kruskall, W., 115, 121
Ku Klux Klan, 6–7

Index

Landry, Curt, 112
Lazarsfeld, Paul, 83
Levitan, Dave, 39
Limbaugh, Rush, 51
limited government orientation
  anti-intellectualism and, 43–44
  between-person differences in
    anti-intellectualism and, 44, 118–120,
    122, 129–131
  climate change and, 43
  measurement of, 118–120
  policy output, as, 44
  politically relevant preferences, relation to, 36–37
  sstatic input, as, 43–44
  Tea Party and, 49–51, 130
  vaccines and, 43
Loewen, P.J., 59
longitudinal public opinion survey data.
    See panel data
Lucid Theorem, 76–77
Lunz-Trujillo, Krissy, 29, 32

macro anti-intellectualism database (MAID)
  generally, 93, 106
  actual legislative behavior and, 94
  fluctuations in anti-intellectual behavior,
    observing, 94
  indicators, 93–95
  limitations of, 96–97
  micro level and, 97
  pluralistic approach of, 93–94
  prevalence of anti-intellectualism in, 106–108
  survey questions, 94–96
Manhattan Project, 38
March for Science, 4–5
McCarthyism, 9–10, 37–38
measurement of anti-intellectualism
  generally, 20, 65–66, 90
  ANES Time Series Pilot Study, 75–76
  content validation, 20, 66, 78
  convergent validation, 20, 66, 78, 85–89
  COVID-19 pandemic and, 75–77
  cross-sectional survey data, 63
  CSPP Panel Study, 72–75
  datasets, 68–69
  GSS Panel Studies, 70–72
  GSS Time Series Study, 70
  limitations of, 66, 74, 214–215
  longitudinal public opinion survey data
    (see panel data)
  macro anti-intellectualism database (MAID)
    (see macro anti-intellectualism database
    (MAID))
  methodological pluralism and, 66
  micro-level public opinion data, 63–64
  panel data (see panel data)

populism and, 73–74
predictive validation, 20, 66, 78
public opinion generally, 20, 68
satisficing behavior, avoiding, 78–80
Science and Policy Rolling Cross-Sectional
  Study (SciPol), 76–77
survey questions, 67–68, 76
trust in experts (see trust in experts,
  measurement of)
trust in scientists, 67–68, 70–71
Mechanical Turk, 80–81
Merkley, E., 59, 105
meta-ignorance, 8–9, 54
methodological pluralism, 66
micro-level public opinion data, 63–64
Miller, Jon, 144–145
Mirosa, O., 58
Mooney, Chris, 37, 48, 51
Mullin, Megan, 5

national affiliation, 15
National Institute of Allergy and Infectious
  Diseases, 13
National Opinion Research Center (NORC)
  GSS Panel Studies, 70–72
  GSS Time Series Studies, 70
National Science Board, 144–145
National Science Foundation, 39, 105
Nixon, Richard, 38–40
Norris, P., 210
Nye, Bill, 5

Obama, Barack
  Affordable Care Act and, 47, 49–50
  evidence-based policies and, 199–200
  growth in anti-intellectualism under, 110,
    130, 132
  Palin and, 50–51
  Tea Party and, 21–22, 49, 114, 136–139
O'Brien, T., 58
Office of Science and Technology Policy, 40
Office of Technology Assessment, 48
Oliver, J.E., 15–16, 67, 73, 76–79, 85–87, 89,
  105, 126, 168

Palin, Sarah, 40, 49–51
panel data
  generally, 63
  ANES Time Series Pilot Study, 75–76
  CSPP Panel Study, 72–75
  GSS Panel Studies, 70–72
  GSS Time Series Study, 70
  long data, 71
  stacked data, 71

324   INDEX

Paris Climate Accord, 4–5, 178
partisan identity
  anti-expert partisan rhetoric, 41–42
  between-person differences in
    anti-intellectualism and, 117–118, 122,
    124–127
  measurement of, 117–118
  politically relevant preferences, relation to,
    36–37
  Republican Party and, 124–126
  Tea Party and, 125–126
partisan polarization
  anti-intellectualism and, 2, 19, 114
  asymmetric polarization, 47–49
  between-person differences in
    anti-intellectualism and, 21–22
  expert dislike and distrust and, 33
  recency of, 2, 19, 21–22, 33, 47, 114,
    125–126, 201
  Tea Party and, 35, 51–52, 114, 136–140, 201
Paul, Rand, 49
Perry, Rick, 188
Pew Research Center, 103–104
Policy Agendas Project, 93, 189–190, 192–193
policy consequences of anti-intellectualism
  generally, 3, 18, 23–24, 166–167, 197–198, 201
  climate change, for, 23, 176–179
  COVID-19 pandemic, for, 23, 179–184
  economic policy, for, 184–186
  environmental policy, for, 176–179
  evidence-based policies, rejection of, 2,
    167–176
  immigration, for, 185
  macroeconomic policy and, 23
  macro level, at, 166–167
  micro level, at, 166–168
  public health, for, 178–184
  robustness checks, 197
  survey questions, 168
  vaccines, for, 179–184
politically relevant preferences, 36–37
PolitiFact, 50
populism
  anti-elitism and, 15
  anti-intellectualism, relation to, 3, 15–18,
    116–117
  bidirectionality thesis and, 61–62
  defined, 15
  economic inequality and, 210–211
  expert dislike and distrust and, 15–16
  intellectuals embracing, 16
  measurement of anti-intellectualism and, 73–74
  national affiliation, 15
  science-related populism, 15–17
predictive validation, 20, 66, 78
prevalence of anti-intellectualism
  generally, 20–21, 91–93, 110–111

aggregated assessments of, 93–94, 96–98,
    105–107, 113
  defined, 104
  dichotomy, lack of as problem, 97–98
  difficulty in measuring, 97
  "don't know" (DK) responses, problem of,
    98–101
  elites versus public, 103
  high level of opinionation, 99–100
  ideological sub-group differences in, 105
  importance of determining, 92
  limitations of determination, 215
  macro anti-intellectualism database (MAID)
    (see macro anti-intellectualism database
    (MAID))
  micro level, at, 100
  middle options, lack of as problem, 98–100
  overstatement of, 103
  pluralistic approach to, 104, 106–110
  problems in measuring, 97–102
  public opinion data, 53
  subjective nature of, 92
  trust in scientists, relation to, 103–105
Pruitt, Scott, 4–5, 40
public health
  Congressional hearings on, 196
  Congressional response to anti-intellectualism
    and, 196–197
  COVID-19 pandemic (see COVID-19
    pandemic)
  policy consequences of anti-intellectualism
    for, 178–184
  survey questions, 168
  vaccines (see vaccines)
public opinion
  longitudinal public opinion survey data, 63
  measurement of anti-intellectualism generally,
    20, 68
  micro-level public opinion data, 63–64
  prevalence of anti-intellectualism, 53

Rahn, W.M., 15–16, 67, 73, 76–79, 85–87, 89,
    105, 126, 168
Reagan, Ronald
  anti-science attitudes of, 21, 48
  partisan polarization and, 114, 125–126, 139
regression models
  between-person differences in
    anti-intellectualism and, 114–117
  bidirectionality thesis and, 155, 162
  expert policy role (EPR) orientations
    and, 162
  within-person changes in anti-intellectualism
    and, 143–144
religiosity
  anti-intellectualism and, 19

Index

between-person differences in
anti-intellectualism and, 120, 122, 131–133
climate change and, 46
measurement of, 120
politically relevant preferences, relation to,
36–37
scientists, among, 45
static input, as, 44–46
Tea Party and, 132
Republican Party
anti-expert partisan rhetoric and, 41–42
anti-intellectualism and, 19, 91, 102–103, 105
climate change, on, 39, 42, 206–207
critical race theory (CRT), on, 203
expert dislike and distrust and, 33, 37–41
historical attitudes toward experts, 21–22, 33,
46–47, 114
partisan identity and, 124–126
symbolic ideology and, 37–42
Tea Party (*see* Tea Party)
restoring trust in experts
generally, 202, 206
communication strategies, 206–207
science interest and, 207–210
system-level reforms, 210–211
unified approach, 206–210
reverse causality
affective and group-centric theory of
anti-intellectualism and, 34
between-person differences in
anti-intellectualism and, 116, 133–136
science interest and, 142, 147–148
science knowledge and, 142, 147–148
within-person changes in anti-intellectualism
and, 142, 147–148
Rigney, D., 6, 8–9, 15–16
Roper Center, 93–95
Rubio, Marco, 49

satisficing behavior, 78–80, 87
Schoonover, Rod, 187–188
Science & Engineering Indicators, 144–145
Science & Engineering Survey, 105
Science and Policy Rolling Cross-Sectional
Study (SciPol), 76–77
science interest
anti-intellectualism, relation to, 145–147, 201
capacity to mitigate anti-intellectualism,
141–142
dynamic input, as, 56–57
evaluation of diverse experts, as affecting,
208–209
higher education, enhancing effects of in, 143,
148–150, 209
lasting trait and temporary trait, as, 208
measurement of, 145

restoring trust in experts and, 207–210
reverse causality and, 142, 147–148
scientists, and public attitudes toward,
142–143, 150–151
short-term and long-term effects of, 208
temporal changes in, 142
young persons, in, 209
science knowledge
anti-intellectualism, relation to, 145–147
capacity to mitigate anti-intellectualism,
141–142
climate change and, 55
dynamic input, as, 54–56
higher education, enhancing effects of in, 143,
148–150
measurement of, 144–145
reverse causality and, 142, 147–148
scientists, and public attitudes toward, 142,
150–151
temporal changes in, 142
science-related populism, 15–17
scientific research, public attitudes toward, 5
scientists
experts, as, 12–15
measurement of trust in, 67–68, 70–71
personal lives, interaction in, 12–13
policy, interaction with, 13
public attitudes toward, 103–104
religiosity among, 45
science interest and public attitudes toward,
142–143, 150–151
science knowledge and public attitudes
toward, 142, 150–151
"science popularizers," 82, 147
trust in, measurement of (*see* trust in scientists,
measurement of)
Scott, Tim, 204–205
Self-Categorization Theory (SCT)
generally, 30–31
affective and group-centric theory of
anti-intellectualism and, 32–33
anti-vaccine social identity (AVISD) and, 32
Shalala, Donna, 26
Shaw, D., 42, 45–46
Skocpol, T., 49–50
Snider, Charlie, 109–110
Social Identity Theory (SIT)
generally, 30–31
affective and group-centric theory of
anti-intellectualism and, 32–33
anti-vaccine social identity (AVISD) and, 32
source credibility effect, 41
Spanish flu, 1
sstatic inputs
generally, 35–37
asymmetric polarization and, 47–49
defined, 35–36

sstatic inputs (*continued*)
   limited government orientation as, 43–44
   politically relevant preferences, relation to,
      36–37
   religiosity as, 44–46
   stability of, 36–37
   symbolic ideology as, 37–41
   Tea Party and, 49–52
Standridge, Rob, 216–217
Stecula, D.A., 105
Steinfeld, Jesse, 39
stem-cell research, 39, 45–46, 48, 156
Stevenson, Adlai, 9–10, 37–38, 188
Stimson, J., 93
Survey Sampling International (SSI), 73–74,
   76–77
Sylvester, Steven, 32
symbolic ideology
   anti-science attitudes and, 42
   between-person differences in anti-
      intellectualism and, 118, 122, 127–129
   measurement of, 118
   politically relevant preferences, relation to,
      36–37
   Republican Party and, 37–42
   sstatic input, as, 37–41

Tea Party
   anti-intellectualism and, 21–22, 51, 136–139
   anti-science attitudes and, 40
   between-person differences in
      anti-intellectualism and, 136–139
   conspiracy theories and, 49–50
   "death panels," on, 50
   expert dislike and distrust and, 51, 139
   limited government orientation and, 49–51,
      130
   Obama and, 21–22, 49, 114, 136–139
   origins of, 49
   partisan identity and, 125–126
   partisan polarization and, 35, 51–52, 114,
      136–140, 201
   religiosity and, 132
   sstatic inputs and, 49–52
technocracy, 60
Thielens, Wagner, 83
Truman, Harry, 38
Trump, Donald
   anti-intellectualism and, 1–2, 91, 94, 108,
      110, 187
   climate change, on, 4–5, 187
   COVID-19 pandemic, on, 47, 61, 112,
      181–182
   critical race theory (CRT), on, 203–204
   economic policy and, 186
   evidence-based policies and, 199–200

expert dislike and distrust and, 10, 37–38, 40,
   47–48, 59, 109–110
higher education, on, 203–204
ideological inconsistency of, 47
immigration, on, 185
March for Science and, 4
populism and, 210
scientists, hostility toward, 187–188
Tea Party and, 49
Wallace compared, 40, 108–110
trust in experts, measurement of
   generally, 67
   public definitions of expert and, 80–82
   satisficing behavior and, 78–79
   survey questions, 67
   trust in scientists compared, 82–89
trust in scientists, measurement of
   generally, 67–68
   convergent validation and, 85–89
   empirical data, 104
   prevalence of anti-intellectualism and, 103–105
   satisficing behavior and, 87
   survey questions, 67–68
   trust in experts compared, 82–89
Turning Point USA (TPUSA), 203–204
Twitter, 138, 203–204
Tyson, Neil deGrasse, 5, 82

University of California, Berkeley, 203
University of Minnesota CSPP Panel Study,
   72–75
unreflective instrumentalism, 8

vaccines
   anti-vaccine social identity (AVISD), 32
   limited government orientation and, 43
   policy consequences of anti-intellectualism
      for, 179–184
   survey questions, 168
Vietnam War, 39–40

Walensky, Rochelle, 88–89
Wallace, George
   anti-intellectualism and, 94, 108–110
   expert dislike and distrust and, 10, 40, 47–48
   Trump compared, 40, 108–110
Walsh, Joe, 51
warning labels, 207
WebMD, 55
Wellcome Global Monitor (WGM), 212–213
Wellcome Global Trust, 212
Whitmer, Gretchen, 154
Williamson, V., 49–50
within-person changes in anti-intellectualism

generally, 141–143, 150–151
affective and group-centric theory of
    anti-intellectualism and, 34–35
between-person differences in
    anti-intellectualism and, 115, 117
data, 144–145
empirical results, 145–147
epistemic abilities, effect of, 22
measurement of, 144–145
motivations, effect of, 22
regression models and, 143–144
reverse causality and, 142, 147–148

science interest, effect of (*see* science interest)
science knowledge, effect of (*see* science
    knowledge)
World Bank, 213

X (Twitter), 203–204

Yellen, Janet, 14, 88
YouGov, 75
Youngkin, Glenn, 216

The manufacturer's authorised representative in the EU for product safety is Oxford
University Press España S.A. of El Parque Empresarial San Fernando de Henares,
Avenida de Castilla, 2 – 28830 Madrid (www.oup.es/en or product.safety@oup.com).
OUP España S.A. also acts as importer into Spain of products made by the manufacturer.

Printed in the USA/Agawam, MA
January 31, 2025

881971.008